THE CONSTITUTIONAL LEGITIMACY OF LAW OFFICERS IN THE UNITED KINGDOM

This book provides a detailed account of each law officer's functions and draws on that account as the basis for a conceptual analysis of their constitutional legitimacy.

In recent years, the constitutional legitimacy of law officers has been questioned repeatedly because of recurring controversies surrounding the discharge of their varied functions. Indeed, it has become increasingly clear that those functions enable law officers to play a highly influential part in the regulation and exercise of public power throughout the United Kingdom.

McCormick argues that the most persuasive framework for analysing the offices which make up this diverse regime involves concentrating on the constitutional values of independence, accountability and trust which underpin it.

Both aspects of the book – namely the explanation of individual functions and the conceptual analysis of collective legitimacy – are written in a holistic way which encompasses critical analyses about the Attorney General and Solicitor General for England and Wales; the Counsel General for Wales; the Lord Advocate, Solicitor General and Advocate General for Scotland, as well as the Attorney General and Advocate General for Northern Ireland.

The Constitutional Legitimacy of Law Officers in the United Kingdom

Conor McCormick

•HART•
OXFORD • LONDON • NEW YORK • NEW DELHI • SYDNEY

HART PUBLISHING

Bloomsbury Publishing Plc

Kemp House, Chawley Park, Cumnor Hill, Oxford, OX2 9PH, UK

1385 Broadway, New York, NY 10018, USA

29 Earlsfort Terrace, Dublin 2, Ireland

HART PUBLISHING, the Hart/Stag logo, BLOOMSBURY and the Diana logo are trademarks of Bloomsbury Publishing Plc

First published in Great Britain 2022

A catalogue record for this book is available from the British Library.

Library of Congress Cataloging-in-Publication data

Names: McCormick, Conor, author.

Title: The constitutional legitimacy of law officers in the United Kingdom / Conor McCormick.

Description: Oxford ; New York : Hart, 2022. | Based on author's thesis (doctoral – Queen's University of Belfast, 2019). | Includes bibliographical references and index.

Identifiers: LCCN 2022010936 | ISBN 9781509944118 (hardback) | ISBN 9781509944156 (paperback) | ISBN 9781509944132 (pdf) | ISBN 9781509944125 (Epub)

Subjects: LCSH: Attorneys general—Great Britain.

Classification: LCC KD7105 .M33 2022 | DDC 353.4/2293—dc23/eng/20220430

LC record available at https://lccn.loc.gov/2022010936

ISBN: HB: 978-1-50994-411-8
ePDF: 978-1-50994-413-2
ePub: 978-1-50994-412-5

Typeset by Compuscript Ltd, Shannon

PREFACE

The doctoral thesis from which this book evolved was supervised by Gordon Anthony and John Morison at Queen's University Belfast. To Gordon, my primary supervisor and most inspirational mentor, I owe more thanks than I am able to articulate. I strive to be half the lawyer he is. To John, my second supervisor, I also owe my stoutest gratitude. I would not have searched for most of the conceptual arguments in this book without his encouragement.

In addition to my supervisors, I would like to record my appreciation to the Department for Employment and Learning (NI), which has since been renamed the Department for the Economy (NI), for funding the doctoral research which led to this volume.

I would also like to note how grateful I am to my wider colleagues at Queen's, for facilitating the sabbatical which made it possible for me to convert my thesis into a monograph with considerably less stress than would otherwise have been the case. Equally, I take this opportunity to express my thanks to everyone at Hart – especially Kate Whetter, Rosie Mearns and Linda Staniford – for their kind support with the publishing process.

I have benefitted from an abundance of advice from many more sounding boards over the years, whom I hesitate to list on an individual basis only because I will almost certainly omit someone important. With that said, I have decided that it is worth risking special mentions for Brice Dickson, Rory O'Connell, Colm O'Cinneide, Christopher McCrudden, Alex Schwartz, John Stannard, Claire Archbold, Graeme Cowie, David Torrance, Thomas Stewart, Anurag Deb, Sarah Craig, Róise Connolly, Allison McAreavey, Patricia O'Lynn, Christopher McCorkindale and Ben Yong.

I am also thankful to the law officers, past and present, who have sustained my interest in the subject of this research by speaking to me about their work at different intervals, and likewise to the many helpful officials from their offices.

My partner, James Nelson, has caringly buoyed me throughout every stage of my academic career while continually reminding me of the good things in life beyond it. I dedicate this book to him. My closest family – especially Mum, Gerry, Eoin, Claire, Jack, Blaíne and Caítlyn – also keep me grounded and motivated in ways only they can. I dedicate it to them too.

Last, but not least, I would like to thank you for choosing to read my work. I sincerely hope that you find it useful and interesting.

TABLE OF CONTENTS

TABLE OF CASES

TABLE OF STATUTES

TABLE OF STATUTORY RULES AND INSTRUMENTS

1

Introduction

The constitutional legitimacy of law officers in the UK is a relatively under-examined element of its multi-textured scheme of government, despite a long record of recurring controversies surrounding the discharge of their varied functions. Indeed, this diverse set of functions – ranging from the provision of binding legal advice within government, to a gatekeeping role in connection with proceedings about the investigation of unexplained deaths – means that law officers play a highly influential part in the regulation and exercise of public power throughout the UK. The under-examined nature of this influence is understandable, however, given both the considerable degree of constitutional complexity that underpins it and the absence of a persuasive framework for measuring the legitimacy of those who wield it. While some scholars have attempted to identify the client supposedly served by each function and to assess the legitimacy of a law officer's performance by measuring the extent to which they advance the *interests* of that client, for example, this book adopts a different approach for reasons that will be explained more fully below. That said, it should perhaps be noted here at the outset that, at its most basic, the approach of this book centres on legitimising constitutional *values* and the ways in which controversy can arise when they are poorly understood or inappropriately weighted. Thus, the first aim of this book is to argue that a values-based framework of analysis is the most persuasive conceptual basis for considering the constitutional legitimacy of law officers in the UK – with the constitutional values of independence, accountability and trust proving fundamental to that analysis. The second aim of the book, which is to provide a detailed account of the functions performed by each law officer in the UK, is of course closely linked to the first. Though it may be needless to say, it is nevertheless acknowledged that the robustness of the conceptual argument depends to a large extent on an accurate understanding of the law and practice associated with each law officer's functions. As such, it should be clearly emphasised that this is a book which attempts to combine academic theories with practical legal doctrines. The results, it is hoped, contribute to the knowledge of both domains.

Rather than opening with an outline of how these aims have been explored and realised, this chapter begins by addressing an important preliminary matter about how the UK law officer regime has been defined and classified throughout the book. Having introduced the dramatis personae, the next section presents a critical analysis of several works that have made major contributions to existing scholarship about the UK law officers to date. The following section then expands on the general nature of the values-based framework of analysis that distinguishes this book from its forerunners and provides a chapter outline in the course of those expository notes. It also unpacks how the remainder of the book could be said to consist of several analytical dimensions that work in tandem to produce an account of the law officers which is as theoretically and jurisdictionally holistic as possible. The chapter concludes with a short summary of the foregoing sections.

Labelling the Law Officers

The task of deciding which offices to qualify for inclusion in the UK law officer regime has vexed most writers on this subject for one reason or another. Writing in 1964, for example, Edwards restricted the scope of his main study to 'Law Officers of the Crown'; a category which he took to refer to certain legally qualified Ministers of the Crown who were responsible for discharging a unique combination of (quasi-)judicial and (narrowly construed) political obligations that had accumulated in the portfolios for their offices over time.[1] However, while Edwards was content to recognise the Lord Chancellor within that regally patented bracket of law officials to the extent that the title was 'used to indicate the Chancellor's constant availability as one of the principal legal advisers to the Prime Minister and the Cabinet, of which he [was and] is a member',[2] Kyriakides has since highlighted several reasons why it would be 'incorrect and improper to describe the Lord Chancellor as a Law Officer of the Crown' today.[3]

It should also be noted that there are three further groups of office-holders who were not accorded Law Officer of the Crown status by Edwards and who are similarly excluded from the UK law officer regime as defined for the purposes of this book. First, Edwards' definition appears to have precluded the inclusion of law officers who were dignitaries of royal appointment but who lacked a ministerial rank. So it was that the still-extant offices of the Attorney General for the Duchy of Lancaster;[4] the Attorney General and Solicitor General of the County Palatine

[1] John Ll J Edwards, *The Law Officers of the Crown: A Study of the Offices of Attorney-General and Solicitor-General of England with an Account of the Office of the Director of Public Prosecutions of England* (Sweet & Maxwell 1964).

[2] ibid 2.

[3] Klearchos A Kyriakides, 'The Law Officers of the Crown and the Rule of Law in the United Kingdom' in Gabrielle Appleby, Patrick Keyzer and John M Williams (eds), *Public Sentinels: A Comparative Study of Australian Solicitors-General* (Routledge 2014) 188–189. Kyriakides' point is based on those substantial reforms to the office of Lord Chancellor brought about by the Constitutional Reform Act 2005, pt 2, which have had the effect of 'virtually extinguishing his [or her] status as an Olympian legal personality within the Cabinet'.

[4] The Duchy of Lancaster is a title that comprises a range of estates and jurisdictions which, for the most part, still raises revenue for the monarch in her personal capacity. For further information about the Duchy, see: *Halsbury's Laws of England* (2014) vol 29, Crown and Crown Proceedings, para 214. On the Attorney General for the Duchy, see: *Halsbury's Laws of England* (2014) vol 20, Constitutional and Administrative Law, para 274.

of Durham;[5] the Attorney General for the Duchy of Cornwall,[6] together with the Attorney General and Solicitor General of the Queen Consort,[7] were all forgivably consigned to a footnote in his original treatise.[8] Likewise, this book does not explicitly consider the constitutionality of those offices because of their limited functions and their particularly parochial significance. Perhaps the most important point to note in this respect is that a familiar title cannot be relied upon to denote modern law officer status. The titles given to members of the UK law officer regime vary considerably in modern times – something which underlines the fact that relevant office-holders are better grouped by the similarity of their functions and rank rather than by reference to commonly used official titles.

The second group of offices which are not studied in any detail herein concerns those which are now defunct or extraneous to the UK as a jurisdiction. Historical information of this nature is therefore limited, in the main, to matters of interest which pertain to offices which still exist in the UK today. There is insufficient space to consider, for example, fascinating antecedents such as the King's Advocate General in any detail.[9] Nor has the scope of this book allowed for thorough research into the constitutional legitimacy of former colonial law officers from a historical standpoint, though there is useful literature surrounding the modern offspring of such offices which has helpfully informed critical appraisals of the current UK models.[10] Moreover, law officers in the 53 countries comprising the Commonwealth of Nations,[11] as well as law officers in the three Crown Dependencies,[12] are specifically excluded on account of their constitutional independence from the

[5] These office-holders were formally responsible for carrying on the interests of the Crown in courts belonging to the County Palatine of Durham, however they do not appear to have enjoyed any automatic preferment in the allocation of such briefs for a long time. See: James William Norton-Kyshe, *The Law and Privileges Relating to the Attorney-General and Solicitor-General of England* (Stevens and Haynes 1897) 61–63.

[6] The Prince of Wales – a title granted to the heir apparent to the UK monarch – appoints an Attorney General to represent him as the Duke of Cornwall in court matters related to that duchy. For more historical information, see: Edmund Robert Daniell, *A Treatise on the Practice of the High Court of Chancery with Some Practical Observations on the Pleadings in That Court: Volume 1* (J & WT Clarke 1837) 21.

[7] These offices are in abeyance as the current sovereign is female, but the wife of a male sovereign remains entitled to appoint both an Attorney General and a Solicitor General to carry out her legal affairs and thereby shield her own name from attack in the courts. The same facility is not extended to the Queen Dowager when there is one. See: ibid 20.

[8] Edwards, *The Law Officers of the Crown* (n 1) 27.

[9] Edwards records that this office-holder was, until 1872, 'standing adviser to the Crown upon questions of international law, maritime and ecclesiastical law'. See: ibid 119 and 131–140.

[10] The evolution of former colonial law officers in the USA, Canada, Australia, New Zealand and Ireland have been most closely considered for this purpose. Edwards himself considered some of these in his second volume on the law officers. See, in particular: John Ll J Edwards, *The Attorney General, Politics and the Public Interest* (Sweet & Maxwell 1984) ch 12.

[11] The Commonwealth is a voluntary association of independent sovereign states. Most of its members are former British colonies or dependencies of those colonies.

[12] The Crown Dependencies of Jersey, Guernsey and the Isle of Man are self-governing domestic jurisdictions represented on the international law plane by the UK, as they have no international legal personality of their own. The UK Government remains responsible for their defence, international relations and good governance.

UK as a jurisdiction. Law officers in the 14 UK Overseas Territories are also excluded from consideration, despite their continuing constitutional links to the UK,[13] on account of their comparatively unique and autonomous genealogies. In the same vein, the law officers for regions within supranational and international organisations to which the UK is or was once a party also fall outside of present parameters.[14] There is certainly a case to be made for examining the constitutional legitimacy of such offices using the framework advanced in this book, just as there is a strong case to be made for an in-depth comparison between such offices and their counterparts in nations from predominantly civil law traditions, but limitations of space and resources have again supplemented the methodological reasons for leaving those studies to one side and reinforced a decision to focus on law officers in the four countries which form the UK itself; namely, England, Wales, Scotland and Northern Ireland.

Finally, although Edwards justifiably included an account of the Director of Public Prosecutions alongside his initial study of the Law Officers of the Crown, he was careful to distinguish the Director as a separate entity because that office was and remains a creature of statute rather than one of royal decree, and because the office was only represented at a ministerial level by proxy.[15] Consonant with that approach, but for slightly different reasons, this book only offers specific analyses on the roles of the Directors of Public Prosecutions across the UK today in so far as it is necessary to explain their important relationships to the UK law officer regime. In the same way, while a panoply of other offices which operate tangentially to the law officers are noted where appropriate, the UK law officer regime itself is not intended to encompass figures such as the Treasury Solicitor;[16] First Parliamentary Counsel;[17] the Crown Solicitor for Northern Ireland;[18] the

[13] UK Overseas Territories are each constitutionally unique – with varying degrees of self-government – but they are unified by their continued recognition of UK sovereignty, with the Queen as Head of State and automatic British citizenship flowing from that recognition.

[14] Special care should perhaps be taken to distinguish the Advocates General to the Court of Justice of the EU from UK law officers and their comparators – roles which, according to Burrows and Greaves, 'cannot be compared to any judicial or legal being in the common law system'. See: Noreen Burrows and Rosa Greaves, *The Advocate General and EC Law* (Oxford University Press 2007) 3.

[15] Edwards, *The Law Officers of the Crown* (n 1) 2.

[16] The Treasury Solicitor's non-ministerial Department was renamed the Government Legal Department in 2015, though, in both manifestations, the relevant Department was and is a subordinate of the Attorney General's Office in the bureaucratic hierarchy of the UK Government. By virtue of the Treasury Solicitor Act 1876, however, the Treasury Solicitor is a corporation sole vested with a bespoke range of powers and responsibilities. Moreover, the Treasury Solicitor enjoys the rank of a permanent secretary in the UK Civil Service and, in that capacity, is responsible for managing about 2,800 officials across a range of practice areas (though most advisory lawyers are physically stationed in the Department to which their expertise relates).

[17] First Parliamentary Counsel refers to the person in charge of the Office of Parliamentary Counsel, which is responsible for drafting primary legislation on the instruction of departmental lawyers (who normally draft secondary legislation themselves) and for advising the UK Government on constitutional and legislative matters. The devolved equivalents of this office, which have slightly different titles, are also excluded from the scope of this work.

[18] The Crown Solicitor for Northern Ireland is a statutory appointment made by the Advocate General for Northern Ireland. The Crown Solicitor's Office carries out most Northern Ireland litigation on behalf of UK Government Ministers and Departments, inter alios, under authority conferred by the

Departmental Solicitor for Northern Ireland;[19] the Solicitor to the Attorney General for Northern Ireland;[20] the Solicitor to the Advocate General for Scotland;[21] the Solicitor to the Scottish Government;[22] the Director of the Welsh Government Legal Services Department,[23] or any other senior government lawyers who do not enjoy 'ministerial status', 'cabinet rank', or a closely equivalent governmental status at the devolved level. Senior parliamentary lawyers are likewise treated as belonging to a fundamentally different stratum of officials.[24]

As mentioned above, these three updated groups of office-holders have been excluded from the UK law officer regime as defined for the purposes of this book for 'slightly different reasons' than those which ostensibly underpinned Edwards' 'Law Officers of the Crown' classification. Whereas Edwards' inclusion criteria consisted of an office involving both hybrid governmental responsibilities and royal approval, the latter criterion is replaced in this book with the criterion of 'ministerial status', 'cabinet rank', or a closely equivalent governmental status at the devolved level. This formulation also differs from the approach of Kyriakides, whose focus on the law officers at a UK Government level precluded anything more

Northern Ireland Constitution Act 1973, s 35, as amended by Justice (Northern Ireland) Act 2002, Sch 7, para 14. Among the list of non-departmental public bodies and public officers advised and represented by the Crown Solicitor is the Chief Constable of the Police Service for Northern Ireland.

[19] This office closely resembles the role of the Treasury Solicitor in the context of the devolved arrangements for Northern Ireland, though it is a business area within the devolved Department of Finance rather than being structurally subordinate to the Office of the Attorney General for Northern Ireland (which would be more precisely akin to the administrative position of the Treasury Solicitor in the UK Government). The post-holder is nonetheless considered Head of the Government Legal Service for Northern Ireland, carrying the ultimate responsibility for a wide range of legal services arising from the work of the Northern Ireland Executive, Ministers, and Departments.

[20] The Solicitor to the Attorney General for Northern Ireland is second from the top in the bureaucratic management structure of the Attorney's Office, but the Solicitor is unrecognised by statute and may not, for example, act as a legal deputy for the Attorney in quite the same way that the Solicitor General for England and Wales may act as a legal deputy for the Attorney General for England and Wales under the Law Officers Act 1997 (explained further below).

[21] The Solicitor to the Advocate General for Scotland is the Director of the Office of the Advocate General, which is responsible for advising and litigating on behalf of all UK Government Departments in matters relating to Scots law, as well as instructing Parliamentary Counsel in relation to UK legislation that applies to Scotland. The office is roughly equivalent to the Crown Solicitor for Northern Ireland, though it is a non-statutory appointment. There is also a Deputy Solicitor to the Advocate General for Scotland but, unlike the Advocate General himself, both office-holders are simply senior civil servants. They report to the Advocate General.

[22] The Solicitor to the Scottish Government is Director for the Scottish Government Legal Directorate, which is responsible for providing legal services to the devolved Scottish Government. The Solicitor is a senior civil servant and reports to the Lord Advocate and the Solicitor General for Scotland. Although the work of the office is largely akin to the Departmental Solicitor for Northern Ireland, the bureaucratic line of command in Scotland leads directly to the devolved law officers.

[23] This post-holder has responsibility for providing legal advice and legislative drafting services, inter alia, to Ministers and Director Generals across the Welsh Government. The post resembles the Solicitor to the Scottish Government and the Departmental Solicitor for Northern Ireland.

[24] For an introduction to the various legal advisers to the UK Parliament, see: Andrew Kennon, 'Legal Advice to Parliament' in Alexander Horne, Gavin Drewry and Dawn Oliver (eds), *Parliament and the Law* (Bloomsbury Publishing 2013). Also see: Ben Yong, Greg Davies and Cristina Leston-Bandeira, 'Tacticians, Stewards, and Professionals: The Politics of Publishing Select Committee Legal Advice' (2019) 46 *Journal of Law and Society* 367, 378–381.

than passing consideration of the devolved law officers.[25] In contrast, the UK law officer regime as defined herein merges the office-holders traditionally described as 'Law Officers of the Crown' with devolved office-holders who enjoy comparable governmental responsibilities and status. In particular, the fact that, for historical reasons, the Attorney General for Northern Ireland is not formally appointed by the Queen[26] (unlike the Counsel General for Wales,[27] together with the Lord Advocate and Solicitor General for Scotland[28]) is not a matter of definitional determination in this context. Moreover, it has been necessary to refer to offices with the broadly construed 'status' of a government Minister or Cabinet member because there exists a constitutional debate to be explored at later junctures about whether law officers should in principle be accorded any of those politically controlled labels or whether, instead, they ought simply to be either entitled or regularly invited to attend the meetings at which others who are so labelled gather.

It is arguable that the conferral and retention of labels in general is an expression of power by law officers' patrons, from which a certain type of legitimacy can flow but which only partially explains the broader constitutional position of the offices in question. For example, while the prosaic but history-laden title of 'law officer' itself may, in some circumstances, have the effect of increasing the expected trustworthiness of an office-holder in administrative and governmental circles, that effect may not be as likely in political and judicial circles. Placing trust in a title-bearer normally follows from the assumption that their appointment has been considered and approved by, to continue the last example, representatives of the executive. Where appointment and removal procedures require legislative approval, however, knowledge of those procedures is likely to enhance an office-holder's expected trustworthiness among members of the legislature in later encounters.[29] The judicial role prescribed for removing the Attorney General for Northern Ireland from office might even affect an office-holder's relationship with members of the judiciary in similarly interesting ways.[30] To repeat this point in general terms, one part of assessing the legitimacy of law officers involves considering the roles played by various legitimating patrons in the process by which

[25] Kyriakides (n 3).

[26] It is normally for the First Minister and deputy First Minister of Northern Ireland acting jointly to appoint the Attorney General for Northern Ireland: Justice (Northern Ireland) Act 2002, s 22(2). There is normally no formal role for the Northern Ireland Assembly in this process. Due to the abnormal circumstances that prevailed in Northern Ireland between January 2017 and January 2020, however, it was made possible for a UK Minister to perform this appointment function: Northern Ireland (Executive Formation and Exercise of Functions) Act 2018, s 5, as amended by the Northern Ireland (Ministerial Appointment Functions) Regulations 2019.

[27] It is for the First Minister of Wales to recommend to the Queen that a person should be appointed to or removed from the post of Counsel General, but he or she may only do so with the agreement of the National Assembly for Wales: Government of Wales Act 2006, s 49.

[28] It is for the First Minister of Scotland to recommend to the Queen that a person should be appointed to or removed from the posts of Lord Advocate and Solicitor General, but he or she may only do so with the agreement of the Scottish Parliament: Scotland Act 1998, s 48.

[29] For the statutory provisions requiring legislative involvement in current appointment procedures, see nn 26–28. Neither the Northern Ireland Assembly nor the UK Parliament have any formal role in appointment and removal procedures.

[30] Justice (Northern Ireland) Act 2002, s 24.

they acquire and keep the titles attached to their office. This claim applies both to office-holders with the above-prescribed responsibilities and status at the devolved level and to those who work within the UK Government centrally, which further justifies the wide taxonomy adopted herein.

By way of concluding these preliminary remarks about the scope of the UK law officer regime as defined for the purposes of this book, it is worth noting that the list of office-holders emerging from the definition set out above compares quite favourably to the following list recognised by the UK Parliament in section 35 of the Freedom of Information Act 2000 (as amended): 'the Attorney General [for England and Wales], the Solicitor General [for England and Wales], the Advocate General for Scotland, the Lord Advocate, the Solicitor General for Scotland, the Counsel General to the Welsh Government and the Attorney General for Northern Ireland'. The only additional office recognised for the purposes of this book is the Advocate General for Northern Ireland. It is unclear whether the Advocate's omission from section 35 was an oversight or a deliberate exclusion, which is an interesting though irrelevant exception to the exemption created by that provision in respect of public requests for information about legal advice provided by the law officers so defined. In any event, the Advocate's office conforms sufficiently well to the above definition to warrant some attention towards its unique constitutional position hereinafter. For the avoidance of any doubt, a full list of the law officers recognised for the purposes of this book is set out in Table 1.1 alongside the government client(s) with which they are primarily associated and the jurisdiction that forms the focus of their work. In the interests of mellifluousness, however, it should be noted that generic shorthands like 'Attorney General', 'Solicitor General' and 'Advocate General' will be used at various points in the book where the office-holder in question is obvious from their surrounding context.

Table 1.1 The UK Law Officer Regime

Law Officer Title	Primary Government Client(s)	Jurisdictional Focus
The Attorney General for England and Wales	The UK Government	England and Wales
The Solicitor General for England and Wales	The UK Government	England and Wales
The Advocate General for Scotland	The UK Government	Scotland
The Advocate General for Northern Ireland	The UK Government	Northern Ireland
The Lord Advocate	The Scottish Government	Scotland
The Solicitor General for Scotland	The Scottish Government	Scotland
The Counsel General for Wales	The Welsh Government	Wales
The Attorney General for Northern Ireland	The Northern Ireland Executive	Northern Ireland

It would be remiss to discuss the terminological challenges of writing about law officers without reflecting at this point on two grammatical debates which appear to perturb a range of expert commentators on a recurring basis.

The first debate concerns whether law officer titles should be written out as hyphenated compounds (like Attorney-General and Solicitor-General) or open compounds (like Attorney General and Solicitor General). Hyphenated compounds of the former sort have become the norm in New Zealand and Australia, whereas modern writers in the UK, the US and Canada tend to prefer open compounds.[31] The second debate is linked to the first, in that it concerns how a compound word should be pluralised (be it a hyphenated compound word like Attorney-General or an open compound word like Attorney General). This is a textbook example of how pluralising an expression can give rise to confusion when it involves a compound word which was once a short descriptive phrase and is part of the reason why the most commonly pluralised form of the word (Attorneys General) sounds jarring to the ears of anyone who no longer perceives the anatomy of a phrase within the word. Those who do not hear remnants of a phrase within the compound and instead hear a strongly connected string of simple words will prefer to pluralise from the singular to Attorney Generals. The same problem arises with a word like mother-in-law, where those who can still detect the phrase from which the hyphenated compound word was formed will prefer to pluralise it to mothers-in-law (whereas if the originating phrase has faded from cognitive significance a preference for mother-in-laws will seem natural).[32]

There is a further feature of law officer etymology that contributes to this difference in perceptions and usage. Those unacquainted with the word Attorney General, for instance, might at first glance wonder why it is used instead of General Attorney given that an adjective normally precedes a noun in the English language. Helpfully, Pinker has explained that the reason for this ostensibly back-to-front impression is because the word in question was one of several governmental terms taken from French after the Norman conquest of England and because adjectives can come after a head noun in French (as in the case of *États-Unis*, meaning United States).[33] Consequently, Pinker has pointed out that anyone who insists on analysing (and therefore pluralising) words like Attorney General as they were analysed 'in the minds of the original speakers of Norman French' are, by extension, arguing in favour of unintuitive pluralisations like 'majors general' because 'a *major-general* was once a general major (from the French *major-général*)'.[34] For practical purposes, while these explanations make it clear that there is grammatical logic

[31] Appleby, Keyzer and Williams decided to 'maintain the different norms across jurisdictions' in their excellently edited comparative collection on law officers: Gabrielle Appleby, Patrick Keyzer and John M Williams (eds), *Public Sentinels: A Comparative Study of Australian Solicitors-General* (Routledge 2014) xvii.

[32] Steven Pinker, *Words and Rules: The Ingredients of Language* (Basic Books 1999) 27–28.

[33] ibid 29.

[34] ibid.

to support either pluralisation style – Attorneys General and Attorney Generals – the weight of historical 'custom and authority'[35] in the UK most certainly points toward Attorneys General as the most widely accepted formulation among past and present office-holders and onlookers. Thus, given that Pinker regards custom and authority as the strongest measure of 'correctness' in grammatical debates of this nature,[36] it follows that fidelity to tradition is likely to prevail over any argument driven by a desire for cross-jurisdictional consistency in this context. As such, Attorneys General is the open compound word pluralisation used throughout this book.

Leading Critiques of the Law Officers

There are three scholars who have made notable contributions to academic debates about the constitutional legitimacy of law officers in the UK: Edwards, Walker and Appleby. This section will outline the main ideas that have emerged from each of these critical contributions. It does not, therefore, explore the commentary of every writer who has either endorsed or denounced the constitutional legitimacy of law officers in the UK for one reason or another. Though literature of that kind will certainly feed into the analysis of constitutional controversies in Chapter 7, as is explained further below, the present discussion is confined to academic contributions that offer theoretical insights into some fundamental tensions that beset the UK law officer regime.

Edwards authored two complementary vade mecums in 1964[37] and 1984[38] which continue to be sources of leading authority on the historical origin and practical operation of law officers in the UK, at least in so far as they remain relevant in light of the constitutional changes that have occurred since their publication. The 1964 volume exposed many of the potentially conflicting interests at the centre of different functions for which law officers were responsible at the time, likening the 'agility and sure-footedness' required to tread the constitutional paths that separate these roles to that of a tight-rope walker.[39] The historical view of this volume revealed that these potentially conflicting interests were not always a burden of the law officers, but that they developed over time. It charted the changing nature of a law officer's role, from one of a legal adviser to one with political objectives, as a result of the growth in their responsibilities to Parliament (and notions of the broader public interest) alongside the evolution of their services to the monarch (and narrower notions of governmental interests).

[35] ibid 26.
[36] ibid 26–28.
[37] Edwards, *The Law Officers of the Crown* (n 1).
[38] Edwards, *The Attorney General, Politics and the Public Interest* (n 13).
[39] Edwards, *The Law Officers of the Crown* (n 1) ix

The 1984 volume built on this realisation by delineating some of the 'philosophic differences in approach' to the office of the Attorney General for England and Wales; some accounts of public controversies surrounding that office at the time, and some attempts to change mechanisms for ensuring its accountability to the public accordingly.[40] It emphasised that the central theme of public debate on law officers had been 'the necessity of ensuring to the maximum extent possible the independent and impartial exercise of the very considerable powers associated' with them.[41]

Edwards explored 'philosophical differences in approach' to the role of a law officer primarily through the lens of a debate on whether the Attorney General ought to attend meetings of the UK Cabinet, as it was said to epitomise conflicting characterisations of the role.[42] He recounted how those in favour of Cabinet attendance, such as the former Labour Attorney General Sam Silkin, suggested it was a necessary means of keeping his political colleagues out of court (which Silkin regarded as his primary duty, over and above representing them in the courts).[43] He also set out a countervailing approach, held by Silkin's Conservative predecessor Peter Rawlinson, whereby the proper relationship between an Attorney General and the inner council of government was one with emphasis on symbolic distance between the two.[44] Edwards saw shortcomings in both the former 'doctrine of intimate but independent involvement' and the latter 'doctrine of independent aloofness',[45] but reserved his most disapproving remarks for proposals made by the former Labour Attorney General Sir Hartley Shawcross.[46] Shawcross' proposal to defuse the potential for constitutional controversies inherent in the position of the Attorney General by completely de-politicising the office was rejected outright by Edwards because his concern to ensure a place for political accountability in the relevant constitutional framework was uncompromising.[47]

In a less widely cited but deeply insightful book chapter published in 1995, Edwards also placed emphasis on the importance of having 'several lines of accountability that must be taken into account by any attorney general wishing to fulfil his or her constitutional obligations as the responsible member of the executive'.[48] He consequently criticised the 'total insulation' of prosecutorial powers

[40] Edwards, *The Attorney General, Politics and the Public Interest* (n 13).

[41] ibid 61.

[42] ibid 62.

[43] Sam Silkin, 'The Functions and Position of the Attorney-General in the United Kingdom' (1978) 59 *The Parliamentarian* 149.

[44] Peter Rawlinson, 'A Vital Link in the Machinery of Justice' (1977) 74 *Guardian Gazette* 798.

[45] Edwards, *The Attorney General, Politics and the Public Interest* (n 13) 67–79.

[46] Hartley Shawcross, Letter to *The Times* (3 August 1977), as cited in ibid 61.

[47] ibid 66–67.

[48] John Ll J Edwards, 'The Office of Attorney General – New Levels of Public Expectations and Accountability' in Philip C Stenning (ed), *Accountability for Criminal Justice: Selected Essays* (University of Toronto Press 1995) 309. For two further publications by Edwards which touch upon the functions of UK law officers but focus on Canadian equivalents, see: John Ll J Edwards, *Ministerial Responsibility for National Security as it relates to the Offices of Prime Minister, Attorney General and Solicitor General of Canada* (A Study Prepared for the Commission of Inquiry Concerning Certain Activities of the Royal Canadian Mounted Police 1980); John Ll J Edwards, 'The Attorney General and the Charter of Rights' in Robert J Sharpe (ed), *Charter Litigation* (Butterworths 1986).

from judicial review at the time,[49] and objected to 'any legislative immunity that is designed to insulate the holder of the office of attorney general from *all* forms of professional accountability' exercisable by the disciplinary arm of a governing professional body – such as the Law Society or the Bar Council – in the event of ethical misconduct.[50] Ultimately, however, Edwards maintained that

> no matter how entrenched constitutional safeguards may be, in the final analysis it is the strength of character, personal integrity and depth of commitment to the principles of independence and the impartial representation of the public interest … which is of supreme importance.[51]

He argued, moreover, that even an office-holder with such 'elevated personal qualities' would not warrant 'total independence' in the exercise of prosecutorial functions.[52] The 'principle of independence without the accompanying sanction of parliamentary accountability' was, in his view, 'too high a price for any society to pay in achieving the goal of keeping partisan political pressures away from the exercise of prosecutorial discretion'.[53]

Walker, analysing the position as it stood in 1999, agreed with the conclusion reached by Edwards in so far as he dismissed the existence of any 'neat constitutional formula' capable of resolving the tensions inherent in the functions of law officers, such as 'doomed' suggestions to separate their legal and political functions.[54] In addition, Walker advanced theoretical understandings about the tension between certain law officers' functions by making a number of original insights of his own. Most significantly, perhaps, he highlighted that various commentators on public controversies surrounding the law officers tended to falsely characterise the tensions in their role. He was dismissive of those who viewed them as tensions between the need to be a partisan politician and the need to be an independent lawyer, as well as those who viewed them as a tension between a guardian of the public interest and a government legal advisor.[55] Both of these views, he argued, grasped 'only one element of a more complex truth' about the role of law officers, namely that they are impaired by 'parallel antimonies', or simultaneous contradictions, between legal and political conceptions of their roles.[56] He made the compelling argument that these notions run in parallel

> in the sense that the notion of the law officer as agent of government closely corresponds to a partisan conception of the role, whereas the idea of the law officer as independent custodian of independent values is linked to a public interest conception of the role.[57]

[49] Edwards, 'New Levels of Public Expectations and Accountability' (n 48) 322.
[50] ibid 303.
[51] Edwards, *The Attorney General, Politics and the Public Interest* (n 13) 67.
[52] Edwards, 'New Levels of Public Expectations and Accountability' (n 48) 310.
[53] ibid.
[54] Neil Walker, 'The Antinomies of the Law Officers' in Maurice Sunkin and Sebastian Payne (eds), *The Nature of the Crown: A Legal and Political Analysis* (Oxford University Press 1999) 161–162.
[55] ibid 145.
[56] ibid.
[57] ibid.

At the core of both conceptualisations, Walker submitted, is a universal challenge for every constitutional order faced with articulating a legitimate role for the law officers:

> [to reconcile] their attachment to a particular government and its political objectives with their commitment to a broader set of values associated with the integrity of the legal and political order.[58]

This revelation paved the way for another of Walker's important insights, namely that theoretical debates about the appropriate role of law officers can be related to more general debates about constitutionalism, such as the ideological quarrels between positivist and natural law jurists, or between liberal and republican schools of political thought.[59] Moreover, by recognising that these perspectives need not be mutually exclusive – and that it may be possible for theorists to agree on the correlation of an appropriate role conception to well-defined areas of responsibility – Walker also enabled more thoughtful consideration about how to ensure that appropriate modes of accountability are applied to particular law officer functions.[60]

While drawing upon Edwards and Walker for its historical backdrop, Appleby's contribution to the academic scholarship on law officers is primarily concerned with the role played Solicitors-General in modern-day Australia.[61] She published what is widely regarded as an instant 'locus classicus'[62] on the subject in 2016.[63] However, in addition to being highly significant in its own context and in its own right, Appleby's ideas are also of undoubted relevance to this jurisdiction given that Appleby repeatedly highlights the importance of her findings with reference to the UK position. There can be no doubt, moreover, that Appleby has a strong command of the constitutional history in connection with the UK law officer regime, which adds credibility to her comparative claims on the merits of the law officer models in use across different jurisdictions.[64] Appleby's place as a modern authority in this field is also reinforced by her role as co-editor of an insightful comparative study on law officers that was published in 2014.[65]

At the forefront of Appleby's contribution to UK law officer debates is her view that previous scholars and governments have 'failed to address the importance of

[58] ibid 135.

[59] ibid 146.

[60] ibid 147–148.

[61] Gabrielle Appleby, *The Role of the Solicitor-General: Negotiating Law, Politics and the Public Interest* (Hart Publishing 2016).

[62] The Honourable Justice W Sofronoff, 'Book Review: The Role of the Solicitor General' (2017) 91 *Adelaide Law Journal* 683, 684. See also: Anne Twomey, 'Book Review: The Role of the Solicitor General' (2016) 39 *UNSW Law Journal* 1466; Yee-Fui Ng, 'Book Review: The Role of the Solicitor General' (2017) 26 *Social & Legal Studies* 658.

[63] Appleby, *The Role of the Solicitor-General* (n 60).

[64] See, in particular, Appleby (n 61) ch 2.

[65] Appleby, Keyzer and Williams (n 31). See: Conor McCormick, 'Book Review: Public Sentinels: A Comparative Study of Australian Solicitors-General' (2017) 10 *Irish Yearbook of International Law* 315.

maintaining *public confidence*' in the ability of law officers to navigate the tensions in their constitutional role,[66] as aside from the importance of detecting and sanctioning actual episodes of impropriety. This view appears to be premised on Appleby's prior conclusion that the constitutional position of the Attorney General and Solicitor General for England and Wales is inferior, in its design, to the position of the Attorney-General and Solicitor-General in Australia.[67] The position of the Attorney General and Solicitor General for England and Wales will be fully explained in Chapter 3 of this book, but for now let it suffice to say that it involves politically appointed ministerial office-holders with a shared portfolio of functions that are both ostensibly legal and political in nature. The Australian model which Appleby prefers, on the other hand, involves a highly politicised Attorney-General who is responsible for holding to account a 'non-political' Solicitor-General carrying responsibilities primarily relating to the provision of government legal advice and advocacy.

Appleby argues that a structural bifurcation in the responsibilities between an Attorney-General and a Solicitor-General can assist in combatting public perceptions of impropriety arising from the universal challenge identified by Walker (namely the need to discharge varied functions while displaying fidelity to fundamental societal values, but without departing from party political loyalties). She is critical of the UK Government's rejection of a 2007 parliamentary recommendation in favour of bifurcation which was made in the context of some serious law officer controversies that will be analysed in Chapter 7 of this book.[68] The UK Government's preference for addressing misconceptions about impropriety by way of efforts to improve public awareness instead of structural reform can be challenged on principle, Appleby submits, because the very same reasoning was *not* followed by a previous UK Government as part of its decision to undertake major reforms to the office of Lord Chancellor in 2005.[69] Inconsistencies of principle aside, Appleby has also set out detailed arguments in favour of implementing a law officer model akin to the Australian system in the UK. Some of these arguments will be explored at relevant junctures throughout this book, but her main point in favour of bifurcation along Australian lines is that it may *lessen* tensions within the role. In brief, Appleby's central thesis is that

> while the non-political grounding of Australia's Solicitor-General has in some respects removed the office from the immediate tensions between the public interest, the law and politics, the office's continuing relationship with the democratic government means that these tensions resurface in practice and must be negotiated by individual officeholders.[70]

[66] Appleby, *The Role of the Solicitor-General* (n 60) 47. Original emphasis.

[67] Appleby (n 61) 47–48; Gabrielle Appleby, 'Reform of the Attorney General: Comparing Britain and Australia' [2016] *Public Law* 573, 594.

[68] Appleby, 'Reform of the Attorney General: Comparing Britain and Australia' (n 66).

[69] ibid 579.

[70] Appleby, *The Role of the Solicitor-General* (n 60) 286.

Presenting a Fresh Perspective on the Law Officers

Overall, it should be clear from the previous section that what limited scholarship there is on the UK law officer regime falls far short of a rounded constitutional analysis for modern times. While Appleby's contributions have been published relatively recently, they arise mainly from an examination of the position of the Attorney General and Solicitor General for England and Wales on account of the understandable need to draw some boundaries around the comparative reach of her research. As a result, even Appleby has paid little attention to the various law officer models that have been tested elsewhere in the UK and which pertain in some devolved regions at present. Indeed, the consequences that have flowed from a rapid redistribution and introduction of law officers' functions in response to the needs of devolution is a significant omission from all existing studies. This book seeks to plug that gap by analysing different expressions of the legitimising constitutional values for UK law officers in order to substantiate a workable framework for evaluating them generally. In fact, the book differs from existing scholarship quite fundamentally in this respect. While Edwards, Walker and Appleby have generally analysed the position of law officers by considering how to appropriately define and weight *legitimate constitutional interests* which may be taken into account in the discharge of various functions (be they interests of the executive or of society at large, for example), this book approaches the subject by considering how to appropriately define and weight *legitimising constitutional values* in multifarious circumstances.

It was indicated above that one of the main aims of this book is argue that the constitutional legitimacy of law officers in the UK is best understood by reference to three interacting values (independence, accountability and trust) that derive their constitutional status from a range of relevant factors. To that end, while the conceptual meanings that have been accorded to each of those values for the purposes of this book will be examined more substantively in Chapter 2, the purpose of this section is to clarify the general nature of the values-based framework of analysis in advance of that context-specific discussion. It should be made clear, in particular, that while this approach is undoubtedly novel in the context of the UK law officer regime, it is a relatively well-established approach to legal scholarship more widely.

Perhaps the first thing to highlight about this approach is that it rests on the assumption that values 'exist at varying levels of generality in the legal system and in various sectors within it'.[71] This underscores the importance of delineating the intended scope of any particular framework composed of values. As such, it should be reiterated at this point that the scope of this book is strictly limited to the UK law officer regime and does not, therefore, make any claims about the constitutional legitimacy of offices which lie beyond the regime as defined earlier in this

[71] Dawn Oliver, *Common Values and the Public-Private Divide* (Butterworths 1999) 55.

chapter. Moreover, it should be explained that the values-based framework of analysis proposed herein consists of several theoretical dimensions. These dimensions roughly reflect those developed by Daly in the context of an attempt to analyse the legitimacy of judicial review.[72] As such, this analysis has a *historical* dimension, a *descriptive* dimension, an *interpretive* dimension, a *prescriptive* dimension, and an *evaluative* dimension. Moreover, and unlike Daly's framework, this book has an expressly *comparative* dimension that will be duly unpacked further below.

The *historical* and *descriptive* dimensions of the analysis involve putting forth an accurate representation of how the UK law officer regime has developed into the form it now takes in conjunction with a description of that contemporary form. Chapters 3 to 6 of this book serve these dimensions of the analysis by way of a historical and structural overview of the law officers in the regime together with detailed information about the variety of their modern functions.

The *interpretive* dimension of the analysis involves seeking to reveal 'an *intelligible order* in the law, so far as such an order exists'.[73] This element of the analysis is weaved throughout this book as a result of its 'reflective' method, to borrow Daly's term for a similar process.[74] Daly identified and formulated the values he argues are most relevant to understanding the legitimacy of judicial review by 'starting with understanding of the values drawn from legal and political theory but revising those understandings to bring them into line with those manifest in the case law'.[75] This book adopts a similar approach by setting out existing understandings of the three values that were identified as being central to the legitimacy of the UK law officer regime during the historical and descriptive phases of the research underpinning it, before adding new depth to those understandings by applying an interpretive lens to episodes of controversy that have not been studied in this kind of analytical context before. The interpretive dimension of the theory therefore consists of an '*ex post facto* rationalisation'[76] about what appears to legitimise the UK law officer regime, based on values 'immanent'[77] in the historical and contemporary materials associated with it.

However, it should be strongly emphasised here that the three values chosen for the purposes of this book do not exhaust every legitimising value that might be

[72] Paul Daly, 'Administrative Law: A Values-Based Approach' in John Bell and others (eds), *Public Law Adjudication in Common Law Systems: Process and Substance* (Hart Publishing 2016); Paul Daly, 'Administrative Law: Characteristics, Legitimacy, Unity' in Mark Elliott, Jason NE Varuhas and Shona Wilson Stark (eds), *The Unity of Public Law? Doctrinal, Theoretical and Comparative Perspectives* (Hart Publishing 2018). Also see: Paul Daly, *Understanding Administrative Law in the Common Law World* (Oxford University Press 2021) ch 1.

[73] Stephen A Smith, *Contract Theory* (Oxford University Press 2004) 5, as cited in Daly, 'Administrative Law: A Values-Based Approach' (n 72) 102.

[74] Daly, 'Administrative Law: A Values-Based Approach' (n 72) 23; Daly, 'Administrative Law: Characteristics, Legitimacy, Unity' (n 72) 108; Daly, *Understanding Administrative Law* (n 72) 248.

[75] Daly, 'Administrative Law: Characteristics, Legitimacy, Unity' (n 72) 108.

[76] Allan Beever and Charles Rickett, 'Interpretive Legal Theory and the Academic Lawyer' (2005) 68 *Modern Law Review* 320, 324.

[77] Daly, 'Administrative Law: Characteristics, Legitimacy, Unity' (n 72) 108; Daly, 'Administrative Law: A Values-Based Approach' (n 72) 25.

suggested from a close reading of the leading literature about law officers. Rather, they have been formulated at a deliberately high level of abstraction resulting from a search for the most fundamental elements of legitimacy evident in those materials. Both Oliver's value-based analysis of commonalities between public and private spheres of the common law[78] and Daly's value-based analysis concerning judicial review of administrative actions[79] adopted a particular level of abstraction that reflected the degree of generality which their theses called for. Daly, in particular, explains that the values he selected were aimed at finding a 'middle ground' between those chosen by Oliver that were broad enough to cover the whole common law landscape and 'those so specific that they cover only a small part of the modern administrative law map'.[80] The values at the centre of this book are of the more specific sort envisaged by Daly, in that they apply only to the UK law officer regime as one part of a much broader constitutional picture, though they operate at a high level of abstraction within that context. This book is therefore more similar in its scope (but not in its overall method, which is mostly doctrinal and theoretical) to Richards' empirically supported study of 'responsiveness' as a 'legitimating value' within the narrower context of administrative bureaucracies.[81]

The *prescriptive* dimension of this framework is borne from the understanding that its values can be given different weight in different contexts and that such exercises are capable of guiding law officer conduct in the interests of maintaining their constitutional legitimacy. As Bottoms and Tankebe put it, values can be used to understand limits 'that define the conditions within which legitimate power may be exercised' in addition to supplying power-holders 'with rules and resources within which they can seek to realize certain societal objectives'.[82] In some situations, 'one of the values will prove more compelling than the others'[83] and in that sense determine the appropriate exercise of a law officer's function. In other situations, 'each of the values can be accommodated' in a way which reflects their appropriate weight in a given context 'rather than treating any one value as determinative'.[84] In this way, the values can provide an alternative perspective on conflicts between different interests (such as public interests and government interests) and provide a structured way of balancing them with reference to broadly accepted tools of conceptual analysis (such as independence, accountability and trust). Daly describes the overlapping and interlocking nature of the values involved in an analytical framework like this as a facilitative and 'pluralist' feature.[85]

[78] Oliver, *Common Values and the Public-Private Divide* (n 71) 56–60.
[79] Daly, 'Administrative Law: A Values-Based Approach' (n 72) 31.
[80] ibid.
[81] Zach Richards, *Responsive Legality: The New Administrative Justice* (Routledge 2018) ch 3.
[82] Anthony Bottoms and Justice Tankebe, 'Beyond Procedural Justice: A Dialogic Approach to Legitimacy in Criminal Justice' (2012) 102 *Journal of Criminal Law and Criminology* 119, 142.
[83] Daly, 'Administrative Law: A Values-Based Approach' (n 72) 24.
[84] ibid.
[85] ibid 24–25; Daly, 'Administrative Law: Characteristics, Legitimacy, Unity' (n 72) 120.

It is a feature which obviates a rigid approach to the demands of legitimacy in wide-ranging constitutional contexts. It is accepted, therefore, that the value-based framework used in this book is normative in so far as it provides benchmarks for criticism when law officers fail to appropriately calculate the weighting of their legitimising constitutional values in certain contexts.[86] Indeed, benchmarking assessments of this sort encapsulate the *evaluative* dimension of the framework.

As highlighted above, Chapters 3 to 6 of this book give form to its historical and descriptive dimensions by explaining how the UK law officer regime has historically developed into its current state alongside a detailed description of the modern functions that the law officers who constitute the regime must perform. It can be further noted at this stage that these studies also contain an embedded *comparative* dimension, though not in the traditional comparative law sense which is predominantly concerned with comparing 'legal formants' (i.e. individuals and groups who are 'institutionally involved in the activity of creating law') within multiple *states*.[87] Rather, the term 'compare' is used in its more literal sense in this book because the comparisons involved are concerned with offices that have developed differently in devolved *regions* within the UK as a single unitary state.[88] It is important to note, however, that there is no premise of assimilation underlying the goals of this project. Instead, its main goal of devising a conceptual framework that can be used to understand what legitimises different UK law officer models is to some extent premised on explaining the legitimate legal diversity embodied in those models.[89] Thus, while appreciating that the 'merits of the rules in one jurisdiction can show up more sharply the defects of the other' and that 'the successful practical operation of rules in one can most convincingly counter the theoretical fears which inhibit their adoption in the other',[90] the comparative research for these chapters was conducted with no negative preconceptions about the presence or absence of constitutional differences.

Having explained the rationale for including a literal form of comparative analysis throughout this book, a separate note on the theoretical framework adopted for the purposes of differentiating between the *levels* of difference discernible throughout them remains necessary. To this end, the five categories of difference first developed by McHarg as a means of conceptually distinguishing varying

[86] Daly, 'Administrative Law: A Values-Based Approach' (n 72) 24.

[87] Pier Giuseppe Monateri, 'Methods in Comparative Law: An Intellectual Overview' in Pier Giuseppe Monateri (ed), *Methods of Comparative Law* (Edward Elgar 2012) 7.

[88] Sergio Bartole, 'Internal Ordering in the Unitary State' in Michel Rosenfeld and András Sajó (eds), *The Oxford Handbook of Comparative Constitutional Law* (Oxford University Press 2012).

[89] For a useful review of some literature on legal pluralism and plurinationalism that supports the accommodation of constitutional diversity within a unitary state, see: Aileen McHarg, 'Public Law in Scotland: Difference and Distinction' in Aileen McHarg and Tom Mullen (eds), *Public Law in Scotland* (Avizandum 2006) 15–20.

[90] JDB Mitchell, 'The Merits of Disharmony' [1956] *Public Law* 6, 8; Roger Cotterrell, 'Is It So Bad to Be Different? Comparative Law and the Appreciation of Diversity' in Esin Orucu and David Nelken (eds), *Comparative Law: A Handbook* (Hart Publishing 2007).

degrees of difference between the public law rules of Scotland and those in the rest of the UK were identified and applied to the more limited range of provisions covered in Chapters 3 to 6.[91] McHarg's framework is, of course, extended beyond its original purpose in this context, to the extent that her categories are applied both vertically (in respect of differences between the law officers associated with the central UK Government as compared with those who are associated with the devolved administrations) and horizontally (in respect of differences between the various law officer models in operation at the devolved level alone). However, it is submitted that the conceptual distinctions supplied by McHarg are plainly abstract enough to be helpfully transferable.[92]

McHarg's first category will be used to describe *trivial* differences between the law officers, namely differences which do not reflect a substantive alteration in the underlying policy objective pursued by a nominally different set of rules.[93] This category is relevant, for example, where a devolved legislature has enacted legislation delineating certain powers or duties for a law officer which does not pursue radically different policy goals from similar but separate legislation enacted by another legislature.[94] Most functional differences between the Attorney General and the Solicitor General for England and Wales as set out in Chapter 3 fall into this category.[95] The second category encompasses *contextual* differences, including any distinctions thought to exist because of the legal and governance environment in which they apply, or because they involve issues which have 'no direct parallels elsewhere in the UK'.[96] Disparities arising from the unique Scottish legal system and the consociational form of government in Northern Ireland, for example, give rise to differences of this nature.[97] Differences resulting from *conservationism* fall into the third category, which holds more substantive divergences in the sense that they 'embody alternative value judgments about the appropriate constitution, regulation or scope of governmental power'.[98] Most likely to be categorised as such

[91] McHarg, 'Public Law in Scotland: Difference and Distinction' (n 89) 9–15. See also: Aileen McHarg, 'Unity and Diversity in the United Kingdom's Territorial Constitution' in Mark Elliott, Jason NE Varuhas and Shona Wilson Stark (eds), *The Unity of Public Law? Doctrinal, Theoretical and Comparative Perspectives* (Hart Publishing 2018). In the latter piece, McHarg adopts a different system for classifying territorial differences with reference to empirical evidence of institutional diversity, diversity in constitutional values, and differences in how the state itself is theorised. Her original approach is preferred for present purposes.

[92] Indeed, McHarg has since accepted that had she not confined the focus of her original framework to an evaluation of how aspects of public law in Scotland diverged from those elsewhere in the UK, she 'may have found more significant territorial diversity in the UK's constitutional arrangements' (particularly in relation to Northern Ireland). See: McHarg, 'Unity and Diversity' (n 91) 279.

[93] McHarg, 'Public Law in Scotland: Difference and Distinction' (n 89) 10.

[94] ibid.

[95] This observation is supported by Daintith and Page, for example, who 'speak no further' of the Solicitor General for England and Wales after concluding that there is a 'lack of any distinctiveness' in the modern office when compared with the Attorney General: Terence Daintith and Alan Page, *The Executive in the Constitution: Structure, Autonomy, and Internal Control* (Oxford University Press 1999) 233.

[96] McHarg, 'Public Law in Scotland: Difference and Distinction' (n 89) 10–11.

[97] ibid.

[98] ibid 11–13.

are differences which endure either because of a political desire to maintain the status quo in a certain region and those which endure simply because their reform has not been regarded as a sufficiently high priority by those with power to make the relevant changes.[99] The penultimate category is likely to attract fewer issues than the others in that it is intended to cope with *symbolic* constitutional differences that are largely a matter of 'rhetoric – rather than having any major practical effects on the operation of particular institutions'.[100] McHarg suggests the contestability of parliamentary sovereignty under Scots constitutional law as one such example,[101] to which the minimisation of royal rituals in constitutional matters affecting Northern Ireland might be added as a further example.[102] Fifth and finally, *genuine* differences are so categorised where there is evidence of a different path having been taken deliberately and which has real practical significance.[103] The statutory independence of the Attorney General for Northern Ireland is a highly significant example of many genuine differences that will be highlighted in due course. Indeed, provisions which fall into all five categories of difference – whether they be trivial, contextual, conservationist, symbolic or genuine – are highlighted by functional examples at appropriate junctures throughout Chapters 3 to 6, before all the offices within the UK law officer regime are compared on a more general basis at the beginning of Chapter 7.

Chapter 7 consolidates the interpretive dimension of the values-based framework of analysis by reflecting on how controversies about the functions described in Chapters 3 to 6 can be better understood with reference to the legitimising constitutional values set out in Chapter 2. In this way, Chapter 7 seeks to bring some intelligible order to the broad range of controversial episodes in recent history that have brought the legitimacy of the UK law officer regime into question. This is achieved by exploring how those episodes are normally justified with reference to either independence or accountability or both. The exploration of these values includes an overview of several historically significant controversial episodes. These overviews are analysed, in turn, through the interpretive lenses supplied by the conceptual literature in Chapter 2 before the underestimated value of trust is presented as an overlooked but nonetheless implicit value of importance to all such constitutional controversies. From this foundation, Chapter 8 proposes a trifocal and relativistic model for understanding the legitimacy of UK law officers and attempts to substantiate that model by reference to the findings made throughout this book. It develops those claims further, moreover, by proposing

[99] ibid.

[100] ibid 13–14.

[101] ibid.

[102] While the Crown defines executive power in Northern Ireland, and the Royal Assent is required for an Act of the Assembly, monarchical references have been minimised in various ways besides, such as in the wording of constitutional oaths and affirmations. In respect of those applicable to the judiciary and Northern Ireland Ministers, respectively, see: Justice (Northern Ireland) Act 2002, s 19; Northern Ireland Act 1998, s 16A(9) and Sch 4.

[103] McHarg, 'Public Law in Scotland: Difference and Distinction' (n 89) 14–15.

a structured way of evaluating and, to some extent, prescribing the conduct of UK law officers that takes account of all three legitimising constitutional values and which respects the synergistic and polydimensional nature of the analytical framework proposed. That chapter brings the book to its conclusion by summarising the original results of this study and considering how future studies on the UK law officer regime might make use of them.

Conclusions

This chapter began by setting out how the UK law officer regime has been defined and classified for the purposes of this book, before conducting a focused analysis of the leading literature about UK law officers to date. The significance of Edwards' historical insights were highlighted, together with his efforts to identify several philosophical differences in the way that past office-holders have approached the role of Attorney General, for instance, just as the weight of Walker's theoretical insights in connection with the internal contradictions associated with the role of a law officer were duly considered. The relevance of Appleby's potent argument in favour of addressing the significance of public confidence in respect of a law officer's conduct (as aside from the identification and punishment of actual misconduct) was also noted in this context. Subsequent to this review of the leading literature, there followed an explanation of the values-based framework for analysing the constitutional legitimacy of law officers in the UK that sets this book apart from its forerunners. In particular, a number of the dimensions involved in this approach – ranging from the historical, to the descriptive, to the interpretive, to the prescriptive, to the evaluative, to the comparative – were each examined in turn. In addition, a breakdown of the way in which various categories of difference are to be recorded in later chapters – ranging from the trivial, to the contextual, to the conservationist, to the symbolic, to the genuine – was also noted by way of explaining the comparative dimension of the book. Thus, having set the methodological scene as transparently as possible, it is now time to lift the curtain on some of the core concepts that form a necessary part of the backdrop for fully appreciating the constitutional legitimacy of the UK law officer regime.

2

Conceptualising Law Officers in the UK Constitution

Introduction

It is important, in a book of this kind, to be particularly careful about invoking normatively loaded words and concepts that may otherwise appear to be simplistic, vague or ill-defined. With that risk in mind, the purpose of this chapter is to demystify and define some of the most significant concepts that are drawn upon for evaluative purposes throughout the rest of the book. It is perhaps obvious by now that the conceptual development of the argument in this volume does not fit easily within the analytical methodologies that are most familiar to traditional legal scholars, because of the novel way in which it has been framed by reference to legitimising constitutional values rather than legitimate constitutional interests. On account of this break with tradition, both generally and in respect of the existing literature on law officers, it has been necessary to borrow from literature across a wide range of disciplines in order to construct functionally effective meanings for the core concepts that are needed in order to assess the constitutional legitimacy of the law officers with appropriate rigour. As such, the theoretical mind maps that are outlined below in connection with the constitutional values of independence, accountability and trust have been established not only from socio-legal studies literature but also from works of philosophy, history, political science, public administration, sociology, criminology and economics. Summaries of the main conceptual understandings that have been moulded from a combination of those disciplines are presented in each of the following sections of this chapter, after an initial summary in connection with the overarching concept of constitutional legitimacy is outlined in the first instance. They are followed, by way of conclusion, with an explanation of how these under-utilised resources will inform the remainder of this book.

The Concept of Constitutional Legitimacy

The concept of legitimacy is fundamental to the argument developed in this book, as demonstrated by the references to legitimate constitutional interests and legitimising constitutional values above. Thus, in accordance with the overarching significance of that argument, the aim of this section is to clarify which conception of legitimacy is intended throughout.[1] Schaar is to be credited, by way of background, for highlighting some important differences between 'traditional and lexical' definitions of legitimacy as compared with more recent 'professional definitions'.[2] The former, he explains, 'rest the force of a claim … upon foundations external to and independent of the mere assertion or opinion of the claimant'.[3] Such definitions of legitimacy may resonate with traditional legal scholars who adhere to Hart's conception of the rule of law, given that it is predicated on a secondary 'rule of recognition' which is accepted and used for the identification of 'primary rules of obligation'.[4] The 'professional' definitions assessed by Schaar, on the other hand, all 'dissolve legitimacy into belief or opinion' by trimming the traditional definitions of their normative and philosophical aspects.[5] Beetham singles out Max Weber's influence on the subject of legitimacy among social science professionals, for instance, as 'an almost unqualified disaster' on the part of an otherwise enormously important thinker in that domain.[6] Beetham heavily criticises Weber's definition of legitimacy (namely that 'legitimacy derives from people's belief in legitimacy') for conflating the concept with popular consent.[7] Lipset, in line with this normatively neutral Weberian tradition, later defined legitimacy as 'the capacity of a political system to engender and maintain the belief that the existing political institutions are the most appropriate ones'.[8] Beetham is similarly critical of that definition of the concept. He points out that, when taken to their logical conclusion, all such definitions would imply that the reason why constitutional systems fail is as a result of 'a deficiency of public relations',[9] which he rightly regards as an unsatisfactory explanation.

The 'received' definition of legitimacy borne from Weberian thought is generally defective for two persuasive reasons put forward by Beetham.[10] The first was touched on above, in that it concerns a misrepresentation of the relationship between legitimacy and people's beliefs. The legitimacy of a given system is not achieved simply because people believe in its legitimacy, he submits, but 'because

[1] For a helpful commentary on the intellectual history of legitimacy across a range of research disciplines, see: Robert D Lamb, *Rethinking Legitimacy and Illegitimacy: A New Approach to Assessing Support and Opposition Across Disciplines* (Rowman & Littlefield 2014) ch 2.

[2] John H Schaar, *Legitimacy in the Modern State* (Transaction 1981) 20.

[3] ibid.

[4] HLA Hart, *The Concept of Law* (3rd edn, Oxford University Press 2012) 100.

[5] Schaar (n 2) 20–21.

[6] David Beetham, *The Legitimation of Power* (Palgrave 1991) 8.

[7] ibid.

[8] Seymour Martin Lipset, 'Some Social Requisites of Democracy: Economic Development and Political Legitimacy' (1959) 53 *The American Political Science Review* 69, 86. See further: Seymour Martin Lipset, 'Social Conflict, Legitimacy, and Democracy' in William Connolly (ed), *Legitimacy and the State* (Basil Blackwell 1984) 88–103.

[9] Beetham (n 6) 9–10.

[10] ibid 11–12.

it can be *justified in terms of* their beliefs'. As such, when seeking to assess the legitimacy of a regime – like the UK law officer regime – it is necessary to evaluate how far the regime 'satisfies the normative expectations' of it or 'how far it conforms to [relevant] values'.[11] The exercise is not an assessment against 'universal criteria of the right or the good' that are often the concern of moral and political philosophers, but rather an assessment of the values which pertain within the context of a given regime.[12] This book conducts an evaluative exercise of this type by way of its values-based framework for analysing the legitimacy of the UK law officer regime.

The nature of that values-based framework of analysis was introduced in Chapter 1, but it should be noted at this juncture why a *polydimensional* understanding of its constituent values is necessitated by the concept of legitimacy overarching this book. The reason is that modern criminological scholars have extended social scientific understandings of legitimacy through several empirical studies, based on Beetham's modified Weberian framework together with some comparable theoretical models, which have 'shown that legal officials sometimes have to consider their legitimacy in relation to more than one audience and that these audiences might have significantly different priorities'.[13] Bottoms and Tankebe, in particular, have emphasised the importance of considering the dialogic relationship between self-beliefs about legitimacy held by power-holders in conjunction with the beliefs of their audiences.[14] In this way, Bottoms and Tankebe regard legitimacy as iterative in character because, unlike 'a single transaction', they conceptualise it as being 'more like a perpetual discussion, in which the content of power-holders' claims will be affected by the nature of the audience response'.[15] As such, the values-based framework of analysis used in this book takes full account of how different law officers' patrons can be expected to bring different interpretations of constitutional legitimacy driven by differing constitutional priorities. The intricacies of this framework will be developed further in Chapter 7, but the core point to note here is that the understandings of legitimacy contained in existing literature support the argument in this book about the importance of law officers' position between the main units of UK government and how this generates uniquely polydimensional conceptions of their legitimising constitutional values.

The second reason why Beetham disagrees with 'received' Weberian definitions of legitimacy is because they ignore other elements of the concept which are unrelated to people's beliefs. Beetham isolates both '*consent expressed through actions* which are understood as demonstrating consent', and *legality* (namely

[11] ibid 11.

[12] ibid 13.

[13] Anthony Bottoms and Justice Tankebe, 'Beyond Procedural Justice: A Dialogic Approach to Legitimacy in Criminal Justice' (2012) 102 *Journal of Criminal Law and Criminology* 119, 122–123, citing Alison Liebling, 'A "Liberal Regime Within a Secure Perimeter"?: Dispersal Prisons and Penal Practice in the Late Twentieth Century' in Anthony Bottoms and Michael Tonry (eds) *Ideology, Crime and Criminal Justice* (Routledge 2002).

[14] Bottoms and Tankebe (n 13) 129.

[15] ibid.

whether 'power is or is not acquired and exercised within the law') as two significant components of legitimacy that are independent of people's beliefs.[16] Other modern accounts of legitimacy with respect to a particular regime have considered whether its sources might also include factors such as its moral purpose, its methods, and its effectiveness at delivering specified outputs.[17] This book adopts Beetham's concept of legitimacy in light of his persuasive critiques of older Weberian definitions; because its emphasis on values is consistent with the analytical framework proposed, and because there appear to be no strong criticisms of his ideas in subsequent commentaries on legitimacy.[18] To summarise, Beetham's theory is that legitimacy is achieved by at least three cumulative factors. First, there is 'the legal validity of the acquisition and exercise of power'.[19] Second, there is 'the justifiability of the rules governing a power relationship in terms of the beliefs and values' that are prominent within a given regime.[20] Third, there is 'the evidence of consent derived from actions expressive of it'.[21]

This conception of legitimacy is helpful for the purpose of articulating legitimising constitutional values for law officers in the UK because it lays the necessary groundwork for realistic research methods. Beetham himself highlights that unmodified Weberian definitions would involve 'a quite misleading research strategy for determining whether power is legitimate: that of asking people whether they believe it is'.[22] In an empirical study, educating the respondents to such a question about the meaning of legitimacy would be highly problematic and, Beetham suggests, is ultimately unnecessary given that questions about the factors which animate his definition of legitimacy 'can in principle be answered from evidence in the public domain'.[23] In a normative book about legitimacy, like this one, it is more appropriate to explore whether a regime exercises its functions lawfully; whether

[16] Beetham (n 6) 12. Emphasis added.

[17] See, for example: Fiona de Londras and Kanstantsin Dzehtsiarou, *Great Debates on the European Convention on Human Rights* (Palgrave 2018) 1–10. Also see: Mark Elliott, *The Constitutional Foundations of Judicial Review* (Hart Publishing 2001) 10–21.

[18] This is not to say that others have not suggested *alternatives* to Beetham's conception of legitimacy, only that his ideas do not appear to have been attacked or undermined in any important sense by other thinkers in this field. See, for instance: Lamb (n 1); Wojciech Sadurski, Michael Sevel and Kevin Walton (eds), *Legitimacy: The State and Beyond* (Oxford University Press 2019).

[19] Beetham (n 6) 12. There is, of course, a rich debate about what amounts to valid law among legal philosophers that is not sufficiently relevant to be recounted here, but which is well encapsulated in the following book chapter: David Dyzenhaus, 'The Legitimacy of the Rule of Law' in David Dyzenhaus, Murray Hunt and Grant Huscroft (eds), *A Simple Common Lawyer: Essays in Honour of Michael Taggart* (Bloomsbury Publishing 2009).

[20] Beetham (n 6) 12. Beetham in fact refers to the beliefs and values operating within a 'particular society', but this book adopts his definition for the purposes of a small-scaled regime that has a standalone basis of legitimacy within a particular society. Nicole Roughan recently called for more studies of 'micro-legitimacy' such as this. See: Nicole Roughan, 'The Legitimacy of Whom?' in Wojciech Sadurski, Michael Sevel and Kevin Walton (eds), *Legitimacy: The State and Beyond* (Oxford University Press 2019).

[21] Beetham (n 6) 13.

[22] ibid.

[23] ibid.

the exercise of those functions in practice is congruent with relevant constitutional values and whether there is sufficient evidence to suggest that those most affected by the regime consent to be bound by it. This task has an obvious resemblance to the classic requirements for identifying constitutional conventions proposed by Jennings – namely evidence of a rule supported by reason that can be shown to have set a precedent that those affected feel bound by[24] – but its scope of application is broader in that it is capable of recognising both legal and political facets of constitutionalism.

The definition of legitimacy adopted for the purposes of this book is, in fact, premised on a related conception of constitutionalism that sees it as a 'politico-legal process', as opposed to a conception of constitutionalism focused primarily on the limitation of political power by law.[25] Feldman describes two characteristics of politico-legal constitutionalism that add clarity to the theoretical context of this study. The first characteristic provides that debates and disputes about the control, allocation and use of public power must be explored through whatever combination of political and legal processes is acceptable to those involved.[26] This understanding rationalises why many functions of UK law officers do not fit comfortably into purely political or legal models of constitutional analysis (as highlighted in the summary of Walker's critiques of past law officer scholarship in Chapter 1). The second characteristic provides that institutions and procedures for resolving constitutional debates and disputes must be continuously used in practice to secure a contemporaneously acceptable solution without expecting decided solutions to remain authoritative forevermore.[27] This further illuminates the significance of law officers given that they are expected to facilitate internal and external government debates and disputes while avoiding the trappings of an approach to their resolution which relies on constitutional entrenchment. Such an understanding of constitutionalism in the UK recognises 'a stable and effective set of norms, diverse in both form and in weight', which guide the conduct of law officers without necessarily owing their existence to legislative will or judicial protection.[28] In a similar vein, Casey and Kenny argue that 'the conventions, norms, and structure' within which law officers must operate 'will probably dictate the structure and culture' of their working environment.[29] When viewed from this perspective, it is clear that 'the processes and substantive norms governing the

[24] Ivor Jennings, *The Law and the Constitution* (University of London Press 1959) 136.

[25] David Feldman, 'Constitutionalism, Deliberative Democracy, and Human Rights' in John Morison, Kieran McEvoy and Gordon Anthony (eds), *Judges, Transition, and Human Rights* (Oxford University Press 2007) 444–447.

[26] ibid 445.

[27] ibid.

[28] Terence Daintith and Alan Page, *The Executive in the Constitution: Structure, Autonomy, and Internal Control* (Oxford University Press 1999) 19.

[29] Conor Casey and David Kenny, 'The Gatekeepers: Executive Lawyers and the Executive Power in Comparative Constitutional Law' (2022) *International Journal of Constitutional Law*, forthcoming.

work of executive legal advisors are of great importance to the exercise of public law in constitutional democracies, and our understanding of executive authority'.[30]

Having outlined the concept of constitutional legitimacy that underpins this book, the understandings of independence, accountability and trust that emerged from an analysis of pertinent literature on those concepts are summarised in the next three sections of this chapter. Chapters 7 and 8 will reflect on the manifestation of these legitimising constitutional values within the UK law officer regime, before advancing a theory about the synergistic relationship between them in that context. It is to be remembered, therefore, that the following summaries should be read as no more than an anchoring backdrop to the more specific conceptual analyses about law officers to come.

The Concept of Independence

One of the most striking features about the existing literature on independence is the extent to which it is fused with commentary on the judiciary and therefore understood as a distinctively judicial trait which other constitutional actors and institutions simply mirror to different degrees.[31] Some of the existing law officer scholarship discussed in Chapter 1 displayed this quality, often by characterising certain law officers' functions as 'quasi-judicial' in nature.[32] Rubin argues strongly against this approach, however, because it is premised on 'the idea that government consists of three separate branches' with clearly differentiated characteristics and powers, which bypasses 'the more basic question about what the concept of independence really means, as an operational matter'.[33] As he puts it, '[t]he judiciary, after all, is part of the government, acts in close conjunction with other governmental units, and generally contributes to the maintenance of a single governmental system'.[34] In light of these points, and in order to properly develop a theory of independence capable of capturing relevant governance techniques that are deployed across the state, Rubin prefers to envision the government by reference to 'the image of a network of interconnected institutions'.[35] The main

[30] ibid.

[31] Edward L Rubin, 'Independence as a Governance Mechanism' in Stephen B Burbank and Barry Friedman (eds), *Judicial Independence at the Crossroads: An Interdisciplinary Approach* (Sage 2002) 56. Also see: Edward L Rubin, *Beyond Camelot: Rethinking Politics and Law for the Modern State* (Princeton University Press 2007) 65.

[32] See, for example, Edwards' coverage on the prosecutorial independence of the Attorney General for England and Wales: John Ll J Edwards, *The Law Officers of the Crown: A Study of the Offices of Attorney-General and Solicitor-General of England with an Account of the Office of the Director of Public Prosecutions of England* (Sweet & Maxwell 1964) 223.

[33] Rubin, 'Independence as a Governance Mechanism' (n 31) 56–57.

[34] ibid 57.

[35] ibid 61. A similar image is presented by Bamforth in his thesis on the importance of institutional interdependence in the UK constitution, although he focuses almost exclusively on the specific relationship between courts and legislatures (the legislature being dependent on courts for clarifications

takeaway from this element of Rubin's argument is that analyses of independence are often damaged by their failure to identify the most relevant interacting governmental units with sufficient specificity.[36]

Rubin's theorisation of independence as a general rather than a judicial concept is a useful perspective for the purposes of this book. It enables a more accurate way of modelling the relationships between governmental units of different sizes and levels,[37] when compared with cruder models that are derived from eighteenth century legal philosophy.[38] The real strength of Rubin's model lies, first, in its taxonomy of 'signals' that flow through the linkages between different units and, second, in its classification of various 'interferences' with those signals that have the effect of producing escalating levels of independence between interacting units.

Inspired by the earlier efforts by Austin,[39] Searle[40] and Habermas,[41] Rubin breaks down the types of signal that flow through linkages between different units into three sorts: *informative* signals, *performative* signals, and *expressive* signals.[42] Informative signals 'describe a state of the world' and can include, for example, statements relating to the subject matter that a receiving unit is responsible for regulating or statements about the planned activities of the unit sending a signal.[43] Performative signals, by contrast, 'act in the world by making promises, delivering requests or issuing commands'.[44] Whereas promises and requests are types of signal typically sent between units that enjoy a collegial relationship with one another, commands are a type of signal typically sent between one unit that is authorised to control or supervise another.[45] Expressive signals, finally, consist

of its powers, for example). See: Nicholas Bamforth, 'Ultra Vires and Institutional Interdependence' in Christopher Forsyth (ed), *Judicial Review and the Constitution* (Hart Publishing 2000).

[36] Rubin, 'Independence as a Governance Mechanism' (n 31) 62.

[37] ibid 63.

[38] Most notably: Baron de Montesquieu, *The Spirit of Laws* (Thomas Nugent tr, Batoche Books 2001). Montesquieu's work was originally published in 1748 and translated by Nugent in 1752. For a short summary of its apparent influence over UK constitutional law, see: Colin R Munro, *Studies in Constitutional Law* (2nd edn, Oxford University Press 1999) 299–332. Laudable attempts to depart from the strictures on legal thought set by Montesquieu have been made in Australia through efforts to recognise a 'fourth branch' of government, though those developments are arguably hampered by similarly crude structural limitations. See: James Spigelman, 'The Integrity Branch of Government' (2004) 78 *Australian Law Journal* 724. Likewise, for a comparatively broader and more recent perspective, see: Mark Tushnet, *The New Fourth Branch: Institutions for Protecting Constitutional Democracy* (Cambridge University Press 2021).

[39] John L Austin, *How to do Things with Words* (2nd edn, Harvard University Press 1962), cited in Rubin, 'Independence as a Governance Mechanism' (n 31) 63.

[40] John R Searle, *Speech Acts: An Essay in the Philosophy of Language* (Cambridge University Press 1969), cited in Rubin, 'Independence as a Governance Mechanism' (n 31) 63.

[41] Jürgen Habermas, *The Theory of Communicative Action* (Thomas McCarthy tr, Beacon Press 1984) 273–338, cited in Rubin, 'Independence as a Governance Mechanism' (n 31) 63.

[42] Rubin, 'Independence as a Governance Mechanism' (n 31) 63.

[43] ibid 63–64.

[44] ibid 63.

[45] ibid 64.

of statements regarding the moral, political or emotional viewpoint of one unit about the conduct of another.[46] These signals can be positive (where, for example, the shadow Minister in charge of scrutinising a Government department speaks with approval about the actions of the Minister responsible for that department) or negative (where, for example, a judge declares the decision of a governmental official unconstitutional without any coercive order in accompaniment). Rubin submits that, in a network model, 'governmental units affect one another by means of signals' that fall within one of these three group types and that independence, 'as a structural feature of government', is 'produced when the signals from one unit to another are interfered with in some manner'.[47]

Though he recognises that other possibilities may exist, Rubin focuses on three forms of interference that have the effect of achieving independence between governmental units in different ways: the *prohibition* of certain signals between units, the *attenuation* of certain signals between units, and *expert filtering* on the part of a receiving unit.[48] He emphasises that the variety of ways in which these interferences can manifest themselves depends to a large extent on whether they are specific or global in their application, and on whether they are enforced by direct or indirect means.[49] Prohibitive interferences also vary in specific ways depending on the types of signals that are prohibited – a phenomenon which Rubin believes the term judicial independence fails to capture by virtue of its uniform connotations.[50] A 'low level of independence' is achieved when one unit is prohibited from sending performative signals to another, thereby precluding any direct or hierarchical control.[51] A higher, 'medium level' of independence is achieved when the first unit is also forbidden from sending an informative signal to the other, because such signals are influential in their nature (though the degree of influence they carry will increase depending on whether they are promises, requests or commands).[52] Finally, the 'highest level of independence' between two units is achieved when all types of signal between them are prohibited, to include not only performative and informative signals but also expressive signals, albeit the prohibition of expressive signals will only have an effect, of course, where a unit is capable of being influenced by the approval or disapproval of another.[53]

Attenuated interferences, meanwhile, can reduce the effect of different signal types 'without sacrificing so much of the control or coordination that the signals provide'.[54] This is easier said than done, but norms, protocols and 'widely shared

[46] ibid 64–65.
[47] ibid 65.
[48] ibid 66–69.
[49] ibid 67–68.
[50] ibid 66.
[51] ibid.
[52] ibid.
[53] ibid.
[54] ibid.

understanding[s]' providing that a unit is only supposed to send signals to another in certain circumstances is one means of achieving a partial increase in independence without closing down communication between them altogether.[55] Lastly, the application of expert filtering to information received by a particular unit is also suggested by Rubin as a mechanism for producing independence.[56] An obvious example of expert filtering interference would be the exclusion of signals where they fail to adhere to specific procedures, formats or qualifications that a receiving unit is trained to require (as, for instance, is the case in respect of certain court documents). The distinction between attenuated interferences and interferences produced by way of expert filtering is perhaps one of the weaker aspects of Rubin's model, given that they appear to overlap somewhat, but the overall framework remains helpful.

Rubin demonstrates the utility of his independence theory by using it to consider the extent to which judicial functions should be discharged independently in the US, and in what ways.[57] His sophisticated analysis shows how most of the features of judicial independence that are normally listed by writers on that subject can be accommodated by the theory set out above. Such features have been summarised in recent times by Smith, for example, as 'impartiality, insularity, exclusive competence, and compliance'.[58] Gee and others, on the other hand, define features of judicial independence in the UK with greater granularity by reference to ten 'conditions' which include guaranteed tenure; a merit-based appointment process; fair and secure remuneration; adequate funding for the overall system; exclusive jurisdiction; immunity from suit, and misconduct procedures which ensure that complaints are not used to influence how individual judges decide particular cases.[59] By microanalysing features of this sort using his theoretical framework for understanding independence, Rubin is able to suggest prescriptive recommendations for institutional improvement by reference to other legitimising constitutional values associated with the American judiciary, such as fairness. This book borrows from aspects of Rubin's understanding of independence in order to analyse the UK law officer regime in a similar vein, but with a different focus (on the functions of law officers) and by reference to the other legitimising constitutional values that have been identified in connection with members of that regime (namely accountability and trust).

[55] ibid 67.

[56] ibid. Rubin actually uses the term 'bias' to refer to this method of achieving independence, drawing on a definition of the word as it is understood in engineering sciences, but the term 'expert filtering' is used here instead to avoid any confusion with the concept of bias as it is commonly understood in UK administrative law – namely a disposition to decide something contrary to the interests of a particular party: see Timothy Endicott, *Administrative Law* (5th edn, Oxford University Press 2021) ch 5.

[57] Rubin, 'Independence as a Governance Mechanism' (n 31) 69–91.

[58] BC Smith, *Judges and Democratization: Judicial Independence in New Democracies* (Routledge 2017) ch 2.

[59] Graham Gee and others, *The Politics of Judicial Independence in the UK's Changing Constitution* (Cambridge University Press 2015) 10–11.

The Concept of Accountability

Much literature on the value of independence discusses it in tandem with the value of accountability.[60] Burbank and Friedman, for instance, describe the values as 'different sides of the same coin' and place writers who dichotomise them on the same par of misunderstanding as those who insist that 'achieving a proper balance' between the two values is 'a challenge unique to the judiciary'.[61] Gee and others recognise that Burbank and Friedman's coin metaphor is helpful 'insofar as it encourages us to grasp that independence and accountability are not in inevitable and irreconcilable tension' but warn that it could be 'misleading if it is taken to suggest that there are easy answers about how best to promote independence while also ensuring adequate accountability'.[62] They illustrate the point by explaining how it is unsurprising to find judges who regard themselves as unaccountable because of their attachment to a particular conception of independence.[63] This problem arises, in their view, where judges fail to appreciate a distinction between 'sacrificial' and 'explanatory' accountability.[64] Moreover, while they broadly agree that the value of independence requires steps to 'insulate judges against the types of sacrificial accountability found in the political sphere' (namely sanctions, penalties or dismissals in the event of poor performance), the demands of explanatory accountability (which mainly involve duties to provide specified types of information) are in fact consistent with many of the conditions for judicial independence.[65] As such, the negotiation of 'issues like judicial appointments or the management of judicial misconduct' are transactions about both independence and accountability.[66] Within the rubric of Rubin's theory of independence, negotiations like this might be understood as a process for establishing ground rules in relation to the types of interference that it is legitimate to impose upon signals between the relevant units of government.

Helpful though it is for introductory purposes, the distinction between sacrificial and explanatory accountability is not the most precise theoretical understanding that might be used. Rather, it is just one of many 'disconnected' approaches

[60] For a full edited volume that grapples with the relationship between both values, albeit only in a judicial context, see: Guy Canivet, Mads Andenas and Duncan Fairgrieve (eds), *Independence, Accountability and the Judiciary* (British Institute of International and Comparative Law 2006).

[61] Stephen B Burbank and Barry Friedman, 'Reconsidering Judicial Independence' in Stephen B Burbank and Barry Friedman (eds), *Judicial Independence at the Crossroads: An Interdisciplinary Approach* (Sage 2002) 15–16. Also see: Stephen B Burbank, 'The Architecture of Judicial Independence' (1999) 72 *Southern California Law Review* 315, 339–340.

[62] Gee and others (n 59) 21.

[63] ibid 19–20.

[64] ibid 19. The terms 'sacrificial' and 'explanatory' accountability are derived from Vernon Bogdanor. See: Vernon Bogdanor, 'Parliament and the Judiciary: The Problem of Accountability' (*UK Public Administration Consortium*, 9 February 2006), available at https://ukpac.wordpress.com/bogdanor-speech/.

[65] Gee and others (n 59) 19–22.

[66] ibid 22.

contained in a mass of accountability literature.[67] This body of disjointed scholarship has been criticised for being largely unsusceptible to systemic or comparative research due to the inconsistencies in approach that pervade it – as 'every volume and author tries to redefine accountability in his or her own way'.[68] Bovens has been ground-breaking in this respect, not only because he has recognised the dangers in a multiplicity of conceptually incoherent definitions but also because he has reduced the variances into two clear ways of thinking about accountability that have been very influential on the trajectory of accountability studies since.[69] His conceptualisation of accountability is thus slightly better refined and more widely used than the excellent work of Oliver[70] and Harlow[71] in this area, though their perspectives are fairly congruent with Bovens' in any event.

Bovens distinguishes between accountability as a 'virtue' and accountability as a 'mechanism' in academic research. Studies about the 'virtue' of accountability involve analysing different factors that induce accountable behaviour and evaluating whether the resulting behaviour conforms to certain standards (such as democracy, constitutionality and effectiveness). Normative research of this sort is about identifying deficits or excesses in accountability phenomena.[72] Whichever standards are applied in these assessments of accountability relations will normally yield separate and potentially conflicting results.[73] If democratic standards are applied, for instance, a deficit might be identified that would not arise as a concern if the relevant standard of assessment was good governance or efficient administration.[74] Bovens' arguments on this point overlap with the complementary research of Mashaw as developed by Adler, who has suggested a range of competing models of administrative justice (bureaucratic, professional, legal, managerial, consumerist, market) that are driven by different normative goals (accuracy, public service, legality, improved performance, consumer satisfaction,

[67] Mark Bovens, 'Two Concepts of Accountability: Accountability as a Virtue and as a Mechanism' (2010) 33 *West European Politics* 946, 946.

[68] ibid 947.

[69] Mark Bovens, 'Analysing and Assessing Accountability: A Conceptual Framework' (2007) 13 *European Law Journal* 447; Mark Bovens, Thomas Schillemans and Paul 't Hart, 'Does Public Accountability Work? An Assessment Tool' (2008) 86 *Public Administration* 225; Bovens, 'Two Concepts of Accountability' (n 67); Mark Bovens, Robert E Goodin and Thomas Schillemans, 'Public Accountability' in Mark Bovens, Robert E Goodin and Thomas Schillemans (eds), *The Oxford Handbook of Public Accountability* (Oxford University Press 2014).

[70] Dawn Oliver, 'Accountability and the Foundations of British Democracy – the Public Interest and Public Service Principles' in Nicholas Bamforth and Peter Leyland (eds), *Accountability in the Contemporary Constitution* (Oxford University Press 2013); Dawn Oliver, *Constitutional Reform in the United Kingdom* (Oxford University Press 2006) ch 3; Dawn Oliver, *Government in the United Kingdom: The Search for Accountability, Effectiveness and Citizenship* (Open University Press 1991).

[71] Carol Harlow, 'Accountability as a Value in Global Governance and for Global Administrative Law' in Gordon Anthony and others (eds), *Values in Global Administrative Law* (Hart Publishing 2011); Carol Harlow and Richard Rawlings, 'Promoting Accountability in Multilevel Governance: A Network Approach' (2007) 13 *European Law Journal* 542.

[72] Bovens, 'Analysing and Assessing Accountability' (n 69) 462.

[73] ibid.

[74] ibid 463–464.

economic efficiency) and which should therefore be assessed using different modes of accountability.[75] Perhaps the most important point that Bovens makes about the variety of normative perspectives that can be applied to studies of accountability as a virtue, which is reinforced by the administrative justice scholarship of Mashaw and Adler, is that they ultimately feed into 'a far bigger, more abstract concern of accountability'.[76] The biggest concern of accountability when viewed through these normative frameworks, as Bovens understands them, is legitimacy.[77] His understandings therefore dovetail well with the conception of legitimacy overarching this book, and its relationship with constitutional values like accountability, as already outlined above.

In studies about the 'mechanism' of accountability, on the other hand, the objective is to understand whether certain institutional relations really amount to accountability at all (as opposed to related but distinct phenomena such as transparency, responsiveness and participation) and, if so, what types of accountability are in use.[78] In these studies, the primary object 'is not so much the behaviour of public agents as it is the way in which these institutional arrangements govern the behaviour of public agents'.[79] Bovens helpfully supplies a definition of accountability and a four-way classification of the types of accountability that fall within it for the benefit of detailed but consistent analyses of this sort. He defines accountability as a specific social relation as follows:

> Accountability is a relationship between an actor and a forum, in which the actor has an obligation to explain and to justify his or her conduct, the forum can pose questions and pass judgement, and the actor may face consequences.[80]

Several brief points of elaboration about Bovens' definition may be useful. The first is that he accepts that both individuals and organisations can be actors and forums,[81] which coincides with the flexible conception of government units in the theory of independence developed by Rubin. Secondly, Bovens recognises that the obligation that lies between an actor and a forum where an accountability relationship exists can be both formal and informal, regular and irregular.[82] It can even be self-imposed, as in the case of voluntary audits for instance.[83] These

[75] For an overview of these models, see, in particular: Michael Adler, 'Understanding and Analysing Administrative Justice' in Michael Adler (ed), *Administrative Justice in Context* (Hart Publishing 2010). For the main contribution of Mashaw that inspired Adler's scholarship in this field, see: Jerry L Mashaw, *Bureaucratic Justice: Managing Social Security Disability Claims* (Yale University Press 1983). Also see: Nicholas R Parrillo (ed), *Administrative Law from the Inside Out: Essays on Themes in the Work of Jerry L. Mashaw* (Cambridge University Press 2018).

[76] Bovens, 'Analysing and Assessing Accountability' (n 69) 464.

[77] ibid.

[78] ibid 450–454.

[79] Bovens, Goodin and Schillemans (n 69) 8.

[80] Bovens, 'Analysing and Assessing Accountability' (n 69) 450. Emphasis removed.

[81] ibid 450–451.

[82] Bovens, 'Analysing and Assessing Accountability' (n 69) 451.

[83] ibid.

points complement Feldman's conception of UK constitutionalism as a politico-legal process, a conception which underpins this book in the manner discussed earlier. Lastly, Bovens distinguishes between three main phases in the actual account giving between an actor and a forum. During the first phase, the actor is obliged to inform the forum about his or her conduct.[84] During the second phase, the forum must be given an opportunity to 'interrogate the actor and to *question* the adequacy of the information or the legitimacy of the conduct'.[85] During the third phase, the forum may pass judgement on the actor. Judgement can take many forms – positive or negative, sanction or reward, implicit or explicit – but will normally involve consequences of some kind or other.[86]

While Bovens' definition of accountability alone exceeds the analytical capabilities provided by a relatively blunt distinction between sacrificial and explanatory accountability, he makes another significant contribution to this strand of thinking by delineating four dimensions to the concept that revolve around some seemingly simple questions: 'who is accountable to whom, for what, by which standards, and why?'.[87] Bovens emphasises that every accountability relation can be mapped onto each of these dimensions because the dimensions themselves are largely distinctive and unrelated.[88] As such, each will be considered in turn before this section reaches its conclusion – first the nature of the *forum* involved, then the nature of the *actor*, then the nature of the *conduct*, followed by the nature of the *obligation*.

There are at least five types of forum that organisations and officials operating in a constitutional democracy may encounter, Bovens submits, and hence at least five different kinds of accountability.[89] Political forums call for political accountability, first and foremost, which is exercised along a chain of principal–agent relationships in the UK context.[90] That is to say, 'public servants and their organisations are accountable to their minister, who must render a political account to parliament' and, in some sense at least, parliamentary representatives 'render account to the voters at election time'.[91] On this conventional understanding of the UK constitution, each link in the chain is 'not only principal and agent, but also forum and actor' for the purposes of analysing accountability, with the exception of the two ends of the chain (the voters and the frontline officials), where there is no need to multi-role.[92] Legal forums like courts, meanwhile, involve legal accountability which is rather less ambiguous because it is usually based on specific responsibilities that have been legally conferred upon authorities.[93]

[84] ibid.
[85] ibid.
[86] ibid 451–452.
[87] Bovens, Goodin and Schillemans (n 69) 10. Emphasis removed.
[88] Bovens, 'Analysing and Assessing Accountability' (n 69) 461.
[89] ibid 455.
[90] ibid.
[91] ibid.
[92] ibid.
[93] ibid 456.

Administrative forums like ombudsmen and auditors require a different form of accountability again, often on the basis of specifically prescribed norms such as maladministration and financial misconduct,[94] and professional forums like law societies and bar councils also lay down codes of practice which are monitored and enforced vis-à-vis respected peers within a given profession.[95] Finally, Bovens further recognises a range of social forums like 'civil interest groups, charities and associations of clients' that are capable of forming social relations amounting to accountability with public actors, but cautions that in many cases such forums are unable to sanction or reward actors in a way meaningful enough to bring them within scope.[96] Where social forms of accountability do come into being, however, they can be particularly effective at 'providing policy-makers with feedback about the legitimacy and effects of their policies'.[97] In any event, it is quite clear that all five of these forums 'generally demand different kinds of information and apply different criteria as to what constitutes responsible conduct', and that public actors must therefore be prepared to face the 'problem of many eyes' as they strive toward legitimising perceptions of their conduct.[98]

Accountability forums of all varieties often face a similarly diverse variety of actors, as it can be 'difficult to unravel who has contributed in what way to the conduct of an agency' and who, therefore, should be brought to account for it.[99] Bovens characterises this as the 'problem of many hands'[100] and draws particular attention to the fact that organisational conduct is often the result of an 'interplay between fatherless traditions and orphaned decisions' as personnel come and go.[101] He identifies a range of strategies for overcoming this problem, the first and bluntest being the incorporation of an organisation so that its actions are treated unitarily.[102] Another is the 'one for all' approach, where an institution is organised hierarchically and processes for calling to account 'start at the top, with the highest official'.[103] In this sort of system, superior officials hold their subordinates to account by way of internal accountability in accordance with the chain of command between each principal and agent, or, in other words, between each forum and actor.[104] The convention of ministerial responsibility in the UK befits this model, for instance, and can be contrasted with the 'all for one' approach inherent in the convention of collective cabinet responsibility wherein every member of the unit agrees to account for a given matter irrespective of their actual contribution

[94] ibid.
[95] ibid; Bovens, Goodin and Schillemans (n 69) 11.
[96] Bovens, 'Analysing and Assessing Accountability' (n 69) 457.
[97] Bovens, 'Two Concepts of Accountability' (n 67) 956.
[98] Bovens, 'Analysing and Assessing Accountability' (n 69) 455.
[99] ibid 457.
[100] ibid.
[101] ibid 458.
[102] ibid.
[103] ibid.
[104] ibid.

to it.[105] This reflects the formal legal position, of course, given that UK ministers are regarded as a 'single body' by the law.[106] However, when such accountability strategies fail on account of moral objections related to the proportional allocation of wrongdoing and blame, Bovens suggests that individual accountability is the appropriate solution, in which 'individual officials are held accountable in so far as they have contributed to or are responsible for the acts of the organization'.[107]

In terms of the scope of the conduct that actors can be called upon to explain and provide justification for, Bovens submits that this will normally 'concur with the classification made according to the type of forum' and does not therefore call for lengthy analysis.[108] Some forums, like auditors, may only consider financial conduct, while other forums, like legislatures, may consider a broad range of conduct including the content of policy decisions.[109]

The last dimension open to consideration is, in fact, a cumulatively relational one, in that the nature of the obligation involved in any given accountability situation will depend to a large extent on the relationship between an actor and a forum as well as any limits on the type of conduct that is recognised for account giving purposes between them. The key distinction that Bovens highlights here is between mandatory and voluntary obligations, which give rise to vertical and horizontal lines of accountability, though he also recognises an intermediary suite of relations which give rise to what he calls diagonal accountability. Mandatory obligations, as he conceptualises them, lie upon an actor where a particular forum wields formal power over them, as in the case of an administrative body that is accountable to a government minister, who is in turn accountable to Parliament. These relations are emblematic of vertical accountability.[110] Voluntary obligations, meanwhile, arise where there is no hierarchical relationship between an actor and a forum.[111] The horizontal line of accountability that occurs in these situations is normally explicable by reference to some sort of moral obligation.[112] Bovens notes, however, that administrative accountability relations normally fall somewhere between these two extremes.[113] Although ombudsmen lack formal enforcement powers, for instance, they normally report to a government minister

[105] ibid 458–459; Bovens, Goodin and Schillemans (n 69) 10. For a detailed constitutional account of the above-mentioned conventions, see: Geoffrey Marshall, *Constitutional Conventions: The Rules and Forms of Political Accountability* (Oxford University Press 1987) ch 4.

[106] *R (BAPIO Action Ltd) v Secretary of State for the Home Department* [2008] UKHL 27, [2008] 1 AC 1003 at [33]. Note, however, that the legal position differs significantly in respect of the Northern Ireland Executive. See: Conor McCormick, 'The Three Tiers of Executive Power in Northern Ireland' in Brice Dickson and Conor McCormick (eds), *The Judicial Mind: A Festschrift for Lord Kerr of Tonaghmore* (Hart Publishing 2021).

[107] Bovens, 'Analysing and Assessing Accountability' (n 69) 459; Bovens, Goodin and Schillemans (n 69) 10.

[108] Bovens, 'Analysing and Assessing Accountability' (n 69) 459.

[109] Bovens, Goodin and Schillemans (n 69) 11.

[110] Bovens, 'Two Concepts of Accountability' (n 67) 953.

[111] Bovens, 'Analysing and Assessing Accountability' (n 69) 460.

[112] ibid.

[113] ibid.

or to Parliament, which gives rise to an 'indirect, two-step relation with the forum' that Bovens describes as diagonal accountability, or 'accountability in the shadow of hierarchy'.[114]

Both of the frameworks developed by Bovens for studying accountability as a virtue and accountability as a mechanism are relevant to this book. Care will be taken to avoid conflating the two sets of analytical apparatus, which Bovens warns against, as the complementary perspectives they enable are considered.[115] The latter type of analysis will be used, in particular, to assess which law officer functions are subject to accountability mechanisms and, for those that are, whether they involve any excesses or deficits in feedback and control. The former type of analysis will contribute to an assessment of law officers' engagement with accountability mechanisms in times of controversy, as part of a broader assessment of how their legitimacy is damaged or sustained in those circumstances.

The Concept of Trust

Trust is the final constitutional value that will be used to inform an evaluative assessment of legitimacy in respect of the UK law officer regime in this book. The following summary of established understandings about the concept begins by introducing its broad relevance alongside the values of independence and accountability discussed above, followed by some clarification about its relationship to several more important concepts. An overview on predominant schools of sociological thought about the underlying rationale of trust scholarship will be provided thereafter, before this section ends by setting out a theoretical model of trust that seeks to demonstrate how it can be applied practically.

Beginning with the relevance of trust to this book, the first point to note is that the concept is prevalent throughout a significant proportion of the literature on independence and accountability set out above, although it is not normally given the same weight or attention as the other two values. Appleby even touches on connections between the concept and its two counterparts in her work on Australian law officers, albeit in passing, when explaining that a Solicitor-General 'must maintain accountability, ensure professional independence and gain trust' when 'negotiating the at times competing tensions that are inherent in the office'.[116] In the independence literature, moreover, some theorists have posited that courts enhance their independent authority by strategically earning the trust of governmental audiences,[117] and, in the accountability literature, a decrease in

[114] ibid.

[115] Bovens, 'Two Concepts of Accountability' (n 67) 961–963.

[116] Gabrielle Appleby, 'Navigating a Complicated Relationship: The Role of the Solicitor-General' (2016) 29 *Law Society of NSW Journal* 70, 71.

[117] See, for example: Clifford James Carrubba, 'A Model of the Endogenous Development of Judicial Institutions in Federal and International Systems' (2009) 71 *The Journal of Politics* 55.

public trust tends to be suggested as a potential justification for the introduction of different accountability mechanisms.[118] The potential for excessive or badly tailored accountability to obstruct trust in the UK judiciary is, moreover, a well-documented risk in judiciary-focused scholarship, where it is also considered an important 'part of the rationale for protecting judicial independence'.[119] While these acknowledgements about the relevance of trust to legal research questions are positive, most academics do not position the relevance of trust on a par with more familiar legal concepts. This book is therefore unique in this regard, partly as a result of the values-based methodology guiding it and the fundamental importance of trust that emerged from its historical and structural study of the UK law officer regime, but also in response to a group of legal scholars who have called 'for more attention to be paid to the concept of trust in our study of law'[120] (including public law).[121]

Hardin emphasises the close relationship of trust to a range of appurtenant concepts by way of his contention that it is 'not a simple primitive term' but rather one 'constituted by certain things, including expectations and cognitive judgments of the motivations of others, motivations that would make them more or less trustworthy in particular contexts'.[122] The distinction between trust and trustworthiness is often misunderstood, to Hardin's repeated frustration,[123] because writers fail to distinguish between the properties of trust itself (such as a degree of risk, reliance

[118] Bovens, 'Analysing and Assessing Accountability' (n 69) 457. Also see: Hassan Danaee Fard and Ali Asghar Anvary Rostamy, 'Promoting Public Trust in Public Organizations: Explaining the Role of Public Accountability' (2007) 7 *Public Organization Review* 331. Cf Genki Kimura, 'Towards Persuasive Accountability: Accountability in the Post-Truth Era' (Questions of Accountability Conference, Online, November 2021). Kimura argues that 'accountability deficits' and 'accountability overloads' actually tend to coexist because governments often attempt to regain public trust by way of bureaucratically demanding institutional reforms, when really they ought to reorientate their practices towards 'persuasive accountability' techniques that translate scientifically rigorous justifications for their decisions into rhetorically appealing messages to the public.

[119] Gee and others (n 59) 20–21; Andrew Le Sueur, 'Developing Mechanisms for Judicial Accountability in the UK' (2004) 24 *Legal Studies* 73, 74–75. Both these works refer to the important consciousness-raising work of Onora O'Neill's BBC Reith Lectures: Onora O'Neill, *A Question of Trust* (Cambridge University Press 2002). Also see: Onora O'Neill, 'Trust, Trustworthiness, and Accountability' in Nicholas Morris and David Vines (eds), *Capital Failure: Rebuilding Trust in Financial Services* (Oxford University Press 2014).

[120] David Vitale, 'A Trust Network Model for Social Rights Fulfilment' (2018) 38 *Oxford Journal of Legal Studies* 706, 706. Vitale refers to the following leading lights, among others: Frank B Cross, 'Law and Trust' (2004) 93 *Georgetown Law Journal* 1457; Roger Cotterrell, 'Trusting in Law: Legal and Moral Concepts of Trust' (1993) 46 *Current Legal Problems* 75; Mark A Hall, 'The Importance of Trust for Ethics, Law, and Public Policy' (2005) 14 *Cambridge Quarterly of Healthcare Ethics* 156. Also see: David Vitale, 'Leaving the EU: A Matter of "Trust"?' (*UK Constitutional Law Association Blog*, 9 April 2019). Available at: https://ukconstitutionallaw.org/2019/04/09/david-vitale-leaving-the-eu-a-matter-of-trust/.

[121] Paul Reynolds, 'Legitimate Expectation and the Protection of Trust in Public Officials' [2011] *Public Law* 330. Also see: Raquel Barradas de Freitas and Sergio Lo Iacono (eds), *Trust Matters: Cross-Disciplinary Essays* (Hart Publishing 2021).

[122] Russell Hardin, *Trust* (Polity Press 2006) 27.

[123] ibid; Russell Hardin, *Trust and Trustworthiness* (Russell Sage Foundation 2004) 29–31; Karen S Cook, Russell Hardin and Margaret Levi, *Cooperation Without Trust?* (Russell Sage Foundation 2005) ch 2.

on another, and so on) and the qualities or actions of an individual or unit that make them trustworthy (such as honesty, capability and reputation). Trust and trustworthiness therefore demand some definitional clarification that Hardin deals with well by delineating a number of their elements and relatives.[124] According to Hardin, foremost among these elements and relatives are notions of reliance, risk and expectation. He points out that all standard accounts of trust 'assume that it involves some reliance on someone or some agency when there is at least some risk that the agent will fail the trust'.[125] Matters that distinguish the conditions for discretionary trust from obligatory reliance are debated among scholars, however, with some arguing the distinction flows from some moral faith in the cooperative nature of humanity and others insisting it comes from a 'prudential assessment' of trustworthiness on the part others – neither of which are necessary in cases of reliance (as where someone relies on the sun to rise).[126] Risk is almost universally regarded as an essential component of trust, moreover, because 'acting on a trust involves giving discretion to another to affect one's interests', something which creates an inexorable risk 'that the other will abuse their discretion'.[127] As for expectations, Hardin explains that 'virtually all conceptions of trust' contain an element of expectation, though he admits that not all conceptions conform to his view that trusting involves the inherent expectation that a person who trusts another does so because it is in the other's interests to act cooperatively.[128]

Hardin is to be credited for acknowledging the contested approach to trust on which some of his definitions are premised. Hosking has explained that Hardin's approach appears to be a derivative of both functionalism and rational choice theory, which he contrasts with approaches to trust that are based on plainly normative foundations.[129] Functionalist theories generally posit an ultimate role or purpose for trust.[130] Luhmann, for example, believes that the function of trust is to reduce the complexity of the modern world. On this account, trust deals with complexity 'by going beyond available information and generalising expectations of behaviour in that it replaces missing information with an internally guaranteed security'.[131] Functionalist theories which borrow from rational choice theory are driven by the view that 'social life constitutes the aggregated outcomes of all individual's rational choices', in which 'rationality is understood in utilitarian terms as a matter of satisfying the individual's preference'.[132] Hosking notes that Hardin, as

[124] Hardin, *Trust* (n 122) 27–31.
[125] ibid 27.
[126] ibid 27–28.
[127] Hardin, *Trust and Trustworthiness* (n 123) 11–12; Hardin, *Trust* (n 122) 28–29.
[128] Hardin, *Trust* (n 122) 29.
[129] Geoffrey Hosking, *Trust: A History* (Oxford University Press 2014) 34–37.
[130] Barbara Misztal, *Trust in Modern Societies: The Search for the Bases of Social Order* (Polity Press 1996) ch 3.
[131] Niklas Luhmann, *Trust and Power* (Wiley & Sons 1979) 93.
[132] Misztal (n 130) 77–78.

an exponent of this approach, 'sees trust as an expression or indirect manifestation of one's own self-interest'.[133] As a result, Hardin thinks that trust comes about where two or more people encapsulate the interests of each other in their conceptions of self-interest.[134] This normally occurs, he says, because of a mutual desire to maintain an ongoing relationship that is justified by a positive assessment of the risk that purely personal interests may trump the encapsulated interests.[135]

The main alternatives to these 'cognitive' approaches to trust are founded on normative or 'affective' precepts.[136] Hollis, who is a leading writer of this optimistic sort, contests the notion that individuals are free-standing rational actors and instead prefers to view the world as a place where 'we who construct the action are social beings before we are particular individuals and are plural before we are singular'.[137] He criticises Hardin's conceptualisation for its inability to explain 'what motivates car-drivers to give lifts to hitchhikers or donors to give blood', where there is 'no obvious return' and 'no likelihood of a continuing relationship such as would justify an interest-based explanation'.[138] He associates, instead, with communitarian political traditions which work from the assumption that 'human beings exercise trust because they would like others to trust them and accept that this entails being trustworthy oneself'.[139] Seldon also firmly commits himself to this way of thinking by describing trust as an 'innate' trait of human beings, a claim which substantiates his view on the importance of intrinsic motivations to trust.[140] He believes that extrinsic motivations like 'rigid laws and harsh punishments' can lead to compliance at most, but never trust.[141] He also regards 'middle-ground' accountability mechanisms (which he defines broadly to include contracts and target duties) as an imperfect route to trust,[142] leaving only intrinsic trust as a sure way of achieving a society in which trust 'becomes the dominant value'.[143] As this objective makes clear, Seldon favours trust 'as the best overarching idea for reinvigorating society and bringing back purpose and legitimacy to government'.[144] In this regard, he differs from a broad range of contemporary political philosophers who each stress 'the need for one goal to be placed above all others: Justice (Rawls); Liberty (Nozick); Happiness (Layard); or Capabilities (Sen)'.[145]

[133] Hosking (n 129) 34.
[134] Hardin, *Trust* (n 122) 18–25.
[135] ibid 19.
[136] Hosking (n 129) 36; Cross (n 120) 1463–1471. Also see: Rutger Bregman, *Humankind: A Hopeful History* (Bloomsbury Publishing 2020).
[137] Martin Hollis, *Trust Within Reason* (Cambridge University Press 1998) 115; Hosking (n 129) 36.
[138] Hosking (n 129) 36.
[139] ibid.
[140] Anthony Seldon, *Trust: How We Lost It and How to Get It Back* (Biteback 2009) 25.
[141] ibid 14.
[142] ibid 25.
[143] ibid 14.
[144] ibid 56.
[145] ibid.

The more moderate stance of Cross and Hosking stands out as the most preferable take on these debates about cognitive and affective trust, however, namely that 'any individual instance of trust probably contains both affective and cognitive components' and that any satisfactory theory therefore needs 'both rational-choice and moral conceptions of trust'.[146] A combination of both types is regarded as essential for 'optimal trust' in this light, though the ratio between affective and cognitive trust need not be constant in all contexts.[147] Indeed, Cross highlights that individuals 'may trust affectively in some contexts (such as interpersonal relations) while being more cognitively calculating in others (such as business dealings)'.[148] On this view, the real distinction between each type of trust lies in the 'leap of faith' that each calls for in different degrees, with the breadth of that leap being 'much narrower' where cognitive trust is concerned.[149]

As this book has identified trust as a constitutional value capable of legitimising perceptions of certain governmental conduct, it is necessary to consider how the concept might be realised and measured in practice. A model of trust proposed by Seldon, which involves measuring all actions against a conceptual 'trust test', is instructive in this respect.[150] Seldon's trust test assesses actions on the basis of whether they add or detract from trust, which he sees as a qualitative judgement best informed by reference to two interacting continuums: an individualist–collectivist continuum and an ideology–regulation continuum.[151] To judge an action with reference to the individualist–collectivist continuum involves thinking about whether it strikes an appropriate balance between the needs of an individual and the needs of society more generally in any given context.[152] An action that registers at the individualist end of the continuum will be regarded as selfish and is therefore likely to fail the trust test, just as an action which is too collectivist will fail by reason of its potential to stifle individual and corporate enterprise.[153] To judge an action with reference to the ideology–regulation continuum, on the other hand, involves striking a balance between conduct which furthers an ideological goal and managerial regulation designed to provide certainty.[154] Seldon points to 'Marxism or extreme environmentalism' to illustrate ideologies which can be damaging to the extent that 'they place the achievement of their ends above human needs', and berates 'the modern drive for scientific managerialism in the form of regimentation and accountability' by way of an example of excessive control.[155]

[146] Cross (n 120) 1469; Hosking (n 129) 37.
[147] Cross (n 120) 1469.
[148] ibid.
[149] ibid.
[150] Seldon (n 140) 28.
[151] ibid 26–29.
[152] ibid 26–27.
[153] ibid.
[154] ibid 27.
[155] ibid.

As such, Seldon argues that it is only by identifying a middle ground between both poles on both continuums that trust can be realised and measured to some useful degree.[156] Empirical research projects involving public surveys or game experiments could also be developed in order to build on this model by refining sociological understandings of where the appropriate balance lies with respect to certain controversial proposals.[157]

Conclusions

This chapter has defined the concept of constitutional legitimacy and the values of independence, accountability and trust that will be used to anchor the values-based analysis of constitutional controversies in Chapters 7 and 8. In addition, having introduced the core concepts relevant to that analysis at this stage in the book, it will be possible to highlight and foreshadow some features of the UK law officer regime that intersect with these concepts during the historical and structural examination of the regime in Chapters 3 to 6. It should be recalled at this point that much of the existing academic literature containing historical and structural studies of the UK law officer regime is outdated, incomplete and fragmentary.[158] Cognisant of these deficiencies, one of the main objectives of Chapters 3 to 6 it is to provide a fresh historical and structural overview of the law officers; one which places a particular emphasis on the considerable changes ushered in by the advent and growth of devolved government in the UK. Thus, the next four chapters aim to frame future scholarship on the UK law officer regime in a manner which is as constitutionally holistic and balanced as possible. Accordingly, its focus is on the technical modelling of those law officers which collectively constitute the regime. A normative evaluation of the different models at play – with reference to past controversies which appear to have impugned their legitimacy – would be premature and depthless if explicated in tandem with their doctrinal exposition. It is for these reasons that the substantive consideration of such controversies will instead be considered at subsequent junctures, at least in so far as they are relevant to the overarching aims of this book as summarised in Chapter 1. The substantive consideration of relevant controversies is weaved throughout Chapter 7, in particular, by way of advancing context-specific understandings of the three main factors which appear to sustain the legitimacy of the UK law officer regime (that is, law officer-specific understandings of independence, accountability and trust). However, the development of those arguments is, of course, grounded in the foundational framework that has been fashioned in this chapter and the one which preceded it. Thus, another objective of the historical and structural analysis which follows is to begin

[156] ibid 27–29.
[157] Hardin, *Trust* (n 122) 35–38.
[158] For more specific commentary on the existing literature, see ch 1 at 9–13.

contextualising the theoretical narrative introduced hitherto and developed later in the book by detailing the homogeneity and heterogeneity of law officer modelling in the UK. It features passing reference to significant controversies only where they may have constituted drivers of historical change or continuity, and where they usefully highlight conceptual tensions in their overall context. Chapter 3 deals, first, with the offices of the Attorney General and the Solicitor General for England and Wales. Chapter 4 is dedicated to the office of the Counsel General for Wales. Chapter 5 turns to the offices of the Lord Advocate, the Solicitor General and the Advocate General for Scotland, while the focus of Chapter 6 falls on the offices of the Attorney General and the Advocate General for Northern Ireland. Many of the similarities and differences between these offices will be highlighted where relevant along the way, but a short review of those comparative findings will also be provided at the beginning of Chapter 7.

3

The Attorney General and Solicitor General for England and Wales

Introduction

The exact origin of the office of Attorney General is said to be 'lost in the pages of history'.[1] It is known that because a medieval King would not appear as a litigant in royal courts to plead in a case which might affect his own interests, he would appoint an Attorney to discharge this function.[2] Thus, in the beginning, the King's Attorney was simply a partisan servant of the monarch; there being no division of the Crown into legislature, executive and judiciary consonant with the fictional legal definition of the term as we understand it today.[3] Over time, as 'the functions of sovereignty became more complex and extensive and acquired a more public character',[4] the functions of the King's Attorneys expanded to an extent whereby they 'were expected to officiate as advisers and attendants to the peers of the realm'.[5] Some subtle political connotations were first assumed by the office through developments of this nature, whereby the role of legal adviser to the monarch had to be managed alongside commands from his legislature. Less subtly, the concept of the Crown (once firmly attached to the King's figurative head) was fundamentally redefined in response to the constitutional upheavals of the seventeenth century which demanded a rearrangement of the monarchical constitution into one which institutionalised 'partners in authority'.[6] Power-brokers who could not be removed by the monarch were conceptually amalgamated to govern in the name of the Crown by this method,[7] which resulted in more enduring complications around the identity of the Attorney's notional client(s).

[1] Hartley Shawcross, 'The Office of the Attorney-General' (1953) 7 *Parliamentary Affairs* 380, 381. For references to the work of some legal historians who 'were less reluctant to fathom the genesis of the office', see: John Ll J Edwards, *The Law Officers of the Crown: A Study of the Offices of Attorney-General and Solicitor-General of England with an Account of the Office of the Director of Public Prosecutions of England* (Sweet & Maxwell 1964) 12–13.

[2] Shawcross (n 1).

[3] Fiona Hanlon, 'An Analysis of the Office of Attorney General in Australia and Directions for the Future' (PhD thesis, University of Melbourne 2007) 17.

[4] Shawcross (n 1).

[5] Edwards, *The Law Officers of the Crown* (n 1) 4.

[6] Martin Loughlin, 'The State, the Crown and the Law' in Maurice Sunkin and Sebastian Payne (eds), *The Nature of the Crown: A Legal and Political Analysis* (Oxford University Press 1999) 44.

[7] ibid.

The early origin of the office of Solicitor General is beset by a lack of agreement among historians, though it is by comparison a more 'modern creation of smaller stature'.[8] While the post of King's Solicitor is 'universally recognised as the original precursor to the modern office',[9] it is unclear whether that nominally distinct title was devised out of recognition towards some specialist knowledge of equitable procedures executed by agents of that name or, more simply, because the original office-holders had a similar relationship to the King's Attorney as that which existed between private solicitors and attorneys of the time.[10] In any case, it is clear that after the title of Solicitor General emerged in 1525 its bearers were clearly regarded as deputies to the Attorney General.[11] The prestige attached to the role and the relevant experience it provided for was such that a strong convention in favour of promotion to the post of Attorney General in the event of a vacancy quickly came into being,[12] although the modern-day currency of that convention is very weak.[13]

It is a largely unfortunate by-product of historical conservationism that the Solicitor General is not known as the Assistant or Deputy Attorney General, given that most of those who have held the office have been barristers rather than solicitors ever since that professional division came into existence, and because nearly 'all that may be said about the Attorney-General applies to the Solicitor-General, who stands in his [or her] place and acts for him [or her] when his [or her] office is vacant, or when for any other reason he [or she] is unable to take action'.[14] While this basic dynamic has long been recognised at common law,[15] it was placed on a specific statutory footing by the Law Officers Acts of 1944 and 1997. The 1944 Act provided that functions authorised or required to be discharged by the Attorney General could be discharged by the Solicitor General in one of three circumstances, namely (a) if the office of the Attorney General was vacant, (b) if the Attorney General was unable to act owing to absence or illness, or (c) if the Attorney General authorised the Solicitor General to act in any particular case.[16]

[8] George W Keeton, *A Liberal Attorney-General: Being the Life of Lord Robson of Jesmond (1852–1918) with an Account of the Office of Attorney-General* (James Nisbet & Co 1949) 127.

[9] Edwards, *The Law Officers of the Crown* (n 1) 28.

[10] ibid 28–29 and 121–123.

[11] ibid 29.

[12] ibid.

[13] As Hand has pointed out, none of the ten Solicitors General since Sir Nicholas Lyell in 1992 had gone on to become Attorney General until Michael Ellis was promoted to cover for Suella Braverman during a period of maternity leave in 2021: James Hand, 'The Attorney-General, Politics and Logistics – A Fork in the Road?' (2022) *Legal Studies*, forthcoming. For some useful comments on the background to the Ministerial and other Maternity Allowances Act 2021, which made Braverman's maternity leave possible, see: James Hand, 'Ministerial Maternity Leave' (*UK Constitutional Law Association Blog*, 1 March 2021). Available at: https://ukconstitutionallaw.org/2021/03/01/james-hand-ministerial-maternity-leave/.

[14] James William Norton-Kyshe, *The Law and Privileges Relating to the Attorney-General and Solicitor-General of England* (Stevens and Haynes 1897) 4–5.

[15] *R v John Wilkes* (1768) 97 ER 123 (HL).

[16] Law Officers Act 1944, s 1(1).

The 1997 Act remedied two practical difficulties which arose from the limitations of the 1944 Act by, first, removing the cumbersome need for specific delegations in particular cases and, second, clarifying that it was permissible for 'any function' to be delegated. The standalone authority of the Solicitor General was also made clear by a provision affirming that 'the validity of anything done in relation to the Attorney General, or done by or in relation to the Solicitor General, is not affected by a vacancy in the office of Attorney General'.[17]

Given the unique constitutional position of the Attorney General, there are a number of practical advantages in having a fully-fledged deputy like the Solicitor General. These include his or her ability to take control of cases involving constituency matters linked to the political interests of the Attorney General, and his or her ability to appear in the same case as the Attorney General representing a different one of the law officers' clients. While the latter scenario is scarcely likely in modern times due to the availability of civil panel counsel, from a historical point of view it is clearly illustrated by the *Dean and Canons of Windsor* case, for instance, where the Attorney General represented the public interest by virtue of his historical role in proceedings concerning charitable trusts,[18] while the Solicitor General represented the private interests of the Crown in the same case.[19]

Appleby published a comprehensive review of the literature exploring various stages in the evolution of both these offices in 2016,[20] but only some of it is relevant for present purposes. As such, the historical outline above is provided simply to explain, by way of background, why the odd mixture of functions which inhere in the modern-day offices first came together and the substantial extent to which the offices themselves have functionally assimilated over time. The remainder of this chapter will focus on cataloguing those modern-day functions under three headings (executive functions; advisory and advocacy functions, and so-called public interest functions). These groupings are somewhat artificial because many of the functions overlap in various ways related to how they are conceptualised. However, outlining the law officers' functions in this manner is, in itself, an instructive exercise given that variants of this three-way taxonomy are commonly used as a framework for explicating their roles in official papers.[21] Whether this taxonomy notionally inflates the apparent tensions between different functions is a question that will be considered at a later stage.

Moreover, the sheer number of functions which fall within these loose groupings is often noted with interest. This explains in part why it is usually necessary to provide illustrative examples for each category – despite the contestability of

[17] Law Officers Act 1997, s 1(3).
[18] See below at 69–70.
[19] *Attorney General v Dean and Canons of Windsor* (1860) 11 ER 472, 476; 478.
[20] Gabrielle Appleby, *The Role of the Solicitor-General: Negotiating Law, Politics and the Public Interest* (Hart Publishing 2016) ch 2, especially at 19–32.
[21] See, e.g., *Governance of Britain: A Consultation on the Role of the Attorney General* (Cm 7192, 2007) 5.

those categories – in lieu of comprehensive discussion. However, while reference is commonly made to an overall figure of 42 functions which emanates from a 2007 government consultation paper,[22] various dangers associated with precisely quantifying the law officers' changeable business provide pause for thought. For example, the 2007 list of functions includes at least five itemised roles which have since been transferred to the Attorney General, the Advocate General and the Director of Public Prosecutions for Northern Ireland on foot of the devolution of policing and criminal justice functions in 2010.[23]

Executive Functions

The formal status of the Attorney General and the Solicitor General in the executive branch of the UK Government requires careful explanation. They are both salaried ministers of the Crown,[24] appointed by the Queen on the recommendation of the Prime Minister,[25] with ministerial responsibility for a range of so-called 'Law Officers' Departments'. The powers which flow from their appointments are subject to the temporariness that applies to all ministerial offices. That is to say, unless they are dismissed by the Prime Minister, once appointed all office-holders enter and leave office with a particular government which, of course, only ever stays in power for so long as its Prime Minister can command a majority in the House of Commons. Despite their historical initiation to Parliament as aides to the House of Lords, since approximately 1700 both law officers have normally been drawn from the House of Commons.[26] There are, however, several examples of office-holders drawn from the Lords in more recent times[27] and, indeed, some exceptional instances of tenure in the absence of a seat in either the Upper or Lower House of Parliament.[28]

[22] ibid Annex A. References to this list can be found here: Appleby, *The Role of the Solicitor-General* (n 20) 32; Klearchos A Kyriakides, 'The Law Officers of the Crown and the Rule of Law in the United Kingdom' in Gabrielle Appleby, Patrick Keyzer and John M Williams (eds), *Public Sentinels: A Comparative Study of Australian Solicitors-General* (Routledge 2014) 191.

[23] See ch 6 at 140–159.

[24] House of Commons Disqualification Act 1975, Sch 2.

[25] Note, however, that new office-holders are also typically 'sworn in' at the Royal Courts of Justice in London at a ceremony normally headed by the Lord Chancellor, the Lord Chief Justice of England and Wales, and the Chair of the Bar Council. See, for instance, the following press release concerning the swearing in ceremony for the current law officers (at which, unusually, a new Lord Chancellor was also sworn in): 'Law Officers sworn in' (*Attorney General's Office*, 23 September 2021). Available at: www.gov.uk/government/news/law-officers-sworn-in.

[26] Edwards, *The Law Officers of the Crown* (n 1) ch 3.

[27] For example, Prime Minister Tony Blair appointed Lord Goldsmith of Allerton as Attorney General and Lord Falconer of Thoroton as Solicitor General.

[28] For example, in 1931 William Jowitt held the office of Attorney General without a seat, while, in 1924, Henry Slesser held the office of Solicitor General without a seat.

The Attorney General (and, at least by implication of the Law Officers Acts, the Solicitor General) enjoy 'Cabinet level membership of the Government',[29] but they are not in fact members of the Cabinet. This distinction is not a point of mere pedantry. As highlighted in Chapter 1,[30] and as will be explored further in Chapter 7, it is viewed as an important characteristic of the offices that is indissociable from debates and controversies about the degree of independence from the executive that the law officers should exhibit when discharging functions which are thought of as ill-suited to partisan political consideration (such as prosecutorial decisions). Formal exclusion has also been thought of as a professional protection for the law officers themselves, who ostensibly benefit from avoiding complications that could arise if they were members of the Cabinet and faced a difficult policy decision to be determined on a collective basis with reference to legal advice received from the Attorney General and/or the Solicitor General.[31]

Having evolved from being 'a grouping of the King's closest confidential advisors', the modern-day Cabinet is essentially a gathering of senior government figures who enjoy 'the confidence of Parliament and the Prime Minister'.[32] Traditional writers have characterised it as a representative decision-making body responsible for collectively settling departmental conflicts and establishing the political imperatives of the government for the purpose of presenting major policies to the public on a unified basis,[33] but others have argued it is better understood as a principle rather than an institution of government given that 'the ministerial combinations in which decisions are effectively made rarely coincide with Cabinet membership'.[34] The latter interpretation certainly seems to dovetail more accurately with contemporary practices involving the law officers for England and Wales. While the maintenance of an official distinction between the law officers and full Cabinet members might demonstrate Prime Ministerial recognition of the continuing importance in some symbolic distance between them, in modern practice the distance appears to be almost entirely superficial. When questioned about his role as the Attorney General in 2015, a recent office-holder explained that while he attended Cabinet by invitation rather than as of right, both he and his predecessor had in fact accepted invitations to attend *all* Cabinet meetings held during their respective tenures.[35] This convention was further affirmed by Sir Geoffrey Cox qua the Attorney General who, in giving evidence to Parliament, stated there was an 'expectation' that Attorneys General 'attend each and every

[29] Cabinet Office, *List of Ministerial Responsibilities Including Executive Agencies and Non-Ministerial Departments* (March 2021) 8–9. Available at: https://assets.publishing.service.gov.uk/government/uploads/system/uploads/attachment_data/file/968352/List-of-Ministerial-Responsibilities.pdf.

[30] See 6–7.

[31] Shawcross (n 1) 383.

[32] Rodney Brazier, *Ministers of the Crown* (Oxford University Press 1997) 15.

[33] John P Mackintosh, *The British Cabinet* (Stevens 1962).

[34] Colin Seymour-Ure, 'The Disintegration of the Cabinet and the Neglected Question of Cabinet Reform' (1971) 24 *Parliamentary Affairs* 196, 203.

[35] Justice Committee, *Oral Evidence by the Rt Hon Jeremy Wright QC MP on the Work of the Attorney General* (HC 409, 15 September 2015).

Cabinet' meeting.[36] The present-day office-holder was initially less definitive on this point, but recently clarified that she too attends all Cabinet meetings in practice.[37] In any event, the Attorney's membership of no less than six high-powered Cabinet Committees at the time of writing[38] provides added weight to the second interpretation of the Cabinet considered above, bearing in mind such committees are defined as 'groups of ministers that can take collective decisions that are binding across government',[39] which further minimises the significance of her official status in reality.

Leaving the question of Cabinet membership to one side for now, the law officers' responsibility for a range of so-called 'Law Officers' Departments' requires some brief elaboration. The Law Officers' Departments are technically varied in terms of the extent to which the law officers are in charge of their governance and, therefore, the level of accountability expected of them. The Attorney General's office, which supports both the Attorney General and the Solicitor General with all their functions, is the only ministerial department and therefore the only one the law officers are expected to lead in day-to-day policy terms. In addition, there are three non-ministerial departments with agency status which the law officers are responsible for 'superintending': the Government Legal Department, the Crown Prosecution Service, and the Serious Fraud Office. The second and third of these agencies are headed by directors whom the law officers have specific statutory duties to superintend,[40] whereas their duty to oversee the Treasury Solicitor's management of the Government Legal Department is non-statutory. The law officers are also responsible for overseeing another public body which does not have any departmental or agency status, namely Her Majesty's Crown Prosecution Service Inspectorate – though the legislative authority for the law officers' relationship of superintendence over the Inspectorate supposed by prominent government documentation[41] is, in fact, phrased as a duty on the Chief Inspector to 'report to the Attorney General on any matter connected with the operation of the Service which the Attorney General refers to him'.[42] Lastly, the law officers are also expected to

[36] Justice Committee, *Oral Evidence by the Rt Hon Geoffrey Cox QC MP on the Work of the Attorney General* (HC 1887, 23 January 2019).

[37] Justice Committee, *Oral Evidence by the Rt Hon Suella Braverman QC MP on the Work of the Law Officers* (HC 962, 25 January 2022). Cf: Justice Committee, *Oral Evidence by the Rt Hon Suella Braverman QC MP on the Work of the Attorney General* (HC 462, 21 July 2020).

[38] Namely the National Security Council; the Global Britain (Strategy) Committee; the Global Britain (Operations) Committee; the Crime and Justice Taskforce; the Parliamentary Business and Legislation Committee, and the Domestic and Economic Implementation Committee.

[39] Cabinet Office, *List of Cabinet Committees* (21 October 2021). Available at: www.gov.uk/government/publications/the-cabinet-committees-system-and-list-of-cabinet-committees.

[40] For the legislative provisions providing that all functions of the Director of Public Prosecutions and the Director of the Serious Fraud Office, respectively, shall be discharged under the superintendence of the Attorney General, see: the Prosecution of Offences Act 1985, s 3(1) and the Criminal Justice Act 1987, s 1(2).

[41] Cabinet Office, *List of Ministerial Responsibilities* (n 29) 8.

[42] Crown Prosecution Service Inspectorate Act 2000, s 2(1)(b). Moreover, for a recently agreed Protocol which emphasises the independence of the Inspectorate, see: Attorney General's Office,

exercise 'non-statutory general oversight' of the Services Prosecuting Authority as well as all government prosecutors stationed in departments with their own prosecuting apparatus (such as the Prosecution Division of the Department for Work and Pensions).[43]

The difficulty for the law officers when it comes to exercising appropriate levels of ministerial oversight as required by the different formulations above, which does not arise in respect of the Attorney General's Office itself, of course, is a need to respect the independence of the office-holders designated to lead each relevant organisation. This difficulty is compounded by a need to stay apprised of the activities carried out by each organisation and, where appropriate, to influence the direction of those activities so as to be in a position to answer for them in Parliament and thereby maintain parliamentary trust. As one former Attorney General put it in 2015, 'superintendence is a strange beast in a way because it is not direct control'.[44] Some of the controversies connected to this limitation, which have usually been framed as an accountability dilemma, will be analysed in Chapter 7 together with the interacting importance of independence and trust in such episodes. It is worth noting here, however, that most controversies have arisen in connection with the Serious Fraud Office in particular.[45] Current practices in this area were, until recently, governed by a protocol setting out how the law officers and the two superintended directors were expected to exercise their functions in relation to each other, which was developed as a direct consequence of such controversies.[46] This protocol has recently been replaced, however, with two separate framework agreements which perform the same regulatory function but with greater specificity.[47] The law officers also issue guidelines to the prosecution services regarding subjects they wish to regulate with particular specificity.[48]

The final ministerial role of the law officers concerns their 'tripartite responsibility for criminal justice policy' which, as the quotation suggests, they share with the Home Secretary and the Secretary of State for Justice.[49] The appropriate ambit

Protocol between the Law Officers and Her Majesty's Chief Inspector of the Crown Prosecution Service (29 January 2020), especially at para 7.

[43] Cabinet Office, *List of Ministerial Responsibilities* (n 29).

[44] Justice Committee, *Oral Evidence by the Rt Hon Jeremy Wright QC MP on the Work of the Attorney General* (HC 409, 15 September 2015).

[45] See, especially: *R (Corner House Research & Ors) v Director of the Serious Fraud Office* [2008] UKHL 60, [2008] 1 AC 756. Also see ch 7 at 184–192.

[46] Attorney General's Office, *Protocol between the Attorney General and the Prosecuting Departments* (July 2009).

[47] Attorney General's Office, *Framework Agreement between the Law Officers and the Director of the Serious Fraud Office* (21 January 2019); Attorney General's Office, *Framework Agreement between the Law Officers and the Director of Public Prosecutions* (18 December 2020). Also see ch 7 at 190–192.

[48] See, e.g., Attorney General's Office, *Use of the Common Law Offence of Conspiracy to Defraud* (November 2012). Available at: www.gov.uk/guidance/use-of-the-common-law-offence-of-conspiracy-to-defraud--6.

[49] *Governance of Britain: A Consultation on the Role of the Attorney General* (Cm 7192, 2007) 8.

of the law officers' input into such policy formation appears to be confined, for the most part, to matters concerning the prosecution services for which they are responsible, though past office-holders have succeeded in promoting an interpretation of the role expansive enough to justify the introduction of their own Bills to Parliament.[50] The narrowness of this role as shaped by more modern law officers can be illustrated by reference to the reflections of a relatively recent former Attorney General, Dominic Grieve, who cites tri-lateral conversations about where to position the Serious Fraud Office in the machinery of government – be it beneath the law officers or otherwise – as a contemporary example of the role.[51] Indeed, the same office-holder has confessed to having deliberately adopted a minimalist approach to this role in light of the comparatively small number of staff in the Attorney General's Office and a personal determination to 'focus on the advisory side of the work'.[52] It is to that category of work that this chapter now turns.

Advisory and Advocacy Functions

The Attorney General and the Solicitor General are well established as the chief legal advisers to the Crown. However, as Kyriakides has pointed out, while enduring constitutional theories insist that they have only one client in the form of the Crown as a singular and indivisible entity, in reality that client seeks the advice of the law officers in a variety of potentially conflicting manifestations.[53] As such, the law officers are expected to provide advice to the Sovereign; to the government (sometimes in the guise of the Cabinet); to individual ministers in both their official and personal capacities (to the extent permitted by the Ministerial Code), and to Parliament in certain circumstances.[54] In any of these roles the law officers may also be expected to represent their client(s) in court, should the circumstances call for it. Indeed, before briefly considering the relationship between the law officers and each of these notional clients in turn, it is worth stressing the potential for conflict between them. The minister with individual responsibility for one department will normally have different views and priorities from the minister for another which, despite the aspirations of the convention on collective ministerial responsibility, can lead to confrontation over the scope and meaning of ambiguous

[50] Sam Silkin, 'The George Bean Memorial Lecture' (A Speech by the Attorney General in Manchester, 29 October 1978) 11; John Ll J Edwards, *The Attorney General, Politics and the Public Interest* (Sweet & Maxwell 1984) 214.

[51] 'Ministers Reflect: Dominic Grieve' (*Institute for Government*, 2015). Available at: www.instituteforgovernment.org.uk/ministers-reflect/person/dominic-grieve/.

[52] ibid.

[53] Kyriakides, 'The Law Officers of the Crown and the Rule of Law' (n 22) 191–192.

[54] ibid.

legal provisions.[55] Occasionally, the nature and level of these disputes can be very serious indeed.[56] The law officers may be placed in a theoretically challenging position in such circumstances, particularly given the impression that their 'legal advice', if it is requested as appropriate, is generally expected to come not as a formal opinion on the law but, rather, as one which takes account of the various policy objectives of the government in so far as acceptable interpretations of the law fused with political judgement will allow.[57] This can clearly make it difficult for the law officers to reconcile their range of responsibilities without fracturing trust in one quarter or another.

The Monarchical Client

There is relatively little on record about the law officers' relationship with their sovereign client the Queen or how it compares to Her Majesty's relationship with the Attorney General for the Duchy of Lancaster, mentioned in Chapter 1,[58] among other royal appointments concerned with the Queen's legal powers and duties. Writing in 1992, the former Attorney General Sir Patrick Mayhew did state that law officers had a 'special role to play in peerage cases' and, as a hypothetical example of personal legal representation, that the Attorney General might represent Her Majesty 'if a Palace servant were to breach the confidence of the Sovereign'.[59] More recently, the Attorney General was recognised by the President

[55] For an example requiring judicial resolution, see: *R (BAPIO Action Ltd) v Secretary of State for the Home Department* [2008] UKHL 27, [2008] 1 AC 1003, where at [60] Lord Mance ruled with the support of a majority in the House of Lords that the effects of an inconsistency between guidance issued by the Secretary of State for Health 'as one emanation of the Crown' and rules issued by the Home Secretary as 'another emanation of the Crown' were 'so profound as to render such guidance invalid'. For further commentary, see: Conor McCormick, 'The Three Tiers of Executive Power in Northern Ireland' in Brice Dickson and Conor McCormick (eds), *The Judicial Mind: A Festschrift for Lord Kerr of Tonaghmore* (Hart Publishing 2021) 226–227.

[56] Consider, for example, the disagreement over whether use of military force would be legal under international law in the context of the 1956 Suez Crisis. Opposing views as between the Lord Chancellor and the Legal Adviser to the Foreign Office who formulated the legal opinions of the foreign secretary at the time placed the law officers, who broadly sided with the Foreign Office opinion that force would not be legally justifiable, in a position of serious constitutional conflict with the Lord Chancellor. See: Ben Yong, 'Risk Management: Government Lawyers and the Provision of Legal Advice within Whitehall' (The Constitution Society 2013) 86–87; Geoffrey Marston, 'Armed Intervention in the 1956 Suez Canal Crisis: The Legal Advice Tendered to the British Government' (1988) 37 *International and Comparative Law Quarterly* 773.

[57] Terence Daintith and Alan Page, *The Executive in the Constitution: Structure, Autonomy, and Internal Control* (Oxford University Press 1999) 297; Yong, 'Risk Management' (n 56) 60. Also see Kieran McEvoy, Louise Mallinder and Anna Bryson, *Lawyers in Conflict and Transition* (Cambridge University Press 2022) ch 5, where the idea of 'creative compliance' is explored, i.e. the propensity of government lawyers to advise their clients 'on how to escape legal controls without technically violating the law, in order to ensure that the policy choices of elected officials [are] implemented', which is contrasted with the propensity of other government lawyers to 'look beyond formal legality' when determining what is required of them by the public interest.

[58] See fn 4 in ch 1 at 2.

[59] Patrick Mayhew, 'The Role of the Law Officers in England and Wales' (1992) 1 *Inter Alia* 18, 19.

of the Family Division of the High Court as 'sole defendant' to a summons about whether, among other things, the will of the late Prince Philip, Duke of Edinburgh, could be sealed and withheld from public inspection.[60] Although the Attorney was said to have been summoned by virtue of his responsibility 'to represent the public interest'[61] – rather than the private interests of the Queen or the Royal Family as such – his view of the public interest nevertheless favoured a decision which would, inter alia, 'protect the dignity of the person of the Sovereign, by protecting the privacy of those family members closest to Her'.[62] Beyond these rare glimpses into the relationship between the law officers and the Queen, however, there is not enough documentary evidence on which to base a more extensive description of their responsibilities in this sphere.

The Governmental and Ministerial Clients

There is a formal hierarchy of legal advice within the UK Government.[63] All government officials dealing with controversial or contested questions of law are required to refer their queries along a chain of command which, via a number of intermediaries, ultimately leads to the law officers.[64] The fact that the law officers sit at 'the apex of the legal hierarchy'[65] is an important constitutional provision for satisfying the seeming need for legal advice to the government which is 'final and determinative' and also the need to secure some degree of consistency in public sector decision making.[66] In fact, it has been said that matters about which the law officers have given opinions are 'subject to advice which is so authoritative as to be binding' until 'different advice is given or a court gives a contrary judgment'.[67] In this sense the law officers 'occupy a position analogous to that of the "final Court of Appeal" on matters of strictly legal advice' within government,[68] though from a departmental perspective the law officers are not always viewed as the most suitable source of 'external' advice.[69] This can occur, for example, where

[60] *Re The Will of His late Royal Highness The Prince Philip, Duke of Edinburgh* [2021] EWHC 77 (Fam).

[61] ibid [2]. Also see ibid [53]. The public interest functions of the law officers are discussed in more detail at 62–71 below.

[62] ibid [37]. For a critique that queries the role of the Attorney General as the exclusive representative of the public interest in this context, see Paul Magrath, 'Why Can't We Read Prince Philip's Will?' (*Transparency Project*, 26 September 2021). Available at: www.transparencyproject.org.uk/why-cant-we-read-prince-philips-will/.

[63] Yong, 'Risk Management' (n 56) ch 4.

[64] ibid 56–57.

[65] ibid 57.

[66] ibid.

[67] Alan Trench, 'Washing Dirty Linen in Private: The Processes of Intergovernmental Relations and the Resolution of Disputes' in Alan Trench (ed), *Devolution and Power in the United Kingdom* (Manchester University Press 2007) 195.

[68] Edwards, *The Attorney General, Politics and the Public Interest* (n 50) 185.

[69] Daintith and Page (n 57) 307.

the law officers' expertise is known to be inferior to specialist civil panel counsel. Therefore, as Daintith and Page put it, while the 'political pre-eminence' of law officers' advisory opinions is unquestionable, their lack of 'a monopoly of external advice' and the limits of their own specialist knowledge must be properly weighted in any evaluation of their authority among government officials.[70]

Ministers of every kind are also expected to familiarise themselves with the circumstances in which is it is appropriate to consult the law officers in accordance with the current Ministerial Code, which is a document of high importance in so far as it provides a written outline of the fundamental expectations of any given Prime Minister.[71] The latest Code vaguely requires that the law officers 'must be consulted in good time before the Government is committed to critical decisions involving legal considerations'; though the general meaning of this obligation, which has been heavily abbreviated over the course of several editions, is apparently well understood within Whitehall.[72] It is also the Code which requires ministers to seek guidance from the law officers before any personal legal proceedings which may have implications for them in their official capacity are initiated or, indeed, where they become embroiled in proceedings as a defendant or a third party.[73]

By convention, however, the advice of the law officers 'is confidential and may not be divulged outside government without the consent of both the person seeking the advice and the law officers themselves'.[74] The accountability of the law officers to Parliament is thus limited to a significant extent.[75] As such, Trench and Hazell have characterised the law officers' advice as a variety of 'private public law'.[76] They have investigated opinions formulated primarily in relation to devolution matters and found that, initially at least, all members of the UK law officer regime 'consulted each other and gave joint opinions'[77] which would be disseminated via a government intranet network.[78] This must have represented a remarkable constriction of individual independence on the part of each law officer, entered into voluntarily in the interests of constitutional stability and consistency.

[70] ibid 308.

[71] See: Andrew Blick, *The Codes of the Constitution* (Hart Publishing 2016).

[72] Cabinet Office, *Ministerial Code* (August 2019) para 2.10. Available at: www.gov.uk/government/publications/ministerial-code; Yong, 'Risk Management' (n 56) 58.

[73] Cabinet Office, *Ministerial Code* (n 72) paras 7.16–7.17.

[74] Trench (n 67) 195. This longstanding convention is fortified to some extent by the Freedom of Information Act 2000, s 35, first mentioned in ch 1 at 7. It should be noted, however, that neither the convention nor s 35 are insurmountable barriers to the public disclosure of a law officer's legal advice either in practice or in principle. For a simple illustration, see: *HM Treasury v Information Commissioner & Evan Owen* [2009] EWHC 1811 (Admin).

[75] Gabrielle Appleby, 'Reform of the Attorney General: Comparing Britain and Australia' [2016] *Public Law* 573, 583.

[76] Trench (n 67); Robert Hazell, 'Out of Court: Why Have the Courts Played No Role in Resolving Devolution Disputes in the United Kingdom?' (2007) 37 *Publius: The Journal of Federalism* 578, 590.

[77] Trench (n 67).

[78] Hazell (n 76).

The resulting 'corpus of authoritative and known legal rulings to which lawyers and officials across the UK government can (and do) have regular recourse'[79] is clearly a very significant constitutional phenomenon.

While the presumption of confidentiality in respect of the law officers' legal advice precludes a comprehensive study on the contemporary nature of their advisory services to governmental and ministerial clients,[80] it is possible to state two general propositions and five specific propositions about this role with relative certainty. The two general propositions are succinctly reflected in the following quotation:

> [T]he advisory function of the Attorney General is regarded as embracing an intertwined pair of consequential duties. One requires the Attorney General to ensure that his legal advice is not simply received by the appropriate persons in the Government but, where appropriate, is integrated into the policy-making, decision-making and legislative processes. The second duty requires the Attorney General to ensure that the Government operates within the law, especially in circumstances where he has tendered legal advice or is aware of a breach, or possible breach, of the law.[81]

The advisory role of the law officers in relation to five aspects of the modern legislative process can, however, be stated with greater specificity by reference to some more disparate sources.

First, as highlighted above in respect of Trench and Hazell's research, the Attorney General and (therefore) the Solicitor General have statutory powers to refer to the UK Supreme Court any questions they have regarding the competence of the three devolved legislatures to enact any proposed legislation – albeit the Attorney General must be acting in his or her capacity as Advocate General for Northern Ireland where legislative competence issues arising from Northern Ireland are concerned.[82] Where such a power is exercised,[83] it is clearly symptomatic

[79] Trench (n 67).

[80] Klearchos A Kyriakides, 'The Advisory Functions of the Attorney-General' (2003) 1 *Hertfordshire Law Journal* 73, 76.

[81] Kyriakides, 'The Law Officers of the Crown and the Rule of Law' (n 22) 192. Also see: Peter Goldsmith, 'Government and the Rule of Law in the Modern Age' (A Speech by the Attorney General for the LSE Law Department and Clifford Chance, 22 February 2006). Available at: www.lse.ac.uk/website-archive/publicEvents/pdf/20060222-Goldsmith.pdf.

[82] References in respect of the legislative competence of the Welsh Parliament/Senedd Cymru, the Scottish Parliament and the Northern Ireland Assembly are made under the Government of Wales Act 2006, s 112; the Scotland Act 1998, s 33, and the Northern Ireland Act 1998, s 11, respectively. For more information about the office of the Advocate General for Northern Ireland, see ch 6 at 141–142.

[83] See *United Nations Convention on the Rights of the Child (Incorporation) (Scotland) Bill – Reference by the Attorney General and the Advocate General for Scotland, and European Charter of Local Self-Government (Incorporation) (Scotland) Bill – Reference by the Attorney General and the Advocate General for Scotland* [2021] UKSC 42, [2021] 1 WLR 5106; *UK Withdrawal from the European Union (Legal Continuity) (Scotland) Bill – Reference by the Attorney General and the Advocate General for Scotland* [2018] UKSC 64, [2019] AC 1022; *Agricultural Sector (Wales) Bill – Reference by the Attorney General for England and Wales* [2014] UKSC 43, [2014] 1 WLR 2622; *Local Government Byelaws (Wales) Bill – Reference by the Attorney General for England and Wales* [2012] UKSC 53, [2013] 1 AC 792. Note that a reference was also made by the Attorney General in respect of a Bill which became the

of intergovernmental conflict and controversy,[84] though it has also been characterised more positively as an important way of safeguarding 'clarity around the parameters of the devolution settlements'.[85] This should not be over-emphasised, however, given that some of the most important judicial statements about devolution in the UK have been delivered in cases initiated by private parties.[86] Moreover, it should be noted that there is now a distinct but similar power available to the Attorney General and (therefore) the Solicitor General to refer to the UK Supreme Court questions about whether a Bill of the Scottish Parliament[87] or the Welsh Parliament/Senedd Cymru[88] relates to a 'protected subject-matter', i.e. a matter requiring a two-thirds super-majority vote in order for said Bill to be passed validly in those legislatures. All members of the UK law officer regime also have related powers to initiate court proceedings concerning 'devolution issues' as defined by the relevant devolution statutes,[89] as well as the right to defend proceedings relating to a devolution issue in certain jurisdictions; the right to be notified of such issues if raised by others in certain jurisdictions; the right to participate in all proceedings so notified, and the right to require a court or tribunal in any proceedings to which they are party to refer a devolution issue to the UK Supreme Court.[90] The Attorney General and the Solicitor General are therefore expected to formulate legal views in a fairly vast but clear set of contentious contexts connected to the devolution settlement. The precise identity of the law officers' notional client is unclear in such contexts, but there is certainly some evidence to suggest that in practice they tend to adopt interpretations of the relevant devolution statutes which, broadly speaking, coincide with those of the UK Government. Moreover, past office-holders have clearly indicated that the law officers 'assist the government in its search for

Law Derived from the European Union (Wales) Act 2018, but the reference was subsequently withdrawn and thereby obviated any judicial consideration.

[84] For example, as McCorkindale has pointed out, the Scottish Government portrayed the reference of the United Nations Convention on the Rights of the Child (Incorporation) (Scotland) Bill, ibid, as 'morally repugnant'. The Scottish Government, in turn, was accused of 'weaponising' children's rights to 'stir up constitutional chaos'. See Christopher McCorkindale, 'The UNCRC and European Charter of Self-Government Bill References: Once (and Twice) More unto the Breach?' (*Centre on Constitutional Change*, 26 April 2021). Available at: www.centreonconstitutionalchange.ac.uk/news-and-opinion/uncrc-and-european-charter-local-self-government-bill-references-once-and-twice.

[85] Robert Buckland, 'Role of Law Officers on Devolution and Bills' (A Speech by the Solicitor General to Public Law Wales, 20 December 2016). Available at: www.gov.uk/government/speeches/role-of-law-officers-on-devolution-and-bills.

[86] Prominent examples include *AXA General Insurance Ltd & Ors v Lord Advocate & Ors* [2011] UKSC 46, [2012] 1 AC 868 and *R (Miller) v Secretary of State for Exiting the European Union* [2017] UKSC 5, [2018] AC 61.

[87] Scotland Act 1998, s 32A, as inserted by the Scotland Act 2016, s 11.

[88] Government of Wales Act 2006, s 111B, as inserted by the Wales Act 2017, s 9.

[89] The Attorney General and (therefore) the Solicitor General only have power to do so in courts in England and Wales under the Government of Wales Act 2006, Sch 9, para 4; the Scotland Act 1998, Sch 6, para 15(1), and the Northern Ireland Act 1998, Sch 10, para 12, respectively. The comparable powers of other law officers under each statute will be pinpointed at more appropriate junctures below.

[90] See, generally: the Government of Wales Act 2006, Sch 9; the Scotland Act 1998, Sch 6, and the Northern Ireland Act 1998, Sch 10, respectively.

a lawful and proper way to achieve its policy objectives' through their role in the legislative process generally.[91]

Second, the law officers 'have a specific role in ensuring that human rights implications of proposed primary legislation are given careful consideration' on account of the obligations imposed on the UK Government by the Human Rights Act 1998.[92] It is *not* the role of the law officers to routinely advise individual ministers seeking to introduce a Bill to Parliament about the compatibility of their proposed legislation with human rights law for the purpose of making ministerial statements of compatibility to Parliament, which ministers are required to make under section 19 of the 1998 Act. Departmental lawyers ordinarily perform this task, *unless* 'a difficult question' arises which is referred to the law officers 'for a binding opinion'.[93] In most cases this does not happen, however, so the law officers normally scrutinise proposed legislation for its compatibility with human rights at a later stage in the legislative process. As members of the Cabinet Committee on Parliamentary Business and Legislation, the law officers are supplied with all of the memoranda prepared by departmental lawyers in order to inform a minister's opinion on the strengths and weaknesses of human rights issues raised by a particular Bill for the purpose of making his or her statement to Parliament under section 19.[94] When considering these memoranda, the law officers first satisfy themselves that the legal reasoning of the legislation-proposing department is correct, before providing assurances to the Cabinet Committee (and therefore the government) to that effect.[95] In this way, the law officers are viewed as having a fundamental role in reducing the susceptibility of government-led legislation to later challenge on human rights grounds.

Third, the oversight of the law officers in respect of departmental lawyers' advice concerning human rights law constraints on government policy appears to apply in a similar way to departmental legal advice provided in respect of Brexit-related and other international law restrictions affecting ministers seeking to propose government legislation and indeed in respect of Brexit and international law related decision making more generally. Before the UK acceded to the European Economic Communities, as they were then, the level of advisory work that accession was expected to create actually prompted some discussion about the creation of an additional law officer to the UK Government.[96] Although this

[91] Oliver Heald, 'The Role of the Law Officers' (A Speech by the Solicitor General to Kent Law School, 18 October 2012). Available at: www.gov.uk/government/speeches/the-role-of-the-law-officers.

[92] Dominic Grieve, 'The Role of Human Rights in a Law Officer's Work: Challenges Facing the HRA and the ECHR' [2012] *Judicial Review* 101, 102.

[93] Edward Garnier, 'The Law Officers and Legislative Procedure' (A Speech by the Solicitor General to the Constitutional and Administrative Law Bar Association, 17 July 2010). Available at: www.gov.uk/government/speeches/speech-to-the-constitutional-and-administrative-law-bar-association.

[94] Grieve (n 92).

[95] ibid.

[96] Edwards, *The Attorney General, Politics and the Public Interest* (n 50) 177–178.

proposal was not acted upon, and the nature of the relevant advisory work has no doubt changed beyond recognition as a result of Brexit,[97] the relevant responsibilities of the Attorney General and the Solicitor General in connection with all three of the specific propositions outlined so far are, of course, now shared at a territorial level with additional office-holders since created to serve the devolved governments. Brexit has, however, clearly increased and complicated the number of challenges which have attached to these roles in this context.[98]

Finally, the fourth and fifth specific propositions about the law officers' advisory role in the law-making process relate to government bills containing provisions that would permit either retrospective effect or early commencement. In both cases, there are constitutional conventions which mean that departmental proposals containing provisions of either sort are not allowed to proceed without the consent of the law officers.[99] As such, where a minister is proposing legislation which would have retrospective effect, the law officers will consider whether the public interest in doing so would outweigh the notion that it is only fair to pass laws which citizens can comply with by prospectively guiding their conduct appropriately.[100] In addition, it is well established that retrospectivity in the criminal sphere attracts a particularly heavy burden of justification under the European Convention on Human Rights.[101] Moreover, where a minister proposes legislation which would come into effect after the Royal Assent sooner than the conventional two-month waiting period thereafter, which customarily occurs so that those affected by the law can learn about it and adjust their behaviour accordingly, the law officers are again expected to consider whether any purported justification for so legislating really outweighs the reasons underlying the convention against early commencement.[102] The 'main effect' of these conventions, according to a former

[97] For an authoritative window into some of this workstream, written by two former departmental lawyers, see: Eleonor Duhs and Indira Rao, *Retained EU Law: A Practical Guide* (The Law Society 2021). For the broader picture, see: Paul Craig and Gráinne de Búrca, *EU Law: Text, Cases and Materials (UK Version)* (7th edn, Oxford University Press 2020). For an introduction to the wider international law framework, see James Crawford, *Brownlie's Principles of Public International Law* (9th edn, Oxford University Press 2019).

[98] For a general overview of the Brexit challenges that have led to litigation so far, see: Christopher McCorkindale and Aileen McHarg, 'Litigating Brexit' in Oran Doyle, Aileen McHarg and Jo Eric Khushal Murkens (eds), *The Brexit Challenge for Ireland and the United Kingdom* (Cambridge University Press 2021).

[99] Garnier (n 93).

[100] ibid.

[101] *AXA General Insurance Ltd & Ors v Lord Advocate & Ors* [2011] UKSC 46, [2012] 1 AC 868 at [119]–[120] (Lord Reed). Article 7(1) of the ECHR provides, in so far as is relevant here, that 'no one shall be held guilty of any criminal offence on account of any act or omission which did not constitute a criminal offence under national or international law at the time when it was committed'.

[102] This custom was placed under considerable strain by the pressure for immediacy during the COVID-19 pandemic, of course, alongside a larger suite of rule of law based concerns, on which, see: Katie Lines, *18 Months of Covid-19 Legislation in England: A Rule of Law Analysis* (Bingham Centre for the Rule of Law, 16 October 2021) paras 81–87. Available at: https://binghamcentre.biicl.org/publications/18-months-of-covid-19-legislation-in-england-a-rule-of-law-analysis.

Advocate General for Scotland,[103] 'is that the minds of those civil servants preparing and instructing the legislation will be concentrated' by the knowledge that law officers will not 'allow a Bill to proceed to Parliament' unless their 'concerns on the law … are addressed'.[104]

Each of the above propositions about the law officers' advisory roles might have been considered in the context of their public interest functions, below, to the extent that categorising the roles as such is warranted by the claim that they are or should be discharged with a mindset disconnected from the goals of the government in a party-political sense. As explained earlier, however, the overlapping nature of these loose categories renders the sequence of discussion unimportant at this stage, as it would be premature to adopt a settled view on whether such a conceptual division of the roles is either possible or desirable.

Before moving on, it is also important to note that the law officers are only regarded as the most appropriate *advocates* to represent their governmental and ministerial clients in exceptionally important cases. This reality is obscured somewhat by the Crown Proceedings Act 1947, which requires that the Attorney General must be named as the claimant in any civil proceedings instituted by the Crown unless a specific government department has been authorised to sue in its own name,[105] and likewise that civil proceedings against the Crown must be instituted against the Attorney General unless an authorised government department is clearly more appropriate.[106] In practice, however, the vast majority of government departments are so authorised and so targeted. That being said, even where the law officers are named in civil proceedings involving the Crown in accordance with these rules they do not appear personally in court in the vast majority of that litigation.[107] The processes for appointing a range of civil panel counsel to receive and carry out these briefs instead of the law officers are administered by the Treasury Solicitor, whose work is overseen by the law officers at a general level. There are principled reasons for maintaining this arrangement, given the theoretical possibility that some government-led legislation and government-made decisions more broadly may be pursued contrary to the preferred view of the law officers, which could at the very least lead to a perception of conflicting interests. The confidentiality of law officers' opinions, however, makes it impossible to know whether that theoretical problem manifests itself in practice with any frequency.

[103] For more information about the office of the Advocate General for Scotland, see ch 5 at 109–116.

[104] Lord Wallace of Tankerness, 'The Role of the Advocate General and its Constitutional Context' (A Speech by the Advocate General for Scotland to a 1st Year Public Law Class at Edinburgh University, 10 June 2013). Available at: www.gov.uk/government/speeches/the-role-of-the-advocate-general-and-its-constitutional-context.

[105] Crown Proceedings Act 1947, s 17(2).

[106] Crown Proceedings Act 1947, s 17(3).

[107] For an insight into the range of court appearances made by one former Attorney General, on behalf of a range of nominal clients, see: Constitutional Affairs Committee, *The Constitutional Role of the Attorney General* (HC 2006-07, 306) 70–91.

The Parliamentary Client

The law officers are normally MPs or members of the House of Lords and, as with other ministers, they are answerable to Parliament both for the activities of their department and for those of the agencies for which they are responsible.[108] Questions to the Attorney General is a regular item of Commons (or Lords) business, normally held at six-week intervals on a Thursday. In addition, both Ministerial Statements and Responses to Urgent Questions are routinely repeated in the Lords (and vice versa if the law officer is a peer). Beyond those traditional forms of parliamentary accountability, however, there is also an expectation that the law officers must, in some circumstances, 'advise' Parliament in its own right. Indeed, the law officers still receive a writ when they are appointed which requires them to attend the House of Lords 'to treat and give [their] advice' along with the royal patents for their offices, though these are now purely historical artefacts which office-holders have not 'obeyed or taken seriously … since 1742'.[109] Thus, references to the law officers' parliamentary client are normally used to denote the House of Commons in its plenary and committee formations, with the law officers normally being MPs.

It is important, however, that the different incarnations of the Lower House are appreciated in this context, for the conventional willingness of the law officers to advise on the floor of the Commons and before its general committees differs from their general reluctance to be called upon by Select Committees of the House. Whereas *Public Bill Committees* (which are a type of general committee formerly known as Standing Committees[110]) of the House of Commons routinely conduct clause-by-clause debates on proposed legislation at the committee stage of a Bill, for example, *Select Committees* carry out a range of tasks which are generally geared towards probing the efficacy of government departments (sometimes in isolation and sometimes on a cross-departmental basis) and standalone subject matters of contemporary significance.[111] Care must also be taken to differentiate the law officers' relationship with committees of the Lower House from their membership of the *Cabinet Committees* considered earlier.[112]

The law officers' reluctance to advise select committees stems from a proliferation of those committees during the last century, bringing with them broader

[108] See 48–49 above.

[109] Edwards, *The Attorney General, Politics and the Public Interest* (n 50) 207. Also see: Robert Buckland, 'The History and Role of the Law Officers' (*Inner Temple Lecture*, 18 February 2019). Available at: www.robertbuckland.co.uk/news/history-and-role-law-officers, where the former Solicitor General (and Lord Chancellor) states that the law officers' 'historic role as legal advisers to Parliament has been somewhat supplanted by the Clerks and Speaker's Counsel … On very rare occasions in recent history have the law officers provided impartial advice to the House, which was the purpose of their medieval writ to the Lords'. Moreover, it is perhaps worth emphasising that, while a small number of law officers have been appointed from the Upper House in recent times, this has no real bearing on the practical significance of the writ mentioned here.

[110] HC Standing Order 84(b).

[111] Edwards, *The Attorney General, Politics and the Public Interest* (n 50) 227.

[112] Appleby, for example, appears to confuse the advisory role of the law officers as members of the Parliamentary Business and Legislation Committee of the Cabinet in relation to the human rights

and more aggressive forms of scrutiny which have not been met with universal governmental enthusiasm. This proliferation has led to the claim that it is beyond the practical capabilities of the already heavily burdened law officers to advise them on demand.[113] Principled reasons for minimising the regularity of such advisory interactions have also been suggested; mainly relating to the potential for a conflict of interest that would arise if a select committee sought to procure advice on a question of law about which the law officers had already advised the government, and which would therefore be subject to the convention in favour of keeping such opinions confidential unless both law officer and ministerial consent to disclose them was in place.[114] A notable departure from the generally recalcitrant approach to select committees by the law officers occurred between 2006 and 2008, however, when inquiries into the constitutional role of the Attorney General were conducted by both Houses;[115] prompting and informing a government consultation on the same subject which, in turn, led to some minor reforms.[116] It should also be noted that over the past several years, Attorneys General have voluntarily attended hearings before the Justice Committee of the House of Commons in order to give evidence and answer questions about their work.[117] Interestingly, moreover, Robert Buckland qua the Solicitor General gave evidence and answered questions of a similar nature for the first time in April 2019.[118]

In relation to Public Bill committees, the law officers have been much more historically willing to accept invitations to advise on the meaning and effect of proposed legislation,[119] and indeed to attend not by invitation but by virtue of their right to do so ex officio under the Standing Orders of the House.[120] Whenever the law officers are in attendance at a Public Bill Committee, they are present not as members but as participants in its deliberations – much like their position vis-à-vis the Cabinet – and are not therefore entitled to vote; to make any motions; to move any amendments, or to be counted in the quorum.[121] The same rules

compatibility of government-led legislation, discussed above at 56, with their role as advisors to various committees in the Houses of Parliament: Appleby, *The Role of the Solicitor-General* (n 20) 36.

[113] Edwards, *The Attorney General, Politics and the Public Interest* (n 50) 229–230.

[114] ibid 219–220.

[115] Constitutional Affairs Committee, *The Constitutional Role of the Attorney General* (HC 2006–07, 306); Select Committee on the Constitution, *Reform of the Office Attorney General* (HL 2007–08, 93). It may be helpful to note for completeness here that, as this book was being finalised for the printers, the House of Lords Constitution Committee launched a fresh inquiry into the *Role of the Lord Chancellor and the Law Officers*. See: https://committees.parliament.uk/work/6540/role-of-the-lord-chancellor-and-the-law-officers/.

[116] *Governance of Britain: A Consultation on the Role of the Attorney General* (Cm 7192, 2007); *The Government's Response to the Constitutional Affairs Select Committee Report on the Constitutional Role of the Attorney General* (Cm 7355, 2008). For a useful summary of the context to these reports, see: Alexander Horne, *The Law Officers* (HC Library Standard Note SN/PC/04485, 2014) 8–18.

[117] For a transcript of the most recent session, see: Justice Committee, *Oral Evidence by the Rt Hon Suella Braverman QC MP on the Work of the Law Officers* (HC 962, 25 January 2022).

[118] Justice Committee, *Oral Evidence by Robert Buckland QC MP on the Work of the Solicitor General* (HC 1837, 4 April 2019).

[119] Edwards, *The Attorney General, Politics and the Public Interest* (n 50) 221.

[120] HC Standing Order 87(1).

[121] ibid.

apply to every variety of general committee *other than* the Scottish,[122] Welsh,[123] Northern Ireland[124] and European[125] Grand Committees (the first three of which are exclusively composed of MPs representing Scottish, Welsh and Northern Ireland constituencies respectively), wherein any minister of the Crown (which qualifies the law officers) may both take part in deliberations *and* make motions, though they still cannot vote or be counted in the quorum. There are also some obvious practical limitations layered over these formal restrictions on the participation of the law officers, again arising mainly from the potential for conflicts of interest created by their general duty to keep any advice they have provided to the government confidential in the absence of ministerial consent to do otherwise.

The law officers enjoy all the privileges that attach to every other minister of the Crown on the floor of the Lower House, but there is an accepted understanding that they must 'advise the House in an entirely non-party way' when called upon by any parliamentarian for legal advice.[126] This understanding does not, of course, prevent the law officers from speaking defensively on behalf of the governing party at other times. Parliamentary business qualifying as 'legal advice' and therefore calling for impartiality in this context is broadly restricted to matters 'in relation to the constitution of and conduct of proceedings in the House, the conduct and discipline of members, and the effect of proposed legislation'.[127] For example, recent office-holders have emphasised their readiness to advise the Lower House on the enforcement of its sub judice rule, which provides that the absolute privilege that is afforded to Members of Parliament is self-restricted to the extent that 'matters in debates, questions, or motions which are awaiting adjudication in a court of law' are disallowed.[128] This is an interesting example of the law officers' part in mediating power tensions between parliamentarians and the judiciary which, to foreshadow later arguments, vividly demonstrates how the performance of a particular function can act as an indicator of polydimensional independence, accountability and trust.

Indeed, the Attorney General can also intervene in court proceedings to assert the privileges of either House of Parliament. The Attorney General is entitled to do so at his or her own motion, ex proprio motu; at the request of the House, or at the request of the court.[129] The role of the Attorney General in *Pepper v Hart*

[122] HC Standing Order 93.
[123] HC Standing Order 102.
[124] HC Standing Order 109.
[125] HC Standing Order 119.
[126] Shawcross (n 1) 388.
[127] Sam Silkin, 'The Functions and Position of the Attorney-General in the United Kingdom' (1978) 59 *The Parliamentarian* 149, 155; Edwards, *The Attorney General, Politics and the Public Interest* (n 50) 218–220.
[128] Dominic Grieve, 'Parliament and the Judiciary' (A Speech by the Attorney General to BPP Law School, 25 October 2012). Available at: www.gov.uk/government/speeches/parliament-and-the-judiciary; Buckland (n 85).
[129] Constitutional Affairs Committee, *The Constitutional Role of the Attorney General* (HC 2006-07, 306) 11.

is a frequently cited example of such an intervention,[130] but the operative identity of the law officer's notional client(s) in that case requires careful contemplation. It is true that the Attorney General did unsuccessfully attempt to persuade the court that recourse to Hansard's record of parliamentary proceedings prior to the enactment of legislation for the purpose of interpreting the legislation would be an infringement of the privileges of the Commons.[131] However, while the Attorney General '*appeared* for the Crown'[132] in a widely-encompassing sense, and which is theoretically capable of including the Lower House, at a practical level he was *instructed* by a government department.[133] That the Inland Revenue stood to gain from a judicial interpretation of the relevant legislation which was more likely to be handed down in the absence of reference to Hansard is enough to suggest that the strategy of the Attorney General to assert Parliament's privileges in the manner that he did was not done in aid of Parliament's interests alone.[134] This high-profile example serves as a useful reminder of the potential for the purported interests of law officers' clients to overlap, whether consciously or coincidentally and, therefore, the polydimensional nature of the forces which may guide their tactical conduct in various circumstances.

Public Interest Functions

A number of things ought to be noted about the third and final category of the law officers' functions in advance. It should first be said that this category contains perhaps the most malleable, contestable and ill-defined roles of the law officers. It could be argued that certain topics discussed above should have been featured at this juncture instead, such as the advisory role of the law officers in relation to human rights and devolution. Indeed, it is possible to characterise all the law officers' functions as having the public interest at their core. Dilemmas of this sort are inexorably connected to a more fundamental debate about which functions give rise to an expectation that they will be discharged 'in the public interest' or 'quasi-judicially', which is essentially a blunt definitional manoeuvre used to denote an expectation of strong independent mindedness. Framing functions in this way plainly disintegrates the applicability of specific expectations derived from the rules of professional ethics that would ordinarily apply between an identifiable client and their adviser, such as duties of confidentiality. The client served by the law officers when discharging their so-called public interest functions is a

[130] *Pepper (Inspector of Taxes) v Hart* [1993] AC 593 (HL). See: Andrew Kennon, 'Legal Advice to Parliament' in Alexander Horne, Gavin Drewry and Dawn Oliver (eds), *Parliament and the Law* (Bloomsbury Publishing 2013) 127; Appleby, *The Role of the Solicitor-General* (n 20) 36.

[131] *Pepper (Inspector of Taxes) v Hart* [1993] AC 593 (HL) 604–610.

[132] ibid, 623. Emphasis added.

[133] Kennon (n 130) 127.

[134] ibid.

purely theoretical one, depending largely on their own conception of the role as conditioned by the constitutional values of independence, accountability and trust which sit at the heart of this book. It is therefore essential to emphasise that there is no fixed standard of decision making for the functions in this contested category. Labelling particular decision making powers and duties as 'public interest functions' is not a clear and accurate heuristic technique for explaining the appropriate calibrations of independence, accountability and trust needed to legitimise such decisions.

The Criminal Law Context

With respect to their so-called public interest role in the criminal law context, a distinction can be drawn between the law officers' statutory functions and their prerogative functions recognised at common law.

The law officers' statutory duties to appoint and superintend the Director of Public Prosecutions[135] and the Director of the Serious Fraud Office[136] have already been mentioned; however, there are three further sets of statutory powers and duties to consider, the first of which concerns the requirement for a law officer's consent to the commencement of a very broad range of offences.[137] A Law Commission report on this subject indicated that although various justifications have been suggested as to why Parliament may have inserted clauses of this nature into so much legislation over the years, 'many take the view that there is no unifying principle to account for the variety of offences' that now call for a law officer's consent to prosecute.[138] Generally speaking, suggested justifications for including a statutory restriction on the bringing of prosecutions in legislation all relate back to a perceived risk of criminal proceedings being instituted in 'inappropriate circumstances'.[139] In relation to offences under the Official Secrets Acts 1911–1989, for example, control by the law officers has been justified on the basis that such prosecutorial decisions ought to be taken with regard to 'important considerations of public policy or of a political or international nature',[140] about which the law officers are 'able to consult colleagues in government' by virtue of

[135] Prosecution of Offences Act 1985, s 2(1) and s 3(1).

[136] Criminal Justice Act 1987, s 1(2).

[137] Over 60 such offences were listed by the Law Commission in 1998: *Consents to Prosecution* (Law Com No 255, 1998) Annex A. A less precise but updated list is maintained on the CPS website: *Consents to Prosecute* (Crown Prosecution Service) Annex 1, Part 1. Available at: www.cps.gov.uk/legal-guidance/consents-prosecute.

[138] *Consents to Prosecution* (Law Com No 255, 1998) para 3.8 and paras 3.27–3.35.

[139] *Consents to Prosecution* (Law Com No 255, 1998) para 3.33, citing the Home Office Memorandum to the Departmental Committee on Section 2 of the Official Secrets Act 1911 (Cmnd 5104, 1972).

[140] ibid. For an in-depth study on this example, see: Rosamund M Thomas, *Espionage and Secrecy: The Official Secrets Acts 1911–1989 of the United Kingdom* (Routledge 1991) ch 4.

their 'special position'.[141] To take another example, for comparative purposes, it is interesting to note that the consent of the Attorney General or Solicitor General is required before it is possible for somebody to challenge before the High Court the sufficiency of an inquest which they believe should be quashed and reheard in the interests of justice.[142] Consent must be obtained even where the need for a further inquest is uncontested, as was the case in a recent decision wherein a responsible coroner responding to fresh DNA evidence was required to seek the consent of the Attorney General for England and Wales.[143] This arrangement, requiring an applicant to seek consent in order to proceed to the High Court for a substantive decision, can be interestingly contrasted with the power of the Attorney General for Northern Ireland to decide *him- or herself* whether a fresh inquest should be held where he or she considers it 'advisable' to do so.[144]

There are also a range of offences for which the consent of the Director of the Crown Prosecution Service or the Serious Fraud Office is required rather than that of the law officers,[145] though the relevant director still acts under the superintendence of the law officers in accordance with the terms of mutually agreed framework documents.[146] It should be remembered, moreover, that in respect of all the prosecutorial 'consent duties' considered above the relevant office-holders are statutorily *required* to decide whether or not the prosecution in question should proceed, which means that they are unable to abdicate from that responsibility even in controversial circumstances.[147]

The second set of relevant statutory provisions from the criminal domain concern those which enable the law officers to bring certain types of criminal proceedings in the interests of protecting the administration of justice. Contempt of court proceedings may be brought by the law officers, for example, against the publisher of any material which risks damaging an unfinished trial or, to take another example, against a juror who discloses the content of jury deliberations while a trial is ongoing.[148] In addition, the law officers have power to apply to the

[141] Jeremy Wright, 'The Attorney General on Who Should Decide What the Public Interest Is' (A Speech at University College London's Law Faculty, 9 February 2016). Available at: www.gov.uk/government/speeches/the-attorney-general-on-who-should-decide-what-the-public-interest-is.

[142] Coroners Act 1988, s 13. The need for a law officer's consent is implied by this provision, which states that the High Court can make orders where, 'on an application by or under the authority of the Attorney-General', it is satisfied the conditions laid out in the section are met. For a critical account of this arrangement, see: Emma Norton, 'Applications to the Attorney-General and s 13 of the Coroners Act 1988' (*Liberty*, 6 October 2016). Available at: www.publiclawproject.org.uk/data/resources/249/PLP-paper-Emma-Norton.pdf.

[143] *Re HM Senior Coroner for North West Wales* [2017] EWHC 2557 (Admin).

[144] Coroners Act (Northern Ireland) 1959, s 14.

[145] See, e.g., the Bribery Act 2010, s 10(1)(a). For further examples and guidance, see: *Consents to Prosecute* (Crown Prosecution Service) Annex 1, Part 3. Available at: www.cps.gov.uk/legal-guidance/consents-prosecute.

[146] See n 47 above.

[147] Peter Goldsmith, 'The Role of the Attorney General in Changed Constitutional Circumstances' (A Lecture at Birmingham College of Law, 2006).

[148] Contempt of Court Act 1981. On the background and architecture of this Act, see: Edwards, *The Attorney General, Politics and the Public Interest* (n 50) 161–176. For the current approach to these

High Court for a 'criminal proceedings order' against a person whom they allege has 'habitually and persistently and without reasonable ground … instituted vexatious prosecutions (whether against the same person or different persons)'.[149] If granted, the effect of such an order is to prevent the person involved from bringing further proceedings without leave of the High Court.

Thirdly, there are a set of statutory powers which enable the law officers to prompt appellate court reconsideration of decisions taken at first instance in certain contexts. An important example of this concerns the power of the law officers to refer, with leave of the Court of Appeal, the sentence given to a person in Crown Court proceedings which they believe to be 'unduly lenient'.[150] Only indictable offences and offences triable either way listed in an order made by the Home Secretary by statutory instrument can be so referred,[151] but upon receiving such a reference the Court of Appeal may quash the sentence of the Crown Court and replace it with another sentence which may be more severe but no greater than one which the Crown Court itself could have passed.[152] Some early studies on the operation of this scheme suggested that the Court of Appeal was strongly inclined to increase a sentence referred to it by the law officers. Shute, for instance, tracked a 97 per cent 'success rate' for referrals made within the first five years of the scheme.[153] Rozenberg's analysis of some more recent figures, on the other hand, 'confirm a steady decline in the number of unduly lenient sentences being increased by the Court of Appeal over the past five years, even though the scheme's scope has been extended twice during the period'.[154] In 2017, for instance, Rozenberg notes that while the Court of Appeal increased the sentences of 79 per cent of the offenders whose cases were referred to it by the law officers, by 2020 that figure had dropped to just 63 per cent.[155]

Under a different statutory authority, the law officers also have the power to refer to the Court of Appeal a point of law arising from the decision of a Crown Court which has acquitted a person tried on indictment.[156] Given that prosecutors did not have a right to appeal against any rulings in a trial on indictment until such a power was conferred by section 58 of the Criminal Justice Act 2003; a position which, until the commencement of section 58, stood in contrast with

powers, see: Attorney General's Office, *The Law Officers' Approach to Contempt of Court Referrals* (15 September 2021). Available at: www.gov.uk/guidance/the-law-officers-approach-to-contempt-of-court-referrals. Also see: Dominic Grieve, 'Contempt of Court: Why It Still Matters' (A Lecture by the Attorney General in Honour of Michael Kalisher, 12 October 2010).

[149] Senior Courts Act 1981, s 42(1)(c).

[150] Criminal Justice Act 1988, s 36.

[151] Criminal Justice Act 1988, s 35.

[152] Criminal Justice Act 1988, s 36(1)(b).

[153] Stephen Shute, 'Prosecution Appeals Against Sentence: The First Five Years' (1994) 57 *Modern Law Review* 745, 754.

[154] Joshua Rozenberg, 'New Figures Suggest Better Sentencing: Steady Decline in Proportion of Unduly Lenient Sentences Increased on Appeal' (*A Lawyer Writes*, 26 August 2021). Available at: https://rozenberg.substack.com/p/new-figures-show-better-sentencing?r=8r17o&utm_campaign=post&utm_medium=web&utm_source=.

[155] ibid.

[156] Criminal Justice Act 1972, s 36.

the prosecution's longer standing right to appeal by way of case stated in respect of proceedings tried summarily,[157] the law officers' referral power was introduced as a means of challenging incorrect statements of law made in the Crown Court which might otherwise form damaging precedents for future cases. Although the opinion of the Court of Appeal in any such case will not affect the acquittal giving rise to the referral,[158] it can help to ensure that the correct interpretation of a criminal law is applied prospectively.[159]

The prerogative powers of the law officers that are recognised at common law in the criminal context are now vanishingly thin by comparison with their statutory rights and responsibilities. The Attorney General used to be entitled to file a criminal information ex officio, for example, but that power was displaced by statute some time ago.[160] Nowadays, the only remaining prerogative of note is the power of the law officers to enter a *nolle prosequi* on any indictment. This broad discretionary power has the effect of staying proceedings, though formally speaking it is merely 'an undertaking entered on record by leave of the Attorney-General, to forbear to continue proceedings wholly or partially'.[161] In modern times, the procedure appears to be used mainly where there are compassionate grounds for discontinuing a criminal trial for indictable offences, as the case may be where defendants standing accused of crime fall very ill or are otherwise incapacitated.

It is worth emphasising again, by way of a closing reminder, that the law officers' discretion in respect of so-called public interest decisions in the criminal law context, statutory and non-statutory alike, appears to be implicitly constrained by definition. In particular, constitutional discourse surrounding the exercise of these functions tends to emphasise the need for a high standard of independent mindedness, perhaps most prominently encapsulated by an official statement on the contours of that standard by the former Attorney General Sir Hartley Shawcross. A short extract of that important statement, which has been widely endorsed by various judicial, parliamentary and executive patrons over the years,[162] is reproduced below:

> … [I]t is the duty of an Attorney-General, in deciding whether or not to authorise the prosecution, to acquaint himself with all the relevant facts, including, for instance, the effect which the prosecution, successful or unsuccessful as the case may be, would have upon public morale and order, and with any other considerations affecting public policy. In order so to inform himself, he may, although I do not think he is obliged to, consult with any of his colleagues in the Government; and indeed, as Lord Simon once said, he would in some cases be a fool if he did not. On the other hand, the assistance of his colleagues is confined to informing him of particular considerations which might affect his own decision, and does not consist, and must not consist, in telling him

[157] Magistrates' Courts Act 1980, s 111.
[158] Criminal Justice Act 1972, s 36(7).
[159] See, e.g., *Attorney General's References (Nos 1 and 2 of 1979)* [1980] QB 180, [1979] 3 WLR 577.
[160] Criminal Law Act 1967, s 6(6).
[161] *Consents to Prosecution* (Law Com No 255, 1998) para 2.17, fn 31.
[162] Kyriakides, 'The Law Officers of the Crown and the Rule of Law' (n 22) 197–198; Edwards, *The Attorney General, Politics and the Public Interest* (n 50) 319–320.

> what that decision ought to be. The responsibility for the eventual decision rests with the Attorney-General, and he is not to be put, and is not put, under pressure by his colleagues in the matter. Nor, of course, can the Attorney-General shift his responsibility for making the decision on to the shoulders of his colleagues. If political considerations which, in the broad sense that I have indicated, affect government in the abstract arise, it is the Attorney-General, applying his judicial mind, who has to be the sole judge of those considerations.[163]

Edwards' contention that the constitutional value of independence inherent in this statement existed alongside the principle of accountability to Parliament '*after the termination of the particular criminal proceedings*'[164] was a good-willed but inadequate attempt to reconcile the two concepts. This is because greater legitimacy can be achieved by real-time adjustments to the weighting of these values with reference to indicators of patronal trust; rather than by the automatic apportionment of greater weight to a one-dimensional understanding of each value at a fixed stage in proceedings by implication.

The Civil Law Context

With respect to the so-called public interest functions of law officers in the civil law context, a similar distinction applies between those which are statutory and those which derive from prerogative powers recognised at common law. In contrast to the above discussion about criminal cases, however, it is the law officers' prerogative functions which attract greater attention than their statutory counterparts in civil cases. It should be remembered, moreover, that all these functions are united by their purported separation from the civil cases in which law officers advise and act for the variety of notionally identifiable Crown clients discussed earlier. Most particularly, there is a familiar refrain in the literature which emphasises the importance of distinguishing 'between proceedings in which the Attorney-General represents the government, and an action undertaken by him to enforce the law on behalf of the general community'.[165] This sub-section focuses on civil cases of the latter sort, where the law officers are again expected to act 'wholly independently of the government'.[166]

As mentioned above, most of the law officers' statutory functions in this context have attracted relatively little real argument. They include, for example, a power to apply to the High Court for a 'civil proceedings order' against vexatious litigants (akin to the 'criminal proceedings order' noted above) or, if applicable, an

[163] HC Deb 29 January 1951, vol 483, cols 683–684.
[164] Edwards, *The Law Officers of the Crown* (n 1) 224–225.
[165] Rosamund M Thomas, 'The Attorney-General for England and Wales, and Northern Ireland: His Role in Civil and Criminal Proceedings' (1991) 57 *International Review of Administrative Sciences* 209, 210.
[166] ibid.

'all proceedings order' (which has the combined effect of the two other orders).[167] They also include the statutory power to intervene in family law applications for a declaration as to marital status; as to adoptions effected overseas; and of parentage, legitimacy or legitimation.[168] Such interventions are permitted regardless of whether a family court has sent relevant papers to the Attorney General for consideration, which it can do either of its own motion or at the request of a party.[169]

The law officers, moreover, have a statutory power to appoint 'special advocates' to represent defendants before the High Court when it has been 'seised of relevant civil proceedings', normally involving counter-terrorism measures, and therefore granted an application to permit the use of closed material therein.[170] Closed material proceedings enable parties to rely upon 'material the disclosure of which would be damaging to the interests of national security',[171] without disclosing that evidence to other parties in the proceedings and, instead, disclosing it to the special advocate who is charged with considering the evidence on behalf of the other parties while being prohibited from communicating with them.[172]

The law officers also have a more general role in appointing 'Advocates to the Court', or amici curiae, in civil cases where 'there is a danger of an important and difficult point of law being decided without the court hearing relevant argument'.[173] The role of an Advocate to the Court has been described as the fulfilment of 'a non-partisan advisory function' and is to be contrasted with third-party interveners which can be granted permission to advocate in favour of one party's position on the law.[174] Advocates to the Court are requested in accordance with a Memorandum agreed between the Lord Chief Justice and the Attorney General in 2001, which emphasises the need for such requests to be made sparingly and not, for example, as a routine substitute for professional legal opinions in self-represented litigation.[175] There is also some authority providing for a personal intervention by one of the law officers as an amicus curiae in civil proceedings in order for them to advocate in 'matters of public interest and importance involving the policy of Her Majesty's Government'.[176] The conflation of the public interest with the government's interest in this respect is a further reminder of the conceptual complexity underpinning certain functions.

[167] Senior Courts Act 1981, s 42.
[168] Family Law Act 1986, s 59(2).
[169] Family Law Act 1986, s 59(1).
[170] Justice and Security Act 2013, s 9(1). The law officers have similar powers for the appointment of special advocates in closed material proceedings under other statutes which are not considered here.
[171] Justice and Security Act 2013, s 6(11).
[172] Justice and Security Act 2013, s 8(1).
[173] James Munby, 'The Role of the Attorney General in Appointing Advocates to the Court or Special Advocates in Family Cases' (Guidance from the President of the Family Division, 26 March 2015).
[174] *Re Northern Ireland Human Rights Commission* [2002] UKHL 25, [2002] NI 236 at [15].
[175] Munby (n 173).
[176] *Rio Tinto Zinc Co & Ors v Westinghouse Electric Co* [1978] AC 547, 589; Silkin, 'The Functions and Position of the Attorney-General in the United Kingdom' (n 127) 152.

Although closed material proceedings themselves are highly controversial,[177] criticism about the law officers' role in the appointment of special advocates and amici curiae alike has been relatively muted. In 2003, for example, the Court of Appeal did express the view that there was a potential for conflicting interests on the part of the law officers when appointing amici curiae given that they are also responsible for superintending the litigating authorities, and that therefore the court itself should be empowered to appoint special counsel in the exceptional circumstances presented by so-called public interest immunities from the disclosure of relevant evidence.[178] Those views were categorically dismissed, however, by the late Lord Bingham while sitting on the Appellate Committee of the House of Lords in 2004.[179] Commenting that the Attorney General acted 'as an independent, unpartisan guardian of the public interest' when discharging these functions, Lord Bingham went on to note that counsel had 'roundly acknowledged the complete integrity shown by successive holders of the office in exercising this role'.[180] Since then it has not gone unnoticed, all the same, that the law officers' role in this area amounts to 'an unusual intersection between the judiciary and the executive' in so far as it frequently involves judges coming directly to the law officers and 'asking for safeguards to the trial process'.[181]

The role of the law officers in civil proceedings relating to charities, meanwhile, is partly governed by statute and partly by prerogative power. They have, for instance, statutory powers to intervene before the First-tier and Upper Tribunal in any charity proceedings,[182] as well as powers to refer questions involving the operation or application of charity law to the relevant Tribunal.[183] While most of the law officers' formal functions in this sphere are now carried out by the Charity Commission, many of the Commission's powers derive from the continuing prerogative powers of the Attorney General ex officio,[184] who can prevent the Commission from exercising those powers without his or her agreement.[185] As the technicalities in this area are somewhat complex, no more than a general statement of the law officers' position is possible here.[186] Their position is a historical

[177] See, e.g., *Belhaj & Anr v Director of Public Prosecutions & Anr* [2018] UKSC 33, [2019] AC 593; John Jackson, *Special Advocates in the Adversarial System* (Routledge 2021).

[178] *R v H & C* [2003] EWCA Crim 2847, 3019.

[179] *R v H & C* [2004] UKHL 3, [2004] 2 AC 134, 157.

[180] ibid.

[181] Wright (n 141).

[182] Charities Act 2011, s 318.

[183] Charities Act 2011, s 326.

[184] See, e.g., the Charities Act 2011, s 114, which empowers the Charity Commission to 'exercise the same powers with respect to (a) the taking of legal proceedings with reference to charities or affairs of charities, or (b) the compromise of claims with a view to avoiding or ending such proceedings, as are exercisable by the Attorney General acting *ex officio*'.

[185] See, with respect to the foregoing example, the Charities Act 2011, s 114(5)(b).

[186] For specifics, see: Hubert Picarda, *The Law and Practice Relating to Charities* (4th edn, Bloomsbury Professional 2010) ch 51; Hubert Picarda, *The Law and Practice Relating to Charities – Supplement to the Fourth Edition* (Bloomsbury Professional 2014) ch 51.

derivative of the Crown's ancient parens patriae prerogative jurisdiction, providing power for an official to act where it is necessary to do so for the protection of vulnerable citizens and charitable interests.[187] There is a pragmatic justification for this power that depends upon a basic understanding of charitable trusts, which recognise both legal and equitable interests over property. Whereas for a non-charitable trust to be valid there must be beneficiaries in possession of equitable interest who are capable of enforcing the trust, charitable trusts do not have beneficiaries (or 'objects') as such, only charitable *purposes* which must benefit the general public. In the resulting absence of individuals with the legal rights that are necessary to take actions for the enforcement of a charitable trust, therefore, the law officers have historically performed tasks of this nature. Unsurprisingly, they have been expected to carry out these roles 'in the public interest' generally, rather than in the interest of the Government or any other Crown client.[188]

Another of the law officers' prerogative powers appears to stem from the Crown's role as parens patriae,[189] namely their ability to seek an injunction from the High Court for the enforcement of public rights or the prevention of public nuisances either by virtue of their office, ex officio, or at the instance of a 'relator' (i.e. an informant), ex relatione. Historically speaking, the latter mode of procedural inception through 'relator actions' has been much more frequent.[190] Relators themselves have thus ranged from being private individuals and companies of different kinds, to administrative authorities and government departments of various sorts.[191] All those who do manage to obtain the consent of the law officers in order to take such an action must conduct the proceedings themselves and carry all costs which arise from doing so.[192] Various attempts by disgruntled respondents and would-be relators to challenge its exercise in circumstances where past office-holders have issued or refused their fiat will be considered further in Chapter 7 of this book.[193] Suffice it to say that controversies have arisen in connection with the possibility of party-political motivations on the part of the law officers when issuing and refusing their consent in certain cases, and on the basis of similar suspicions in relation to proceedings for injunctive relief instigated or not instigated ex officio.[194]

[187] For a judicial affirmation of this principle, albeit in the context of a now outmoded statutory framework, see: *In Re Belling & Enfield London Borough Council v Public Trustee & Ors* [1967] Ch 425, 432–433. For more judicial statements to this effect, see: Robert MacRae, 'The Attorney General's Role in Relation to Charities' [2018] *The Jersey & Guernsey Law Review* 34, 35–36.

[188] For interesting coverage of a recent episode in this area, involving a High Court application by the Attorney General seeking to revisit the valid uses of the National Fund, see: Barbara Rich, 'Small Change: Charity and the National Debt' (2018) 24 *Trusts & Trustees* 741.

[189] Edwards, *The Law Officers of the Crown* (n 1) 286–287.

[190] Conor McCormick, 'Judicial Review of Administrative Action in the United Kingdom: The Status of Standards Between 1890 and 1910' (2018) 10 *Italian Journal of Public Law* 49, 70–73.

[191] ibid.

[192] Edwards, *The Law Officers of the Crown* (n 1) 288.

[193] Most notably *Gouriet v Union of Post Office Workers* [1977] UKHL 5, [1978] AC 435. See ch 7 at 195–199.

[194] ibid.

In addition, there have been debates about whether certain relator actions taken with the consent of past office-holders were, in fact, for the enforcement of rights enjoyed by a narrow stratum of the public, rather than being truly general public rights.[195] These incidents are another potent illustration of the overall conceptual challenges facing this category of so-called public interest functions.

Conclusions

This chapter has considered the functions of the Attorney General and the Solicitor General for England and Wales under three headings relating to their executive functions; their advisory and advocacy functions; and their so-called public interest functions. Throughout this analysis, various allusions to some of the apparent tensions between this 'bewildering'[196] assortment of functions were included to illustrate those issues, though they will be revisited again later in this book.[197] By this stage, however, it should already be clear how some law officers' functions have evolved in a way that has made them prone to confusion and controversy. Frequent references to the challenges of devising an appropriate taxonomy for explicating the law officers' modern-day functions have been necessary in order to emphasise the difficulties which inevitably confront office-holders and onlookers alike.

Walker reduced these difficulties to three related problems in his 1999 study on the law officers:[198] first, the need to 'adopt a schizophrenic approach' to the overall role of a law officer to properly distinguish between interests that can be legitimately taken into account in different contexts;[199] second, the need to give a fixed meaning to concepts like the public interest even where, given 'our pluralist political culture', such conceptual boundaries are uncertain;[200] and third, the need to recognise that 'some spillover in self-understanding and external expectation' over the maintenance of these fragile boundaries may be unavoidable.[201] Overarching these problems, as explained in Chapter 1, Walker also identified 'parallel antinomies' existing within both legal and political conceptions of these roles.[202] In the

[195] See, in particular, *Attorney General (on the Relation of the Spalding Union Rural District Council) and the Spalding Rural District Council v Garner & Anr* [1907] 2 KB 480, 486.
[196] Daintith and Page (n 57) 232.
[197] See chs 7–8.
[198] See ch 1 at 11–12 for an overview of Walker's contributions to law officer scholarship.
[199] Neil Walker, 'The Antinomies of the Law Officers' in Maurice Sunkin and Sebastian Payne (eds), *The Nature of the Crown: A Legal and Political Analysis* (Oxford University Press 1999) 148–150. Also, for some more recent research confirming the challenges of 'state schizophrenia' among government lawyers in various contexts, see: Kieran McEvoy, Louise Mallinder and Anna Bryson, *Lawyers in Conflict and Transition* (Cambridge University Press, 2022) ch 5.
[200] Walker (n 199) 150–158.
[201] ibid 158–161.
[202] ibid 144–145.

terms used by a legal conception, tension arises between the legitimate functions of a professional agent acting on behalf of their client(s) and the functions of an independent custodian of fundamental values.[203] Within a political conception, the relevant tension is between a politically partisan approach to the appropriate exercise of certain functions and one which considers a broader view of the public interest necessary.[204]

The research for this book revealed an increasingly common tendency to characterise the functions of the law officers for England and Wales using language which corresponds to a political conception of their roles. This might be as a result of the difficulties in identifying the notional 'clients' necessary in order to sustain a legal conception, or perhaps as a consequence of the expansion in their political responsibilities in modern times.[205] The latter explanation is arguably reinforced by virtue of the career paths taken by recent law officers after leaving office. Whereas there was once a healthy debate to be had about whether former Attorneys General could expect to be offered a senior judicial office in later life,[206] the reform of judicial appointment procedures together with perceptible changes in the professional trajectory of most modern alumni would render such a debate almost otiose today.[207] Indeed, if there is any trend on the rise, it seems to point departed law officers in the direction of an active political life after leaving office, rather than towards any form of public or private legal practice.[208] This, among other things, has motivated some commentators to argue that it might be necessary to stipulate that a certain amount of legal experience should be required of those who aspire to assume these offices in the future.[209] It has been observed from the same point view, moreover, that a certain level of experience should be made obligatory if the Attorney General's position as the titular head of the Bar, ex officio, is to escape the fictional quality that it has taken on in recent years.[210]

[203] ibid 145.

[204] ibid.

[205] On which, see: James Hand, 'The Attorney-General, Politics and Logistics' (n 13).

[206] Edwards, *The Law Officers of the Crown* (n 1) ch 15; Appleby, *The Role of the Solicitor-General* (n 20) 25.

[207] James Hand, 'The Attorney-General, Politics and Logistics' (n 13).

[208] ibid. The main exceptions here are Lord Goldsmith of Allerton and Sir Geoffrey Cox QC MP. Goldsmith's stormy exit from professional politics in 2007 is presumably one of the reasons why he returned to private legal practice as the London Co-Managing Partner and Chair of European and Asian Litigation in Debevoise & Plimpton following his term as Attorney General: www.debevoise.com/lordgoldsmithqc. Cox, meanwhile, is reported to have earned almost £900,000 from various law firms in the course of a single year following his term: John Hyde, 'Ex-Attorney General Cox Earning £468,000 a Year as Law Firm Consultant' (*The Law Society Gazette*, 30 August 2021). Available at: www.lawgazette.co.uk/news/ex-attorney-general-cox-earning-468000-a-year-as-law-firm-consultant/5109621.article.

[209] James Hand, 'The Attorney-General, Politics and Logistics' (n 13). This would not be unprecedented in the UK law officer regime, given that there is a statutory requirement of ten years' standing in respect of candidates for the office of the Attorney General for Northern Ireland, under the Justice (Northern Ireland) Act 2002, s 22(6).

[210] ibid. Also see: Catherine Baski, 'Out of Balance: Should the AG Lead the Bar?' (*The Law Society Gazette*, 4 February 2022). Available at: https://edition.pagesuite.com/html5/reader/production/default.aspx?pnum=12&edid=fd421366-4bc7-4f50-a30b-51c7ee0a1eae&isshared=true.

Whatever the future may hold for those who have the difficult job of operationalising these demanding portfolios, it will be argued hereafter that their performance as law officers is not best evaluated with reference to the tenets of a simplistic 'legal' or 'political' conception of their roles. In concert with Walker's view that neither of these approaches yield particularly helpful answers,[211] it will be suggested that more useful results can, in fact, be obtained from evaluations based on a trifocal model of legitimising constitutional values (namely independence, accountability and trust). Fuller explanations of this argument must wait, however, until the law officers that operate regionally in respect of Wales, Scotland and Northern Ireland have been considered and compared with the foregoing account of the Attorney General and Solicitor General for England and Wales. This reflects the scheme of the next three chapters.

[211] Walker (n 199) 161.

4

The Counsel General for Wales

Introduction

Devolution in the UK has been defined as 'the transfer to a subordinate elected body, on a geographical basis, of functions at present exercised by ministers and Parliament' at Westminster, and as such represents an attempt to reconcile 'two seemingly conflicting principles' of the constitution, namely 'the sovereignty or supremacy of Parliament and the grant of self-government in domestic affairs to Scotland, Wales, and Northern Ireland'.[1] It is something which was fundamentally at odds with the centralist historical tendencies of the UK constitution until the end of the last century, with the notable and turbulent exception of various schemes for the government of Northern Ireland from 1920 onwards and a range of separate but failed attempts to advance the process in other regions prior to 1998. The political reasons for a substantial devolution of powers to Wales, Scotland and Northern Ireland by centrally enacted legislation passed in 1998 are complex,[2] and the legal architecture of the territorial constitution since that time has been anything but static.[3] However, instead of beginning with a general account of these changes, this chapter on the office of the Counsel General for Wales includes contextual information about the historical backdrop to its creation only in so far as is necessary in order to illuminate some important stages in its development.[4]

[1] Vernon Bogdanor, *Devolution in the United Kingdom* (Oxford University Press 1999) 1–2. Debates about devolution to England have been quite subdued until relatively recently. For information about a parliamentary procedure involving 'English votes for English laws' that was in place between October 2015 and July 2021, however, see: www.parliament.uk/about/how/laws/bills/public/english-votes-for-english-laws/.

[2] Bogdanor (n 1); James Mitchell, *Devolution in the UK* (Manchester University Press 2009); Russell Deacon, *Devolution in the United Kingdom* (2nd edn, Edinburgh University Press 2012).

[3] For an excellent summary of the fundamental legal changes involved in the devolution reforms of 1998, see: Noreen Burrows, *Devolution* (Sweet & Maxwell 2000). For an updated overview of the many developments since Burrows' book was published, see: Richard Rawlings, 'The Welsh Way/Y Ffordd Gymreig' in Jeffrey Jowell and Colm O'Cinneide (eds), *The Changing Constitution* (9th edn, Oxford University Press 2019); Aileen McHarg, 'Devolution in Scotland' in Jeffrey Jowell and Colm O'Cinneide (eds), *The Changing Constitution* (9th edn, Oxford University Press 2019); Brice Dickson, 'Devolution in Northern Ireland' in Jeffrey Jowell and Colm O'Cinneide (eds), *The Changing Constitution* (9th edn, Oxford University Press 2019). See also: Derek Birrell, *Comparing Devolved Governance* (Palgrave Macmillan 2012).

[4] The same approach to contextualisation is taken in respect of the law officers for Scotland and Northern Ireland in chs 5 and 6 respectively.

Notwithstanding some important idiosyncrasies, most of the functions of the Counsel General for Wales can in fact be described using similar categories to those that were used in Chapter 3 to assess the powers and responsibilities of the Attorney General and Solicitor General for England and Wales, namely: executive functions; advisory and advocacy functions; and so-called public interest functions.[5] Thus, the position of the Counsel General for Wales is examined in the next three sections of this chapter in the following order. The first section provides an outline of devolution in Wales; the non-statutory genesis of the Counsel General; and an introduction to the statutory framework for the office. The next section recounts most of the Counsel General's functions as they stand today by way of the three categories noted above, before the third and final section summarises a range of particularly unique and recently created functions that have been added to the Counsel General's portfolio by statute. A comparative dimension to these analyses is weaved throughout, moreover, in accordance with the methodological approach outlined in Chapter 1.[6]

Constituting the Counsel General

The creation and administration of laws for both England and Wales was carried out centrally at Westminster for a long period of time after the two countries merged in the sixteenth century,[7] so the functional history of the Attorney General and Solicitor General provided in Chapter 3 applies to this period. In the late nineteenth century, however, the Liberal governments recognised some calls for localised Welsh policies. By passing the Sunday Closing (Wales) Act of 1881, in particular, Gladstone's government effected 'a change in public law which applied exclusively to Wales' for the first time since the seventeenth century.[8] It was 'soon followed by measures in which an actual element of devolution' existed, leading to the re-establishment of Wales as 'an administrative area in its own right'.[9] With the establishment of a University of Wales in 1893, and then a Welsh Department of the Board of Education in 1906, for example, the trend towards a burgeoning sense of

[5] This is to be contrasted with the approach to functional exposition adopted in respect of the law officers for Scotland and Northern Ireland in chs 5 and 6, where a more chronological style of writing is employed because of the historical complexity of those jurisdictions.

[6] See ch 1 at 17–19.

[7] The Laws in Wales Acts 1536 and 1543. See: Harold Carter, 'Local Government and Administration in Wales 1536–1939' in JA Andrews (ed), *Welsh Studies in Public Law* (University of Wales Press 1970). For an even earlier history of Welsh laws and government, see: Dafydd Jenkins, 'Law and Government in Wales Before the Act of Union' in JA Andrews (ed), *Welsh Studies in Public Law* (University of Wales Press 1970). Also see: Nicholas Barber, *The United Kingdom Constitution: An Introduction* (Oxford University Press 2021) 227–231.

[8] Carter (n 7) 48.

[9] ibid.

national autonomy had begun.[10] That trend was resisted by both the Conservative Party and the Labour Party throughout much of the twentieth century, however, meaning that it 'took seventy-two years from the first attempt to create a Welsh Secretary in Parliament in 1892, until the Labour Government eventually did so in 1964'.[11] The Welsh Office, for which the Welsh Secretary thereafter became responsible, represented, until it was overshadowed in 1999, 'the most obvious example of the devolution of public administration to Wales'; growing as it did from 'a territorial government ministry, with mainly executive oversight responsibilities (commenting on the work of other departments), to a department with its own functional remit'.[12] Throughout all of this time, as stated above, the Attorney General and Solicitor General for England and Wales remained the relevant law officers for all matters affecting Wales. It may also be worth noting here, albeit tangentially, that the heavily hollowed-out Welsh Office was renamed the Office of the Secretary of State for Wales in May 2018 in an effort to draw attention to the continued role of the UK Government (and, accordingly, the Attorney General and Solicitor General) in non-devolved Welsh affairs.

The coming into force of the Government of Wales Act 1998 marked the first in four main phases of modern devolution to Wales. The 1998 Act established a National Assembly, which was the first democratically elected national law-making body for Wales in its history,[13] but which assumed secondary law-making powers only. These executive powers of the National Assembly were limited to several specific areas conferred upon it by the 1998 Act, which comprised statutory functions formerly exercised by the Secretary of State for Wales and other UK Government Ministers. This devolution model of specifically *conferred* powers famously distinguished the initial Welsh arrangements from those created in respect of Scotland and Northern Ireland, which endowed the relevant legislatures with a general competence to legislate on any matter not *reserved* to the UK Parliament (subject to various caveats).[14] The National Assembly for Wales was also unique in that it was founded as a single corporate body, lacking any division between representative and governmental functions. While this corporate form had been devised in tandem with plans to run the Assembly on the basis of a committee system for decision-making,[15] the 'rapid emergence' of a Cabinet

[10] Carter (n 7) 49; Thomas Glyn Watkin, *The Legal History of Wales* (2nd edn, University of Wales Press 2012) ch 9.

[11] Deacon (n 2) 129. See also: Ivor Gowan, 'Government in Wales in the Twentieth Century' in JA Andrews (ed), *Welsh Studies in Public Law* (University of Wales Press 1970).

[12] Deacon (n 2) 130.

[13] David Gardner, *Administrative Law and the Administrative Court in Wales* (University of Wales Press 2016) 26–27.

[14] Lord Reed once explained that under reserved powers models, 'competence is given to the devolved legislatures in respect of all matters, unless the matter is excepted by way of reservation to the UK Parliament'. Under a conferred powers model, on the other hand, there is 'legislative competence only in respect of enumerated matters'. See: *Agricultural Sector (Wales) Bill – Reference by the Attorney General for England and Wales* [2014] UKSC 43, [2014] 1 WLR 2622 at [29].

[15] Deacon (n 2) 170.

system gave immediate rise to both a 'Virtual Parliament' and an 'Executive Committee' within 'the formal legal shell' of the National Assembly.[16]

The emergence of an Executive Committee of the National Assembly created the need, in turn, for a devolved law officer. While the Attorney General and Solicitor General for England and Wales continued to advise the UK Government on matters affecting Wales which had not been devolved – something which itself distinguished the Welsh devolution model from its counterparts in Scotland and Northern Ireland, in respect of which the new offices of the Advocate General for Scotland[17] and Advocate General for Northern Ireland[18] were created – it was thought that 'the role of providing authoritative legal advice to the Assembly Government' could not be carried out by the Attorney General and Solicitor General for England and Wales given that they were members of a different administration.[19] In the presence of this practical demand, albeit in the absence of any express statutory authority for its creation, an experienced barrister by the name of Winston Roddick assumed the role of 'Chief Legal Adviser to the Assembly' before going on to recommend the title 'Counsel General' before leaving his post in 2003.[20] As a civil servant, the Counsel General during this phase of Welsh devolution was not, of course, a member of the Welsh Executive Committee itself but was instead a member of the Assembly's staff and therefore subject to the usual civil service principles of honesty, integrity, impartiality and objectivity.[21] The most relevant line of accountability led to the Permanent Secretary at this time.[22] The office was thus genuinely different in that it had no executive functions comparable to the Attorney General and Solicitor General at this point; only certain advisory, advocacy and – depending on how they are defined – public interest functions. It is particularly notable that the Counsel General was required to help the National Assembly discharge its role in the judicial resolution of devolution issues.[23] Even at this stage in its development, however, the office of the Counsel General is likely to have faced conceptual difficulties associated with carrying out

[16] Richard Rawlings, 'Law Making in a Virtual Parliament: The Welsh Experience' in Robert Hazell and Richard Rawlings (eds), *Devolution, Law Making and the Constitution* (Imprint Academic 2005) 71.

[17] See ch 5 at 109–116.

[18] See ch 6 at 141–142.

[19] Office of the Secretary of State for Wales, *Better Governance for Wales* (Cm 6582, 15 June 2005) para 2.8; Richard Rawlings, *Delineating Wales: Constitutional, Legal and Administrative Aspects of National Devolution* (University of Wales Press 2003) 463.

[20] Russell Deacon, Alison Denton and Robert Southall, *The Government and Politics of Wales* (Edinburgh University Press 2018) 87.

[21] These have been regarded as the 'core values' of the civil service at least since the introduction of a Civil Service Code in 1996. There are now a range of separate codes which take account of devolution and the different arrangements that apply to the Diplomatic Service, which can all be downloaded here: http://civilservicecommission.independent.gov.uk/code/. The codes are now underpinned by the Constitutional Reform and Governance Act 2010, pt 1, with s 7(4) providing that they 'must require civil servants to carry out their duties' with reference to the four core values noted above.

[22] Rawlings, *Delineating Wales* (n 19) 463.

[23] Burrows (n 3) 162; Government of Wales Act 1998, Sch 8 (now repealed).

such varied functions within the rubric of a largely legal role conception. In other words, despite the apparent intention to create a Counsel General who would be 'a high profile legal figure but not a high profile political one',[24] it was still possible for that familiar friction to arise between the functions of a professional agent acting on behalf of a client (the client in this context being 'the Assembly as a whole'[25]) and the functions of an independent custodian of fundamental legal values.[26] However the shield of ministerial responsibility that conventionally protects civil servants from parliamentary and judicial accountability, among other things, would have made it very important to ensure the presumably high calibrations of trust and independence needed to legitimise the office at this time.

No more need be said about that constitutional model for the Counsel General, however, given that it was substantially overhauled by the second phase of modern devolution to Wales given effect by the Government of Wales Act 2006. The 2006 Act formally separated the Executive Committee from the Virtual Parliament by establishing the Welsh Assembly Government as an entity distinct from the National Assembly.[27] The Welsh Assembly Government has since been renamed the Welsh Government,[28] while the National Assembly has since been renamed the Senedd Cymru/Welsh Parliament,[29] which are the titles that will be used to refer to them hereafter. The 2006 Act also expanded the competence of the Senedd in a significant way by enabling it to pass *primary* legislation in the form of 'Assembly Measures'. The Senedd was only entitled to do so, however, via requests to the UK Parliament for 'Legislative Competence Orders' which had the effect of incrementally extending its competence under Schedule 5 to the 2006 Act.[30] This cumbersome process of expanding the conferred powers of the Senedd is why Rawlings has described the years under this arrangement as the 'proto-legislative phase' of Welsh devolution.[31] The 2006 Act did, however, contain provisions which could and would herald the third 'fully-legislative' conferred powers phase of Welsh devolution.[32] Following the commencement of these popularly endorsed provisions in 2011,[33] the cumbersome Legislative Competence Order procedure for expanding competencies under Schedule 5 to the 2006 Act was consigned to modern history and, instead, the Senedd was given the ability to make primary

[24] Burrows (n 3) 163.

[25] Rawlings, *Delineating Wales* (n 19) 464, citing the words of the first Counsel General, Sir Winston Roddick, as published in the Law Supplement to the Western Mail on 28 February 2000.

[26] Neil Walker, 'The Antinomies of the Law Officers' in Maurice Sunkin and Sebastian Payne (eds), *The Nature of the Crown: A Legal and Political Analysis* (Oxford University Press 1999) 145.

[27] Government of Wales Act 2006, s 45(1).

[28] Wales Act 2014, s 4(1).

[29] Senedd and Elections (Wales) Act 2020, s 2. Consistent with the approach of this legislation, 'the Senedd' will also be used as a convenient shorthand hereafter.

[30] For an exact outline of the statutory process, see: Gardner (n 13) 29.

[31] Richard Rawlings, 'The Strange Reconstitution of Wales' [2018] *Public Law* 62, 63.

[32] ibid.

[33] The relevant provisions could only be commenced subject to a referendum held under s 103 of the Government of Wales Act 2006. A vote was held on 3 March 2011, which endorsed the commencement of those provisions by a majority of 63.5 per cent.

'Acts of the Assembly' in any area related to a subject listed in Schedule 7 to the 2006 Act,[34] subject to certain limitations on that legislative competence.[35]

The restructuring and accrual of primary legislative power on the part of the Senedd also meant that its secondary law-making powers could pass to newly created Welsh Ministers in accordance with more conventional approaches to the institutional division of governmental powers.[36] Under the Government of Wales Act 2006, a First Minister is appointed by the Queen after being nominated by the National Assembly.[37] Welsh Ministers can be appointed then from the ranks of the Senedd by the First Minister, although such appointments are subject to approval by the Queen.[38] Notably, however, the newly configured office of the Counsel General for Wales created by section 49 of the statute, the essence of which has endured throughout all subsequent devolution phases, is not granted the status of a Welsh Minister (partly because the office-holder need not be drawn from the elected Senedd, about which more will be said below). The Counsel General is instead styled as a member of the Welsh Government[39] with 'ministerial status'.[40] This fact, together with the special status of the First Minister,[41] means that despite there being a statutory restriction on the total number of Welsh Ministers (including Deputy Welsh Ministers) to the effect that they cannot exceed 12 in number,[42] the Welsh Government can nonetheless comprise up to 14 members.

Within the Welsh Government there was, until recently, a non-statutory distinction between Welsh Ministers who are in charge of a department, such as the *Cabinet Secretary for* Education, and Welsh Ministers who serve under them, such as the *Minister for* Welsh Language and Lifelong Learning.[43] This distinction appears to have been replaced, however, with a simpler division between Cabinet Ministers and deputy Ministers.[44] Both variations correspond approximately to the more traditional distinction between Cabinet Ministers and Junior Ministers which prevails at Westminster. The Counsel General attends the Cabinet at the invitation of the First Minister but evades these distinctions in status by virtue

[34] Government of Wales Act 2006, s 107.
[35] Government of Wales Act 2006, s 108.
[36] Gardner explains that on 25 May 2007 'those functions previously transferred to the National Assembly for Wales by Order in Council under s 22 of the GOWA 1998 (the most wide-ranging of which being the National Assembly for Wales (Transfer of Functions) Order 1999) and any functions specifically conferred on the National Assembly by enactments made subsequent to the passing of GOWA 1998 were transferred to the Welsh Ministers pursuant to GOWA 2006, s 162(1) and Sch 11, para 30'; 25 May 2007 being the date the latter provisions came into force under s 161(5) of the Government of Wales Act 2006. See: Gardner (n 13) 119–120.
[37] Government of Wales Act 2006, ss 46–47.
[38] Government of Wales Act 2006, s 48.
[39] Government of Wales Act 2006, s 45(1)(c).
[40] Explanatory Notes to the Government of Wales Act 2006, para 231.
[41] Government of Wales Act 2006, s 45(1)(a) and ss 46–47.
[42] Government of Wales Act 2006, s 51.
[43] Welsh Government, 'Cabinet, Cabinet Secretaries and Ministers' (3 November 2017).
[44] Welsh Government, 'Cabinet Members and Ministers' (1 November 2021). Available at: https://gov.wales/cabinet-members-and-ministers.

of the perceived seniority of the office itself.[45] There is a subtle difference here between the ministerial position of the Counsel General and that of the Attorney General and Solicitor General for England and Wales which is largely contextual but also genuinely distinct. It will be recalled that while the Attorney General and Solicitor General are Ministers of the Crown and therefore 'full' members of the UK Government, they attend the UK Cabinet as attendees rather than members of it in order to, inter alia, denote some detachment and independence from the requirements of collective ministerial responsibility in respect of their so-called public interest functions. While the Counsel General is also both a member of the Welsh Government and an invited attendee at Cabinet, the office-holder is not, by contrast, a Welsh Minister ex officio.[46] There is thus an additional measure of institutional distance between the Counsel General and his or her ministerial colleagues in comparison to that which exists in respect of the Attorney General and Solicitor General for England and Wales.

As noted above, the Counsel General is distinguished from his or her ministerial colleagues in this manner partly because office-holders are not appointed in quite the same way as other members of the Welsh Government. Like ordinary Welsh Ministers,[47] the Counsel General can only be appointed or removed by the Queen on the recommendation of the First Minister and may resign from office at any time (though their resignation only takes effect when it is accepted by the Queen).[48] Unlike his or her colleagues, however, the Counsel General does not have to be appointed from the pool of elected Members of the Senedd and is instead selected via a 'recruitment process' which places a premium on professional legal qualifications and expertise that might not otherwise be available from within the Senedd.[49] To date, this process has led to the selection of four appointees from within the Assembly and one appointee from outside it.[50] Moreover, and significantly, the Counsel General cannot be appointed (or removed) unless a First Minister's proposal is approved by way of a resolution of the Senedd moved by the First Minister.[51] If these procedures have been satisfied in respect of a proposed appointment, the Counsel General designate is thereafter formally sworn into office at a ceremony undertaken by the Presiding Judge of the Wales Circuit on behalf of the Queen.[52]

[45] Welsh Government, 'Ministerial Code' (August 2021) para 6.17. Available at: https://gov.wales/cabinet-members-and-ministers.

[46] Note, however, that this arrangement has precluded neither Jeremy Miles nor Mick Antoniw from assuming Ministerial offices *concurrently* with their appointments to the office of Counsel General. For more information and analysis about this, see the text at fns 64–65 below and ch 7 at 177–179.

[47] Government of Wales Act 2006, s 48.

[48] Government of Wales Act 2006, s 49(1)–(4).

[49] Deacon, Denton and Southall (n 20) 88.

[50] Theodore Huckle was appointed from outside the Assembly and held office between 2011 and 2016. The four internal office-holders to date have been Carwyn Jones (2007–2009), John Griffiths (2009–2011), Mick Antoniw (2016–2017; 2021–present) and Jeremy Miles (2017–2021).

[51] Standing Orders of the Welsh Parliament (March 2021) 9.1–9.2 and 9.5–9.6

[52] Deacon, Denton and Southall (n 20) 88.

The Government of Wales Act 2006 makes no provision for a deputy to the Counsel General, though it does permit the First Minister to designate a person to exercise the functions of the Counsel General if the office-holder is for any reason unable to act or if the office itself becomes vacant.[53] These provisions bear a potentially confusing similarity to the provisions which originally applied to the Solicitor General for England and Wales, but they differ to the extent that any person designated under them can only exercise the functions of the Counsel General for a maximum of six months.[54] They cannot, therefore, be used as the statutory basis for a long-term deputy to the Counsel General should their functions become unduly onerous. This is not to say that the Counsel General carries out all the functions vested in his or her office single-handedly, only that they are single-handedly responsible, in the ministerial sense, for any work carried out by non-statutory delegates such as First Counsel to the Welsh Government.[55]

The Familiar Functions of the Counsel General

Most of the current functions of the Counsel General for Wales can be discussed through the lens of the same three categories that were used to explicate the functions of the Attorney General and Solicitor General for England and Wales in Chapter 3, albeit in much shorter form. In keeping with that taxonomy, the following sub-sections examine the Counsel General's executive functions; advisory and advocacy functions, and so-called public interest functions.

Executive Functions

Beginning with the executive functions of the Counsel General and leaving to one side the requirements of the Ministerial Code with which the Counsel General must comply to the same extent as the Welsh Ministers,[56] four specific roles are clearly identifiable.

The first role is one of departmental oversight. The Counsel General is expected, for example, to oversee the work of the Legal Services Department which provides legal services to the Welsh Government.[57] He or she must also oversee prosecutions

[53] Government of Wales Act 2006, s 49(6).

[54] Government of Wales Act 2006, s 49(7).

[55] First Counsel to the Welsh Government is the top external lawyer appointed by the Counsel General to assist with advocacy and advisory work. There are several other externally appointed legal panels which supplement the internal support available to the Counsel General from his or her civil servants.

[56] Welsh Government, 'Ministerial Code' (n 45) para 1.8.

[57] Alys Thomas, 'The Counsel General – A Quick Constitution Guide' (*National Assembly for Wales Research Service*, March 2018). Available at: https://senedd.wales/media/0bdjk3cj/18-019-web-english.pdf. Also see: Gruffydd Owen, 'Constitutional Quick Guides – Research Briefing' (*Welsh Parliament/*

on behalf of the Welsh Ministers,[58] though the fact that the majority of prosecutions in Wales are carried out by the Crown Prosecution Service for England and Wales superintended by the Attorney General and Solicitor General means that the demands of this function are much smaller by comparison. At present, the Welsh Government only has authority to bring prosecutions in discrete statutory circumstances concerning matters within its devolved competence, such as prosecutions for the protection of animal health and welfare.[59] It should be noted, however, that this arrangement may soon change if further justice powers are devolved in line with the recommendations of the Commission on Justice in Wales and if, in the exercise of those powers, the Senedd decides 'to establish a single independent prosecution service for Wales'.[60] Indeed, in its final report containing long-term recommendations for the operation of the Welsh justice system, the Commission on Justice formally proposed that such a service 'would properly operate under the arms-length supervision of the Counsel General to ensure that decisions on prosecution were made independently of any political or governmental influence'.[61]

The second significant executive function of the Counsel General relates to his or her 'role in the development of Welsh Government policy on legal matters'.[62] For example, a recent office-holder, Jeremy Miles, conducted a 'rapid review of the Welsh Government's gender and equality policies' in conjunction with another Welsh Minister, Julie James, with the political goal of advancing issues in that realm using the devolved powers available to the Welsh Government.[63] Miles was also appointed 'Brexit Minister' in January 2019, which caused some controversy at the time,[64] though interestingly there was no such backlash when the current office-holder, Mick Antoniw, was appointed 'Minister for the Constitution' concurrently with the office of Counsel General in May 2021.[65] These incidents will be analysed further in Chapter 7,[66] but for now it suffices to note that the broad ability of the Counsel General to play a policy role in all 'legal matters'[67]

Senedd Research, November 2021), 27–29. Available at: https://research.senedd.wales/media/qssa4cmf/21-19.pdf.

[58] ibid.

[59] See, e.g., the Animal Welfare Act 1981, which contains a range of offences which the Welsh Ministers are responsible for prosecuting consequent to the National Assembly for Wales (Transfer of Functions) Order 1999, Sch 1, read alongside the Government of Wales Act 2006, s 162(1) and Sch 11, para 30.

[60] See *Justice in Wales for the People of Wales* (The Commission on Justice in Wales Report, October 2019). Available at: https://gov.wales/commission-justice-wales-report.

[61] ibid, para 12.174.

[62] 'Counsel General for Wales' (*Law Wales*, 15 May 2018).

[63] Jeremy Miles, 'Discrimination and Public Law: Promoting Equalities for a Fairer and More Equal Wales' (A Speech by the Counsel General to the Public Law Wales Conference, 26 March 2018). Available at: https://publiclawproject.org.uk/content/uploads/2018/05/Public-Law-Wales-Project-final-speech-for-publication.pdf.

[64] The Record of Proceedings, Plenary, 8 January 2019, paras 339–363.

[65] The Record of Proceedings, Plenary, 26 May 2021, paras 100–105.

[66] See ch 7 at 177–179.

[67] 'Counsel General for Wales' (n 62).

and 'justice policy'[68] is genuinely different from the ministerial remit of the Attorney General and Solicitor General for England and Wales, which is restricted to their tripartite responsibility for *criminal justice* policy only. Thirdly, and in close connection with this policy role, the Counsel General is statutorily entitled to introduce Government Bills to the Senedd.[69] Finally, the fourth function of relevance to the executive responsibilities of the Counsel General concerns the fact that he or she, along with the First Minister and the Welsh Ministers, is authorised by statute to 'make representations about any matter affecting Wales'.[70] This permits the Counsel General to address both national and international bodies and conferences, for example, about Welsh affairs.

Advisory and Advocacy Functions

The advisory and advocacy functions of the Counsel General are similar to those of the Attorney General and Solicitor General for England and Wales in many ways, though there is no analogous role in respect of the monarch. With regard to governmental and ministerial clients at the devolved level, however, the legal advice of the Counsel General is 'final and authoritative' in much the same way that the advice of the Attorney General and Solicitor General is regarded as such among UK Government officials.[71] The official circumstances in which such advice must be sought are couched in vague language referring to questions of the 'greatest legal complexity, or political controversy or sensitivity, or which have the widest implications'.[72] In all but exceptional circumstances, moreover, the appropriate procedure for seeking formal written advice from the Counsel General is on instruction from the Director of Legal Services and 'in good time before the Welsh Government is committed to critical decisions involving legal considerations'.[73]

The presumption of confidentiality applicable to the legal advice of the Attorney General and Solicitor General for England and Wales[74] applies similarly to the legal advice of the Counsel General: both the fact that the Counsel General has or has not advised and the content of any advice that has in fact been provided 'must not be disclosed outside the Welsh Government without the authority of the Counsel General'.[75] Interestingly, the wording of the Ministerial Code quoted in

[68] 'Mick Antoniw MS: Counsel General and Minister for the Constitution' (*Welsh Government*). Available at: https://gov.wales/mick-antoniw-ms.

[69] Government of Wales Act 2006, s 110(1)(a). The Legislation (Wales) Bill, for example, was introduced to the Senedd by Jeremy Miles qua the Counsel General on 3 December 2018. More will be said about the history and effect of the Act that this Bill became at 91–93 below.

[70] Government of Wales Act 2006, s 62.

[71] Welsh Government, 'Ministerial Code' (n 45) para 6.17.

[72] ibid, para 6.18.

[73] ibid.

[74] See ch 3 at 53–54.

[75] Welsh Government, 'Ministerial Code' (n 45) para 6.19.

the previous sentence leaves open the question whether any consent on the part of the person or body who has sought advice from the Counsel General is required in addition to the consent of the Counsel General him- or herself. If client consent is not required in the Welsh context, this would represent a genuinely different breadth of discretion on the part of the Counsel General when compared with that of the Attorney General and Solicitor General for England and Wales.

In Chapter 3, two general propositions and five specific propositions about the advisory role of the Attorney General and Solicitor General for England and Wales were proffered subject to the caveat that the presumption of confidentiality that applies to most of their advice prevents a more comprehensive analysis.[76] The two general propositions – namely that the law officers have a duty to ensure legal advice is integrated into government policy making, decision making and legislative processes, and to ensure the government acts within the law so advised – appear to apply to the Counsel General with equal force. The nature of the advisory role of the Counsel General has, in fact, been described in tandem with a duty on office-holders to uphold the rule of law in several contexts, which emphasises the weight accorded to these duties.[77]

The five specific propositions mentioned in Chapter 3 – namely that the law officers have a duty to monitor the development of government legislation and decision-making for issues arising from the devolution settlement, human rights, Brexit and international law, retrospective effects and early commencement provisions – also have clear parallels in the Welsh context. In respect of the devolution settlement, the Counsel General can refer questions about the legislative competence of the Senedd to the UK Supreme Court,[78] or initiate court proceedings to determine 'devolution issues' as defined by the statute in much the same way as the Attorney General and Solicitor General for England and Wales.[79] Office-holders also have the right to defend proceedings relating to a devolution issue in other legal jurisdictions within the UK; the right to be notified of such issues if raised by others in those jurisdictions; the right to participate in all proceedings so notified, and the right to require a court or tribunal in any proceedings to which they are party to refer a devolution issue to the UK Supreme Court.[80] Whereas the Attorney General for England and Wales has pursued references to the UK Supreme Court over the legislative competence of the Senedd on two occasions now,[81] though a third challenge was only narrowly avoided,[82] the Counsel General has done so

[76] See ch 3 at 54–58.

[77] See, e.g., *Form and Accessibility of the Law Applicable in Wales* (Law Com No 366, 2016) para 3.41.

[78] Government of Wales Act 2006, s 112.

[79] Government of Wales Act 2006, Sch 9, pt 2, para 4(1).

[80] Government of Wales Act 2006, Sch 9.

[81] *Local Government Byelaws (Wales) Bill – Reference by the Attorney General for England and Wales* [2012] UKSC 53, [2013] 1 AC 792; *Agricultural Sector (Wales) Bill – Reference by the Attorney General for England and Wales* [2014] UKSC 43, [2014] 1 WLR 2622.

[82] A third reference was made but subsequently withdrawn by the Attorney General for England and Wales in respect of the Law Derived from the European Union (Wales) Bill, which duly became the Law Derived from the European Union (Wales) Act 2018. See: *UK Withdrawal from the European Union*

only once.[83] Prior to the commencement of the Government of Wales Act 2006, similar (though not identical) rights were vested in the National Assembly itself rather than the Counsel General.[84] Just as the change in these phases of the Welsh devolution settlement invested the Counsel General with new rights and responsibilities, the recent dawn of a fourth phase in that process – concerned, primarily, with a switch from the conferred powers model of devolution to one with reserved powers[85] – has charged the Counsel General with yet more tasks. In particular, the Counsel General has been given a power under the Wales Act 2017 to refer questions about whether any provision of a Bill passed by the Senedd relates to a 'protected subject-matter',[86] i.e. a matter requiring a two-thirds super-majority vote to be passed validly by the Senedd.[87]

The second and third specific propositions discussed in Chapter 3 – concerning human rights, Brexit-related and other international law restrictions that apply to Ministers who seek to propose government legislation (and indeed in respect of human rights, Brexit and international law related decision-making by Ministers more generally)[88] – also apply to a certain extent in the Welsh context simply by virtue of how 'devolution issues' are defined.[89] The effect of that definition is to condition the legislative competence of the Senedd in a much more vigorous manner than that which applies to the UK Parliament by virtue of the self-imposed constraints in place there. This represents another contextual but genuine difference in the nature of the advisory role between the Attorney General and Solicitor General for England and Wales on the one hand, and, as we will see, all the law officers associated with devolved administrations on the other.

The fourth and fifth propositions concerning proposals to enact legislation with retrospective effect or early commencement also apply to the Counsel General.[90] This clear set of duties is supplemented, however, with some more

(Legal Continuity) (Scotland) Bill – A Reference by the Attorney General and the Advocate General for Scotland [2018] UKSC 64, [2019] AC 1022 at [9].

[83] *Recovery of Medical Costs for Asbestos Diseases (Wales) Bill – Reference by the Counsel General for Wales* [2015] UKSC 3, [2015] AC 1016.

[84] Government of Wales Act 1998, Sch 8 (repealed). The National Assembly could not, for instance, institute proceedings for the determination of a devolution issue in the courts of England and Wales under the 1998 Act as the Counsel General can under the 2006 Act.

[85] Rawlings, 'The Strange Reconstitution of Wales' (n 31) 65.

[86] Government of Wales Act 2006, s 111B, as inserted by the Wales Act 2017, s 9.

[87] Government of Wales Act 2006, s 111A, as inserted by the Wales Act 2017, s 9.

[88] See, in particular, the Government of Wales Act 2006, ss 80–82.

[89] One type of devolution issue is defined as a question whether any provision passed by the Senedd is within its legislative competence: Government of Wales Act 2006, Sch 9, Pt 1, para 1(a). Any provision which is incompatible with Convention rights is outside the competence of the Senedd: Government of Wales Act, s 108A(2)(e). A modification to retained EU law, and the conferral of a power by subordinate legislation to modify retained EU law, is also prohibited so far as the modification is of a description specified in regulations made by a Minister of the Crown: Government of Wales Act, s 108A(2)(e) and 109A(1). As such, if it is suggested that a purported legislative provision fails to comply with Convention rights or that it purports to modify retained EU law in a way which is prohibited, this will automatically give rise to a devolution issue to be considered by the Counsel General.

[90] *Form and Accessibility of the Law Applicable in Wales: A Consultation Paper* (Law Com CP No 223, 2015) para 3.42.

expansive expectations of the Counsel General regarding the protection of legal principles throughout Welsh legislative processes. As such, Bill teams are required to inform the Counsel General where any 'particularly sensitive issues' arise as government legislation is formulated.[91] Such issues further encompass provisions concerning 'powers of arrest or entry, appeals, offences and penalties' and 'codes of practice'.[92] Further still, the Counsel General is said to have a 'general responsibility to consider the justice of provisions, and would expect to be consulted' if there were any concerns about such a question within a Bill team,[93] despite the ambiguity of that instruction.

As is the case in respect of the Attorney General and Solicitor General for England and Wales, the Counsel General only acts as *advocate* for his or her governmental and ministerial clients in exceptionally important cases. In addition to representing the Welsh Government in the UK Supreme Court in the first two challenges to the legislative competence of the Senedd brought by the Attorney General for England and Wales,[94] the Counsel General has represented the First Minister of Wales in analogous challenges to the legislative competence of the Scottish Parliament.[95] As noted above, however, the Counsel General tends to draw on specialist advocates appointed to various government-approved panels to represent his or her office and its clients in court.[96] In all civil proceedings where the Counsel General is acting in a representative capacity on behalf of the Welsh Ministers, or the First Minister, he or she 'must protect the interests of the Welsh Government'.[97]

The Counsel General no longer advises or advocates on behalf of the Senedd, which recruits and instructs its own parliamentary lawyers. Although the legacy of the Counsel General as chief legal adviser and representative of the Senedd mirrors

[91] ibid.
[92] ibid.
[93] ibid.
[94] See (n 81).
[95] *AXA General Insurance Ltd & Ors v Lord Advocate & Ors* [2011] UKSC 46, [2012] 1 AC 868 at [4]. Interestingly, however, this intervention was apparently brought in the name of the First Minister under s 71 of the Government of Wales Act 2006, rather than in the name of the Counsel General under s 67, simply because following the 2011 election to the National Assembly for Wales there was no Counsel General in post at the time the intervention was sought: Email to author from the Director of Legal Services for the Welsh Government, Jeff Godfrey, on behalf of the Counsel General (13 June 2018).
[96] For example, Richard Gordon QC and Tom Pascoe were instructed by the Director of the Welsh Government Legal Services Department when acting for the Counsel General in *R (Miller) v Secretary of State for Exiting the European Union* [2017] UKSC 5, [2018] AC 61, 125, on which, also see: Richard Gordon, '*Miller* and Devolution: How Wales Approached the Issues' in Daniel Clarry (ed), *The UK Supreme Court Yearbook, Volume 8: 2016–2017* (Appellate Press 2018) 359–377. Likewise, Michael Fordham QC, Celia Rooney and Hollie Higgins were instructed by the Welsh Government Legal Services Department to act for the Counsel General in *R (Miller) v Prime Minister* [2019] UKSC 41, [2020] AC 373, 388, on which, also see: The Hon Mr Justice Fordham, 'The Counsel General for Wales' Intervention in the Prorogation Case' in Daniel Clarry (ed), *The UK Supreme Court Yearbook, Volume 10: 2018–2019* (Appellate Press 2021) 421–424.
[97] Welsh Government, 'Ministerial Code' (n 45) para 6.22.

the historical links of the Attorney General and Solicitor General for England and Wales to the Houses of Parliament at Westminster, the advisory and advocacy obligations once owed by the Counsel General to the Senedd have been guillotined by the fundamental restructuring of the Welsh government institutions outlined above. Whether or not they are a member of the Senedd, however, the Counsel General is entitled to participate in its proceedings (though non-members are not permitted to vote).[98] Moreover, office-holders are required to answer oral and written questions asked by other Members of the Senedd and to make oral and written statements.[99] The Counsel General is also entitled to ask questions for written or oral answer from other members of the Welsh Government.[100] In addition, they can and do attend various Committees of the Senedd by invitation. There is no evidence to suggest any parallel reluctance on the part of office-holders when it comes to appearing before Committees concerned with the scrutiny of Welsh Government operations in a particular subject, akin to the historically tense relationship between the Attorney General and Solicitor General for England and Wales and Select Committees of the UK Parliament, because Committees of the Senedd generally perform a mix of legislative and subject area scrutiny. In any Senedd proceedings in which the Counsel General is obliged or elects to participate, however, he or she may 'decline to answer any question or produce any document concerning the operation of the system of criminal prosecution in any particular case' if doing so would either 'prejudice criminal proceedings in the case' or if doing so 'would otherwise be contrary to the public interest'.[101] As the prosecutorial responsibilities of the Counsel General are quite narrow in comparison to the Attorney General and Solicitor General for England and Wales (and, as Chapter 6 will show, likewise in comparison to the Attorney General and Advocate General for Northern Ireland), this limitation on accountability is of less significance in the Welsh context at the time of writing.

Public Interest Functions

Finally, the public interest functions of the Counsel General can be considered by way of concluding this overview of the familiar functions that are currently attached to the office. It will be recalled from Chapter 3 that it is quite possible to contest the categorisation of other functions discussed thus far in this chapter, such as the extensive expectations on the Counsel General to uphold the rule of law in Welsh legislative processes, as anything other than public interest functions

[98] Government of Wales Act 2006, s 34(1); Standing Orders of the Welsh Parliament (March 2021) 9.4.

[99] Standing Orders of the Welsh Parliament (March 2021) 11, 12 and 14.

[100] ibid.

[101] Government of Wales Act 2006, s 34(3).

given the independent mindedness they appear to call for. However, this is still not the place to explore those arguments.

There is little to say about the limited functions of the Counsel General in the criminal law context that has not already been said, other than noting that it is possible for the Counsel General to institute a criminal prosecution in the public interest independently of the Welsh Government[102] and, where a prosecution function is vested in the Counsel General, the Ministerial Code provides specifically that 'that function is to be exercised by him or her independently of the Welsh Government'.[103] The Shawcross statement reproduced on pages 66–67 of Chapter 3 is echoed somewhat by the following part of the Code which provides that other members of the Welsh Government 'must not interfere in, or be involved in any way with, the exercise of such a function'.[104] This formulation appears to mandate a rather stronger conception of independence on the part of the Counsel General than that which the Shawcross statement requires of the Attorney General and Solicitor General for England and Wales, at least in so far as the words 'in any way' might be interpreted as forbidding ministerial consultations about the exercise of a prosecutorial function. That is another potentially genuine difference between these models.

There are also comparatively few specific public interest roles in civil law contexts, with the exception of a noteworthy statutory power for the Counsel General to institute, defend or appear in any legal proceedings – criminal or civil – 'relating to matters with respect to which any functions of the Welsh Ministers, the First Minister or the Counsel General are exercisable' so long as the Counsel General considers it appropriate to do so 'for the promotion or protection of the public interest'.[105] The Counsel General has relied on this power on quite a number of occasions now, such that several Brexit-related instances may be offered by way of thematic illustration.

First, it was this power which was used as the basis for an intervention by the Counsel General in Gina Miller's application to judicially review the UK Government's intention to serve notice under Article 50 of the Treaty on the Functioning of the European Union by way of a prerogative power and, likewise, to intervene in the same applicant's case in connection with the prerogative power to prorogue Parliament.[106] The Counsel General decided to intervene in the Article

[102] Government of Wales Act 2006, s 67. See, e.g., the following report concerning a sea fisheries prosecution brought by the Counsel General under s 67 wherein the skipper of a Cornish fishing vessel was fined £50,000 for illegal scallop dredging in breach of the Scallop Fishing (Wales) (No 2) Order 2010: Robin Turner, 'Cornish Fisherman Ordered to Pay £50,000 for Taking Scallops from Welsh Waters' (*Wales Online*, 3 April 2014). Available at: www.walesonline.co.uk/news/wales-news/cornish-fisherman-ordered-pay-50000-6915013.

[103] Welsh Government, 'Ministerial Code' (n 45) para 6.20.

[104] ibid.

[105] Government of Wales Act 2006, s 67.

[106] *R (Miller) v Secretary of State for Exiting the European Union* [2017] UKSC 5, [2018] AC 61; *R (Miller) v Prime Minister* [2019] UKSC 41, [2020] AC 373. Also see (n 96) above.

50 case because it raised devolution issues which, in his view, required clarification in the public interest, namely 'whether prerogative powers could be used to side-step the established constitutional mechanisms by which Parliament legislates to change the legislative competence of the National Assembly for Wales'.[107] Similarly, his intervention in the prorogation case was justified, inter alia, on the basis that he had a responsibility to explain to the UK Supreme Court 'the particular and distinct consequences of the prorogation for Wales', including its propensity to impede the ability of the Senedd 'to engage in dialogue with the UK Parliament'.[108]

Second, and likewise related to Brexit, the Counsel General relied on this power to intervene in court proceedings when the Attorney General for England and Wales and the Advocate General for Scotland made a devolution issue reference in respect of the UK Withdrawal from the EU (Legal Continuity) (Scotland) Bill passed by the Scottish Parliament, on the basis that the questions they referred had 'significance for the constitutional balance between Parliament and all the devolution settlements, for the justiciability of that balance, for legislative and ministerial competence, and for the interpretation of primary legislation.'[109]

Third, the Counsel General further relied on this public interest power to institute legal proceedings in his own right (rather than intervening in proceedings brought by others, as in the previous examples) after the United Kingdom Internal Market Act 2020 was enacted at Westminster in breach of the Sewel Convention.[110] The Counsel General's decision to issue these proceedings was framed as a measure 'to protect the Senedd from the attack on its competence made by the UK Internal Market Act 2020' by way of 'two central submissions', namely that

> the Act impermissibly, impliedly repeals parts of the Government of Wales Act 2006 in a way that diminishes the Senedd's legislative competence and that the Act confers

[107] Email to author from the Director of Legal Services for the Welsh Government, Jeff Godfrey, on behalf of the Counsel General (13 June 2018).

[108] Fordham (n 96) 421–422.

[109] ibid. Also see: Alys Thomas, 'Why did the Counsel General intervene in the Supreme Court?' (*In Brief*, 3 August 2018). Available at: https://seneddresearch.blog/2018/08/03/why-did-the-counsel-general-intervene-in-the-supreme-court/. For the judgment, see: *UK Withdrawal from the European Union (Legal Continuity) (Scotland) Bill – Reference by the Attorney General and the Advocate General for Scotland* [2018] UKSC 64, [2019] AC 1022. For a judgment arising from a more recent set of law officer references where the Counsel General intervened for similar (albeit non-Brexit related) reasons, see: *United Nations Convention on the Rights of the Child (Incorporation) (Scotland) Bill – Reference by the Attorney General and the Advocate General for Scotland, and European Charter of Local Self-Government (Incorporation) (Scotland) Bill – References by the Attorney General and the Advocate General for Scotland* [2021] UKSC 42, [2021] 1 WLR 5106.

[110] See Jeremy Miles, 'Written Statement: Legal Challenge to the UK Internal Market Act 2020' (*Welsh Government*, 19 January 2021). Available at: https://gov.wales/written-statement-legal-challenge-uk-internal-market-act-2020, where the Counsel General's grounds of review can be downloaded as a pdf. At [2] of that pdf, the Counsel General is described as 'the Chief Law Officer for the Welsh Government, with statutory authority to bring litigation in the public interest under s 67 of [the Government of Wales Act 2006]'. Also note that the Sewel Convention was breached notwithstanding the statutory recognition accorded to it by the Government of Wales Act 2006, s 107(6), as inserted by the Wales Act 2017, s 2.

> power on the UK Government, by way of wide Henry VIII powers, which could be used by UK Ministers to substantively amend the Government of Wales Act in a way that cuts down the devolution settlement.[111]

Given that the Counsel General's claim was 'said to raise issues of constitutional importance', it was argued before Lewis LJ and Steyn J sitting as a Divisional Court at first instance.[112] However a difficulty for the claim, as counsel for the Secretary of State argued, arose from the fact that it had been brought before the Senedd had actually passed any legislation giving rise to issues involving the 2020 Act and because the Secretary of State had not yet exercised any power to make regulations under the Act.[113] The High Court agreed with these submissions and therefore refused to grant the Counsel General permission to apply for judicial review on the basis that his claim was premature.[114] Interestingly, the Court suggested that there were constitutional reasons why it should refrain from issuing 'advisory declarations'[115] in the circumstances, as it would be more appropriate for the provisions of proposed legislation to be referred to the UK Supreme Court 'if the Counsel General or the Attorney General consider that a question of legislative competence arises' or, 'if that that does not occur, a person with sufficient interest in the matter may seek judicial review in an appropriate case'.[116] This is perhaps a useful indication of the Court's view on the appropriate ambit of the Counsel General's power to institute proceedings in the public interest, particularly given that the Court of Appeal has since dismissed an appeal against the judgment of the High Court.[117]

Leaving these Brexit-related examples of the Counsel General's role in public interest litigation to one side, however, it is important to note that more often than not the Welsh Ministers tend to defend and institute civil litigation under their own name rather than in the name of the Counsel General acting in the public interest.[118] This suggests that care has been taken to avoid conflating court appearances in the public interest from civil litigation on behalf of the Welsh Government, which is genuinely different from the default approach required in respect of the Attorney General and Solicitor General for England and Wales under the Crown

[111] ibid.

[112] *R (Counsel General for Wales) v The Secretary of State for Business, Energy and Industrial Strategy* [2021] EWHC 950 (Admin) at [7].

[113] ibid [6].

[114] ibid [37]–[38].

[115] ibid [33]–[34].

[116] ibid [35].

[117] See *R (Counsel General for Wales) v The Secretary of State for Business, Energy and Industrial Strategy* [2022] EWCA Civ 118 at [35] in particular (Nicola Davies LJ, with whom Sir Geoffrey Vos MR and Dingemans LJ agree).

[118] See, e.g., *R (Roberts) v Welsh Ministers & Cardiff County Council* [2012] EWCA Civ 507; *Welsh Ministers v Price* [2017] EWCA Civ 1768, [2018] 1 WLR 738. Likewise, note that the Welsh Ministers tend to intervene in their own name, as in *R (Driver) v Rhondda Cynon Taf County Borough Council & Ors* [2020] EWCA Civ 1759.

Proceedings Act 1947 (which, as explained in Chapter 3,[119] requires that the Attorney General must be named as the claimant in any civil proceedings instituted by the Crown unless a specific Government Department has been authorised to sue in its own name and that civil proceedings against the Crown must normally be instituted against the Attorney General).[120]

Furthermore, the Counsel General is not tasked with an assortment of statutory and non-statutory functions in civil litigation akin to the Attorney General and Solicitor General for England and Wales as, for example, in respect of special advocates and vexatious litigants. This is largely due to the fact that the court system in Wales remains connected to the English system by a single legal jurisdiction, and the Attorney General and Solicitor General for England and Wales therefore retain a monopoly over such roles. There is, however, a growing campaign for reform. Indeed, most Counsels General have been politically instrumental in arguing the case in favour of such reforms.[121]

Unique and Recently Created Functions of the Counsel General

The Legislation (Wales) Act 2019 has given rise to several unique and far-reaching functions that the Counsel General must now carry out on an ongoing basis, though they have no obvious parallels with the functions of the Attorney General and Solicitor General for England and Wales and are genuinely different from the functions vested in those offices.

The 2019 Act forms part of the Welsh Government's wider programme of 'improving the accessibility of Welsh law and clarifying and simplifying the operation of Welsh legislation'.[122] It was developed as a result of several inquiries,[123] with perhaps the most influential being a report by the Law Commission for England and Wales on how to improve the 'Form and Accessibility of Law in Wales'.[124] That report made a number of significant recommendations which beckoned an amplification in the constitutional role of the Counsel General,[125]

[119] See ch 3 at 58.

[120] Crown Proceedings Act 1947, s 17.

[121] See, e.g., 'Counsel General Calls for Distinct Welsh Legal System' (*Welsh Government*, 7 October 2016). Available at: https://gov.wales/newsroom/improvingpublicservices/2016/58652062/?lang=en. For further examples, see: Huw Pritchard, 'Revisiting Legal Wales' (2019) 23 *Edinburgh Law Review* 123, 123.

[122] Explanatory Notes to the Legislation (Wales) Act 2019, para 4.

[123] ibid, paras 5–9.

[124] *Form and Accessibility of the Law Applicable in Wales* (n 77).

[125] See: Conor McCormick, 'Expanding the Portfolio of the Counsel General to the National Assembly for Wales' (*UK Constitutional Law Association Blog*, 28 July 2016). Available at: https://ukconstitutionallaw.org/2016/07/28/conor-mccormick-expanding-the-portfolio-of-the-counsel-general-to-the-national-assembly-for-wales/.

and the Welsh Government agreed, at least in principle, with the vast majority of those recommendations.[126] Following two consultations on the mechanics of implementing these duly adapted proposals,[127] inter alia, a Legislation (Wales) Bill was introduced to the Senedd by Jeremy Miles qua the Counsel General on 3 December 2018. The Solicitor General for England and Wales subsequently wrote to the Counsel General to express the UK Government's view 'that the application of the Bill to subordinate legislation made by Welsh Ministers under Acts of Parliament' was outwith the legislative competence of the Senedd.[128] The Counsel General replied in robust terms that sought to defend the Senedd's competence to pass the Bill.[129] The Solicitor General later responded that, notwithstanding continued disagreement as to the Counsel General's conclusions with respect to the legislative competence of the Senedd, he would not be referring the Bill to the UK Supreme Court under section 112 of the Government of Wales Act 2006.[130] The Bill subsequently received the Royal Assent on 10 September 2019.

Part 2 of the 2019 Act concerns the interpretation and operation of legislation made by the Senedd and is intended to supplement the Interpretation Act 1978 of the UK Parliament. Significant though these provisions are in so far as they add bespoke clarity to the meaning and effect of Welsh legislation, it is Part 1 of the Act which carries the most relevance with respect to the new and unique functions of the Counsel General. Section 1(1) places a duty on the Counsel General to 'keep the accessibility of Welsh law under review'. This is similar to an obligation imposed on the Law Commission for England and Wales,[131] requiring 'a focus on the law as a collective, be that the law on a particular subject and the statute book as a whole'.[132] The Explanatory Notes to the Act explain that

[126] Final Response Letter from the Welsh Government to the Law Commission (19 July 2017). Available at: https://s3-eu-west-2.amazonaws.com/lawcom-prod-storage-11jsxou24uy7q/uploads/2016/06/2017-07-19-Law-Commission-Final-Response.pdf; Annex to Final Response Letter from the Welsh Government to the Law Commission (19 July 2017). Available at: https://s3-eu-west-2.amazonaws.com/lawcom-prod-storage-11jsxou24uy7q/uploads/2016/06/2017-07-19-Law-Commission-Final-Response-Annex.pdf; Final Law Commission Response to the Welsh Government (20 July 2017). Available at: https://s3-eu-west-2.amazonaws.com/lawcom-prod-storage-11jsxou24uy7q/uploads/2016/06/20-July-Chair-to-CG-as-posted.pdf.

[127] Welsh Government, 'Interpreting Welsh Legislation: Considering an Interpretation Act for Wales' (WG32209, June 2017); Welsh Government, 'Draft Legislation (Wales) Bill' (WG 34368, March 2018).

[128] Letter to the Counsel General for Wales, Jeremy Miles AM, from the Solicitor General for England and Wales, Robert Buckland QC MP (25 April 2019), available at https://business.senedd.wales/documents/s87487/Letter%20from%20the%20Solicitor%20General%20to%20the%20Counsel%20General%20-%2025%20April%202019.pdf.

[129] Letter to the Solicitor General for England and Wales, Lucy Frazer QC MP, from the Counsel General for Wales, Jeremy Miles AM (26 June 2019). Available at: https://business.senedd.wales/documents/s90524/Letter%20from%20the%20Counsel%20General%20to%20the%20Solicitor%20General%20-%2026%20June%202019.pdf.

[130] Letter to the Counsel General for Wales, Jeremy Miles AM, from the Solicitor General for England and Wales, Michael Ellis QC MP (6 August 2019). Available at: https://business.senedd.wales/documents/s92937/Letter%20from%20the%20Solicitor%20General%20to%20the%20Llywydd%20-%206%20August%202019.pdf.

[131] Law Commissions Act 1965, s 3(1).

[132] Explanatory Notes to the Legislation (Wales) Act 2019, para 11.

this duty 'means that the Counsel General's obligation to keep the accessibility of Welsh law under review will be relevant when the Welsh Ministers are considering whether to propose new legislation'.[133] They add that, in such situations, 'regard should be had to how the approach taken to legislating could impact on the accessibility of the law'.[134]

Section 2(1) of the Act, moreover, imposes a separate obligation on the Welsh Ministers and the Counsel General to 'prepare a programme setting out what they intend to do to improve the accessibility of Welsh law'. The Act specifies that each programme must include proposed activities for contributing to 'an ongoing process of consolidating and codifying Welsh law'; for maintaining 'the form of Welsh law (once codified)'; for promoting 'awareness and understanding of Welsh law', and for facilitating 'use of the Welsh language'.[135] Consolidation of the law, which is said to involve 'bringing all legislation on a particular topic together', is clearly distinguished from the process of codification envisaged by the Act, which 'is intended to bring order to the statute book' by reference to its content rather than the date on which it was made.[136] The Counsel General is specifically required to lay a copy of the programme for reviewing the accessibility of Welsh law before the Senedd within six months of the appointment of the First Minister after a general election,[137] and must thereafter 'report annually to the Senedd on progress made under the programme'.[138]

In the Law Commission report which first recommended functions of this nature, the Counsel General was identified as the appropriate duty bearer in this context because of 'the measure of independence from the government' that he or she is said to enjoy.[139] As such, having been passed into law, these new functions arguably represent a recent example of the trust that has been placed in the Counsel General by the Senedd after fairly extensive constitutional deliberations about the appropriate measures of accountability and independence that are needed to maintain that trust.

Conclusions

The Counsel General for Wales has become an increasingly powerful member of the UK law officer regime over time. Correspondingly, it has been explained in this chapter that while the Counsel General initially emerged in the mould of a

[133] ibid.
[134] ibid.
[135] Legislation (Wales) Act 2019, s 2(3)(a)–(d).
[136] Explanatory Notes to the Legislation (Wales) Act 2019, paras 21–23. Also see the definition of codification provided in the Legislation (Wales) Act 2019, s 2(8).
[137] Legislation (Wales) Act 2019, s 2(5). For details about the first such programme, see 'The Future of Welsh Law: A Programme for 2021 to 2026' (*Welsh Government*, 21 September 2021). Available at: https://gov.wales/the-future-of-welsh-law-accessibility-programme-2021-to-2026-html.
[138] Legislation (Wales) Act 2019, s 2(7).
[139] *Form and Accessibility of the Law Applicable in Wales* (n 77) para 6.14.

senior civil servant responsible for advising the Senedd several years before the Welsh Government was formally recognised as a distinct legal entity, the constitutional basis of the office has been radically remoulded in a way which means that it now resembles the offices of the Attorney General and Solicitor General for England and Wales in many respects. With that said, it is clear that neither the constitutional credentials nor the functions of the Counsel General are precisely analogous to those of the Attorney General and Solicitor General for England and Wales. Recall, for instance, that while the Counsel General has been styled as a member of the Welsh Government with ministerial status, which means that the office-holder is not a Welsh Minister per se, the Attorney General and Solicitor General for England and Wales are, by contrast, recognised as 'full' Ministers of the Crown and regarded as closer in status to their ministerial peers in the UK Government ex officio. Equally, while most of the functions of the Counsel General have been explicated by way of the same three categories that were used to examine the functions of the Attorney General and Solicitor General for England and Wales in Chapter 3 – namely, executive functions; advisory and advocacy functions, and so-called public interest functions – it should now be evident that there are a number of notable differences. It should be emphasised, too, that the nature of such differences ranges from the trivial (e.g. the statutory basis of the law officers' powers to refer certain devolution issues to the Supreme Court), to the genuine (e.g. the Counsel General's unique responsibilities in connection with the accessibility of Welsh law). Together with the Counsel General's progressively prominent place in various debates and conversations about the constitutional future of Wales,[140] these findings clearly reinforce the need for a context-sensitive approach to any assessment relating to the constitutional legitimacy of the UK law officer regime as a whole.

[140] See, e.g., Mick Antoniw, 'A National Civic Conversation About Our Constitutional Future' (A Speech by the Counsel General to the Wales Governance Centre at Cardiff University, 5 July 2021). Available at: www.cardiff.ac.uk/__data/assets/pdf_file/0003/2532405/Counsel-General-Speech.pdf.

5

The Lord Advocate, Solicitor General and Advocate General for Scotland

Introduction

Like the Counsel General for Wales, the Advocate General for Scotland is a fairly modern addition to the UK law officer regime. The Lord Advocate and the Solicitor General for Scotland, on the other hand, are of a much greater vintage than the Counsel General and do not lend themselves easily to a similar framework of exposition for that reason. Thus, whereas most of the functions of the Counsel General for Wales were outlined under the same headings used to explicate those of the Attorney General and Solicitor General for England and Wales in Chapter 3, a different approach is required in this context. As such, the ancient origins of the Lord Advocate and Solicitor General for Scotland as servants of the Crown are set out in the opening pages of this chapter, before a short explanation in connection with the 'political' prominence of the Lord Advocate during the nineteenth century is provided thereafter. The 'predominantly legal' portfolio of the Lord Advocate that continuously evolved in later centuries is examined in the following section. With a clear account of these previously uncharted historical developments in place, the remaining sections of this chapter focus on the functions of the Scottish law officers as they stand today, with particular attention being paid to the significant reconfigurations introduced with and since the devolution reforms of 1998.

As alluded to above, the decision not to contain the historical digressions in this chapter within the functional categories used previously has been taken mainly in order to highlight how the constitutional functions of the Lord Advocate and Solicitor General for Scotland have been characterised rather differently at various stages, primarily by reference to competing 'political' and 'legal' conceptions of their legitimate role in Scottish affairs (however doubtful that distinction may be as a tool for normative evaluation). Moreover, the historical evolution of these ancient Scottish offices is analysed in greater depth than the equivalent historical analysis of the Attorney General and Solicitor General for England and Wales because the latter is well-developed in existing literature whereas a fitting account of the former required some considerable synthesis for the purposes of this book.[1] The largely chronological structure employed hereafter also allows appropriate weight to be placed at relevant junctures on the uniquely significant prosecutorial functions of the Lord Advocate and Solicitor General for Scotland that have developed over time and thereby operates as another way of highlighting the contestability of the different functional taxonomies that can be used to frame the work of the UK law officer regime.

The Monarchical Phase

Most commentary suggests that there was a 'King's Advocate' pleading in Scottish civil suits on behalf of the Crown and as a representative 'of the King's interest in Parliament at the trial of certain persons for resisting the King's forces' as long ago as 1478 and 1479 respectively.[2] Finlay, however, casts doubt on whether these dates really do, in fact, mark the origin of the office of King's Advocate in Scotland – warning that it is 'only too easy to confuse the title' as it appears in historical records with 'the substantive role' of the Advocate which, Finlay argues, does not appear to have been consistently or fully formed until slightly later, during the reign of King James IV.[3] While a very general timeframe about the end of the fifteenth century can thus be agreed upon as the temporal birth of the first King's Advocate, there is further disagreement among legal historians over the constitutional derivation of the role. Omond and Gordon think it is probable that, in light of a long series of alliances between France and Scotland, the French office of *procureur du roi* may have inspired Scottish sovereigns to appoint a King's Advocate.[4] The functions of a *procureur du roi* involved maintaining public order, defending and protecting the King's interests, and the positive extension of royal authority ('by defending royal officers who had encroached on non-royal jurisdictions'); functions which were indeed 'substantially carried on by the King's Advocate in the Scotland of James IV'.[5] Edwards, however, relies on two reasons to suggest that the office 'derived its roots from the same soil that gave sustenance to the English office of

[1] It may be recalled, in particular, that Appleby has published a comprehensive review of the literature exploring various stages in the evolution of the Atttorney General and Solicitor General for England and Wales, which meant that the historical analysis in ch 3 of this book could be truncated somewhat. See: Gabrielle Appleby, *The Role of the Solicitor-General: Negotiating Law, Politics and the Public Interest* (Hart Publishing 2016) ch 2.

[2] Lord Clyde, 'Memorandum on the Law Officers of Scotland' *The Times* (London, 7 February 1924), reproduced in James Casey, 'The First Labour Government and Office of Lord Advocate' (1975) 26 *Northern Ireland Legal Quarterly* 18, 26–29.

[3] John Finlay, 'James Henryson and the Origins of the Office of King's Advocate in Scotland' (2000) 79 *The Scottish Historical Review* 17, 19–23.

[4] George WT Omond, 'The Lord Advocates of Scotland: Second Series: 1834–1880' (Andrew Melrose 1914) v; Lionel I Gordon, 'Lord Advocate and the Crown Office' in MR McLarty and G Campbell H Paton (eds), *A Source Book and History of Administrative Law in Scotland* (William Hodge and Company 1956) 55.

[5] Finlay (n 3) 33.

King's Attorney'.[6] First, he cites medieval records dating back to 1243 supporting the existence of a practising King's Attorney in England. Edwards implies that this then century-long practice in England was a more probable source of derivation for the Scottish office by the time of the fifteenth century than the *procureur du roi*. Second, he explains that similar claims of French inspiration for the practice of appointing early King's Attorneys to Scotland's highest judicial body are 'unsupportable historically'.[7] The latter reason offered by Edwards is arguably of limited assistance in understanding why a Scottish law officer was commissioned in the first instance, but there is some merit in his first argument. Finlay, furthermore, highlights that 'although several Scots men of law of this period' were 'educated in France, there is no evidence of any conscious attempt to transplant or adapt the office of *procureur du roi* to Scotland'.[8]

While it seems slightly more likely that the first King's Attorney in Scotland was inspired by the English model implemented in the early thirteenth century, Scottish sovereigns of the time may have been inspired to employ a professional attorney to represent their interests in court by more than one foreign jurisdiction. Alternatively, the office may have been devised independently of outside influence from within Scotland. In the absence of any compelling historical evidence to support one or other of these theories, the true origin story of the Lord Advocate must be left open to speculation.

As regards the ancestry of the Solicitor General for Scotland, Scottish sovereigns went without such an office-holder until 1587.[9] Until that time the services of the Church's Solicitor, an appointment made by the General Assembly of the Church of Scotland subject to confirmation by the sovereign, sufficed to meet their needs.[10] For most of the time thereafter the 'King's Solicitor' and the 'Church's Solicitor' acted independently,[11] though they were both concerned with the same business of protecting the sovereign's financial interests (the sovereign being 'entitled to a surplus of dues' payable to Church ministers).[12] Indeed, over the course of time, some of the King's Solicitors would become fiercely protective of their remit.[13] Their powers expanded in due course. During the seventeenth century, in particular, the King's Solicitors were 'authorised to prosecute exactly as did the King's Advocate'.[14] Indeed, like the Solicitor General for England and Wales in respect of promotion to the post of Attorney General for England and Wales, the Solicitor's office eventually came to be recognised as 'the natural stepping stone to

[6] John Ll J Edwards, *The Attorney General, Politics and the Public Interest* (Sweet & Maxwell 1984) 271.
[7] ibid 272.
[8] Finlay (n 3) 33.
[9] CA Malcolm, 'The Solicitor General for Scotland (Part I)' (1942) *Juridical Review* 67, 68.
[10] Edwards, *The Attorney General, Politics and the Public Interest* (n 6) 287.
[11] Malcolm (n 9) 69.
[12] Edwards, *The Attorney General, Politics and the Public Interest* (n 6) 287.
[13] Malcolm (n 9) 78.
[14] ibid 77.

the senior position of the Lord Advocate'.[15] Once parliamentary government was achieved, however, this would for a long time depend on the continued electoral success of the political party of the Solicitor General for Scotland.[16] Occasional misfortunes were apparently remedied, however, by way of appointments to the judiciary in the majority of cases.[17]

The 'Predominantly Political' Phase

During the sixteenth and seventeenth centuries, prior to the parliamentary union of Scotland and England at the beginning of the eighteenth, the Scottish King's Advocate came to assume a mixture of so-called legal and political functions. Alongside those court and prosecutorial duties outlined above, access to 'the Royal presence' meant he (and it was always a 'he') was able to take 'a leading part in the general business of government' for some time before becoming an official member of the King's Privy Council in Scotland.[18] Then, as a member of the Scottish Government – along with the Chancellor, High Treasurer, Justice-General, Privy Seal, Treasurer-Depute, Clerk-Register and Secretary of State[19] – the King's Advocate was given the title 'Lord'.[20] Moreover, by virtue of being a senior member of the Government, the Lord Advocate sat and voted ex officio in the Estates (i.e. the Scottish Parliament) during this period.[21] Since then it has been customary, though not without exception, for office-holders to be a member of the legislature.[22]

After the parliamentary union of 1707 the Lord Advocate briefly competed for governmental authority with incumbents of the offices of Secretaries of State in Scotland[23] but, by 1725, those offices were vacated and the Lord Advocate became '*de facto* the only minister for Scotland'.[24] Barring a brief revival of the office of Third Secretary between 1741 and 1746, the Lord Advocate enjoyed an unrivalled level of influence over Scottish affairs for an extended period of time thereafter.[25] While the 'technical right' to control Scottish matters in their various departments

> no doubt belonged to the various Ministers of the Crown … so little was known in London about Scotland and the country was in so disturbed and backward a condition

[15] Edwards, *The Attorney General, Politics and the Public Interest* (n 6) 289.
[16] CA Malcolm, 'The Solicitor General for Scotland (Part II)' (1942) *Juridical Review* 125, 141.
[17] ibid.
[18] Gordon (n 4) 56; David Milne, *The Scottish Office and Other Scottish Government Departments* (George Allen & Unwin 1957) 8–9.
[19] Edwards, *The Attorney General, Politics and the Public Interest* (n 6) 277.
[20] Gordon (n 4) 58; Omond (n 4) v–vi.
[21] Milne (n 18) 9.
[22] Ian S Dickinson, 'The Office of Lord Advocate' [1980] SLT 69. Some of the exceptions to this custom are discussed further at 118–121 below.
[23] Milne (n 18) 9.
[24] *The Laws of Scotland: Stair Memorial Encyclopaedia*, Constitutional Law Reissue, para 427.
[25] David Milne (n 18) 11.

> that responsibility was easily devolved upon the only man who knew or cared much about the subject.[26]

The authority of the Lord Advocate over Scottish affairs was in fact so great during the nineteenth century that it was contemporaneously described as 'almost unlimited, and greater than that of any functionary in the British Empire'.[27] Daintith and Page note that this period is remarkable in so far as it differentiates the history of the Lord Advocate from that of the Attorney General for England and Wales.[28] While the former did at this time hold 'real executive power', the latter has never held a similarly sweeping level of authority.[29] Eventually, however, the extent of the legal and political powers of the Lord Advocate began to attract criticism.[30] There were a number of parliamentary debates highlighting the vast range of functions vested in him and some of the difficulties created by that arrangement. Some Scottish Members of Parliament, for example, were dissatisfied because the legal duties of the Lord Advocate 'often required him to be in Edinburgh when Parliament was sitting [in London] and as a result Scottish business in the House [of Commons] was neglected.'[31] It was also said 'that the Government of Scotland should not be a monopoly held by the legal profession'.[32] Such critics of the then prevailing conditions called for 'a greater sense of accountability through the devolution of power' to a dedicated Secretary of State for Scotland;[33] a reform proposal which was eventually acceded to in 1885.[34]

While the statute which established a new Secretary of State for Scotland in 1885 expressly forbade any implied repeal of his existing rights, powers, privileges and duties,[35] its passage marked the beginning of a 'gradual reduction in the political powers' of the Lord Advocate as they then subsequently went to the Secretary of State.[36] Although the Lord Advocate continued to work closely with the Scottish Secretary to discharge the latter's transferred political functions,[37] in 1926 the office was elevated to the status of a Principal Secretary of State.[38] Thereafter, there was to be no doubt about the fact that the Principal Secretary in charge of the UK

[26] Lord Macmillan, *A Man of Law's Tale* (Macmillan & Co 1952) 86.

[27] Omond (n 4) vi.

[28] Terence Daintith and Alan Page, *The Executive in the Constitution: Structure, Autonomy, and Internal Control* (Oxford University Press 1999) 237.

[29] ibid.

[30] Milne (n 18) 12.

[31] ibid 13.

[32] ibid.

[33] Edwards, *The Attorney General, Politics and the Public Interest* (n 6) 278; James Mitchell, *Governing Scotland: The Invention of Administrative Devolution* (Palgrave Macmillan 2003) ch 2.

[34] Secretary for Scotland Act 1885.

[35] Secretary for Scotland Act 1885, s 9.

[36] Gordon (n 4) 59.

[37] *The Laws of Scotland: Stair Memorial Encyclopaedia*, Constitutional Law Reissue, paras 427–428.

[38] Secretaries of State Act 1926. Note, however, that this Act simply created an additional Principal Secretary of State post – it did not create a specific Secretary of State for Scotland as such: *The Laws of Scotland: Stair Memorial Encyclopaedia*, Constitutional Law Reissue, para 427, fn 6.

Government's Scottish Office had assumed primary responsibility for the political affairs of the region.[39] The speed of this shift in constitutional arrangements is captured neatly by Hanham, who records that

> [w]ithin a generation after the passage of the Secretary for Scotland Act, men had ceased to think of the Lord Advocate as primarily a political figure and had come to regard him as little more than the Government's principal legal adviser in Scotland.[40]

So it was that by the end of the nineteenth century the accumulation of political power by the Lord Advocate had reached the end of its peak, with remnants of so-called political responsibilities connected to the office accordingly 'relegated to a subordinate place within the portfolio'.[41] Correspondingly, by the start of the twentieth century, Edwards describes the office as having reverted to its 'original, predominantly legal character'.[42]

The 'Predominantly Legal' Phase

Before providing a brief account of 'predominantly legal' aspects to the work of the Lord Advocate and Solicitor General for Scotland as it was viewed by Edwards and others before the devolution reforms of 1998, it should be noted that some ministerial aspects of the office had expanded once more by the end of the twentieth century (though never reaching the level of dominance over Scottish governmental affairs experienced during the eighteenth and nineteenth centuries). The following sub-section elaborates on the historical executive functions of the Lord Advocate and Solicitor General for Scotland during this long and significant phase in their development. Thereafter, those functions of the Lord Advocate and Solicitor General for Scotland, once contestably regarded as primarily legal in nature, are set out under three bespoke headings (historical advisory functions, litigation functions and prosecutorial functions) which have been tailored to them by dint of the reasons provided above. For context concerning the relationship between the ancient Scottish law officers during this phase of their development and after, it should also be noted that under section 2(1) of the Law Officers Act 1944 the Solicitor General for Scotland was empowered to discharge 'any functions authorised or required' of the Lord Advocate 'by any enactment or otherwise'. The latter provision meant that the Solicitor General for Scotland was (and remains)

[39] It should be noted that the Scottish Office was renamed the Office of the Secretary of State for Scotland in May 2018, ostensibly for the purpose of drawing attention to the continued relevance of the largely diminished UK Minister in charge of non-devolved Scottish affairs. The change in nomenclature was effected in tandem with the transformation of the Wales Office to the Office of the Secretary of State for Wales, as noted in ch 4.

[40] HJ Hanham, 'The Creation of the Scottish Office 1881–1887' (1965) *Juridical Review* 205, 244.

[41] Edwards, *The Attorney General, Politics and the Public Interest* (n 6) 280.

[42] ibid.

permitted to perform both the statutory and non-statutory functions of the Lord Advocate when necessary, something which genuinely distinguished the office-holder from their English equivalent until the Solicitor General for England and Wales was given clear authority to discharge the non-statutory functions of the Attorney General for England and Wales when the 1944 Act was amended in 1997.[43]

Historical Executive Functions

Prior to the devolution reforms of 1998, both the Lord Advocate and Solicitor General for Scotland were appointed by the Queen based on a recommendation by the UK Prime Minister and thus served as Ministers of the Crown subject to the normal whims of a political office (i.e. they would 'go out of office with the government') in the same manner as the Attorney General and Solicitor General for England and Wales.[44] The custom, followed by numerous Prime Ministers, of ordinarily recommending for appointment Scottish law officers who were either MPs or peers, meant that those office-holders were positioned to pilot legislation promoted by the Scottish Secretary of State through whichever House of Parliament they belonged to.[45] Indeed, as one post-devolution Lord Advocate has observed: 'any idea that Law Officers were not legally involved in policy matters [pre-devolution] is an illusion' given that they used to steer government legislation through Parliament, 'including both the 1978 and the 1998 Scotland Acts'.[46] Moreover, the Scottish law officers were able to exercise considerable influence over some executive business by virtue of their regular attendance at various UK Cabinet Committees prior to devolution. For example, another former Lord Advocate recounts having had 'no difficulty in obtaining agreement to a complete re-drafting of the main clause' in a Bill under consideration by the then Legislation Committee on account of deference to his legal expertise on the relevant subject matter.[47]

A particularly large inflation to the ministerial work of the Lord Advocate occurred in 1973, when a range of functions were transferred from the then over-burdened Secretary of State for Scotland.[48] The effect of this seismic reallocation of responsibility has been summarised succinctly as follows:

> [it conferred] on the Lord Advocate statutory functions relating to the Scottish Law Commission formerly exercised by both ministers, functions relating to the Council

[43] Law Officers Act 1997.

[44] David M Walker, *The Scottish Legal System: An Introduction to the Study of Scots Law* (7th edn, Sweet & Maxwell 1997) 356–357.

[45] *The Laws of Scotland: Stair Memorial Encyclopaedia*, Constitutional Law Reissue, para 428.

[46] Elish Angiolini, 'The Lord Advocate in the 21st Century' (Speech by the Lord Advocate at the KPMG Annual Law Lecture, 28 February 2007).

[47] Gordon Stott, *Lord Advocate's Diary 1961–1966* (Aberdeen University Press 1991) 140–141.

[48] Transfer of Functions (Secretary of State and Lord Advocate) Order 1972.

> on Tribunals and its Scottish committee, certain of which he exercised with the Lord Chancellor, powers relating to rules regulating procedure in connection with statutory inquiries and proceedings before certain tribunals held in Scotland, and laying before Parliament memoranda in relation to certain statute law consolidation.[49]

The transfer also added several discrete policy areas to the ministerial portfolio of the Lord Advocate, including:

> the jurisdiction and procedure of Scottish courts in civil proceedings, the law of evidence and the law relating to prescription and limitation of actions, the law relating to arbitration and the law relating to fatal accident inquiries.[50]

In addition to these expressly enumerated matters, the Lord Advocate had acquired further ministerial responsibilities by the end of the twentieth century. These related to functions for which the Lord Advocate had assumed 'a very real de facto responsibility, the de jure responsibility resting with the Secretary of State', such as in relation to the identification of nominees for judicial appointment.[51] Various functions of this nature were added to the unofficial workload of the Lord Advocate because Scotland did not have a direct equivalent to the office of the Lord Chancellor as it existed before undergoing extensive reform in 2005.[52] With the portfolio of the Lord Advocate most closely resembling that of a Minister of Justice, it was natural for the Secretary of State – who was not normally a lawyer – to 'place strong reliance on the judgment of his senior legal colleague' in respect of the administration of justice.[53]

Historical Advisory Functions

As regards the advisory functions connected to the office, the Lord Advocate was well-established as chief legal advisor to the UK Government on matters of Scots law.[54] His advice constituted 'the ultimate source of advice as to the legal correctness in terms of Scots law of proposed government legislation'.[55] His role in providing detailed (sometimes policy-changing) advice to executive and parliamentary committees has already been mentioned. The extent to which that role should be characterised as legal or political is, of course, a matter of debate and interpretation. As Daintith and Page note, Law Officers of the Crown (a category to which the Lord Advocate and Solicitor General for Scotland belonged at this time) did not 'necessarily have to take a wholly passive attitude to being asked for

[49] *The Laws of Scotland: Stair Memorial Encyclopaedia*, Constitutional Law Reissue, para 430.
[50] ibid.
[51] ibid. Italics removed.
[52] Constitutional Reform Act 2005, Pt 2.
[53] Edwards, *The Attorney General, Politics and the Public Interest* (n 6) 293.
[54] Angiolini, 'The Lord Advocate in the 21st Century' (n 46).
[55] *The Laws of Scotland: Stair Memorial Encyclopaedia*, Constitutional Law Reissue, para 432.

advice'.[56] Indeed, they say that the Scottish law officers were able to reverse what was seen as 'a growing tendency of Great Britain departments to neglect to take their advice on the Scots law aspect of legal issues' at their own motion.[57]

The more standard course for seeking advice, however, was via the establishment of a direct relationship between lawyers in the appropriate Scottish Office department and lawyers in the Lord Advocate's Department on each occasion a request for advice was made.[58] The Scottish approach to the provision of legal advice was notably more 'direct and personal' in this respect than that practiced by both the Attorney General and Solicitor General for England and Wales.[59] References to the Lord Advocate and Solicitor General for Scotland were made in the first instance where criteria laid out in a section of the Ministerial Code on when the opinions of law officers should be sought were satisfied.[60] Despite this filtering mechanism, as many as approximately 30–40 written references per year were sent to the Lord Advocate's Department on account of its 'broad span of action'.[61] It was not unusual for the advice of the Lord Advocate and Solicitor General for Scotland to be given in conjunction with the Attorney General and Solicitor General for England and Wales. Indeed, they held 'frequent meetings' 'to settle particular opinions'.[62] Like the individual opinions of the Attorney General and Solicitor General for England and Wales, however, the fact and content of opinions provided by both the Lord Advocate and Solicitor General for Scotland were kept confidential by constitutional convention.[63]

The Lord Advocate's Department was located in Westminster and staffed by a small group of advocates and solicitors in the civil service known as Legal Secretaries.[64] Legal Secretaries were responsible for assisting the Scottish law officers and advising the staff of any government department without its own Scottish legal advisers.[65] They also acted as Parliamentary Counsel; drafting Bills for Parliament in full or in part where they related to matters affecting Scotland.[66] Being based at Westminster had the significant practical effect of ensuring that the Lord Advocate's officials 'acquired a wide expertise and familiarity with current

[56] Daintith and Page (n 28) 308.
[57] ibid 308–309.
[58] ibid 301.
[59] ibid.
[60] ibid 303. The 1997 version of the Ministerial Code is reproduced by Daintith and Page on this page, which lays out precisely the criteria applied by the Scottish Office just prior to devolution. They note that little had changed in the wording of the relevant section since it was first included in the 1976 version of the Code.
[61] Daintith and Page (n 28) 305.
[62] Elish Angiolini, 'Legislation, Litigation and Prosecution: The Role of a Scottish Law Officer' (2003) *Juridical Review* 219, 220.
[63] Daintith and Page (n 28) 309–315.
[64] Walker (n 44) 357–358.
[65] ibid.
[66] ibid.

thinking in Whitehall' on a wide range of constitutional matters.[67] The eventual loss of this physical presence in Whitehall, post-devolution, would make a framework for ensuring continued cooperation between the Scottish law officers and Whitehall an important operational priority.[68]

Historical Litigation Functions

The civil litigation functions of the Lord Advocate and Solicitor General for Scotland prior to devolution can be stated quite briefly. It was customary, at least until 1857, for Scottish suits against the Crown to be brought against the relevant Officers of State.[69] However, under the Crown Suits (Scotland) Act 1857 – which has of course been amended to reflect in particular the changes brought about by devolution – all actions, suits or proceedings to be instituted or defended by or against the Crown were raised at the instance of or directed against 'Her Majesty's Advocate'. As a statutory exception, however, actions against the Secretary of State for Scotland were, and continue to be, brought against him or her directly.[70] This arrangement is similar to the formal position vis-à-vis the Attorney General for England and Wales under the Crown Proceedings Act 1947,[71] and is therefore different from the Counsel General model.[72]

While the Lord Advocate and Solicitor General for Scotland were certainly known to appear on behalf of the UK Government in high-profile cases both domestically and internationally prior to devolution, a steady increase in workload reduced their ability to conduct cases personally.[73] Senior private counsel were thus 'regularly instructed on an ad hoc basis to handle such cases', though the Lord Advocate could apparently be relied upon to be 'involved in an advisory capacity' in any 'case of significance'.[74] In addition, the Lord Advocate had a duty to 'intervene if necessary in certain classes of civil litigation to which no Government department [was] a party but in which the general public interest [was] involved'.[75] The key phrase regarding that function is 'certain classes', because, unlike the Attorney General for England and Wales, the Lord Advocate did not have a *general* right to intervene ex proprio motu in civil litigation to represent the public interest.[76] The right to intervene in this context would arise only where there was 'a statutory

[67] Angiolini, 'Legislation, Litigation and Prosecution' (n 62).
[68] ibid 223–224.
[69] Milne (n 18) 208.
[70] Reorganisation of Offices (Scotland) Act 1939, s 1(8); *The Laws of Scotland: Stair Memorial Encyclopaedia*, Constitutional Law Reissue, para 434.
[71] See ch 3 at 58.
[72] See ch 4 at 90–91.
[73] *The Laws of Scotland: Stair Memorial Encyclopaedia*, Constitutional Law Reissue, para 434.
[74] ibid.
[75] Milne (n 18) 209.
[76] Edwards, *The Attorney General, Politics and the Public Interest* (n 6) 273, fn 27a.

power to do so or where a proprietorial interest of the Crown [was] involved or perhaps where the interests of a public trust [were] involved'.[77] Nor, indeed, did Scots law recognise any equivalent to 'relator actions' which could be commenced with the fiat of the Attorney General for England and Wales.[78] Thus, the Lord Advocate did not have (and still does not have) any similar power to sieve out claims taken by private individuals purporting to enforce the law in the public interest.

Historical Prosecution Functions

Actions for failure to abide by the criminal laws of Scotland were taken almost exclusively at the behest of private individuals until towards the end of the sixteenth century.[79] In order to ensure more consistency in the administration of justice, and in light of the potential for higher revenue payable to the Crown as compensation for criminality, these private arrangements were eventually replaced by a public prosecution system for which the King's Advocate took primary responsibility.[80] While prosecution by indictment has been a power reserved to Scotland's first law officer ever since, private prosecutions by way of 'criminal letters' remain a rarely used but 'healthy' possibility for ordinary citizens who would otherwise be denied justice to this day.[81] Nonetheless, it is notable, for comparative purposes, that Scotland administered a largely public prosecution system long before the Crown Prosecution Service for England and Wales was established in 1986.[82] The current structure has 'been in place since the end of the nineteenth century', having 'slowly developed into its current form over the past century'.[83] The continuous influence of the Lord Advocate and Solicitor General for Scotland on 'the control and co-ordination'[84] of the system as it existed prior and subsequent to devolution should therefore be emphasised as another feature which contextually distinguishes them from the Attorney General and Solicitor General for England and Wales, albeit partially for conservationist reasons.

As head of the systems for criminal prosecution and the investigation of deaths prior to devolution, the Lord Advocate discharged the sizeable duties attached to

[77] ibid.

[78] HWR Wade and CF Forsyth, *Administrative Law* (10th edn, Oxford University Press 2009) 494.

[79] Gordon (n 4) 57; WG Normand, 'The Public Prosecutor in Scotland' (1938) 54 *Law Quarterly Review* 345, 345–346.

[80] Gordon (n 4) 56–58; Normand (n 79) 346–347; *The Laws of Scotland: Stair Memorial Encyclopaedia*, Criminal Procedure 2nd Reissue, paras 26–27.

[81] Edwards (n 6) 275, 300–309; WG Normand (n 79) 347–349. This unusual private prosecution procedure was in fact considered by the High Court of Justiciary relatively recently: *Stewart v Payne* [2016] HCJAC 122, [2017] JC 155.

[82] Prosecution of Offences Act 1985.

[83] Barry T Smith, 'Scottish Public Prosecution, Policy and Practice: Issues of Independence and Accountability' (1999) *Juridical Review* 141, 141.

[84] ibid 142.

that title with the assistance of a clearly defined hierarchy of prosecutorial deputies. Aside from the normal assistance provided by the Solicitor General for Scotland at the apex of the system, the Lord Advocate was supported in these matters by the Crown Agent in charge of the Crown Office. The Crown Agent was invariably an experienced solicitor who administered business for the Lord Advocate in relation to the Procurator Fiscal Service.[85] The Procurator Fiscal Service was composed of civil servants acting on behalf of the Lord Advocate while allied to particular Sherriff Courts across Scotland, where they carried responsibility for, among other things, 'investigating and instituting proceedings for criminal offences within their districts, and for presenting the cases in court' as well as making inquiries into 'sudden and suspicious deaths'.[86] This is, of course, a function performed by coroners in other UK jurisdictions, which makes it important to recall for comparative purposes that there are no coroners in Scotland.[87] To this day, the responsibility for investigating any death that requires further explanation in Scotland rests with the Crown Office and Procurator Fiscal Service, as overseen by the Scottish law officers. Such proceedings are referred to in Scotland as Fatal Accident Inquiries (as opposed to coroner's inquests).[88] The role of the Lord Advocate and Solicitor General for Scotland in connection with the investigation of sudden and suspicious deaths therefore amounts to a significant contextual difference in their functions as compared with other members of the UK law officer regime.

Procurators Fiscal were accountable to the Crown Agent, who responded with 'instructions, requests and general guidance' on behalf of the Lord Advocate.[89] In more particular terms, the Lord Advocate would appoint a small band of Advocates Depute to the Crown Office. Known collectively as Crown Counsel,[90] they were trusted to 'decide whether a prosecution should proceed and issue such instructions as [were] necessary' to the Procurators Fiscal, in addition to their delegated responsibilities for prosecutions in the High Court.[90] Interestingly, the Solicitor General for Scotland was technically described as one of the Lord Advocate's 'Depute Advocates' in his or her commission of appointment, but unlike other Advocates Depute was not precluded from membership of the House of Commons.[91] Moreover, consequent to the 'dual location' of the law officers' headquarters, the Solicitor General for Scotland is said to have spent more time

[85] Edwards, *The Attorney General, Politics and the Public Interest* (n 6) 294–300.
[86] Walker (n 44) 368.
[87] Milne (n 18) 208.
[88] Inquiries into Fatal Accidents and Sudden Deaths etc. (Scotland) Act 2016. For a recent review on the operation of the modified system introduced by this Act, see: Inspectorate of Prosecution in Scotland, 'Follow-Up Review of Fatal Accident Inquiries' (*Scottish Government*, August 2019). Available at: www.gov.scot/publications/follow-up-review-fatal-accident-inquiries/. For information on the statutory basis of earlier inquiry systems, see: Gillian Mawdsley, 'The Historical Purpose and Role of Fatal Accident Inquiries' [2021] SLT 157.
[89] Walker (n 44) 367.
[90] ibid.
[91] *The Laws of Scotland: Stair Memorial Encyclopaedia*, Constitutional Law Reissue, para 436, fn 2.

than the Lord Advocate carrying out Crown Office work in Edinburgh while the Lord Advocate dealt with more business in London.[92]

As Smith has pointed out, this hierarchy was 'vitally important to the effective operation of the system'; providing the Lord Advocate and Solicitor General for Scotland with their sole method for controlling and coordinating prosecution policy.[93] Although it was widely accepted that the Procurators Fiscal had considerable autonomy when exercising their 'vast discretionary powers' over prosecutions,[94] their discretion was not unlimited. One of the only ways a degree of 'consistency and control' could be achieved by the Lord Advocate or one of the Deputes acting on his behalf was by issuing prosecution policy guidelines which Fiscals were bound to follow.[95] Policies could take a general form, or be formulated to cover 'specific cases or classes of cases'.[96] Policies likely to have wider social or political impact would be referred routinely to the Lord Advocate and Solicitor General for input.[97] For example, all cases involving the prosecution of a police officer would be so referred.[98] Indeed, where there was any doubt about the appropriate course of action to take in a particular case, consultations between the Lord Advocate, the Solicitor General for Scotland, the Crown Agent, Crown Counsel and even the Procurators Fiscal would be held in order to secure 'uniformity of administration'.[99] The circulation of prosecution policy guidelines also enabled the Lord Advocate and Solicitor General for Scotland to implement commitments made to Parliament about refraining from prosecutions of certain sorts and thereby reshaping the law in effect. For example, although the *skean-dhu* (a small knife) could technically be classed as an offensive weapon,

> the possession of such items was effectively decriminalised when the Lord Advocate at the time gave an undertaking to Parliament that no one would be prosecuted for having a *skean-dhu* in a public place, so long as they were wearing the dagger as part of Highland dress.[100]

Although these 'informal constraints' on the considerable prosecutorial discretion existing at different levels of the Scottish system during this period were capable of at least securing 'a measure of consistency and control', Smith was very critical of the fact that most policy guidance was not available for public or even parliamentary scrutiny.[101] He submitted that the problem was not that prosecution policy

[92] Daintith and Page (n 28) 237.
[93] Smith (n 83) 142.
[94] ibid 143.
[95] ibid.
[96] ibid 144.
[97] ibid 145.
[98] ibid, citing Lord Mackay as quoted in Ian D Willock, 'Some Lessons of Khaliq' (1984) *Scottish Legal Action Group* 124.
[99] Normand (n 79) 352.
[100] Pamela R Ferguson and Claire McDiarmid, *Scots Criminal Law: A Critical Analysis* (2nd edn, Edinburgh University Press 2014) 129.
[101] Smith (n 83) 143; 150.

did not exist but that it was 'unknown, unconstrained and unclear'.[102] Though it is not entirely accurate to claim prosecution policy was unconstrained and unclear, in light of Smith's own discovery of informal though secret constraints on prosecutorial discretion at this time, his reasoning in respect of the value of greater transparency is laudable. Having acknowledged the constitutional rationale for imbuing public prosecutors with a 'quasi-judicial' level of independence, namely for the purpose of ensuring a degree of apolitical 'finality and fairness to a potential accused, to victims and to witnesses',[103] Smith agreed that this notion of independence should 'be maintained at an acceptable level'.[104] He did not agree, however, that the 'shield of independence' should be used to 'hide prosecutors from reasonable scrutiny'.[105] In particular, he recommended drawing a distinction between policy guidelines and criteria used to constrain the discretion of prosecutors and the actual decision-making process.[106] In other words, Smith drew a distinction between the content of policies and the application of them in individual cases. He suggested that this would enable individuals to challenge decisions in those 'rare cases' exhibiting unfairness or unreasonableness.[107] While it will soon be seen that most prosecution policy guidance has indeed become available to the public since devolution, thereby satisfying many of Smith's concerns about governmental transparency, the historical significance of the guidance is notable just the same. Like the legal opinions provided to other government departments by the Lord Advocate and Solicitor General for Scotland, the practice of issuing official policy guidance to prosecutors demonstrates how broad discretionary powers have traditionally been transformed internally into stable constitutional rules for the regulation of government.[108]

The Post-Devolution, Modern-Day Phase

The Scotland Act 1998 substantially changed the historical roles of the Lord Advocate and Solicitor General for Scotland as one consequence of its overall purpose, namely the creation of a devolved Scottish Parliament and Scottish Executive.[109] The remainder of this chapter is concerned with examining those

[102] ibid 150.

[103] ibid 146, citing a statement made on behalf of the Lord Advocate in *Public Enquiry into the Shootings at Dunblane Primary School*, 24 June 1996 (Day 19), Appendix 3.

[104] ibid 146.

[105] ibid.

[106] ibid 147.

[107] ibid 150. Similar arguments are echoed in the following Canadian study: John Ll J Edwards, 'The Attorney General and the Charter of Rights' in Robert J Sharpe (ed), *Charter Litigation* (Butterworths 1986) 65–68.

[108] Daintith and Page (n 28) 398.

[109] For a useful overview of the constitutional context to the Scotland Act 1998, see: Alan Page, *Constitutional Law of Scotland* (Scottish Universities Law Institute Ltd 2015) ch 2. Note that the Scottish

changes. The first set of changes to be discussed concern the creation of a new Scottish law officer, the Advocate General for Scotland, to whom several of the functions formerly exercised by the Lord Advocate and Solicitor General for Scotland have been transferred. The second set of changes relate to status, primarily concerning the fact that the Lord Advocate and Solicitor General for Scotland have ceased to be Ministers of the Crown and instead become members of the devolved Scottish Government; the fact that they have been provided with greater guarantees of tenure by the 1998 Act in several ways; the fact that a broader range of candidates are eligible to become Lord Advocate and Solicitor General for Scotland under the new regime, and the fact that their relationship with the new Scottish Cabinet is contested for various reasons. The third and final set of changes effected by the devolution reforms to be discussed thereafter concern technical and substantive alterations to the advisory, litigation and prosecutorial functions of the Scottish law officers historically outlined above. Throughout this discussion, it should be noted that the functions of the Lord Advocate and Solicitor General for Scotland have remained essentially interchangeable since devolution, in that the Solicitor General is still permitted to discharge 'any functions authorised or required' of the Lord Advocate 'by any enactment or otherwise'.[110]

The Advocate General for Scotland

The office of the Advocate General for Scotland was created in order to fill the void at Westminster which would otherwise have been left by the transfer of the Lord Advocate and Solicitor General for Scotland to the devolved Scottish Government. Recently released papers from the National Archives have revealed that there was some resistance to the creation of a new ministerial office from the Head of the Constitution Secretariat in 10 Downing Street at the time, who proposed 'bringing additional expertise in Scottish law into the Law Officers' Department' instead of creating a full-time ministerial appointment.[111] However the view of the Lord Chancellor ultimately won out, namely that the new workstream would require what he called 'a "career Scots lawyer" … able to proffer a combination of political and legal advice of the kind to which their Ministerial colleagues traditionally look to the existing four law officers'.[112] The Lord Chancellor concluded, as such, 'that this function can not be left to an official' and that the government would 'therefore have to add to the list of Ministers'.[113] During parliamentary debates

Executive was later renamed the Scottish Government by s 12 of the Scotland Act 2012 and is therefore referred to by that title hereinafter.

[110] Law Officers Act 1944, s 2(1).

[111] Letter from Alex Allan to Kenneth Mackenzie (10 June 1997), accessible via the National Archives by reference PREM 49/18.

[112] Letter from Kenneth Mackenzie to Alex Allan (16 June 1997), accessible via the National Archives by reference PREM 49/18.

[113] ibid.

on the legislative provisions establishing the office, moreover, some Conservative opposition speakers were avowedly against its creation. They proposed, instead, that the Lord Advocate would remain the UK Government's principal legal advisor while the Solicitor General for Scotland would serve the devolved Scottish Government.[114] The Labour Government of the day decided, however, that 'the two offices should continue to have the sort of relationship that has existed for more than three centuries',[115] i.e. a relationship of principal and deputy. The office of the Advocate General for Scotland has, as it turns out, mimicked this long-standing arrangement with the establishment of a non-statutory 'Solicitor to the Advocate General', who has assumed responsibility for the legal advisory functions previously performed by the Scottish Office solicitors.[116] Furthermore, provision has even been made for a 'Deputy Solicitor to the Advocate General'.[117]

The Labour Government responsible for the devolution reforms also did not think it was appropriate to prescribe particular qualifications for the post of Advocate General for Scotland,[118] although commentators did speculate as to whether constitutional conventions might develop in any event.[119] True to conjecture, each of the five individuals to hold office in their own right to date have been members of the Faculty of Advocates and either belonged to the House of Commons or been awarded a peerage upon appointment.[120] There have, in fact, been six individuals responsible for the portfolio, if one includes the period between 18 January and 15 March 2006 when the functions of the office were temporarily discharged by the Secretary of State for Scotland while a second permanent incumbent was sought.[121] The Secretary of State for Scotland of the time was,

[114] Lynda Clark, 'The Role of the Advocate General for Scotland in the New Constitutional Settlement' in Alan Boyle and others (eds), *Human Rights and Scots Law* (Hart Publishing 2002) 40.

[115] ibid, citing HC Deb 10 Feb 1998, col 175.

[116] Noreen Burrows, *Devolution* (Sweet & Maxwell 2000) 158; *The Laws of Scotland: Stair Memorial Encyclopaedia*, Constitutional Law Reissue, para 267.

[117] While there is little public information available on this post, a passing reference to it can be found here: *Annual Report for the Scotland Office and the Office of the Advocate General (2011–2012)* (HC 70, 16 July 2012) 31.

[118] Clark (n 115) 41.

[119] CMG Himsworth and CR Munro, *The Scotland Act 1998* (2nd edn, Sweet & Maxwell 2000) 107.

[120] Namely: Baroness Clark of Calton (1999–2006), Lord Davidson of Glen Clova (2006–2010), Lord Wallace of Tankerness (2010–2015), Lord Keen of Elie (2015–2020) and Lord Stewart of Dirleton (2020–present).

[121] This appointment was made possible by s 87(3) of the Scotland Act 1998, which allows the Prime Minister to determine that another Minister of the Crown can validly perform the functions of the Advocate General for Scotland in the event of a vacancy. Selecting the Secretary of State for Scotland to deputise in 2006 was an obvious but not a mandatory choice. Moreover, during the passage of the Scotland Bill, Neil Gow suggested it would have made sense for the functions of the Advocate General for Scotland to be deputed to either the Lord Advocate or the Solicitor General for Scotland in the event of a vacancy. The decision not to adopt such an approach indicated 'the Westminster orientated character of the office' in his view: Neil Gow, 'Judicial Tenure and the Advocate General' [1998] SLT 87, 89. Alternatively, the provision may have been designed to avoid conflicts of interest in the provision of legal advice, especially given that s 99(1) of the Scotland Act 1998 provided for litigation between the central UK and devolved Scottish governments: Clark (n 115) 41.

in any event, a member of the Faculty of Advocates and an MP. Conventions as regards eligibility for the office were therefore adhered to even during this interlude. Substantive appointments to the office are made by Letters Patent issued by the Queen,[122] in contrast to the appointments procedure established by the Scotland Act 1998 in respect of the devolved Lord Advocate and Solicitor General for Scotland (compared further below).

The Advocate General for Scotland is, like the Attorney General and Solicitor General for England and Wales, a Minister of the Crown.[123] In this company, the office-holder is now typically labelled a Law Officer of the Crown. The advice of the Advocate General on matters of Scots law is intended to have the same authority as the advice of the Attorney General and Solicitor General for England and Wales in respect of English and Welsh law.[124] The office-holder is also one of three Ministers in control of the 'Scotland Office and the Office of the Advocate General' (which is the name of the UK Government department responsible for Scottish affairs at Westminster since devolution).[125] The responsibilities of the office can be divided roughly between ministerial and legal roles in the interest of digestible exposition. This further demonstrates the taxonomical variety available in deliberations on the UK law officer regime.

Ministerial Roles

The Advocate General for Scotland is assisted in the exercise of his or her ministerial duties by a 'Legal Secretariat and Private Office' located in London.[126] Most of these ministerial duties relate either to the Advocate General's membership of Cabinet Committees or to the demands of parliamentary questions. In respect of the former, it is worth restating that decisions taken at Cabinet Committee level in the UK Government 'have the same formal status' as full Cabinet decisions and thus the Advocate General for Scotland can enjoy immediate influence

[122] Clark (n 115) 40. Note, however, that like the Attorney General and Solicitor General for England and Wales the Advocate General for Scotland also undergoes a formal 'swearing in' ceremony. In the case of the Advocate General, however, the ceremony typically takes place before judges of the Court of Session in Edinburgh. See the following press release about the ceremony held in respect of the current office-holder: 'Lord Stewart of Dirleton QC Sworn in as Advocate General for Scotland (*Office of the Advocate General for Scotland*, 8 December 2020). Available at: www.gov.uk/government/news/lord-stewart-of-dirleton-qc-sworn-in-as-advocate-general-for-scotland.

[123] The Scotland Act 1998, s 87(2), created the new Ministerial post by amending the House of Commons Disqualification Act 1975 and the Ministerial and Other Salaries Act 1975. A range of statutory functions were transferred from the Lord Advocate to the Advocate General for Scotland by the Transfer of Functions (Lord Advocate and Advocate General for Scotland) Order 1999, and the Scotland Act 1998 (General Transitory, Transitional and Savings Provisions) Order 1999.

[124] Clark (n 115) 41.

[125] The other two responsible Ministers are the Secretary of State for Scotland and the Parliamentary Under Secretary of State at the Scotland Office. See: *Annual Report for the Scotland Office and the Office of the Advocate General* (n 118) 27–29.

[126] *Annual Report for the Scotland Office and the Office of the Advocate General* (n 118) 20.

over executive decision-making.[127] In respect of the latter, the Advocate General for Scotland has been held to account regularly by way of questions for oral and written answer ranging in subject-matter across a variety of their functions.[128] Convention dictates, however, that no response is normally provided to questions pertaining to matters over which the devolved institutions have competence or to the existence and/or content of the law officers' legal advice to the Government.[129] In recent years office-holders with a peerage have also been designated as the official spokesperson in the House of Lords for the Scotland Office, the Wales Office, the Attorney General's Office and, most recently, the Ministry of Justice.[130] Such roles see the Advocate General for Scotland answering questions and sponsoring legislation through the second chamber of Parliament on behalf of the UK Government.[131]

Legal Roles

There are three divisions in the office of the Advocate General for Scotland which assist in the exercise of predominantly legal duties: the HMRC division; the advisory and legislation division, and the litigation division. The HMRC division deals with, for instance, tax appeals; advisory services in relation to Scottish revenue and customs matters, and some legislative work in relation to Finance Bills.[132] The advisory and legislation division provides legal advice and services to UK Government departments in so far as Scots law and the Scottish devolution settlement are raised by their work.[133] Departmental requests for legal advice are made to the Advocate General for Scotland in accordance with criteria laid down in the

[127] Clark (n 115) 54. The Advocate General for Scotland is currently listed only as a member of the Parliamentary Business and Legislation Committee in the latest public release on committee membership: Cabinet Office, *List of Cabinet Committees* (21 October 2021). Available at: www.gov.uk/government/publications/the-cabinet-committees-system-and-list-of-cabinet-committees. However, the office-holder in 2002 indicated her then membership of committees and sub-committees concerning not only the legislative programme but also nations and regions; incorporation of the ECHR, and freedom of information. See: Clark (n 115) 53–54.

[128] Clark (n 115) 54–55.

[129] ibid 43–44; 55.

[130] *Annual Report for the Scotland Office and the Office of the Advocate General* (n 118) 23; 'Lord Keen of Elie QC Appointed as Lords Spokesperson' (*Office of the Advocate General for Scotland*, 19 July 2016). Available at: www.gov.uk/government/news/lord-keen-of-elie-qc-appointed-as-lords-spokesperson.

[131] The latest annual report for the Scotland Office and the Office of the Advocate General states, for instance, that since taking up his position as Advocate General for Scotland in October 2020, 'Lord Stewart has supported on numerous pieces of Government legislation in the House of Lords. These include: The Covert Human Intelligence Sources (Criminal Conduct) Act (Home Office); the Overseas Operations (Service Personnel and Veterans) Act (Ministry of Defence); and the Counter-Terrorism Sentencing Act (Home Office and Ministry of Justice)'. See: *Annual Report for the Scotland Office and the Office of the Advocate General (2020–2021)* (HC 423, 13 July 2021) 21.

[132] *Annual Report for the Scotland Office and the Office of the Advocate General* (n 118) 20.

[133] ibid.

latest edition of the Ministerial Code.[134] One former office-holder insists she was 'entitled to look after' the interests of ministers and departments when advising them, 'subject to the professional rules applying to advocates'.[135] This suggests an executive client-centred conception of the role rather than one orientated towards the public interest.

The advice of the Advocate General for Scotland may be sought both in relation to the development of policy and legislation in respect of matters reserved to Westminster (which may be formulated in conjunction with the Attorney General and Solicitor General for England and Wales), as well as the impact of proposed policies and legislation made by the devolved Scottish institutions on UK Government departments operating in Scotland.[136] This role appears to encompass general and specific duties in relation to proposed government legislation and decision-making that are largely consistent with those incumbent on the law officers considered in chapters three and four,[137] namely to police the strong presumption against legislation being retrospective or commencing early and so forth.[138]

The Advocate General for Scotland has the power (which is also expressly conferred on the Lord Advocate and the Attorney General for England and Wales) to refer any questions about the competency of the Scottish Parliament to pass a Bill, or any provision of a Bill, to the UK Supreme Court for a determination.[139] It has recently been held, however, that such references only fasten on the legislative competence restrictions set out in section 29 of the Scotland Act 1998 and not, by contrast, on other exceptional grounds for the judicial review of devolved legislation such as inconsistency with fundamental rights.[140] The latter basis for challenging devolved legislation, which might appear to have had a basis in the earlier *Axa* judgment of the Supreme Court,[141] is only an option through ordinary judicial review proceedings.[142] That basis is decidedly not available in proceedings arising from a law officer's reference, however, because the statutory basis of such

[134] Cabinet Office, *Ministerial Code* (August 2019) para 2.10. Available at: www.gov.uk/government/publications/ministerial-code. Note that the current edition of the Code is much less particular than the 2001 edition reproduced by Clark (n 115) at 43.

[135] Clark (n 115) 43.

[136] *The Laws of Scotland: Stair Memorial Encyclopaedia*, Constitutional Law Reissue, para 267.

[137] See ch 3 at 54–58 and ch 4 at 84–86.

[138] Lord Keen, 'The Rule of Law and the Role of the Law Officers' (Speech by the Advocate General for Scotland to the SPLG Conference, 11 June 2018). Available at: www.gov.uk/government/news/the-rule-of-law-and-the-role-of-the-law-officers.

[139] Scotland Act 1998, s 33.

[140] *UK Withdrawal from the European Union (Legal Continuity) (Scotland) Bill – Reference by the Attorney General and the Advocate General for Scotland* [2018] UKSC 64, [2019] AC 1022 at [26].

[141] *AXA General Insurance Ltd & Ors v Lord Advocate & Ors* [2011] UKSC 46, [2012] 1 AC 868 at [47] (Lord Hope) and [149]–[153] (Lord Reed).

[142] *UK Withdrawal from the European Union (Legal Continuity) (Scotland) Bill – Reference by the Attorney General and the Advocate General for Scotland* [2018] UKSC 64, [2019] AC 1022 at [26]. Also see: Aileen McHarg and Chris McCorkindale, 'The Supreme Court and Devolution: The Scottish Continuity Bill Reference' (2019) 2 *Juridical Review* 190, 196.

references is clear that they are specifically restricted to legislative competence queries.[143]

The powers in question have now been exercised three times by the Advocate General for Scotland acting jointly with the Attorney General for England and Wales,[144] with at least partial success on each occasion – first in respect of the European Union (Legal Continuity) (Scotland) Bill;[145] second in respect of the United Nations Convention on the Rights of the Child (Incorporation) (Scotland) Bill, and third in respect of the European Charter of Local Self-Government (Incorporation) (Scotland) Bill.[146] The historically infrequent use of this mechanism is an achievement credited to 'early dialogue and co-operation' between government officials and ministers that have arguably incentivised the Scottish Government to 'focus on keeping within the boundaries of devolved competence'.[147] In addition to making references under this provision, moreover, the Advocate General for Scotland advises the Secretary of State on whether to exercise his or her power to prevent the Scottish Parliament from enacting legislation in certain circumstances.[148] The relatively low profile of this provision appears to be equally reflective of generally positive dialogue and co-operation between the relevant units of government, at least prior to Brexit.

The litigation division advises and supports UK Government departments in litigation raised by or taken against them. This role is taken to include, most notably, 'litigation strategy and handling, including risk management'.[149] This reflects the modern tendency of some government lawyers to offer 'calculations of legal risk' when providing advice, rather than providing 'quasi-judgments' on legal issues.[150] Since coming into existence the Advocate General for Scotland has either

[143] *UK Withdrawal from the European Union (Legal Continuity) (Scotland) Bill – Reference by the Attorney General and the Advocate General for Scotland* [2018] UKSC 64, [2019] AC 1022 at [26].

[144] Note, however, that Law Officers of the Crown do not need to act jointly when deciding whether to refer a Bill to the UK Supreme Court. Indeed, a legislative proposal to this effect was roundly rejected by the law officers in office when the post of Advocate General for Scotland was being established in the run up to the devolution reforms of 1998. John Morris qua the Attorney General for England and Wales, in particular, successfully argued that '[p]rovision for consultation as between the relevant Law Officers and indeed the rest of the government, or as the case may be the Scottish Executive, would … be a matter for internal arrangements'. See: Letter from John Morris to the Rt Hon the Lord Irvine of Lairg (30 June 1997), accessible via the National Archives by reference PREM 49/19.

[145] *UK Withdrawal from the European Union (Legal Continuity) (Scotland) Bill – Reference by the Attorney General and the Advocate General for Scotland* [2018] UKSC 64, [2019] AC 1022.

[146] *United Nations Convention on the Rights of the Child (Incorporation) (Scotland) Bill – Reference by the Attorney General and the Advocate General for Scotland, and European Charter of Local Self-Government (Incorporation) (Scotland) Bill – References by the Attorney General and the Advocate General for Scotland* [2021] UKSC 42, [2021] 1 WLR 5106. Also see ch 3 at 54–55.

[147] Clark (n 115) 51. Also see: Christopher McCorkindale and Janet L Hiebert, 'Vetting Bills in the Scottish Parliament for Legislative Competence' (2017) 21 *Edinburgh Law Review* 319, 341–347.

[148] Scotland Act 1998, s 35; Clark (n 115) 50.

[149] *Annual Report for the Scotland Office and the Office of the Advocate General* (n 118) 20.

[150] Ben Yong, 'Risk Management: Government Lawyers and the Provision of Legal Advice within Whitehall' (The Constitution Society 2013) 52.

represented or intervened on behalf of the UK Government in well over 50 cases, though not always in a personal capacity.[151] Most prominent among these cases are perhaps those raising 'devolution issues', namely cases involving challenges to the legal competence of the devolved institutions.[152] The Advocate General for Scotland may initiate proceedings to determine any devolution issues he or she identifies.[153] In addition, he or she must be informed and allowed to participate in proceedings if they are initiated by others.[154] This function is prone to consuming considerable energy on the part of the Advocate General for Scotland given that, for example, in excess of 1,400 devolution issues were raised between May 1999 and April 2002 alone.[155] The subject-matter of significant devolution cases are discussed at length elsewhere,[156] but a short note on the relevant procedures is perhaps apposite here. Private counsel is normally instructed by the Solicitor to the Advocate General for Scotland to handle such litigation. In cases where the Advocate General for Scotland chooses to appear personally in court, he or she does not require instruction and is therefore said to appear as a litigant in person.[157] These practices are to be contrasted with cases in which the Advocate General for Scotland acts as senior counsel when appearing on behalf of a UK Government department in a representative capacity, and cases taken against the Advocate General for Scotland in name only, when responsibility for the proceedings rests with the relevant department and the legal team they choose to instruct.[158] Care must therefore be taken in this context, as with the law officers discussed in chapters three and four, to separate cases in which the Advocate General for Scotland is advancing a case that represents his or her own views (as a litigant in person) from cases in which he or she is either personally or notionally representing an executive client.

By way of concluding this synopsis of the Advocate General for Scotland, it should be highlighted that there is obvious potential for public contests between

[151] An almost comprehensive list of cases is available at: Office of the Advocate General for Scotland, 'Involvement in Cases' (19 August 2021). Available at: www.gov.uk/government/publications/involvement-in-cases.

[152] Scotland Act 1998, s 98; Sch 6. Note that the Scotland Act 2012, s 36(4), amends para 1 of Sch 6 to exclude issues arising in Scottish criminal proceedings from being characterised as devolution issues.

[153] Scotland Act 1998, Sch 6, Pt 2, para 4.

[154] Scotland Act 1998, Sch 6, Pt 2, paras 5–6. Note that it was the Advocate General for Scotland herself who persuaded the High Court of Justiciary to hold that human rights challenges taken against the Lord Advocate after the commencement of the Human Rights Act 1998 would still give rise to devolution issues under the Scotland Act 1998 and that she had to be notified accordingly in order to 'see that the [devolution] settlement was observed': *Mills v HM Advocate (No 2)* [2001] SLT 1359 [16]–[20].

[155] Clark (n 115) 45.

[156] ibid 44–53; Christopher McCorkindale, Aileen McHarg and Paul F Scott, 'The Courts, Devolution, and Constitutional Review' (2017) 36 *University of Queensland Law Journal* 289; Christopher McCorkindale, 'Devolution in Scotland and the Supreme Court: A Question of Interpretation?' (2020) 1 *Materiali Per Una Storia Della Cultura Giuridica* 67.

[157] Clark (n 115) 53.

[158] ibid.

the Advocate General for Scotland on one hand and the Lord Advocate or Solicitor General for Scotland on the other, by virtue of the different positions they are entitled to advance in their legal roles. The opposing arguments advanced by the Advocate General for Scotland and the Lord Advocate in the litigation on Brexit and devolution issues provide particularly stark examples of this.[159] In general, however, it is difficult to discern the extent to which the varying degrees of good will attenuating such public shows of disagreement conceal 'political career and power struggle[s]'[160] between each of the Scottish law officers, who are now, ostensibly, in competition for the position of Scotland's most authoritative and influential lawyer.

A Contemporary View of the Lord Advocate and the Solicitor General for Scotland

The constitutional status of the Lord Advocate and the Solicitor General for Scotland changed in several fundamental respects upon devolution. Most significantly, as alluded to above, they ceased to be Ministers of the Crown[161] and instead became ex officio members of the Scottish Government.[162] Indeed, other than the First Minister of Scotland, they are the only ministers required by the Scotland Act 1998. The 'shape, nomenclature and size of the ministerial team' is otherwise flexible.[163] As members of the devolved Scottish Government, both are legally permitted to carry out any functions conferred upon the government,[164] while other ministers are not permitted to carry out any so-called 'retained functions' of the Lord Advocate.[165] This means, for example, that the Lord Advocate or Solicitor General for Scotland can in theory exercise health or environmental powers, but a Scottish Health or Environment Minister cannot exercise the powers

[159] *R (Miller) v Secretary of State for Exiting the European Union* [2017] UKSC 5, [2018] AC 61; *R (Miller) v Prime Minister* [2019] UKSC 41, [2020] AC 373; *UK Withdrawal from the European Union (Legal Continuity) (Scotland) Bill – Reference by the Attorney General and the Advocate General for Scotland* [2018] UKSC 64, [2019] AC 1022; *United Nations Convention on the Rights of the Child (Incorporation) (Scotland) Bill, and European Charter of Local Self-Government (Incorporation) (Scotland) Bill – References by the Attorney General and the Advocate General for Scotland* [2021] UKSC 42, [2021] 1 WLR 5106. Also see: *Al-Megrahi v HM Advocate* [2008] HCJAC 15, [2008] SLT 333; *Brown v Stott* [2000] UKPC D3, [2003] 1 AC 681.

[160] Gow (n 122).

[161] Scotland Act 1998, s 48(6).

[162] Scotland Act 1998, s 44(1)(c).

[163] *The Laws of Scotland: Stair Memorial Encyclopaedia*, Constitutional Law Reissue, para 394.

[164] Scotland Act 1998, s 52(3).

[165] This is not, as some commentators have suggested (see, e,g, Himsworth and Munro (n 120) 67), expressly forbidden by the Scotland Act 1998, s 52(5)(b). That provision only exempts the retained functions of the Lord Advocate from the effect of s 52(4) regarding collective government responsibility. It does not apply to s 52(2), which provides for the collective conferral of statutory functions on government Ministers. It is, in fact, s 48(5) which requires the Lord Advocate alone to take such decisions 'independently of any other person'. Retained functions are defined by s 52(6).

of the Lord Advocate to prosecute crimes or investigate suspicious deaths. This is perhaps a possibility of some significance given that many of the de facto and de jure ministerial responsibilities of the Lord Advocate which had been acquired prior to devolution were transferred to the Secretary of State for Scotland in the UK Government as part of the relevant reforms,[166] which both lightened the workload and reduced the individual power of the Lord Advocate; and because a Scottish Minister of Justice was for the first time created, subsuming many of the responsibilities formerly carried out by the Lord Advocate.[167] Another corollary of being members of the Scottish Government is that the Lord Advocate and Solicitor General for Scotland are bound to have the acts and omissions of other ministers regarded as their responsibility jointly and severally, as any acquisitions or liabilities incurred by one Minister are to be treated as the responsibility of all government ministers.[168] However, this notion of collective responsibility does not apply to the retained functions of the Lord Advocate.[169]

Greater Guarantees of Tenure

The methods used for appointing and removing the Lord Advocate and Solicitor General for Scotland also changed upon devolution, with some resulting effects on their constitutional status. Now, it is for the First Minister to recommend to the Queen that a person should be appointed to or removed from the posts of Lord Advocate and Solicitor General for Scotland, but he or she may only do so with the agreement of the Scottish Parliament.[170] Office-holders are then typically sworn in by oath at a traditional ceremony headed by the Lord President of the Court of Session at Parliament House in Edinburgh.[171] Three points can be made about this appointments procedure at this juncture. First, while the First Minister does need the agreement of the Scottish Parliament to request that the Queen appoint any other government minister,[172] he or she does not require its agreement to request that the Queen remove from post any minister other than the Lord Advocate or Solicitor General for Scotland.[173] The Standing Orders of the Scottish Parliament provide, in particular, that in the event of a voting division in respect of a motion to appoint or remove one of these law officers 'the result will only be valid if the number of members who voted is more than one quarter of the total number

[166] Transfer of Functions (Lord Advocate and Secretary of State) Order 1999; HC Deb 22 March 1999, cols 9–10.

[167] *The Laws of Scotland: Stair Memorial Encyclopaedia*, Constitutional Law Reissue, para 431.

[168] Scotland Act 1998, s 52(4).

[169] Scotland Act 1998, s 52(5)(b).

[170] Scotland Act 1998, s 48(1).

[171] See, e.g., 'Lord Advocate Vows to Act Independently as She is Sworn In' (*Crown Office and Procurator Fiscal Service*, 22 June 2021). Available at: www.copfs.gov.uk/media-site-news-from-copfs/1961-lord-advocate-vows-to-act-independently-as-she-is-sworn-in.

[172] Scotland Act 1998, s 47(2).

[173] Scotland Act 1998, s 47(3)(b).

of seats for members'.[174] This requirement for quorate parliamentary agreement means that the Lord Advocate and Solicitor General for Scotland enjoy a stronger degree of political tenure than their ministerial colleagues which, as Munro notes, is

> a reflection of the greater constitutional significance of the Law Officers' role in the administration of justice in Scotland, with a correspondingly greater need for a degree of independence on the Law Officers' part.[175]

Second, the First Minister is only given the power to *recommend* to the Queen that one of the devolved Scottish law officers be appointed, whereas other appointments are merely *approved* by the Queen and, as discussed above, removals do not require any royal involvement at all. The Queen, of course, conventionally acts on the advice of her Ministers. This raises the potential, therefore, for conflicting advice to be proffered by the First Minister of Scotland and UK Ministers of the Crown as regards the appointment and removal of the Lord Advocate and Solicitor General for Scotland. As Seaton has pointed out, the UK Government may effectively 'be able to veto the First Minister's choice of Lord Advocate'.[176] Third, the Lord Advocate and Solicitor General for Scotland may resign of their own accord at any time (a power which can of course be used as a political weapon) and must do so if the Scottish Parliament resolves that the Scottish Government 'no longer enjoys the confidence of the Parliament'.[177] In the latter scenario, the Lord Advocate alone is deemed to continue in office – though only for the purposes of exercising his or her retained functions – until a successor is appointed.[178]

A Broader Range of Eligible Candidates

As with the Advocate General for Scotland, the Scotland Act 1998 does not prescribe that any particular qualifications are required of candidates under consideration for the roles of Lord Advocate and Solicitor General for Scotland. They need not be Members of the Scottish Parliament (MSPs); they need not be members of a political party, and they need not be members of the Faculty of Advocates. Each of these propositions requires some brief elaboration in light of the practices which existed before devolution, as outlined above.

First, the rationale for allowing a proposed Lord Advocate or Solicitor General for Scotland to take office without first having been elected to a Scottish parliamentary seat arose from concerns that 'lawyers of sufficient standing' might not

[174] Standing Orders of the Scottish Parliament, Rules 4.3–4.4 (October 2021).

[175] Jane Munro, *Public Law* (2nd edn, W Green & Son 2007) 141.

[176] Robert Seaton, 'A Monster of the Constitution: Scotland's Lord Advocate' (2001) 1 *Common Law Review* 40, 41.

[177] Scotland Act 1998, s 48(2).

[178] Scotland Act 1998, s 48(3).

be found within that pool of candidates,[179] which echoes the Welsh arrangements outlined in Chapter 4.[180] Office-holders who are not MSPs are still governed by the frameworks for ethical standards applicable to MSPs, such as the requirements regarding registration and declaration of interests and the Members' Code of Conduct.[181] Moreover, such law officers are permitted to participate in parliamentary proceedings to the extent permitted by Standing Orders, but may not vote.[182] While Standing Orders have provided that only the Lord Advocate or the Solicitor General for Scotland may answer written and (unless exceptional circumstances arise) oral questions regarding the systems of criminal prosecution and investigation of deaths,[183] they are statutorily entitled to refuse to answer any question or produce any document relating to those systems if doing so would prejudice criminal proceedings or be otherwise against the public interest.[184] Whether this amounts to a sufficient framework for ensuring the accountability of the law officers is a matter for later debate. It is however notable that Komorowski, in particular, queries whether stultifying both individual *and* collective responsibility in the way provided for by the Scotland Act 1998 can be said to jeopardise the democratic accountability of the Lord Advocate.[185] In addition to answering questions, the Lord Advocate and Solicitor General for Scotland continue to play important parliamentary roles in respect of its legislative business; only now, of course, as champions of the devolved Scottish Government's programme.[186] As well as being required to check whether devolved legislation is intra vires,[187] and their ability to refer a Bill or any of its provisions to the UK Supreme Court for a determination about the legislative competence of the Scottish Parliament to pass it,[188] the law officers have also assumed responsibilities over the planning, management, delivery and accessibility of legislative proposals.[189]

[179] Page (n 110) 75.
[180] See ch 4 at 80.
[181] *The Laws of Scotland: Stair Memorial Encyclopaedia*, Constitutional Law Reissue, para 406.
[182] Scotland Act 1998, s 27(1)(a).
[183] Standing Orders of the Scottish Parliament, Rules 13.5, 13.7 and 13.8 (October 2021).
[184] Scotland Act 1998, s 27(3).
[185] Julius Komorowski, 'The Accountability Deficit: Control of the Lord Advocate in Light of the McKie Case' (2007) *Juridical Review* 73, 74.
[186] 'The Role and Functions of the Lord Advocate' (*Scottish Government*, 16 August 2021). Available at: www.gov.scot/publications/lord-advocate-role-and-functions/.
[187] Scotland Act 1998, s 31(1). This provision requires the Scottish Minister responsible for legislation to state that it is within legislative competence, but this view is reached on the advice of the Scottish law officers.
[188] Scotland Act 1998, s 33. While it might be considered unlikely that the Scottish law officers would make such a reference in respect of a government bill, commentators have suggested they might do so to ward off future challenges by way of judicial review or as a consequence of an undertaking made during debate on a Bill. See: Himsworth and Munro (n 120) 47; McCorkindale and Hiebert (n 148) 348–349.
[189] 'The Role and Functions of the Lord Advocate' (n 187); Alan Page, 'A Parliament that is Different? The Law-Making Process in the Scottish Parliament' in Elaine E Sutherland and others (eds), *Law Making and the Scottish Parliament: The Early Years* (Edinburgh University Press 2011) 21.

Second, there has been an ostensible reduction in the relevance of the political affiliation of a potential Lord Advocate or Solicitor General for Scotland since devolution. This is most dramatically highlighted by the appointment of a former Procurator Fiscal, Elish Angiolini, to the post of Solicitor General for Scotland in 2001. Angiolini's appointment was explicitly recommended by the First Minister (Jack McConnell), then in charge of a Labour-Liberal Democrat Coalition Government, because the time was right, in his view, for a Solicitor General for Scotland appointment based on professional merit rather than party political association.[190] However Angiolini's subsequent appointment to the office of the Lord Advocate in 2006 was recommended, again by First Minister McConnell, on the basis that Angiolini was someone who would 'support and understand the implementation of the Government's policy';[191] which clearly undercut to some extent the non-political styling of her initial appointment as junior law officer.[192] Yet, to the great surprise of many commentators, upon the formation of a Scottish National Party ('SNP') Government in 2007, the new First Minister (Alex Salmond) decided to retain Angiolini. The First Minister claimed this was 'the first time in the democratic era that the Lord Advocate [had] served [a]dministrations of a different political hue'.[193] White, on the other hand, contends that 'anything short of invincible repugnance has long been enough' by way of the party allegiance required of a Scottish law officer, on account of what is still perceived as predominantly legal portfolio.[194] Nonetheless, given that the SNP have remained in Government since 2007, it remains to be seen whether future changes in administration will see any return to the appointment of party-loyal office-holders.

Third, Elish Angiolini's initial appointment as junior law officer was also ground-breaking because she was a solicitor and therefore not a member of the Faculty of Advocates. Though she had extensive experience as a Procurator Fiscal, some controversy was sparked by her career as a government rather than a private lawyer because the 'culture in such employment', it was argued, 'is not one of independence but of service'.[195] However others, including Angiolini herself,[196] robustly rejected 'the proposition that being drawn from a different branch of the profession renders a law officer incapable of impartiality'.[197] This break with

[190] SP (Official Report), 28 November 2001, col 4217.

[191] SP (Official Report), 5 October 2006, col 28322.

[192] Komorowski (n 186) 85–86.

[193] SP (Official Report), 24 May 2007, col 104.

[194] Robin M White, 'The Career Path of Recent Scottish Law Officers Revisited: Lord Advocate Becomes Solicitor, Solicitor Becomes Lord Advocate, and Other Surprises' [2007] 29 SLT 223, 225.

[195] Lord McCluskey, 'Where now for the Lord Advocate?' (*Scotsman*, 10 October 2006). Available at: www.scotsman.com/news/where-now-for-the-lord-advocate-1-1143868.

[196] Elish Angiolini, 'Role still independent' (*Scotsman*, 1 August 2007). Available at: www.scotsman.com/news/role-still-independent-1-911529.

[197] Paul G McBride, 'Law officers are impartial' (*Scotsman*, 2 August 2007). Available at: www.scotsman.com/news/law-officers-are-impartial-1-911758. Also see: Roger McKenzie, 'Interview: Elish Angiolini' (*The Journal of the Law Society of Scotland*, 1 January 2002). Available at: www.journalonline.co.uk/Magazine/47-1/1000046.aspx, where Angiolini indicates having received 'a significant volume of

tradition is still significant if only to the extent that it overrides the unequivocal view of the former Lord President of the Court of Session, namely that it was 'part of the unwritten constitutional law of the land that the Lord Advocate and the Solicitor-General for Scotland are appointed from among the members of the Scottish Bar'.[198] Though there is a 'strong argument' that as a law officer Angiolini would have enjoyed full rights of audience before the High Court of Justiciary ex officio, she was granted silk upon her initial appointment as Solicitor General for Scotland.[199] This avoided any potential doubt over her rights of audience, which might otherwise have arisen with reference to the former Lord President's constitutional view. It may be worth noting, however, that Angiolini's lack of experience as an advocate was unfortunately viewed as a disadvantage by some Justices of the UK Supreme Court when she appeared before them, such that Lord Hope believed it was 'a pity she did not get someone more experienced' to appear on her behalf in an important appeal about a detainee's right to legal representation when questioned under police custody.[200]

A Contested Relationship with the Scottish Cabinet

One further point to consider about the status of the Lord Advocate and Solicitor General for Scotland under the devolution regime, which runs through most of the points made above, concerns the extent to which their relationship with the Scottish Cabinet is compatible with their purported independence in respect of certain functions. The Scottish Cabinet is a non-statutory creature modelled on the UK Cabinet for the purpose of 'reconciling Ministers' individual ministerial responsibilities with their collective responsibility' and providing a forum for the ultimate arbitration of 'all policy on devolved matters'.[201] No mention of it is made anywhere in the Scotland Act 1998, but it sprang immediately into existence when the first newly devolved Scottish Government 'organised its team' into Cabinet Ministers and deputy Ministers.[202] The Lord Advocate was a member of this first Scottish Cabinet, but has since 2002 enjoyed a much less certain level of involvement with it.[203] Indeed, a wave of controversy over the appropriate level of Cabinet participation on the part of the Lord Advocate is clear from several reports over

letters of support and welcome from advocate deputes, members of the Faculty and the judiciary, which diminishes the perception that there is sustained concern about the appointment of a solicitor to the office'.

[198] Lord Clyde, reproduced in Casey (n 2) 26–27.

[199] *The Laws of Scotland: Stair Memorial Encyclopaedia*, Constitutional Law Reissue, para 436, fn 10.

[200] Lord Hope, *Lord Hope's Diaries: UK Supreme Court … and Afterwards (2009–2015)* (Avizandum Publishing Ltd 2019) 42, with reference to *Cadder v HM Advocate* [2010] UKSC 43, 2011 SC (UKSC) 13.

[201] *Guide to Collective Decision Making* (Scottish Government, November 2008) para 4.1; Page (n 110) 81.

[202] *The Laws of Scotland: Stair Memorial Encyclopaedia*, Constitutional Law Reissue, para 396.

[203] ibid para 431.

the years that will be explored in more appropriate depth in the conceptual parts of this book to follow.[204]

Modified Portfolios

The Lord Advocate and Solicitor General for Scotland inherited many of the legal functions vested in their offices prior to devolution, but with some significant variations. In this sub-section, those variations are discussed comparatively with reference to the three main categories historically outlined above, namely: advisory functions; litigation functions, and prosecutorial functions.

Modern Advisory Functions

Starting with the advisory functions of the Lord Advocate and Solicitor General for Scotland under devolution, several of the practical and substantive changes which have taken place should be recognised. Practically speaking, the Lord Advocate's Department – which had been located in Westminster and staffed by Legal Secretaries – relocated to Edinburgh and divided into two branches; one comprising parliamentary draftsmen, the other a Secretariat dedicated to supporting the Lord Advocate and Solicitor General for Scotland with their duties to provide legal advice to the Scottish Government.[205] The Lord Advocate and Solicitor General for Scotland also became operationally responsible for what was originally called the Office of the Solicitor to the Scottish Executive, now known as the Scottish Government Legal Directorate, which is the primary source of legal advice for the Scottish Government.[206] The phrase 'operationally responsible' has been interpreted to mean that they are responsible only at a very general level for the way the Directorate provides legal advice to Scottish Government Departments on a day-to-day basis,[207] which appears to correspond to the oversight function of the Attorney General and Solicitor General for England and Wales in respect of various executive agencies.[208] Scope therefore exists for the Lord Advocate and Solicitor General for Scotland to provide different advice than that provided initially by the Directorate in respect of individual cases if necessary.[209] This new administrative architecture has had the effect of centralising the provision of legal advice and thereby reducing the scope for lawyers within individual Scottish Departments to

[204] See ch 7 at 179–183.
[205] Angiolini, 'Legislation, Litigation and Prosecution' (n 62) 220.
[206] *Scottish Ministerial Code 2018 Edition* (Scottish Government, 8 February 2018) para 2.31.
[207] Angiolini, 'Legislation, Litigation and Prosecution' (n 62) 221.
[208] See ch 3 at 48–49.
[209] Page (n 110) 77.

form different, competing interpretations of the law.[210] In a 2009 speech, the Lord Advocate described the significance of the Directorate's work in this way:

> In their daily roles these lawyers work to ensure that the rule of law is embodied in the work of government, advising Ministers and policy colleagues on what can and cannot be done. Of course ... they are a creative and constructive bunch, who are keen to help and will work hard to find ways of lawfully achieving Ministerial policy. But, just like their counterparts in the rest of the UK, they are also sometimes required to point out the limits on government action. The public will rarely if ever get to hear of this, but in these ways government lawyers serve the ideal of the rule of law.[211]

Moreover, not only does the Directorate refer critical matters to the Lord Advocate and Solicitor General for formal opinions, in keeping with traditional bureaucratic process, they also regularly provide briefs in person.[212] Allowing legal issues at the devolved level to be handled by a single office has, in this way, apparently simplified the law officers' responsibility for identifying legal issues of general application and for attempting to ensure that they are handled consistently.[213]

Page highlights two main reasons why, substantively speaking, the Lord Advocate and Solicitor General for Scotland have become more involved in the work of the Scottish Government than they ever did in respect of the Scottish Office at Westminster prior to devolution.[214] First, the overarching constitutional framework provided by the Scotland Act 1998 has raised the profile of law much higher than at Westminster.[215] By requiring in particular that the Scottish Parliament and the Scottish Government must act compatibly with human rights law,[216] and to refrain from carrying out business reserved to the UK for constitutional reasons,[217] and from modifying certain scheduled provisions,[218] the Scotland Act 1998 has made legal constraints on their competence 'much more of an immediate concern to the Scottish Ministers and administrators than is the case south of the Border'.[219] Nonetheless, it has been emphasised that all of the relevant actors, both at the devolved level and in Whitehall, need to foster 'smooth working relationships' with each other so that each benefits from the expertise of the other in the interests of the devolution settlement.[220] Second, the collective

[210] ibid 78.
[211] Elish Angiolini, 'A Speech by the Lord Advocate to the Law Society of Scotland Annual Conference' (8 May 2009).
[212] Angiolini, 'The Lord Advocate in the 21st Century' (n 46).
[213] ibid.
[214] Page (n 110) 77–78.
[215] ibid.
[216] Scotland Act 1998, s 29(2)(d); s 54.
[217] Scotland Act 1998, s 29(2)(b); Sch 5; s 54.
[218] Scotland Act 1998, s 29(2)(c); Sch 4.
[219] Angiolini, 'Legislation, Litigation and Prosecution' (n 62) 223, also cited in Page (n 110) 77. See also: Colin Boyd, 'Ministers and the Law' (2006) *Juridical Review* 179.
[220] Angiolini, 'Legislation, Litigation and Prosecution' (n 62) 225; McCorkindale and Hiebert (n 148) 348–350.

legal responsibility of the Scottish Government noted above means that the Lord Advocate and Solicitor General for Scotland have a greater interest than ever before in safeguarding the rule of law, and reduces the scope for other Ministers to 'go their own way' on the basis of departmental autonomy.[221] The importance of this role as an internal guardian of the rule of law is well explained in the following words of a former office-holder:

> Much … [legal] regulation will, in the nature of things, never be scrutinised closely by bodies outside Government. That should not and does not relieve the Government from the responsibility of ensuring, so far as is possible, that it is acting within the powers conferred on it by Parliament. And so, even where there is a very low risk of challenge to a piece of legislation or a Ministerial decision, the Executive is actively concerned to make that regulation, or take that decision, within what is allowed by the constitution. At the same time, Ministers naturally wish to be able to do everything which the constitution allows. They have manifestos and policies which they wish to deliver and which they are entitled to deliver.[222]

Indeed, the responsibility of the Lord Advocate and Solicitor General for ensuring 'that the Government acts lawfully at all times' and that, in particular, 'Ministers and officials should therefore ensure that their decisions are informed by appropriate analysis of the legal considerations and that the legal implications of any course of action are considered at the earliest opportunity' is enshrined in the Scottish Ministerial Code.[223] The Code also confirms that the Scottish Government has adopted a variation of the law officers' convention which has long pertained at Westminster, whereby 'Ministers may acknowledge publicly that they have received legal advice on a particular topic, but must not divulge either who provided the advice or its contents (whether it is from the Law Officers or from anyone else)'.[224] However this convention now has four main caveats in the Scottish context, namely: that the existence and/or content of legal advice can be disclosed for compelling public interest reasons if a Minister and the law officers agree;[225] that the existence of law officers' advice in respect of the legislative competence of Government Bills can be divulged because the fact of such advice is broadly acknowledged;[226] that law officers' written opinions, unlike other ministerial papers, will generally be made available to succeeding administrations;[227] and that the views of law officers given in their ministerial capacity are not covered by

[221] Page (n 110) 77–78.
[222] Angiolini, 'The Lord Advocate in the 21st Century' (n 46).
[223] *Scottish Ministerial Code 2018 Edition* (Scottish Government, 8 February 2018) para 2.30.
[224] ibid para 2.38.
[225] ibid para 2.40.
[226] ibid para 2.41.
[227] ibid para 2.37. This caveat apparently rests on 'the professional and objective nature of the advice given' by the law officers – see: *The Laws of Scotland: Stair Memorial Encyclopaedia*, Constitutional Law Reissue, para 433. It could be argued that this rationale is conceptually incoherent, however, because if the advice is non-partisan then the alleged need for it to be kept confidential falls away.

the rule.[228] That last caveat is significant to the extent that it emphasises the need to prevent legal advice privilege being used to stop Scottish law officers' from being scrutinised for their ministerial work. It recognises the possibility of confusion over their dual roles operating as a barrier for accountability.

The net effect of these caveats is to render the nature of the law officers' convention in Scotland both contextually and genuinely different from other UK jurisdictions in certain respects. The fact that legal opinions on the competence of the Scottish Parliament are not covered by the convention by virtue of the well-known fact that they are required to do so is a contextual cause of differentiation from the Attorney General and Solicitor General for England and Wales, for example, while the decision to exclude opinions written in a ministerial capacity appears to be a deliberate change in the interests of constitutional clarity on the part of the Scottish Government. By comparison with the equivalent convention as it applies in Wales, moreover, the Scottish Ministerial Code displays a greater degree of clarity (remembering that, in the Welsh context, there is some uncertainty arising from the wording of the Ministerial Code over whether consent is required from both the Counsel General and the executive recipient of advice before an exceptional departure from the convention would be considered permissible).[229]

Modern Litigation Functions

In respect of their traditional litigation roles, noted above, the Lord Advocate and Solicitor General for Scotland continue to perform a similar range of duties at the devolved level either on behalf of the Scottish Government or in their own right. Indeed, the Scottish Ministerial Code now draws a clear distinction between 'proceedings in which the Law Officers are involved in a representative capacity on behalf of the Government, and action undertaken by them on behalf of the general community to enforce the law as an end in itself'.[230] Moreover, the Code emphasises that the Lord Advocate and Solicitor General for Scotland act 'wholly independently of the Government' in criminal proceedings.[231] These are useful distinctions to draw, because past experience has shown that the role of the law officers in litigation can become confused when uncertainty exists as regards the notional clients they are representing. The Code also requires Scottish Ministers to consult the law officers if they become embroiled in civil litigation in their personal capacities before consulting their own solicitors, 'in order to allow the Law Officers to express a view on the handling of the case so far as the public interest is concerned or, if necessary, to take charge of the proceedings from the outset'.[232] Most civil litigation is carried out by the Directorate in practice, who

[228] *Scottish Ministerial Code 2018 Edition* (Scottish Government, 8 February 2018) para 2.37.
[229] See ch 4 at 83–84.
[230] *Scottish Ministerial Code 2018 Edition* (Scottish Government, 8 February 2018) para 2.42.
[231] ibid.
[232] ibid para 11.16.

routinely instruct counsel selected by the Lord Advocate.[233] When the Lord Advocate or Solicitor General for Scotland appears personally in a civil case on behalf of the government, however, they do so on the instructions of the government (of which they are a member) as a whole.[234] Generally, however, the role of the Lord Advocate or Solicitor General for Scotland in civil litigation appears to remain largely confined to cases where he or she is either joined as a party or possesses a specific statutory or common law right to be involved, though the Scottish Government's webpages have recently been updated in a way which lays claim to 'a general "public interest" role' for the Lord Advocate.[235] This may be true enough, as there is certainly some evidence to suggest that several members of the senior judiciary are willing to recognise a more open-ended approach towards the right of the Lord Advocate or Solicitor General for Scotland to intervene in litigation representing the public interest. Most notably, in the case of *Helow* – which was concerned with unsuccessful allegations of apparent judicial bias against the Palestinian appellant on account of an Israeli-supporting organisational affiliation – Lord Rodger noted that the Appellate Committee of the House of Lords had heard from counsel representing the Lord Advocate 'not only as a Scottish minister with responsibility for the courts but also acting in the public interest'.[236] Lord Rodger's pre-judicial career as Solicitor General for Scotland and Lord Advocate should of course be borne in mind when considering the relative weight that might be placed on *Helow* in the future.

These clarifications and variations to the traditional litigation functions of the Lord Advocate and Solicitor General for Scotland have been supplemented, of course, by a new role in relation to the judicial determination of devolution issues.[237] Thus, both the Lord Advocate and Solicitor General for Scotland – like the Advocate General for Scotland – may initiate proceedings to determine devolution issues;[238] must be informed when proceedings are initiated by others entitled to do so;[239] may participate in such proceedings;[240] and may require a court or tribunal in any proceedings to which they are party to refer a devolution issue to the UK Supreme Court.[241] These powers are, as discussed above, in addition to the power of the law officers to refer questions relating to the legal competence of the Scottish Parliament to enact a Bill or any of its provisions to the UK Supreme

[233] 'The Role and Functions of the Lord Advocate' (n 187).

[234] ibid.

[235] ibid.

[236] *Helow v Secretary of State for the Home Department* [2008] UKHL 62, [2008] 1 WLR 2416, [10]. Also see: *Adams v Advocate General* 2003 SC 171 (OH).

[237] Scotland Act 1998, Sch 6. Note that the Scotland Act 2012, s 36(4), amends para 1 of Sch 6 to exclude issues arising in Scottish criminal proceedings from being characterised as devolution issues.

[238] Scotland Act 1998, Sch 6, Pt 2, para 4(1).

[239] Scotland Act 1998, Sch 6, Pt 2, paras 5–6.

[240] Scotland Act 1998, Sch 6, Pt 3, para 15(2) and Pt 4, para 25(2).

[241] Scotland Act 1998, Sch 6, Pt 5, para 33.

Court.[242] Taken together, they have resulted in a significant increase in the number of cases where the Lord Advocate is a party.[243]

Modern Prosecution Functions

The prosecutorial functions of the Lord Advocate and Solicitor General for Scotland are in many ways unchanged by devolution.[244] Thus, the hierarchy of deputies ranging from Procurators Fiscal to the Crown Agent all continue to support the Lord Advocate in the exercise of his or her duties as the continuing head of the systems of prosecution and investigation of deaths in Scotland. The Scotland Act 1998 simply reinforces this position, in at least four ways. First, it provides that 'any decision of the Lord Advocate in his capacity as head of the systems of prosecution and investigation of deaths in Scotland shall continue to be taken by him independently of any other person'.[245] Second, the Act specifically excludes these 'retained functions' from the general transfer of ministerial functions to the Scottish Government as a whole.[246] Third, it makes it clear that collective ministerial responsibility does not apply to these functions.[247] Fourth, the legislative competence of the Scottish Parliament is expressly limited to the effect that it cannot 'remove the Lord Advocate from his position as head of the systems of criminal prosecution and investigation of deaths'.[248]

These provisions represent an important facet of the devolution framework given that several criminal matters, such as the misuse of drugs,[249] have been reserved to the UK Government. It would therefore be inappropriate for Scottish Ministers to exert influence over decisions related to such matters. They are also important – perhaps more fundamentally – from the perspective of longstanding constitutional principles as regards insulating prosecutorial decisions from inappropriate influences. They are intended to preserve the ability of the Lord Advocate to make decisions independently with reference to his or her conception of the public interest. While some suggest taking decisions in the public interest means resisting partisan pressure exerted by campaigners or the media,[250] others find nothing objectionable about such forces having an influence on a public decision-maker's thinking so long as a broad view of the public interest is considered in lieu of narrow party political interests.[251] There is, as Komorowski puts it, 'a middle

[242] Scotland Act 1998, s 33.
[243] *The Laws of Scotland: Stair Memorial Encyclopaedia*, Constitutional Law Reissue, para 434. Also see James Wolffe, 'The Renton Lecture 2020: Devolution and the Statute Book' (2021) 42 *Statute Law Review* 121, 128.
[244] Angiolini, 'Legislation, Litigation and Prosecution' (n 62) 231.
[245] Scotland Act 1998, s 48(5).
[246] Scotland Act 1998, s 53(2).
[247] Scotland Act 1998, s 52(5)(b).
[248] Scotland Act 1998, s 29(2)(e).
[249] Scotland Act 1998, Sch 5, Pt 2, para B1.
[250] Angiolini, 'The Lord Advocate in the 21st Century' (n 46).
[251] Komorowski (n 186) 82; Edwards, *The Attorney General, Politics and the Public Interest* (n 6) 333.

ground between utterly populist governance and splendid isolation from public opinion' that the concept of the public interest should encourage office-holders to find;[252] something which might bear a strong relation to the results of a trust test as proposed by Seldon.[253] The Lord Advocate and Solicitor General for Scotland, or their delegates, might determine, for example, that the public interest in keeping the intelligence-gathering capabilities of the government secret is more important than prosecuting a spy, regardless of their party's political position on the question.[254] Alternatively, they might determine that it is in the public interest not to prosecute an offender in order to avoid damaging the health of the complainer, again regardless of their party's political position on the question.[255]

Angiolini has argued that conferring the Lord Advocate with this breadth of prosecutorial discretion is more justified than ever before because, since devolution, the office has been subjected to more parliamentary scrutiny for prosecutorial decisions than was ever the case at Westminster.[256] If one starts from the premise that prosecution is a necessary function of government, it follows, Angiolini suggests, that 'the further the prosecution system gets from the central core of government responsibility, the less easy it is to hold Ministers as a collective body responsible for how it is operated'.[257] For this reason, she is firmly against allocating prosecutorial functions 'to some semi-detached outside body'.[258] Whether or not a body equivalent to the office of the Director of Public Prosecutions – which exists in Northern Ireland as well as in England and Wales – would fall foul of Angiolini's preferences is unclear, but such an inference cannot be ruled out. This is a point of some interest considering that Angiolini was commissioned to review the office of the Attorney General for Northern Ireland in 2012, but her recommendations have since been kept confidential by the Northern Ireland Executive Office.[259] One might infer, and an inference is all that is possible at present, that Angiolini would be minded to recommend that the relationship between the Attorney General for Northern Ireland and the Director of Public Prosecutions for Northern Ireland be reformed so as to conform more closely to the Scottish model which she appears to prefer. Angiolini's preference is also notable for the extent to which it differs from the less absolute view of the Court of Session judiciary who, in 2008, provided evidence to the Calman Commission on Scottish Devolution wherein they called it a 'problem' that acts of the Lord Advocate were subject to challenge under the Scotland Act 1998 because it meant the Judicial Committee of the Privy Council

[252] Komorowski (n 186) 83.
[253] See ch 2 at 40–41 and ch 7 at 210–218.
[254] Angiolini, 'The Lord Advocate in the 21st Century' (n 46).
[255] ibid. This particular scenario, formulated in such hypothetical terms by Angiolini, is an obvious allusion to the facts of the infamous 'Glasgow rape case'.
[256] ibid; Angiolini, 'Legislation, Litigation and Prosecution' (n 62) 231.
[257] Angiolini, 'The Lord Advocate in the 21st Century' (n 46).
[258] ibid.
[259] A detailed account of this saga is provided in ch 6 at 161–164 below.

(which was the relevant forum for resolving devolution disputes at the time) was able to review criminal prosecutions in Scotland.[260] The Court of Session judges identified three potential solutions to that problem, one of which was a proposal to transfer the prosecutorial functions of the Lord Advocate to a separate Director of Public Prosecutions.[261] While this proposal was not taken forward, it is indicative of the disagreement which exists over this complex constitutional question. Incidentally, an attempt to remedy this problem was introduced by the Scotland Act 2012 in the form of a narrowly regulated 'compatibility issues' procedure.[262]

It is certainly true that the two Justice Committees of the Scottish Parliament regularly question the Lord Advocate and Solicitor General for Scotland on their prosecutorial functions, which is to say nothing of the wider political pressure that can be brought to bear on the Scottish law officers by parliamentarians from the opposition.[263] In 2017, for instance, one of the Justice Committees published a report containing its findings from an inquiry into the role and purpose of the Crown Office and Procurator Fiscal Service which did not appear to pull any punches.[264] For example, it referred to problems in connection with the efficiency of the service as 'unacceptably high' and claimed that the quality and consistency of prosecutions in summary cases relating to antisocial behaviour, crimes of dishonesty and less violent crimes had been 'under-prioritised' as a result of the Lord Advocate's emphasis on prosecuting domestic abuse cases.[265] However, while such parliamentary investigations do suggest that some degree of effective accountability exists, it must be remembered that the Scottish Parliament can only make full inquiries into the law officers' general *policies* on prosecutions and the investigation of deaths, because the Scotland Act 1998 empowers them to refuse to answer any question or produce any document relating to the operation of those systems '*in any particular case*' if doing so would prejudice criminal proceedings or be otherwise against the public interest.[266] There is some continuing debate over whether such considerations are relevant after a decision has been taken,[267] but the terms of this political accountability restriction appear to be largely indistinguishable from that applicable to the law officers examined in Chapters 3 and 4.

[260] Individual evidence submissions received by the Calman Commission no longer appear to be available online, but, for a letter from the Lord President of the Court of Session correcting how the judiciary's submission had been represented by the media, see: 'Judges' verdict on Lord Advocate' (*The Scotsman*, 8 November 2008). Available at: www.scotsman.com/news/judges-verdict-on-lord-advocate-1-1301097.

[261] ibid.

[262] Scotland Act 2012, ss 34–37.

[263] For a particularly high-profile example, see: 'Opposition Parties Consider Vote of No-Confidence in Lord Advocate' (*Scottish Legal News*, 16 November 2020). Available at: www.scottishlegal.com/article/opposition-parties-consider-vote-of-no-confidence-in-lord-advocate.

[264] Justice Committee, *Role and Purpose of the Crown and Procurator Fiscal Service* (25 April 2017, SP Paper 123.1).

[265] ibid 83.

[266] Scotland Act 1998, s 27(3). Italics added.

[267] Komorowski (n 186) 96–97.

In any event, it has been accepted that the prosecutorial decisions of the Lord Advocate are justiciable in the courts[268] and the courts have in fact been willing to review and, in appropriate cases, overturn decisions in relation to the investigation of deaths.[269] Improved legal accountability for individual decisions of this nature is arguably due, in large part, to the influence of the European Convention on Human Rights as embedded in both the Human Rights Act 1998 and the Scotland Act 1998.[270] Moreover, challenges to individual exercises of prosecutorial discretion might in future be aided by the guidelines for prosecutors published by the Lord Advocate,[271] inter alia;[272] which is a welcome development when it comes to addressing the concerns of Smith in relation to governmental transparency and its consequences for seeking individual redress.[273] Court decisions must be carefully scrutinised, however, to ensure undue deference to political accountability is not inappropriately deployed by members of the judiciary as a reason not to hear complaints about individual cases, given that political accountability of that nature has been statutorily restricted in the devolved context. Indeed, there is arguably a need to guard against this phenomenon apropos the whole UK law officer regime, which is also something that will be picked up for further consideration later in this book.

Conclusions

The extent of the powers and responsibilities of the Lord Advocate and Solicitor General for Scotland have expanded and contracted repeatedly over time. This is clear not only by reference to the emergence of the Secretary of State for Scotland in 1885, and likewise the creation of the Advocate General for Scotland in 1998, but also by reference to a further variety of the historical events that surround those milestones. This chapter has attempted to highlight several of the most significant

[268] Angiolini, 'The Lord Advocate in the 21st Century' (n 46). Also see *Whitehouse & Clark v The Chief Constable and the Lord Advocate* [2019] CSIH 52, 2020 SC 133, wherein the Inner House of the Court of Session overturned the Lord Advocate's immunity from suit in cases of malicious prosecution.

[269] Aidan O'Neill, 'Human Rights and People and Society' in Elaine E Sutherland and others (eds), *Law Making and the Scottish Parliament: The Early Years* (Edinburgh University Press 2011) 51–52.

[270] ibid.

[271] The Lord Advocate's Guidelines are uploaded as individual pdf documents to the following webpage: www.crownoffice.gov.uk/publications/prosecution-policy-and-guidance?showall=&start=4. Some pdfs are dated, while others are not. By way of example, the 'Prosecution Guidance in Relation to Same Sex Marriage' is an undated half-page document outlining the Lord Advocate's view on the probable legality of criticisms of same sex marriage or homosexuality and setting out the approach to be taken by the Crown Office and Procurator Fiscal Service in respect of individual complaints of that nature.

[272] The Lord Advocate's Guidelines are one set of a broader suite of publications regarding prosecution policies and guidance documents, etc. Available at: www.copfs.gov.uk/publications/prosecution-policy-and-guidance.

[273] Smith (n 83) 150.

turning points in this evolution story while paying due regard to the wider historical context which animated the reforms and reconfigurations in question. It has charted, in particular, how the Lord Advocate and Solicitor General for Scotland have been characterised as both 'predominantly political' and 'predominantly legal' roles at various intervals, and how the devolution reforms of and since 1998 have resulted in a number of sweeping changes to the nature of their offices. In addition, a significant number of the differences that mark the Scottish law officers apart from their counterparts in England and Wales (and Wales) have been highlighted in this chapter. Among the most genuine and striking of these differences is the continuing role of the Lord Advocate as head of the systems of criminal prosecution and investigation of deaths, though it should be noted – indeed, emphasised – that there have been mounting calls for this position to be reformed and perhaps even 'radically' changed over the course of the past year or so.[274] Details about the main impetus for those calls – which essentially stem from 'intense scrutiny over the Scottish Government's handling of complaints against former First Minister Alex Salmond and his subsequent acquittal at his criminal trial'[275] – can be read elsewhere.[276] For present purposes, it must suffice to record that the Scottish Government now intends to 'consult on whether the prosecution and government functions of the law officers should be separated'.[277] There can therefore be little doubt that the questions of constitutional legitimacy threaded throughout this book are of considerable contemporary significance.

[274] 'The Role of the Lord Advocate: Time for Radical Change or Cautious Reform?' (*Scottish Legal News*, 4 March 2021). Available at: www.scottishlegal.com/article/the-role-of-the-lord-advocate-time-for-radical-change-or-cautious-reform; 'Scots Lawyers Call for Role of Lord Advocate to be Split' (*Scottish Legal News*, 5 March 2021). Available at: www.scottishlegal.com/article/scots-lawyers-call-for-role-of-lord-advocate-to-be-split; Nick McKerrell, 'The Lord Advocate: A Need for Reform or Reflection?' (*The Constitution Society*, 1 April 2021). Available at: https://consoc.org.uk/the-lord-advocate-a-need-for-reform-or-reflection/; Scott Crichton Styles, 'How the Roles of Lord Advocate Could Be Split and Why It Could Help Pursuit of Indy' (*The National*, 14 June 2021). Available at: www.thenational.scot/news/19369788.roles-lord-advocate-split-help-pursuit-indy/.

[275] McKerrell (n 274).

[276] See (n 274) above.

[277] Scottish Government, 'A Fairer, Greener Scotland: Programme for Government 2021–2022' (September 2021), 103. Available at: www.gov.scot/publications/fairer-greener-scotland-programme-government-2021-22/documents/.

6

The Attorney General and Advocate General for Northern Ireland

Introduction

In common with the Counsel General for Wales and the Advocate General for Scotland, the Advocate General for Northern Ireland is an office conceived in the context of the 1998 devolution reforms. The Attorney General for Northern Ireland, however, is an older office with an origin story stretching back to the creation of Northern Ireland at the beginning of the twentieth century.[1] It is not, therefore, quite so steeped in history as are the offices of Attorney General and Solicitor General for England and Wales, or indeed the offices of Lord Advocate and Solicitor General for Scotland. Moreover, as the following sections in this chapter explain, both the office of the Advocate General for Northern Ireland and the office of the Attorney General for Northern Ireland differ quite fundamentally in several respects from all the law officer models considered in this book so far. The stories of both offices are so intertwined that it was deemed necessary to outline them in a largely chronological sequence generally akin to the chronological analyses of the Scottish law officers in Chapter 5, instead of reverting to the discrete taxonomical approach that was used to frame the functions of the law officers explored in Chapters 3 and 4. This method also made it possible to place appropriate emphasis on the historical importance of the prosecutorial functions that were once discharged by the Attorney General for Northern Ireland. Thus, the nature of the original office created to serve the earliest governments of Northern Ireland is considered in the first instance below, before an explanation of how that office changed in tandem with the introduction of direct rule by the UK Government in 1972. The remainder of this chapter deals with the design, creation and operation of the offices of the Advocate General for Northern Ireland and Attorney General for Northern Ireland that were formally (re-)established in 2010.

[1] For a succinct history of Northern Ireland, see: Rory O'Connell and others, *Applying an International Human Rights Framework to State Budget Allocations: Rights and Resources* (Routledge 2014) 26–36.

The Original Office

As a matter of brief pre-history, it is worth noting that, prior to the partition of Ireland and the consequent establishment of a Northern Ireland Parliament in 1921,[2] there had existed Attorneys General for the whole of Ireland for many years.[3] Indeed, apace with the 'extension of royal authority in Ireland' from the sixteenth century onwards,[4] such office-holders eventually came to be recognised as having the ability to 'exercise a marked influence on general government policy' in Ireland for some time.[5] In fact, the potential of this influence became so great that by 1834 Daniel O'Connell described it in the following words (in the context of an attack on the character on the then Attorney General for Ireland, Francis Blackburne):

> The office of Attorney-General [is] … an office of enormous emolument in the hands of a prosecuting Attorney-General, and of the very first political influence. It is … the most important office all to nothing in the administration of the government of Ireland – consulted upon everything – advising, guiding, directing everything.[6]

The political prominence of the office at this time is thus comparable to that which went with the Lord Advocate and Solicitor General for Scotland throughout much of the nineteenth century. Other rights and responsibilities attaching to the office also differed from the portfolios of the Attorney General and Solicitor General for England and Wales in similarly considerable ways. The Attorney General for Ireland sat at the apex of the prosecution system in Ireland, for example, in contrast to the more residual prosecutorial role of the Attorney General and Solicitor General for England and Wales.[7] The Irish office also carried out legislative drafting for a time and dealt with particularly weighty advisory matters in the context of violent insurrections across the island. Such controversial work 'of a type hardly familiar to their English *confrères*' embraced, for instance, pruning a list of 'Fenian detainees' which had been proposed by the Royal Irish Constabulary down 'from over 1,000 to around 200'.[8] It is also of note that appointments to the office of Attorney General for Ireland gradually became the reserve of individuals affiliated with the governing political party for the majority of its later history, slowly eroding the non-political and non-parliamentary model that was initially contemplated for the office.[9]

[2] Government of Ireland Act 1920.
[3] See, generally: James Casey, *The Irish Law Officers: Roles and Responsibilities of the Attorney General and Director of Public Prosecutions* (Sweet & Maxwell 1996) 6–49.
[4] ibid 10.
[5] ibid 19–20.
[6] Letter from Daniel O'Connell to Lord Duncannon (30 August 1834), quoted in Edward Blackburne, *Life of the Right Hon Francis Blackburne* (Macmillan and Co 1874) 166.
[7] Casey (n 3) 27–30.
[8] ibid 32.
[9] ibid 37–42.

Because the Government of Ireland Act 1920 did not take effect in the twenty-six southern counties of Ireland,[10] there was for a short time a continuity gap in the historical timeline of Irish law officers. The gap was ultimately filled when Hugh Kennedy was appointed to cover the new twenty-six county jurisdiction – first under the title Law Officer to the Provisional Government, and subsequently under the repurposed title of Attorney General.[11] In addition, and more importantly for present purposes, when the 1920 Act came into force in the six counties comprising Northern Ireland there arose need for a separate law officer to serve this newly constituted UK jurisdiction. The Attorney General for Northern Ireland was thus created in the guise of a non-departmental ministerial office appointed by the Lord Lieutenant on the advice of the Prime Minister for Northern Ireland.[12] Before the office was first established, moreover, it was provided that

> … [r]eferences in any enactment to the Attorney-General for Ireland shall from and after such establishment be construed as references to the Attorney-General for Northern Ireland except that the Lord Lieutenant may, if he thinks fit, appoint some other person to act instead of the Attorney-General for Northern Ireland in relation to any matters which are not for the time being within the powers of the Government of Northern Ireland and in that case the references shall in relation to those matters be construed as references to the person so appointed.[13]

The first person to assume the original office of the Attorney General for Northern Ireland was Richard Best, an elected unionist MP for Mid-Armagh who went on to become a Lord Justice of Appeal in 1925.[14] He was succeeded by ten further

[10] For legal accounts of the historical details, see: Arthur S Quekett, *The Constitution of Northern Ireland: Part I – The Origin and Development of the Constitution* (HM Stationery Office 1928) 18–19; Nicholas Mansergh, *The Government of Northern Ireland: A Study in Devolution* (George Allen & Unwin Ltd 1936) ch 6; Brigid Hadfield, *The Constitution of Northern Ireland* (SLS Legal Publications (NI) 1989) ch 2; Christopher McCrudden, 'Northern Ireland and the British Constitution' in Jeffrey Jowell and Dawn Oliver (eds), *The Changing Constitution* (3rd edn, Oxford University Press 1994) 328–330.

[11] Casey (n 3) 3–4.

[12] Harry Calvert, *Constitutional Law in Northern Ireland: A Study in Regional Government* (Stevens & Sons 1968) 362; Arthur S Quekett, *The Constitution of Northern Ireland: Part II – The Government of Ireland Act 1920 and Subsequent Enactments* (HM Stationery Office 1933) 283–284. The Lord Lieutenant was the single representative of the Crown over all of Ireland between April 1921 and December 1922. With the coming into force of the Irish Free State Constitution at the end of 1922, the office of Lord Lieutenant was supplanted by that of the jurisdictionally discrete Governor of Northern Ireland, and it then became the responsibility of the Governor to make subsequent appointments to the office of the Attorney General for Northern Ireland. See: Quekett (n 10) 34–35. The Parliament of Northern Ireland (Disqualification Removal) Order 1921 exempted the Attorney General from being disqualified for membership of the Senate or House of Commons of Northern Ireland by reason of holding office under the Crown, thereby conferring a ministerial status on the office. See: Claire Palley, 'The Evolution, Disintegration and Possible Reconstruction of the Northern Ireland Constitution' (1972) 1 *Anglo-American Law Review* 368, 398.

[13] Supreme Court of Judicature (Northern Ireland) Order 1921, r 2(2). See also: General Adaptation of Enactments (Northern Ireland) Order 1921, r 5; Election Laws Application (House of Commons of Northern Ireland) Order 1921, r 6(1).

[14] Lord Carswell, 'Founding a Legal System: The Early Judiciary of Northern Ireland' in Felix M Larkin and Norma M Dawson (eds), *Lawyers, the Law and History* (Four Courts Press 2013) 25. For

office-holders who were also unionist politicians.[15] As intimated by the excerpt above, the office they held had inherited a range of functions formerly carried out by the Attorney General for Ireland. This conservationist approach left room for uncertainty in relation to certain functions. The power of the Attorney General for Northern Ireland to intervene in litigation in the absence of specific rules allowing it, for example, was objected to in a case concerning the competence of the Northern Ireland Parliament to enact legislation that would deprive a businessman of his property without compensation contrary to the Government of Ireland Act 1920.[16] The objection was dismissed unequivocally by the Court of Appeal, however, which confirmed that such interventions were permissible on the invitation of the Court and,[17] at least according to two members of the court, 'as of right' in any case involving questions of a public nature (unless a specific judge was unwilling to allow an intervention).[18] Significantly, inheriting the former portfolio of the Attorney General for Ireland also meant that local politicians qua the Attorney General for Northern Ireland became directly responsible for the system of criminal prosecutions in Northern Ireland[19] – something which genuinely distinguished office-holders from the more distant responsibility of the Attorney General and Solicitor General for England and Wales in this respect. There were, in fact, calls to establish a consultative advisory committee to reconsider the unique power of the Attorney General for Northern Ireland in determining whether prosecutions should be instituted in individual cases, but those calls were dismissed and so the law officer remained in charge of all prosecutorial matters in Northern Ireland.[20]

Before long, and in response to rising criticism, various office-holders were required to defend the independence of their office and its role in prosecutions. They insisted that the prosecutorial functions of the Attorney General for Northern Ireland were properly carried out independently of inappropriate political and religious influences. For example, John MacDermott prefaced a parliamentary defence of his decision to approve the prosecution of several industrial shipyard workers for leading an illegal strike by emphasising that the decision had been taken by him alone and that members of the Northern Ireland Executive had 'no right to direct a prosecution or to tell the Law Officer what to do'.[21] Similarly, in

further details about the life of Richard Best, including some interesting reflections about his tenure as a law officer, see the memorials published in Issue 2 of the *Northern Ireland Legal Quarterly* (1939) at 55–58 and 59–60.

[15] AR Hart, *A History of the Bar and Inn of Court of Northern Ireland* (The General Council of the Bar of Northern Ireland 2013) 433–434.

[16] *Northern Ireland Road Transport Board v Benson* [1940] NI 133.

[17] *Northern Ireland Road Transport Board v Benson* [1940] NI 133, 140 (Andrews CJ).

[18] *Northern Ireland Road Transport Board v Benson* [1940] NI 133, 165 (Babington LJ); 169 (Murphy LJ).

[19] Robert E Bell, 'The Office of Director of Public Prosecutions for Northern Ireland' (PhD thesis, Queen's University Belfast 1988) 40.

[20] NI Deb 9 May 1933, vol 15, col 740.

[21] NI Deb 5 April 1944, vol 27, col 1046.

response to allegations of inappropriate motivations for various prosecutions (linked, inter alia, to the office-holder's active membership of the Orange Order), Basil Kelly defended his tenure in this speech to the Northern Ireland House of Commons:

> I have tried to carry out my duties with the strictest impartiality in these difficult times independent of Cabinet or Government or political party or religious organisation and I have been unmoved in the matter of public prosecutions by political or religious pressure from any quarter or by popular clamour or public agitation for prosecutions where serious crime has been committed and unsolved and where culprits have not been detected or where sufficient evidence does not exist to justify a prosecution.[22]

Accusations of bias continued to escalate, however, with both sides of Northern Ireland's divided community claiming persecution. Basil Kelly tried to advance the view that his decision to institute prosecutions against prominent unionist figures like Ian Paisley *and* prominent nationalist figures like Bernadette Devlin evidenced a fair and impartial approach to his duties.[23] Despite such efforts to appear accountable, however, the level of public distrust in the independence of the Attorney General for Northern Ireland at this time had become so widespread that even 'a dear lady of very strong political views' from a unionist background akin to that of the office-holder would write sarcastic letters to him addressed, 'Dear Attorney General for the Republicans'.[24] This widespread dissatisfaction came to a head when a formal motion inviting the Northern Ireland House of Commons to censure the Attorney General for Northern Ireland 'in relation to the institution of criminal proceedings arising out of certain disorders and firearms offences' was tabled in 1971,[25] not long before the whole devolution settlement was to collapse. While the motion was defeated by a strong unionist majority,[26] it enabled a lengthy debate on reforming the Northern Ireland prosecution system. Indeed, the Prime Minister for Northern Ireland used his time in the debate to announce that the Northern Ireland Government intended to appoint a separate Director of Public Prosecutions, and that the constitutional position of that office would parallel its counterpart in England and Wales.[27] When the devolution settlement for Northern Ireland was suspended by Westminster in March 1972,[28] however, the Bill that had been developed to provide for this reform was lost and the issue became one of the many pressing responsibilities assumed by the UK Government in lieu of a devolved administration.[29]

[22] NI Deb 13 November 1969, vol 74, col 1348. For some background to this speech, see: John Ll J Edwards, *The Attorney General, Politics and the Public Interest* (Sweet & Maxwell 1984) 259.
[23] NI Deb 13 November 1969, vol 74, col 1351.
[24] ibid.
[25] NI Deb 13 May 1971, vol 80, col 1783.
[26] NI Deb 13 May 1971, vol 80, cols 1905–1906.
[27] NI Deb 13 May 1971, vol 80, cols 1872–1873. See also: Edwards, *The Attorney General, Politics and the Public Interest* (n 22) 261–262.
[28] Northern Ireland (Temporary Provisions) Act 1972.
[29] See: Bell (n 19) 57–82.

The Cognate Office

Dickson explains that the devolution settlement for Northern Ireland was prorogued in 1972 'because of its inability to cope with serious civil unrest that had developed in the province since 1968'.[30] In consequence, a radically new arrangement in respect of the Attorney General for Northern Ireland was established in tandem with the introduction of direct rule from Westminster. The relevant legislative provision provided that

> the Attorney General for England and Wales shall by virtue of that office be Attorney General for Northern Ireland also, and he and the Solicitor General shall by virtue of membership of the bar of England and Wales have in Northern Ireland the same rights of audience as members of the bar of Northern Ireland.[31]

Due to the fact that Northern Ireland had not had a local Solicitor General before this enactment,[32] it was also necessary to provide that the Solicitor General for England and Wales could discharge all of the functions authorised or required to be discharged by the Attorney General for Northern Ireland in the event that that office became vacant or if the Attorney General for Northern Ireland was unable to act owing to absence or illness.[33] Edwards explains that the last of these two contingencies enabled 'the additional burdens to be shared between the two Law Officers of the Crown in a manner best suited to their individual inclinations and changing pressures'.[34]

While most of the functions formerly exercised by the devolved Attorney General for Northern Ireland were passed to the Attorney General for England and Wales qua the Attorney General for Northern Ireland by this 'simple and straightforward' legislative instrument in an unreformed state,[35] the comparatively extensive prosecutorial powers and duties formerly attached to the Attorney General for Northern Ireland were very swiftly remodelled after the introduction of direct rule, bringing the extent of those functions roughly into line with those of the Attorney General and Solicitor General for England and Wales at the time. The change was almost simultaneous, in fact, because the first Order in Council

[30] Brice Dickson, *Law in Northern Ireland* (3rd edn, Hart Publishing 2018) 7–8. For a detailed legal account of the relevant timeline of events, see: Palley (n 12) 406–444.

[31] Northern Ireland (Temporary Provisions) Act 1972, s 1(2).

[32] Proposals to create a Solicitor General for Northern Ireland were in fact considered and dismissed by the Government of Northern Ireland in 1923. Instead, a power for the Governor to appoint an unremunerated Deputy to the Attorney General for Northern Ireland was proposed by the Northern Ireland Government and in due course created by the Northern Ireland Parliament to obviate any difficulties that might arise were the Attorney General to find him- or herself 'unable to act' by virtue of ill health, for example. See: NI Deb 31 May 1923, vol 3, cols 1191–1192; Office of the Attorney General Act (Northern Ireland) 1923, s 2. The 1923 Act was repealed in full by the Northern Ireland (Modification of Enactments–No 1) Order 1973, s 14(2) and Sch 6.

[33] Northern Ireland (Temporary Provisions) Act 1972, Sch, para 3.

[34] Edwards, *The Attorney General, Politics and the Public Interest* (n 22) 237–238.

[35] ibid 238.

which the UK Government proposed and subsequently made in the absence of a devolved administration for the region was for the establishment of a Director of Public Prosecutions for Northern Ireland (DPP).[36] The resulting legislation differed from the Bill that had been developed by the Northern Ireland Parliament prior to its collapse[37] in one particularly significant respect: it provided that the DPP was to discharge his or her functions 'under the superintendence of the Attorney General' and would be 'subject to the directions of the Attorney General in all matters'.[38] This formulation mirrored the statutory relationship between the Attorney General for England and Wales and the Director of Public Prosecutions for England and Wales,[39] but it varied considerably from the dynamic developed by the Northern Ireland Parliament which had envisaged a much stronger conception of independence on the part of the DPP in that he or she would not have been superintended or subject to a power of direction by the Attorney General for Northern Ireland. Instead, the DPP would have been merely 'responsible to the Attorney General for the due performance of the functions' vested in his or her office.[40] Having reviewed the operation of some similar statutory frameworks used in Australia, Bell has expressed a preference for the Northern Ireland developed alternative to a 'superintendence' model on the basis that it represents a better 'balance between giving the Director independence but not completely severing the link with the Attorney General and the accountability' made possible by that relationship.[41]

The 'temporary' legislative position involving superintendence and a power of direction enacted by Westminster did include a provision providing that the formulation preferred by Bell – permitting a greater degree of independence on the part of the director as devised by the Northern Ireland Parliament – would come into force if the primary legislation enabling direct rule by Westminster ceased to have effect.[42] The temporariness of Northern Ireland government by direct rule initially envisaged, however, turned out to be unduly optimistic. The Attorney General for England and Wales qua the Attorney General for Northern Ireland visited Belfast 12 times in the first nine months of direct rule and wrote to the then Secretary of State for Northern Ireland requesting that he publicise those visits 'so as to show that I don't entirely neglect that part of my parish', as he put it, while also seeking to establish official discussions about the future position of the law officers in relation to Northern Ireland.[43]

[36] Bell (n 19) 77.
[37] Prosecution of Offences NI HC Bill (1971–1972).
[38] Prosecution of Offences (Northern Ireland) Order 1972, art 3(2).
[39] Bell (n 19) 78.
[40] Prosecution of Offences NI HC Bill (1971–1972), cl 2(2), cited in ibid 71.
[41] Bell (n 19) 408–411.
[42] Prosecution of Offences (Northern Ireland) Order 1972, art 5(2).
[43] Letter from Peter Rawlinson to William Whitelaw (21 November 1972), accessible via the National Archives by reference CJ 4/265.

Despite several efforts to restore devolution, including the short-lived establishment of a Northern Ireland Assembly in 1974 which resulted in a re-enactment of the legislative arrangement whereby the Attorney General for England and Wales was by virtue of that office the Attorney General for Northern Ireland,[44] several returns to direct rule proved unavoidable.[45] While some brief consideration was given to the establishment of a local Attorney General for Northern Ireland again at this time, Members of Parliament who engaged with the proposition were persuaded that the need for some political accountability over the prosecution system justified a continuation of the cognate office in the absence of a local legislature.[46] Throughout this turbulent period in the history of Northern Ireland government, the ultimate primacy of a politically high profile Attorney General for England and Wales qua Attorney General for Northern Ireland over the decisions of a purportedly independent DPP for the region did, however, raise 'some doubts' as to the impartiality of various controversial prosecution decisions.[47] Suspicions of political interference with decisions in relation to 'the prosecution of members of the security forces, as for instance in the case of the "Bloody Sunday" shootings in Londonderry in January 1972',[48] in particular, rendered the unexpectedly long duration of this constitutional arrangement highly contested.

After a long period of uncertainty, the Northern Ireland Act 1998 once again provided for a locally elected Northern Ireland Assembly subject to a carefully constructed constitutional framework.[49] Under the 1998 Act, as originally enacted, the office of the Attorney General for Northern Ireland continued to be occupied coterminously with the office of Attorney General for England and Wales, albeit certain distinctions were drawn between the two.[50] Moreover, it provided the Attorney General for England and Wales qua the Attorney General for Northern Ireland with an important power to refer an Assembly Bill to the Judicial Committee of the Privy Council, now the Supreme Court of the United Kingdom, for a determination as to its legislative competence under the 1998 Act.[51] Like the other law officers considered earlier in this book, the Attorney General for England and Wales qua the Attorney General for Northern Ireland was also gifted with a significant power to initiate legal proceedings for the determination

[44] Northern Ireland Constitution Act 1973, s 10.

[45] For a succinct account of the context to these attempts at the restoration of devolved government, see: Dickson (n 30) 10–12.

[46] HC Deb 3 July 1973, vol 859, cols 345–349.

[47] Kevin Boyle, Tom Hadden and Paddy Hillyard, *Law and State: The Case of Northern Ireland* (Martin Robertson 1975) 126. Also see: Barry McCaffrey, 'Declassified Documents Reveal Army Lobbied Attorney General Not to Prosecute Soldiers' (*thedetail*, 15 April 2013). Available at: www.thedetail.tv/articles/declassified-documents-reveal-army-lobbied-attorney-general-not-to-prosecute-soldiers.

[48] ibid.

[49] Gordon Anthony, *Judicial Review in Northern Ireland* (2nd edn, Hart Publishing 2014) 156–165.

[50] Noreen Burrows, *Devolution* (Sweet & Maxwell 2000) 161.

[51] Northern Ireland Act 1998, s 11. Also see ss 6(2) and 24 for the various limitations on legislative and executive powers in Northern Ireland and note that compliance with ECHR standards is among them.

of a devolution issue under that Act.[52] The Act also conferred a right to defend proceedings relating to a devolution issue in other legal jurisdictions within the UK; a right to be notified of such issues if raised by others in those jurisdictions; a right to participate in all proceedings so notified, and a right to require a court or tribunal in any proceedings to which the Attorney General for Northern Ireland is a party to refer a devolution issue to the UK Supreme Court.[53] In addition, the Attorney General for England and Wales qua the Attorney General for Northern Ireland enjoyed powers to initiate proceedings to determine in Northern Irish courts Scottish or Welsh devolution issues, prior to the reinstatement of a local Attorney General for Northern Ireland in 2010.[54] The developments which took place between 1998 and 2010 in pursuit of that reinstatement are explained in the following section.

The Current Offices

The Belfast (Good Friday) Agreement 1998, which provided the basis for the Northern Ireland Act 1998, among other things, called for an independent and wide-ranging review of criminal justice.[55] In due course, a Criminal Justice Review panel was established which carried out extensive consultation and commissioned in-depth research relating to its agreed terms of reference. It made its recommendations in a report published in 2000.[56] Safeguarding the independence of the local prosecution system, alongside the need for accountability and transparency, was one of the most important issues considered by the review panel.[57] It concluded that political responsibility for the prosecution system should be devolved to local institutions and, arising from this recommendation, explored suggestions made by consultees that the head of the prosecution service might be accountable to a local Attorney General.[58] While acknowledging that the creation of such a post raised many issues beyond its terms of reference, the review panel recommended the establishment of 'a locally sponsored post of Attorney General who, inter alia, would have oversight of the prosecution service'.[59] The review panel emphasised

[52] Northern Ireland Act 1998, Sch 10, Pt 2, para 4(1).

[53] Northern Ireland Act 1998, Sch 10.

[54] Scotland Act 1998, Sch 6, Pt 4, para 25; Government of Wales Act 2006, Sch 9, Pt 4, paras 22–28. These powers are now in the gift of the Attorney General for England and Wales qua the Advocate General for Northern Ireland.

[55] Northern Ireland Office, *The Belfast Agreement* (10 April 1998) Pt IX, annex B. For some detailed constitutional context to the Agreement and an explanation of its continued importance, see the following publication by a current Judge of the Irish High Court: Richard Humphreys, *Beyond the Border: The Good Friday Agreement and Irish Unity After Brexit* (Merrion Press 2018).

[56] Criminal Justice Review, *Report of the Criminal Justice Review in Northern Ireland* (TSO 2000).

[57] ibid para 4.102.

[58] ibid para 4.160.

[59] ibid.

that it did not recommend a supervisory relationship between the local Attorney General and the head of the prosecution service in Northern Ireland, despite envisaging a less political role 'than almost all its counterparts in other common law jurisdictions'.[60] Instead, it expressed preference towards a consultative model which would further strengthen the insulation of the prosecution service from political influence, but which would enable the Attorney General to be answerable to the Northern Ireland Assembly for the work of the prosecution service 'in general terms'.[61] This recommendation accorded with the conclusions of Bryett and Osborne, commissioned by the review panel to conduct research about international perspectives on criminal prosecutions, who found that 'transparency in a relationship of explanatory accountability' would 'satisfactorily reconcile the imperatives of prosecutorial independence and political accountability'.[62] In addition, they found that 'increased public consciousness and activism would more than adequately compensate for the loss of power of direction by an attorney general'.[63]

The Northern Ireland Office responded to the recommendations made by the Criminal Justice Review by publishing an Implementation Plan in 2001, along with a draft Justice (Northern Ireland) Bill, indicating the Government's intention to adopt the majority of recommendations made. This included those recommendations in relation to the establishment of a local Attorney General with oversight for, but not superintendence over, the local prosecution service.[64] Moreover, the Implementation Plan made it clear that functions relating to the 'excepted' matters then performed by the Attorney General for England and Wales in his or her capacity as Attorney General for Northern Ireland, namely matters beyond the legislative competence of the devolved Assembly,[65] such as national security,[66] would instead be exercised by the Attorney General for England and Wales qua the new office of *Advocate* General for Northern Ireland.[67] Thus, two new offices would be created; one local, and one at Westminster.

However, the statutory framework proposed by the Northern Ireland Office in the Justice (Northern Ireland) Bill was not comprehensive in nature. The Implementation Plan stated that 'additional functions relating to the Assembly and Executive suggested by the Review (such as Legal Advisor to the Assembly)' were matters for those devolved institutions.[68] The distribution of legislative competences at the time therefore resulted in an episodic approach to the delineation of

[60] ibid para 4.162.
[61] ibid paras 4.162–4.163.
[62] Keith Bryett and Peter Osborne, *Criminal Prosecutions Procedure and Practice: International Perspectives* (TSO 2000) 103.
[63] ibid.
[64] Northern Ireland Office, *Criminal Justice Review Implementation Plan* (2 November 2001) 23–24.
[65] Northern Ireland Act 1998, s 6(2)(b) and Sch 2.
[66] Northern Ireland Act 1998, Sch 2, para 17.
[67] Northern Ireland Office (n 64) 23.
[68] ibid.

functions to be vested in the new office of Attorney General for Northern Ireland.[69] Several outstanding issues requiring the attention of the devolved administration were accordingly identified by a Northern Ireland Assembly Ad-hoc Committee on the Justice (Northern Ireland) Bill.[70] In particular, it recommended that the Committee on Procedures examine the extent to which the Attorney General for Northern Ireland may participate in Assembly proceedings and that, after the devolution of justice, appropriate steps be taken to define the future role and extent of the responsibilities of the office.[71] The extent to which these recommendations have been realised will be considered further below, after the statutory underpinnings of the current offices resulting from the developments outlined above are duly considered.

Statutory Underpinnings

The key provisions of the Justice (Northern Ireland) Act 2002 are as follows. The Attorney General for England and Wales is no longer the Attorney General for Northern Ireland[72] but is instead the Advocate General for Northern Ireland by virtue of their primary office.[73] The Attorney General for England and Wales qua the Advocate General for Northern Ireland enjoys the same rights of audience as members of the Bar of Northern Ireland,[74] and is charged with a detailed set of statutory functions listed in Schedule 7 to the 2002 Act. Indeed, the functions of the Advocate General for Northern Ireland have been described as 'solely statutory'.[75] They relate primarily to excepted matters,[76] but also include a mandatory consultative role in relation to a range of statutory decisions connected to the office of the Attorney General for Northern Ireland.[77] To the latter extent, the 2002 Act does not purport to create an entirely clean split between the two new offices. It provides that the Attorney General for Northern Ireland must be appointed by

[69] The Northern Ireland Executive and the Northern Ireland Assembly were consulted by the Northern Ireland Office on the policy areas in the draft legislation that had 'implications for the devolved Administration'. See: HC Deb 21 January 2002, vol 378, col 643.

[70] Ad-hoc Committee, *Second Report on the Justice (Northern Ireland) Bill and the Criminal Justice Review – Implementation Plan* (January 2002).

[71] ibid paras 63–64.

[72] Justice (Northern Ireland) Act 2002, s 22(1).

[73] Justice (Northern Ireland) Act 2002, s 27(1).

[74] Justice (Northern Ireland) Act 2002, s 27(3). This provision also extends rights of audience to the Solicitor General for England and Wales.

[75] HL 3 June 2010, vol 719, col WA9.

[76] The Justice (Northern Ireland) Act 2002, Sch 7, para 23, for example, transfers the power to certify that an offence is not a scheduled offence under the Terrorism Act 2000 to the Advocate General for Northern Ireland.

[77] The Justice (Northern Ireland) Act 2002, Sch 7, para 13, for example, requires the First Minister and deputy First Minister to consult the Advocate General for Northern Ireland before appointing the Attorney General for Northern Ireland.

the First Minister and deputy First Minister 'acting jointly',[78] which averts the sort of party-political associations Alex Salmond voluntarily rejected in the course of making his appointment decisions in respect of the Scottish law officers.[79]

Though the 2002 Act provides that office-holders are subject to a maximum term of five years at a time as Attorney General for Northern Ireland,[80] it also prescribes that they can be removed from office if a judicial tribunal is convened which recommends removal 'on the ground of misbehaviour or inability to perform the functions of the office'.[81] Office-holders must also submit an annual report to the First and deputy First Ministers on how their functions have been exercised,[82] which they must lay before the Assembly before making arrangements for it to be published.[83] The First and deputy First Minister have the power to redact parts of an annual report if publication would, in their opinion, be against the public interest or jeopardise the safety of any person.[84] However, a statement must be published with any annual report which has been redacted indicating that information has been excluded.[85]

Regardless of the method for his or her appointment, the Attorney General for Northern Ireland is not to be considered a political appointee in the orthodox sense because it is a statutory requirement that his or her functions must be exercised 'independently of any other person'.[86] This is a very unique and important statutory requirement, with no analogue in the constitutional arrangements for other members of the UK law officer regime. The requirement is not to be construed as something akin to a judicial review ouster clause, however, as it is intended, rather, to prevent any member of the Northern Ireland Executive or indeed the Assembly from influencing the Attorney General for Northern Ireland in the exercise of *any* of his or her functions to further a particular political cause.[87] The provision thus

[78] Justice (Northern Ireland) Act 2002, s 22(2). There is no legislative involvement in the procedure for appointing the Attorney General for Northern Ireland but there is precedent for a voluntary 'swearing in' ceremony before the Lord Chief Justice of Northern Ireland at the Royal Courts of Justice in Belfast. See: '"Well-qualified" Attorney General is Sworn In' (*Belfast News Letter*, 9 June 2010). Available at: www.newsletter.co.uk/news/well-qualified-attorney-general-is-sworn-in-1-1848319; 'Northern Ireland's New Attorney General Brenda King Sworn In at Belfast's Royal Courts of Justice' (*Belfast Telegraph*, 18 August 2020). Available at: www.belfasttelegraph.co.uk/news/courts/northern-irelands-new-attorney-general-brenda-king-sworn-in-at-belfasts-royal-courts-of-justice-39459371.html. Moreover, as noted in ch 1 at 6, it was made possible for a UK minister to perform this appointment function during the political impasse at the devolved level between 2017 and 2020: Northern Ireland (Executive Formation and Exercise of Functions) Act 2018, s 5, as amended by the Northern Ireland (Ministerial Appointment Functions) Regulations 2019.

[79] See ch 5 at 120 and ch 7 at 180–183.

[80] Justice (Northern Ireland) Act 2002, s 23(2).

[81] Justice (Northern Ireland) Act 2002, s 24.

[82] Justice (Northern Ireland) Act 2002, ss 26(1)–(2).

[83] Justice (Northern Ireland) Act 2002, ss 26(3)–(4).

[84] Justice (Northern Ireland) Act 2002, s 26(5).

[85] Justice (Northern Ireland) Act 2002, s 26(6).

[86] Justice (Northern Ireland) Act 2002, s 22(5).

[87] Conor McCormick, 'Reviewing the Reviewability of the Attorney General for Northern Ireland' [2018] *Public Law* 22, 29.

provides authority for an extremely strong conception of independence in the discharge of all functions vested in the office of the Attorney General for Northern Ireland, which of course differs from the Attorney General and Solicitor General for England and Wales, for example, who can carry out various official functions in accordance with government policy and in light of legitimate consultation with their ministerial colleagues and others. The office itself has stated that it 'has an arm's length relationship with the Executive Office' in order to 'guarantee the independence of the Attorney'.[88] It is noteworthy, therefore, that the form of independence provided for by the 2002 Act has been said to reflect 'a view about the nature of the office that need not, as devolved Government [in Northern Ireland] develops, remain immutable or unreflecting of changed conditions'.[89] This book will return to some of the conceptual complexities underlying these statements later.

While the Attorney General for Northern Ireland cannot be elected to, or be a member of, a district council,[90] the House of Commons,[91] or the Northern Ireland Assembly,[92] a 'modicum of political accountability'[93] is said to exist in so far as he or she may participate in proceedings of the Assembly to the extent permitted by its Standing Orders (while being forbidden from voting in its proceedings under any circumstances).[94] These statutory bars on *membership and voting rights* in the devolved legislature represent another genuine distinction between the constitution of the Attorney General for Northern Ireland and its comparators in the UK law officer regime (though voting rights are, of course, statutorily curtailed in the event of unelected Counsels General, Lord Advocates and Solicitors General for Scotland). Moreover, and also in contrast to other members of the UK law officer regime, the Attorney General for Northern Ireland is not yet regulated by the Standing Orders of the Northern Ireland Assembly in relation to legislative participation rights. While some delay in the drafting of these provisions was to be expected on account of the unique statutory bar on membership of the legislature mentioned above, which clearly calls for a bespoke set of participatory rules, it could be argued that the length of time which has now passed without any

[88] Attorney General for Northern Ireland, 'Solicitor Trainee Scheme' (6 June 2018), 2. Available at: www.attorneygeneralni.gov.uk/sites/ag/files/AGNI18042%202018%20Trainee%20Solicitor%20Terms%20%26%20Conditions%20%28Revised%29.pdf. Note that the Executive Office is the new name for what used to be the Office of the First Minister and deputy First Minister. See the Departments Act (Northern Ireland) 2016, s 1(1).

[89] Attorney General for Northern Ireland, 'Sixth Annual Report – 2015/16', 1. Available at: www.attorneygeneralni.gov.uk/sites/ag/files/media-files/AGNI%20Annual%20Report%202015-16_0.pdf.

[90] Justice (Northern Ireland) Act 2002, s 23(8).

[91] House of Commons Disqualification Act 1975, Sch 1, as amended by the Justice (Northern Ireland) Act 2002, s 23(6).

[92] Northern Ireland Assembly Disqualification Act 1975, Sch 1, as amended by the Justice (Northern Ireland) Act 2002, s 23(7).

[93] Seamus Mulholland, 'An Interview with the Attorney General for Northern Ireland' [2010] *The Verdict* 5, 6.

[94] Justice (Northern Ireland) Act 2002, s 25(1).

progress on the matter has normalised low expectations of accountability over the office to some extent.

The Committee of Procedures only reported findings from the first part of its inquiry into the appropriate level of participation to be made permissible by Standing Orders in 2015,[95] which was subsequently approved by the Assembly but is as yet unimplemented.[96] In the report on the first part of its inquiry, the committee decided that it would not be appropriate to apply the requirements of the Assembly's Code of Conduct to the Attorney General for Northern Ireland.[97] The committee did, however, recommend that a distinct Standing Order be drafted to provide for the registration and declaration of interests and the prohibition of paid lobbying by the Attorney General for Northern Ireland, inter alia, in accordance with the requirements of section 25(4) of the Justice (Northern Ireland) Act 2002 (which stipulates that section 43 of the Northern Ireland Act 1998, on the registration and declaration of interests by Members of the Legislative Assembly, also applies to the Attorney General for Northern Ireland).[98]

Moreover, the committee considered a range of options for enhancing parliamentary accountability over the Attorney General for Northern Ireland in respect of three business areas. In respect of the first two business areas – which dealt with the potential for the Attorney to answer oral and written Assembly questions on a general basis, and accountability arrangements over the ability of the Attorney to refer Assembly Bills to the UK Supreme Court after reaching their Final Stage – the committee decided not to recommend any amendment to Standing Orders.[99] It reached that decision out of recognition towards some risks posed by over-formalisation and because of the existing ability of Assembly Committees to call upon the Attorney General for Northern Ireland in relation to those matters where necessary.[100] In respect of the third business area – namely the statutory requirement to produce an annual report – the committee decided it would be beneficial to codify a process whereby the Attorney General can attend a nominated Assembly Committee at its request to answer questions about the content of an annual report.[101] A fourth business area where greater accountability might have been possible was also considered as part of the committee's inquiry – namely the power of the Attorney to lay two types of statutory rule before the Assembly in relation to human rights guidance,[102] which will be considered further below – but

[95] Committee on Procedures, *Inquiry into the extent to which Standing Orders should permit the Attorney General for Northern Ireland to participate in proceedings of the Assembly: Part 1 – Impartiality of the Office of AGNI, Registration of Interests and Participation of the AGNI in Assembly Proceedings in respect of areas other than Statutory Rules* (NIA 232/11-16, 24 February 2015).

[96] NIA (Official Report), 16 March 2015, vol 103, no 3, 13.

[97] Committee on Procedures (n 95) para 32.

[98] ibid para 31.

[99] ibid paras 64–90.

[100] ibid.

[101] ibid paras 91–101.

[102] The first type of statutory rule the Attorney General for Northern Ireland can lay brings human rights guidance produced by the Attorney into force subject only to the negative resolution procedure

it decided to publish its recommendations about this matter in a second part to its report.[103] While the committee planned to publish part two of its report in May 2016,[104] it did not do so. As noted above, however, none of the recommendations requiring positive action in part one of the committee's report appear to have been implemented yet in any event.

Significantly, the Justice (Northern Ireland) Act 2002 provides that the Attorney General for Northern Ireland may decline to respond to any Assembly requests relating to the operation of the system of prosecution of offences in any particular case which could, in his or her view, prejudice criminal proceedings or which are otherwise against the public interest.[105] This statutory restriction on political accountability applies in respect of both the functions of the Attorney General for Northern Ireland and those discharged by the DPP.[106] It is notable that the DPP is vested with responsibility for making decisions on whether to refer unduly lenient sentences to the Court of Appeal, rather than the Attorney General for Northern Ireland, which is another genuine difference between the arrangements that pertain in England and Wales.[107]

The Attorney General for Northern Ireland is generally accountable for the actions of the DPP because it is he or she who is responsible for appointing the Director;[108] it is he or she who has power to convene a tribunal to consider whether the Director should be removed from office;[109] and it is he or she who has power to suspend the Director from office should a tribunal convened to consider his or her removal recommend it.[110] Apart from a variety of consultative powers,[111] and the requirement that he or she must lay annual reports prepared by the Director before the Assembly,[112] supervision by the Attorney General for Northern Ireland over the DPP effectively stops there. The Attorney General does not have any power to direct or superintend the work of the DPP in keeping with the recommendations of the Criminal Justice Review. The Department of Justice for Northern Ireland conducted a consultation in 2012 reviewing this arrangement,[113] but no

of the Assembly, whereas the second type of rule the Attorney General for Northern Ireland can lay amends the list of organisations to which this human rights guidance may apply subject to the higher requirements of the draft affirmative procedure. The relevant statutory provisions are detailed below.

[103] Committee on Procedures (n 95) para 19.

[104] ibid.

[105] Justice (Northern Ireland) Act 2002, s 25(3).

[106] Assembly and Executive Review Committee, *Second Report on Arrangements for the Devolution of Policing and Justice Matters Volume Two* (NIA 42/09/10R, 25 February 2010) para 3552.

[107] Criminal Justice Act 1988, s 36, as amended by the Justice (Northern Ireland) Act 2002, s 41(5). For a reported example, see: *R v Marcus (DPP's Reference – No 1 of 2013)* [2015] NIJB, [2013] NICA 73.

[108] Justice (Northern Ireland) Act 2002, s 30(1).

[109] Justice (Northern Ireland) Act 2002, s 43(2)(a).

[110] Justice (Northern Ireland) Act 2002, s 43(2)(b).

[111] The Justice (Northern Ireland) Act 2002, s 42(3), in particular, provides that the Attorney General for Northern Ireland and the Director of Public Prosecutions for Northern Ireland may from time to time consult each other on any matter for which the Attorney is accountable to the Assembly.

[112] Justice (Northern Ireland) Act 2002, s 42(6).

[113] Department of Justice, *Governance and Accountability of the Public Prosecution Service* (8 February 2012).

report has been published since because 'no decision was taken on foot of the consultation'.[114]

Pursuant to a Joint Declaration by the British and Irish Governments in April 2003 which, among other things, promised to 'make further provision to promote a human rights culture in the criminal justice system in Northern Ireland',[115] another unique statutory provision emanated from Westminster in the form of section 8 of the Justice (Northern Ireland) Act 2004, for which there is no known parallel in the world.[116] It conferred on the Attorney General for Northern Ireland a power to issue human rights guidance to criminal justice organisations in Northern Ireland from time to time, after consultation with the Advocate General for Northern Ireland,[117] 'in a manner consistent with international human rights standards relevant to the criminal justice system'.[118] The meaning of the word 'international' used in this context was lambasted by several parliamentarians during the passage of the Bill, perhaps most notably by Dominic Grieve (who would later become Attorney General for England and Wales). He said:

> I have simply no idea what such standards may be. They are infinitely flexible, they may change, and they are not subject to any legislation passed by this Parliament: they are meaningless. The human rights standards that this Parliament has chosen to apply, before the incorporation of the Human Rights Act, could be referred to by reference to the human rights convention, to which we are a signatory, and must now be derived from the Act. I would hope that the Human Rights Act is seen to be compatible with nebulous international human rights standards. However, the insertion of the word 'international' is meaningless. It is gobbledegook.[119]

Despite these protestations, an amendment tabled by Grieve to delete the word 'international' did not pass,[120] so it duly made its way into section 8(1) of the enacted legislation. A different critical perspective on this provision during the passage of the Bill called it 'a curious and convoluted formulation' which called for 'doubts over the genuine commitment of the Government to the application of international human rights standards' in Northern Ireland.[121]

The Justice (Northern Ireland) Act 2004 now provides that new guidance comes into effect only after having been published, laid before the Assembly subject to the negative resolution procedure, and commenced by an order provided by the Attorney General for Northern Ireland.[122] The organisations to

[114] Email to author from the Freedom of Information Manager for the Department of Justice for Northern Ireland (17 September 2018).

[115] Joint Declaration by the British and Irish Governments (April 2003) para 24.

[116] Ray McCaffrey, 'Speaking Rights of Attorneys General/Law Officers in Legislatures' (NIAR Briefing Paper 154-13, 19 February 2013) 2.

[117] Justice (Northern Ireland) Act 2004, s 8(1A).

[118] Justice (Northern Ireland) Act 2004, s 8(1).

[119] Standing Committee D, *Justice (Northern Ireland) Bill* (HC 2004) col 91.

[120] ibid col 94.

[121] Clare Fox, 'New Hope for the Criminal Justice Review? A Commentary on the Implementation Process' (2003) 54 *Northern Ireland Legal Quarterly* 437, 445.

[122] Justice (Northern Ireland) Act 2004, s 8(3).

which the guidance applies, which are listed in section 8(4),[123] are required to 'have regard to' it;[124] a provision which does not alter the effect of the obligations on all UK public authorities to act compatibly with human rights incorporated by the Human Rights Act 1998.[125] It has been suggested that so long as 'an organisation can demonstrate that they have made their employees aware of the guidance, whether or not they have adopted it fully, this may act as a *defence* and may make it *easier* for public authorities to withstand legal challenges'.[126] On the other hand, it has also been suggested that 'the guidance could potentially be used to supplement legal challenges against criminal justice organisations should they fail to have "regard to"' it.[127] Further research could usefully investigate the extent to which the guidance is indeed followed by the organisations to which it applies and whether the 'shall have regard to' requirement is thereby satisfied in practice. Research on the extent to which the obligations imposed by the guidance have been cited to courts would also be a useful exercise because, while at present the existence of the guidance is certainly evidence of 'the spread of a discourse of human rights as part of the transitional process',[128] both its practical salience and legal impact are unknown.[129] As Harvey puts it, mere *awareness* of a human rights discourse 'does not mean that implementation is effective, consistent or satisfactory'.[130]

The Attorney General for Northern Ireland may by an order which has been subjected to the draft affirmative procedure of the Assembly amend the list of organisations to which his or her guidance may apply by adding to it, omitting an existing organisation from it, or changing a description used in it,[131] after having

[123] Justice (Northern Ireland) Act 2004, s 8(4), as amended by the Justice (Northern Ireland) Act 2004 (Amendment of section 8(4)) Order (Northern Ireland) 2015.

[124] Justice (Northern Ireland) Act 2004, s 8(2).

[125] Human Rights Act 1998, s 6; Justice (Northern Ireland) Act 2004, s 8(2).

[126] James Fraser, 'Section 8 "Human Rights" Guidance and its Relevance to Practitioners' (2014) 222 *The Writ – The Journal of the Law Society of Northern Ireland* 10, 10. Emphasis in original.

[127] ibid.

[128] Colin Harvey, 'Bringing Humanity Home: A Transformational Human Rights Culture for Northern Ireland?' in Anne-Marie McAlinden and Clare Dwyer (eds), *Criminal Justice in Transition: The Northern Ireland Context* (Hart Publishing 2015) 56.

[129] To take one example demonstrating some form of impact, the Court of Appeal in Northern Ireland recently recognised the applicability of human rights guidance issued by the Attorney General for Northern Ireland to the Public Prosecution Service in the context of a challenge to the DPP by way of judicial review proceedings. The challenge was directed at a decision of the former DPP not to prosecute a soldier for the killing of the applicant's brother and was supported by reference to, inter alia, guidance issued by the Attorney General for Northern Ireland. The applicant submitted that the guidance conveyed an enhanced requirement to bring persons suspected of such serious human rights violations to justice and an enhanced duty to give reasons where a decision not prosecute has been taken in circumstances involving deaths caused by a state actor. It was argued that the DPP had acted other than in accordance with this guidance and had thereby acted unlawfully. The Court of Appeal allowed the application, but its judgment did not engage specifically with these grounds for review in reaching that conclusion. See: *Re Margaret Brady's Application* [2018] NICA 20 [26]; [37]–[39].

[130] Harvey (n 128) 55.

[131] Justice (Northern Ireland) Act 2004, s 8(5)(a)–(c) and s 21(2). The PSNI is the only organisation thus far to have been added to the list in s 8(4), by the Justice (Northern Ireland) Act 2004 (Amendment of section 8(4)) Order (Northern Ireland) 2015. The amendment was met with some criticism by members of the Northern Ireland Assembly who concurred with objections from the Police Service of

consulted the Advocate General for Northern Ireland.[132] Nothing in the guidance which conflicts with a provision in the Code of Practice for the Public Prosecution Service issued by the DPP under section 37 of the Justice (Northern Ireland) Act 2002 must be followed,[133] though a conflict is thought to be highly unlikely.[134] There is no similar provision in respect of potential conflicts with the Code of Ethics for the Police Service of Northern Ireland issued by the Policing Board under section 52 of the Police (Northern Ireland) Act 2000. This difference could be criticised for creating duplicative and potentially conflicting reference points for the police service.

Since 2010, the office of the Attorney General for Northern Ireland has issued 15 guidance documents under the Justice (Northern Ireland) Act 2004.[135] The Attorney General for England and Wales qua the Attorney General for Northern Ireland did not make use of the power between its creation in 2004 and the re-instatement of a local Attorney General in 2010. The first guidance document was issued on a general basis to all the criminal justice organisations then listed under section 8(4).[136] This set out practical measures required of the duty to protect the lives of their employees from the immediate and known risks to

Northern Ireland and the Policing Board Performance Committee, both of whom indicated existing obligations which the police are obliged to have regard to through a human rights focused Code of Ethics under the Police (Northern Ireland) Act 2000, s 52, in addition to further oversight mechanisms provided by the Northern Ireland Human Rights Commission and the Surveillance Commissioner. See, e.g., NIA (Official Report), 16 March 2015, vol 103, no 3, 8.

[132] Justice (Northern Ireland) Act 2004, s 8(5A).

[133] Justice (Northern Ireland) Act 2004, s 8(8).

[134] HL Deb 19 January 2004, vol 657, col 873.

[135] The Attorney General's Human Rights Guidance (Protection of Life) Order (Northern Ireland) 2013; the Attorney General's Human Rights Guidance (Forensic Science Northern Ireland) Order (Northern Ireland) 2013; the Attorney General's Human Rights Guidance (State Pathologist's Department) Order (Northern Ireland) 2013; the Attorney General's Human Rights Guidance (Public Prosecution Service for Northern Ireland) Order (Northern Ireland) 2014; the Attorney General's Human Rights Guidance (Northern Ireland Prison Service – Conditions of Imprisonment) Order (Northern Ireland) 2014; the Attorney General's Human Rights Guidance (Northern Ireland Prison Service – Prison Order and Discipline) Order (Northern Ireland) 2014; the Attorney General's Human Rights Guidance (Northern Ireland Courts and Tribunals Service – Support for Victims and Witnesses) Order (Northern Ireland) 2014; the Attorney General's Human Rights Guidance (Youth Justice Agency – Conditions of Detention) Order (Northern Ireland) 2015; the Attorney General's Human Rights Guidance (Probation Board for Northern Ireland) Order (Northern Ireland) 2015; the Attorney General's Human Rights Guidance (Police Service of Northern Ireland – Protection of Life) Order (Northern Ireland) 2015; the Attorney General's Human Rights Guidance (Youth Justice Agency – Restorative Justice) Order (Northern Ireland) 2015; the Attorney General's Human Rights Guidance (Cooperation and Operational Independence) Order (Northern Ireland) 2016; the Attorney General's Human Rights Guidance (Domestic Abuse and Stalking) Order (Northern Ireland) 2018; the Attorney General's Human Rights Guidance (The Application of Section 5 of the Criminal Law Act (Northern Ireland) 1967 to Rape Victims and Those to Whom They Make Disclosures in Connection With a Claim for Social Security, Child Tax Credit or Anonymous Registration on the Electoral Roll) Order (Northern Ireland) 2018; the Attorney General's Human Rights Guidance (The Use of the Irish Language) Order (Northern Ireland) 2019.

[136] Attorney General's Human Rights Guidance No 1, 'Human Rights Standards Relevant to the Right to Life' (*Office of the Attorney General for Northern Ireland*, 22 March 2013). Available at: www.attorneygeneralni.gov.uk/sites/ag/files/guidance-on-human-rights-protection-of-the-right-to-life.pdf and

which they are exposed.[137] Since then, most documents have been addressed to one organisation at a time in respect of particularised issues. Some listed organisations, such as the Youth Justice Agency, have been individually addressed by more than one guidance document, whereas the Compensation Agency has not been individually addressed as yet. In general, the guidance that has been issued draws on a broad range of sources of international human rights law, which are said to 'encapsulate the international consensus on human rights standards',[138] including many which are otherwise non-binding in domestic law.[139]

There are no published analyses on the content of the guidance documents that assess the extent to which they cover relevant jurisprudence or, in other words, confirming that the standards set out are not cherry-picked from the available sources to avoid reference to particularly onerous or ideologically undesirable duties. Likewise, although the documents state that they are revisited on an annual basis, the extent to which they are properly scrutinised to ensure that they remain in keeping with recent developments in international human rights law is unclear. The need to perform such tasks in the interests of accountability is reflective of the difficulties inherent in the framework at use, which obliges the Attorney General for Northern Ireland to keep abreast of international human rights law developments and to mediate those 'living' standards to the organisations prescribed by way of a non-political executive power, in lieu of simply scheduling the applicable sources of law to the Justice (Northern Ireland) Act 2004. Incorporating the relevant international standards into domestic law, even if the extent of that incorporation was restricted in its application to the practices of criminal justice organisations in Northern Ireland, would surely have been a constitutionally simpler way of meeting the promises made in the Joint Declaration by the British and Irish Governments in April 2003. However, that is not to say that it would necessarily have been more or less effective. It could indeed be argued that the

given effect by the Attorney General's Human Rights Guidance (Protection of Life) Order (Northern Ireland) 2013. The Police Service for Northern Ireland was not a listed organisation when this guidance was first issued.

[137] ibid.

[138] Fraser (n 126).

[139] See, e.g., the Attorney General's Human Rights Guidance No 2, 'Human Rights Guidance for Forensic Science Northern Ireland' (*Office of the Attorney General for Northern Ireland*, 8 May 2013). Available at www.attorneygeneralni.gov.uk/sites/ag/files/human-rights-guidance-for-fsni.pdf and given effect by the Attorney General's Human Rights Guidance (Forensic Science Northern Ireland) Order (Northern Ireland) 2013, which is explicitly based on the following sources: the European Convention for the Protection of Human Rights and Fundamental Freedoms; the International Covenant on Civil and Political Rights; the Council of Europe Convention for the Protection of Individuals with regard to Automatic Processing of Personal Data; the Council of Europe Committee of Ministers Recommendation No R (87) 15 Regulating the Use of Personal Data in the Police Sector; the Council of Europe Committee of Ministers Recommendation No R (92) 1 on the Use of Analysis of Deoxyribonucleic Acid (DNA) within the Framework of the Criminal Justice System; the Council of Europe Committee of Ministers Recommendation No R (99) 3 on the Harmonisation of Medico-Legal Autopsy Rules, and the United Nations Convention on the Rights of the Child.

approach of the 2004 Act conforms to Harlow's 'collaborative model of coordinate construction' in relation to human rights issues, which advocates greater use of institutional 'bridges' between parliament, the judiciary and supranational bodies.[140] While Harlow refers to the 'two-way legislative and judicial focus' of the Joint Committee on Human Rights in this regard,[141] it could be argued that the human rights function of the Attorney General for Northern Ireland falls approximately within the same normative framework.

With that said, the weak accountability over these powers did attract some attention in reaction to a speech made by John Larkin QC shortly after he first assumed the office of Attorney General for Northern Ireland in 2010. Larkin remarked in his speech that the idea of human rights is 'inescapably ambiguous' and that condemnation should not necessarily follow State actions which fall short of '(capital letters) International Human Rights Standards', but rather standards which successfully express 'truths about the dignity of human beings'.[142] Local human rights campaigners highlighted that this candid philosophical position was difficult to reconcile with the Attorney General's statutory duty to devise guidance based on international jurisprudence and therefore called for statutory clarification of the duty.[143] Should these statutory provisions ever be revisited, some consideration could also be given to expanding the list of public authorities to whom the Attorney General can address his or her guidance. As a matter of principle, there is little justification for limiting the potential reach of the guidance documents to criminal justice organisations only. It would perhaps be more prudent, for instance, to either cross-refer to the public authorities who are so designated by section 75 of the Northern Ireland Act 1998 (and the orders thereunder) or to replicate the wording of section 75(3) in any amending legislation that might be brought forward.

Non-Statutory Scaffolding

The statutory provisions in the Justice (Northern Ireland) Act 2002 on the establishment of a local Attorney General for Northern Ireland were conditional upon the devolution of policing and justice functions to Northern Ireland, which

[140] Carol Harlow, 'The Human Rights Act and "Coordinate Construction": Towards a "Parliament Square" Axis for Human Rights?' in NW Barber, Richard Ekins and Paul Yowell (eds), *Lord Sumption and the Limits of Law* (Hart Publishing 2016) 153–174.

[141] ibid 174.

[142] John Larkin, 'Speech at a Conference of the Northern Ireland Human Rights Commission on 16 September 2010', as cited in the Committee on the Administration of Justice's *Commentary on the 'Inquiry into how the Attorney General for Northern Ireland will Participate in Proceedings of the Northern Ireland Assembly* (CAJ Submission No 268, October 2010), 4. Available at: www.caj.org.uk/files/2010/11/01/s._268_Inq_into_how_Attorney_General_NI_will_participate_NIA,_Oct_2010_.pdf.

[143] ibid.

proved to be a protracted process. The St Andrews Agreement of 2006 aimed to catalyse the process, setting a May 2008 deadline for the devolution of relevant competences.[144] Unfortunately, due to continued political disagreements, that deadline passed without a settlement for the way forward being reached. After further negotiations,[145] a date for the devolution of competences was finally agreed in the Hillsborough Agreement of 2010 which, after almost four decades of direct rule over the matters concerned, took effect on 12 April 2010.[146]

During this long period, significant preparations for the expected swearing in of the remodelled Attorney General for Northern Ireland took place. Initially, following a restoration of the Northern Ireland Assembly in 2007, there was an inquiry into the devolution of policing and justice by a Review Committee.[147] During that inquiry, evidence was heard from Northern Ireland Civil Service officials, including representation from the Departmental Solicitor's Office, who assured the committee that 'robust programme management arrangements' had been established which would ensure 'a smooth transfer of powers in whatever form and timescale' agreed by the Assembly.[148] This evidence included a general overview of existing statutory provisions in respect of the Attorney General for Northern Ireland, as well as the following speculative comments in relation to his or her non-statutory functions:

> A raft of functions relating to the Attorney General's non-statutory role in defending the public interest in matters relating to civil law will pass across, because they are carried out currently by the Attorney General for England and Wales. In Northern Ireland, such roles will be carried out by the new Attorney General. However, that is not set in statute though custom and precedent have established that the Attorney General has a role with regard to vexatious litigants on contempt of court proceedings and the appointment of amici curiae in courts, and will continue to have that … The Attorney General might also be given a range of functions by extrapolation from the work that is done by the Attorney Generals in London and Dublin and the Lord Advocate in Scotland – providing legal advice to the Executive, for instance. However, that is not laid down in statute, so it would be for the First Minister and deputy First Minister to decide.[149]

There do not appear to have been any objections by the Review Committee to the proposal that the Attorney General for Northern Ireland would automatically

[144] Gordon Anthony, 'The St Andrews Agreement and the Northern Ireland Assembly' (2008) 14 *European Public Law* 151, 162.

[145] Gordon Anthony, 'The Devolution of Policing and Criminal Justice' (2011) 17 *European Public Law* 197, 200.

[146] Northern Ireland Act 1998 (Amendment of Schedule 3) Order 2010; Northern Ireland Act 1998 (Devolution of Policing and Justice Functions) Order 2010; Northern Ireland Court Service (Abolition and Transfer of Functions) Order (Northern Ireland) 2010.

[147] Assembly and Executive Review Committee, *First Report on the Inquiry into the Devolution of Policing and Justice Matters: Volume 1 – Minutes of Proceedings Relating to the Report, Minutes of Evidence, Papers from the NIO* (NIA 22/07/08R, 26 February 2008).

[148] ibid para 2070.

[149] ibid paras 2101–2102.

inherit the non-statutory functions then exercised by the Attorney General for England and Wales. This is perhaps an indication of the constitutional conservationism which characterised the processes establishing some functions of the new Attorney General for Northern Ireland, in that early opportunities to fully consider how the office could be devised to suit the specific needs of Northern Ireland may have been overlooked.[150] It is also notable from the quotation above that the spokesperson for the Departmental Solicitor's Office confused and misrepresented some functions of the Attorney General for England and Wales to the Review Committee by conflating separate powers in relation to vexatious litigants and proceedings for contempt of court, and by referring to both of them as non-statutory functions.

In a report published in February 2008, the Review Committee acknowledged that arranging an appointment to the post of Attorney General for Northern Ireland was a matter for the First and deputy First Ministers and, having noted that 'no preparatory work had been done in this regard', recommended that such preparations should be taken forward by the First and deputy First Ministers before the devolution of policing and justice matters.[151] It further recommended that the post of Attorney General for Northern Ireland should be a full-time role, at least initially.[152] Its comments on potential governance issues associated with the office of the Attorney General for Northern Ireland included 'the extent of the role and the relationship with, and reporting arrangements to, the Assembly'.[153] It also expressed agreement with the Attorney General's proposed answerability to the Assembly on matters of prosecution policy.[154]

Further to internal political discussions, the First and deputy First Ministers eventually revealed to the Review Committee in November 2008 that it was 'minded that John Larkin QC be invited to become Attorney General'.[155] At the start of 2009, Larkin was then commissioned 'to carry out preparatory work' to establish the office of Attorney General for Northern Ireland and 'to prepare an initial work programme covering the key areas as identified in anticipation of the substantive appointment' upon devolution.[156] Perhaps because this important scoping project

[150] For a critical discussion of some problems arising from this approach to constitutionalism in Northern Ireland, see: John Morison and Stephen Livingstone, *Reshaping Public Power: Northern Ireland and the British Constitutional Crisis* (Sweet & Maxwell 1995) ch 3.

[151] Assembly and Executive Review Committee, NIA 22/07/08R (n 147) para 38.

[152] ibid.

[153] ibid para 44.

[154] ibid.

[155] Assembly and Executive Review Committee, *First Report on the Arrangements for the Devolution of Policing and Justice Matters Together with the Minutes of Proceedings of the Committee Relating to the Report, the Minutes of Evidence and Other Relevant Documents* (6 January 2009, NIA 22/08/09R), Appendix 5, 'Letter from the First Minister and deputy First Minister – 18 November 2008'.

[156] John Larkin, 'Establishing the Office of the Attorney General for Northern Ireland' (August 2009); Office of the First Minister and deputy First Minister, 'Response to the Recommendations on the Report by John Larkin QC on Establishing the Office of the Attorney General for Northern Ireland' (23 March 2010). The author obtained these documents by way of a request to the Office of the First

was, in a 'soft law' sense,[157] as formative of the office as its statutory underpinnings, the Review Committee made concerted efforts to discover its recommendations in order to inform their reporting duties.[158] Its requests to see Larkin's report of August 2009 were at first refused, which did not augur well alongside some of the Committee's concerns about the peculiarity of engaging 'an individual to write his or her own terms of reference',[159] as were its initial invitations for Larkin himself to appear before the Review Committee to answer their questions.[160] One Review Committee member, Alex Atwood, expressed the importance of its inspection in the following words:

> The document concerns the role of the office and the architecture around it, as far as I can conclude from what people have been saying. I do not understand why that document cannot be shared. Knowing what it says does not commit anyone to anything. We are being frustrated from doing our job. Whatever the politics may be in respect of the devolution of justice, we are being frustrated from making the appropriate arrangements, which is part of our mandate. I am exasperated. The document could have been released … without prejudice. We have a duty to try to move these matters forward.[161]

The First and deputy First Ministers subsequently appeared before the Review Committee and, informed by Larkin's report, summarised their conceptions of the expected functions of the Attorney General for Northern Ireland. They explained that they were still considering the report and believed it would be best read in conjunction with their response to its recommendations.[162] Both documents were ultimately provided to the Review Committee in March 2010.[163]

It transpired that the First and deputy First Ministers agreed with most, but not all, of the recommendations made in Larkin's report. Primarily, it was confirmed that the Attorney General for Northern Ireland would assume the non-statutory function of principal legal adviser to the Northern Ireland Executive.[164] Larkin recommended that a very particularised set of circumstances where that advice ought to be sought should be prescribed,[165] but a simpler formulation was favoured by the First and deputy First Ministers (namely that 'it would be appropriate to seek the advice of the Attorney General on the most important and complex legal

Minister and deputy First Minister in April 2016 (before it was renamed the Executive Office by the Departments Act (Northern Ireland) 2016, s 1(1)).

157 See: Greg Weeks, *Soft Law and Public Authorities: Remedies and Reform* (Hart Publishing 2016) ch 1.

158 Assembly and Executive Review Committee, *Second Report on the Arrangements for the Devolution of Policing and Justice Matters: Volume 2 – Together with the Minutes of Proceedings of the Committee Relating to the Report, the Minutes of Evidence and Other Relevant Documents* (NIA 42/09/10R, 25 February 2010).

159 ibid para 2581.

160 ibid paras 3164–3166; 3188–3191. Larkin later offered to brief the Committee, see: ibid para 3204.

161 ibid para 3201.

162 ibid paras 3551–3555.

163 Larkin (n 156).

164 ibid 2.

165 ibid 8.

matters facing the Executive and Ministers'[166]). In relation to the various functions connected to that role, the First and deputy First Ministers did not substantively depart from Larkin's recommendations. Thus, it was agreed that:

(a) the advice of the Attorney General would normally be sought via a reference from the Departmental Solicitor's Office;
(b) regular 'stocktake' meetings between the Attorney General and the Departmental Solicitor's Office would take place;
(c) principles of 'openness, excellence and engagement' would underlie the ethos of the office;
(d) the Attorney General would be entitled to attend all Executive meetings (but it would not be necessary for him or her to always do so);
(e) draft Executive papers would be copied to the Attorney General at the same time as they are first circulated by originating ministers;
(f) the Attorney General should be entitled to attend pre-Executive meetings;
(g) the advice of the Attorney General would normally be shared across all Executive departments unless the Attorney General decides otherwise;
(h) the release of advice by the Attorney General outside the departments of the Executive, or any indication that advice has been sought, should require the permission of the Attorney General;[167]
(i) the office of the Attorney General should lead in litigation arising from matters on which its advice has been provided;
(j) the office of the Attorney General should take responsibility for government civil panels;
(k) the Departmental Solicitor's Office will normally provide solicitor services for litigation to the Attorney General;
(l) in order to fulfil his or her implicit duties with regard to devolution issues, the Attorney General should be provided with the advice given to ministers by the Departmental Solicitor's Office on questions of competence with regard to certification of the Assembly's authority to make the proposed legislation;
(m) ministerial correspondence on legislation is copied to the office of the Attorney General; and
(n) the Attorney General would have oversight of all departmental legal advisers, entitling him or her to see legal advice provided by the Departmental Solicitor's Office.[168]

[166] Office of the First Minister and deputy First Minister Larkin (n 156) para 34.

[167] Larkin's report attached much importance to this provision, noting that given the nature of the Northern Ireland Executive as a mandatory coalition, 'it would be wrong for advice which is provided to the Executive to be released on the decision of one Minister'. See: Larkin (n 156) 12. This, of course, parallels the conventions which apply across the UK law officer regime, and in particular that which appears to apply in Wales (given that there does not appear to be any need for consent on the part of the advice recipient in that context either).

[168] Larkin (n 156) 7–16; Office of the First Minister and deputy First Minister (n 156) paras 36–64.

It was also agreed that, instead of incorporating these arrangements into the Ministerial Code, by which ministers are now bound,[169] they would be published in the form of procedural guidance approved by the Executive.[170] Larkin's report stated that this 'would carry the necessary weight' – signifying that the more formal option of Ministerial Code amendment was not considered desirable. The status of the relevant constitutional document covering these functions is therefore genuinely different from that used elsewhere in the UK law officer regime (though the Ministerial Codes applicable in other UK jurisdictions do not apply with the force of statute, of course, as is the case in Northern Ireland). Moreover, the First and deputy First Ministers diverged from an aspect of Larkin's report in connection with the relevant document in so far as Larkin recommended that the procedural guidance should include an indication that it was expected that legal advice provided by the office of the Attorney General for Northern Ireland would be followed.[171] Instead of 'making this implicit principle explicit',[172] the First and deputy First Ministers carefully stated that while such advice 'would normally be followed', the undertaking was 'without prejudice to the ultimate decision-making responsibilities of the Executive'.[173] The First and deputy First Ministers also qualified their agreement with the proposal to establish a legal secondee in the Northern Ireland Executive Office in Brussels in the interests of identifying local implications of legislative proposals made by the EU[174] by providing that this proposal would be dependent on budgetary considerations.[175]

While Larkin's report recognised that in accordance with the Justice (Northern Ireland) Act 2002 the extent to which the Attorney General for Northern Ireland would be permitted to participate in Assembly proceedings was a matter for the Assembly itself,[176] it nonetheless suggested four areas where such participation might be considered useful,[177] with which the First and deputy First Ministers agreed.[178] The first area concerned the exercise of the Attorney General's responsibilities in relation to the Public Prosecution Service; the second area concerned issues of legislative competence; the third area concerned the general work of the General's office; and the fourth area was not so much an area but a residue option, suggesting that the Attorney General might be called upon in 'certain other circumstances', such as upon the discussion of technical legal proposals.[179]

[169] Northern Ireland Act 1998, s 28A, inserted by the Northern Ireland (St Andrews Agreement) Act 2006, s 5.

[170] Larkin (n 156) 17; Office of the First Minister and deputy First Minister (n 156) para 66.

[171] Larkin (n 156) 17; Office of the First Minister and deputy First Minister (n 156) para 67.

[172] Larkin (n 156) 17.

[173] Office of the First Minister and deputy First Minister (n 156) para 67.

[174] Larkin (n 156) 18.

[175] ibid 17–18; Office of the First Minister and deputy First Minister (n 156) para 71.

[176] Justice (Northern Ireland) Act 2002, s 25.

[177] Larkin (n 156) 20.

[178] Office of the First Minister and deputy First Minister (n 156) para 77.

[179] Larkin (n 156) 20–21.

It was further agreed that the Attorney General would be provided with a base in Parliament buildings.[180] The agreed proposals as regards Assembly participation have since, of course, been supplanted by the more detailed recommendations of the Committee on Procedures at the Assembly, as outlined above.

Arrangements as regards the relationship between the Attorney General for Northern Ireland and the Public Prosecution Service contained in Larkin's report were prefaced by remarks emphasising the importance of 'regularity of contact; sufficiency of information; and frankness of challenge', premised on the belief 'that a consultative relationship can be a challenging relationship'.[181] In order to operationalise the Attorney General's 'curious position of being accountable for something for which he is not ultimately responsible under the [Justice (Northern Ireland) Act 2002] since the Director [of Public Prosecutions] is the arbiter of policy',[182] Larkin's report recommended that a 'memorandum of understanding' be put into place immediately following devolution of justice,[183] for which a specimen was provided[184] and to which the First and deputy First Ministers agreed.[185] This arrangement has strong parallels with the framework agreements in place between the Attorney General and Solicitor for England and Wales and the prosecuting departments they are responsible for superintending,[186] though of course the content of it differs on account of the absence of superintendence on the part of the Attorney General for Northern Ireland.

Larkin's report suggested that a dedicated unit should be established within the office of the Attorney General for Northern Ireland to develop human rights guidance under section 8 of the Justice (Northern Ireland) Act 2004,[187] but the First and deputy First Ministers responded that this would also be dependent on budgetary considerations and the Attorney General's own prioritisation.[188] A similar caveat was applied to the First and deputy First Ministers' agreement with proposals in respect of a pedagogical role for the office of the Attorney General for Northern Ireland consonant with the Attorney General's 'inherent'[189] responsibility for the rule of law,[190] and likewise regarding the employment of an education and communications officer.[191] There was complete agreement with a proposal to have the Attorney General tied into a wider network of related post-holders in the UK, Ireland and the EU,[192] but no comment was made in respect of the proposed

[180] ibid 21; Office of the First Minister and deputy First Minister (n 156) para 79.
[181] ibid 22.
[182] ibid 19.
[183] ibid 23.
[184] ibid Annex D.
[185] Office of the First Minister and deputy First Minister (n 156) para 84.
[186] See ch 3 at 48–49.
[187] Larkin (n 156) 24.
[188] Office of the First Minister and deputy First Minister (n 156) para 89.
[189] Larkin (n 156) 4.
[190] Larkin (n 156) 26–27; Office of the First Minister and deputy First Minister (n 156) para 99.
[191] Larkin (n 156) 27; Office of the First Minister and deputy First Minister (n 156) para 100.
[192] Larkin (n 156) 27; Office of the First Minister and deputy First Minister (n 156) para 103.

development of a 'relationship of encouragement' with the Bar derived from the presumptively inherited role of the Attorney General as the titular head of that organisation.[193]

In relation to a significant catalogue of 'miscellaneous' public interest functions that were listed in Larkin's report – namely in respect of inquests; contempt of court proceedings; vexatious litigants; amici curiae;[194] and the regulation of charities[195] – the response document of the First and deputy First Ministers was silent, or at least those sections of it which have been released to the public. The functions which have passed to the Attorney General for Northern Ireland in these areas should be studied with care, however, because they differ from the equivalent provisions and practices for other members of the UK law officer regime in several respects. It was noted in Chapter 3, for example, that the Attorney General for Northern Ireland is empowered to order that an inquest be held even if a coroner has decided not to do so under the legislation that applies in Northern Ireland,[196] which differs from the (lesser) filtering power of the Attorney General and Solicitor General for England and Wales.[197] By way of a second example, moreover, it could be noted that the legislation which empowers the Attorney General for Northern Ireland to bring proceedings against vexatious litigants in the High Court or in any inferior court or tribunal in Northern Ireland does not distinguish between criminal and civil proceedings in the way that would be more precisely equivalent to the powers of the Attorney General and Solicitor General for England and Wales.[198] In addition, since coming into operation, the office of the Attorney General for Northern Ireland has been conferred with uniquely remodelled powers of this general ilk in connection with the reformed services of the Public Services Ombudsman for Northern Ireland, whereby the Ombudsman may request that the Attorney General for Northern Ireland apply to the High Court for relief where he or she has upheld a complaint of maladministration involving an injustice which is both systemic and ongoing.[199]

Larkin's report did not set out a clear vision for the presumptively inherited ability of the Attorney General for Northern Ireland to intervene in court cases

[193] Larkin (n 156) 28. The extent to which this presumptively inherited leadership role has been accepted by the Bar Council of Northern Ireland, which elects its own Chair and Vice Chair biannually, is unclear.

[194] ibid.

[195] ibid 25–26.

[196] Coroners Act (Northern Ireland) 1959, s 14. For an important (and controversial) decision about the scope of this power in the context of a stillbirth, see: *Attorney General for Northern Ireland & Siobhan Desmond v Senior Coroner for Northern Ireland* [2013] NICA 68, [2015] NI 14. For a discussion of some recent attempts to challenge decisions taken by the Attorney General for Northern Ireland under this provision, see: McCormick, 'Reviewing the Reviewability of the Attorney General for Northern Ireland' (n 87).

[197] Coroners Act 1988, s 13. See ch 3 at 64.

[198] Judicature (Northern Ireland) Act 1978, s 32. For cases where this power has been exercised, see: *Morrow v Attorney General for Northern Ireland* [2015] NICA 69; *Attorney General for Northern Ireland v Sherrie* [2018] NIQB 48. The comparable power of the Attorney General and Solicitor General for England and Wales, as noted in ch 3, can be found in the Senior Courts Act 1981, s 42.

[199] Public Services Ombudsman Act (Northern Ireland) 2016, s 54.

to notionally represent the public interest ex officio.[200] It did, however, suggest an expansive approach to the presumptively inherited ability of the Attorney General to intervene in litigation ex relatione by way of relator actions (which, it will be recalled from an analogous explanation in Chapter 3, enable the law officer to enforce a breach of the criminal law or to instigate proceedings to remedy a nuisance against the public as a whole at the request of an individual).[201] The First and deputy First Ministers agreed with its intriguing proposal 'to explore with public authorities the scope for the relator to assist them in the achievement of their strategic aims',[202] which is a revealing insight into the strategy envisaged for exercising this function in the newly devolved context.[203] Indeed, consultation exercises between government bodies and the Attorney General for Northern Ireland designate, like those embodied in this proposal, perhaps epitomise scenarios in which the potential for that 'uncertain boundary' between 'the narrow political interests of government and the wider public interest' to be conflated are to be expected.[204]

The remainder of Larkin's report dealt with questions of finance, recruitment, logistics, governance and forward work planning which are not pertinent for present purposes. What the above points arguably make clear, however, is the extent to which that report supplemented in substance the statutory functions vested in of the office of Attorney General for Northern Ireland when, on 25 May 2010, John Larkin QC was appointed as its first occupant.

Operational Developments

Since coming into being, the workings of the office of the Advocate General for Northern Ireland have proved somewhat impervious to public notice on account of its cognate nature and solely statutory portfolio, whereas the office of the Attorney General for Northern Ireland has attracted rather more attention from various quarters. Much of the work that has been carried out by the Attorney General's office is detailed in the ten annual reports which have been published

[200] For a recent case where the Attorney General for Northern Ireland intervened ex officio to make unsuccessful oral submissions arguing that existing mental health legislation should be read so as to provide the statutory basis for a deprivation of liberty on the part of a person received into guardianship, see: *X v The Official Solicitor* [2019] NI Fam 9. For a wider overview of the Attorney General's ability to influence judicial decision-making by way of court interventions, see: Brice Dickson and Conor McCormick, 'Northern Ireland Dimensions to the First Decade of the United Kingdom Supreme Court' (2020) 83 *Modern Law Review* 1133, 1157–1165.

[201] Larkin (n 156) 24–25. See ch 3 at 70–71.

[202] Larkin (n 156) 25; Office of the First Minister and deputy First Minister (n 156) para 94.

[203] For an example where, in due course, the Attorney General for Northern Ireland applied for an injunction because Belfast City Council was unable to take a case in its own name, see: *Attorney General for Northern Ireland & Belfast City Council v Campbell & Ors* [2014] NICh 28.

[204] Neil Walker, 'The Antinomies of the Law Officers' in Maurice Sunkin and Sebastian Payne (eds), *The Nature of the Crown: A Legal and Political Analysis* (Oxford University Press 1999) 150.

in accordance with the Justice (Northern Ireland) Act 2002 to date,[205] together with some published interviews with the first office-holder.[206] The following four sub-sections seek to convey a general overview of the constitutional developments which have accompanied that work.

Guardian of the Rule of Law

A particularly strong theme which has emerged in connection with the office of the Attorney General for Northern Ireland is an overarching conception of the role as a 'guardian of the rule of law'. That concept has been framed as 'chief' among the responsibilities of the Attorney General's office from the beginning of its operation and continues to be regarded as central to the role today.[207] Indeed, guardianship of the rule of law has been repeatedly described as a general responsibility which 'governs the discharge' of all the more specific duties of the office,[208] with the notional interests of the rule of law ranking higher than those of the government 'on any occasion that a conflict between them ever comes into being' according to the first office-holder.[209] This narrative appears to bolster a predominantly legal characterisation of the office consistent with the strong conception of independence imbued in it by section 22(5) of the Justice (Northern Ireland) Act 2002. Such a characterisation is reminiscent of how certain functions belonging to other members of the UK law officer regime have been framed in order to give rise to high expectations of independence during their discharge, as with the responsibility of the Counsel General for Wales to screen Assembly Bills for their compatibility with the rule of law, for example, but no office other than the Attorney General for Northern Ireland has such a fixed and universal conceptual architecture over all of its functions.[210] Moreover, even this ostensibly 'shared' convention for upholding for the rule of law in the UK is manifested in some contextually distinct ways by different members of the UK law officer regime in subtle (perhaps even trivial) respects. When asked in 2017 whether conventions as regards the referral of draft

[205] Each of these annual reports is available to download at www.attorneygeneralni.gov.uk/publications.

[206] See, e,g., 'Guardian of the Rule of Law: The Office of Attorney General for Northern Ireland' (2013) 87 *Frontline* 8–9 and 26.

[207] See e.g., Attorney General for Northern Ireland, 'First Annual Report – 2010/11' (n 78) para 3; Attorney General for Northern Ireland, 'Tenth Annual Report – 2019/20', para 2. Available at: www.attorneygeneralni.gov.uk/sites/ag/files/media-files/Attorney%20General%20for%20Northern%20Ireland%20Annual%20Report%20201920_0.pdf.

[208] ibid.

[209] Committee on Procedures, *Standing Orders in Respect of the Attorney General for Northern Ireland* (28 September 2010). Available at: http://archive.niassembly.gov.uk/record/committees2010/Procedures/100928_StandingOrdersinRespectofAttorneyGeneral.htm.

[210] Interestingly, there emerged a consensus among the Lord Advocate, Counsel General for Wales and Attorney General for Northern Ireland to the effect that they all 'shared' a responsibility to uphold the rule of law at a Constitutional Law Summer School session on 'Law Officers and the Constitution: Irish, Scottish and Welsh Perspectives' (8 August 2018, Clayton Hotel, Belfast). This was notwithstanding the substantial differences between each office, and the politically active nature of the Counsel General for Wales at the time.

legislation containing provisions with early commencement or retrospective effect which apply elsewhere in the UK also burden the Attorney General for Northern Ireland, the office-holder at that time indicated that no similarly formal conventions of this nature had yet been established in the Northern Ireland context but that similar considerations would be assessed as a 'quality of law' issue during legislative competence screening exercises.[211]

The Partial Review by Dame Elish Angiolini

On 16 April 2012, the First and deputy First Ministers finalised terms of reference for an independent review of the Attorney General for Northern Ireland's relationship with the Northern Ireland Executive and departments which involved giving consideration to certain reforms.[212] In particular, the review tasked its executor to:

(a) examine the arrangements for when the Executive and ministers seek legal advice from the Attorney General;
(b) examine and make recommendations about the disclosure of legal advice given to the Executive and departments (including ministers);
(c) examine and make recommendations about the role of the Attorney General when departments (including ministers) seek legal advice from the Departmental Solicitor's Office;
(d) make recommendations concerning the respective roles of the office of the Attorney General and the Departmental Solicitor's Office in relation to their dealings with the Executive and ministers; and
(e) examine and make recommendations about any tensions between the Attorney General's role as chief legal advisor to the Executive and his statutory responsibilities, including under Schedule 10 to the Northern Ireland Act 1998.[213]

These terms of reference for the report make it clear that its remit was mostly concerned with advisory functions but also that it did not extend over a further range of functions that have been vested in the Attorney General's office. The Attorney General's obligation to prepare human rights guidance under section 8 of the Justice (Northern Ireland) Act 2004 did not fall within the scope of the review, for instance. The First and deputy First Ministers commissioned the former Lord Advocate, Dame Elish Angiolini, to carry out this review,[214] which was duly delivered in October 2012.

[211] Both the Attorney General for Northern Ireland at the time, John Larkin, and the Solicitor General for England and Wales at the time, Robert Buckland, provided helpful explanations to a question about these conventions during a Constitutional Law Summer School session on 'Our Common Birthright? Access to Law and Legal Education' (9 August 2017, Clayton Hotel, Belfast).

[212] Dame Elish Angiolini, 'Review of the Attorney General's Relationship with the Executive and Departments (Extracts from the Introduction and Background Sections of the Report)' (31 October 2012). The author obtained these extracts by way of a request to the Office of the First Minister and deputy First Minister in April 2016 (before it was renamed the Executive Office by the Departments Act (Northern Ireland) 2016, s 1(1)).

[213] Angiolini (n 212) Annex A.

[214] See ch 5 at 120–121 and 128–129.

There has been considerable interest in Angiolini's report to the First and deputy First Ministers for a number of reasons. Firstly, some have speculated on whether it addresses what was perceived as a 'maximalist approach to the post' adopted by John Larkin.[215] The existence of some report content on this matter was confirmed in 2013 by the First Minister of the time, Peter Robinson, in the following exchange with an MLA from the Social Democratic and Labour Party:

> *Mr Attwood*: Given the current Attorney General's inclination to join in Supreme Court cases, European Court cases and, indeed, cases involving the alleged scandalising of a judge, do you think that, in retrospect and given the review that you referred to, the role that the Executive gave to the Attorney General in July 2010 was too generous and now needs to be constrained?
>
> *Mr P Robinson*: I think that the Member has put his finger on one of the key issues: there is the difficulty with, at one and the same time, the Attorney General being the adviser to the Executive and, on the other hand, having the role independently. His independent role has on occasions required him to take actions against the Executive. We will not deal with what the outcome of that may have been, but it is clearly one of the issues that Dame Elish has looked at, that we are looking at and that will form part of any proposals that we bring to Executive colleagues.[216]

Secondly, when questioned about operational reform ideas, John Larkin qua the Attorney General for Northern Ireland has said that the viability of the office's statutory independence as it stands presently is a matter that continues to be reflected on.[217] Whether the relationship between the Attorney General and the DPP should be reformed has also been suggested as an issue for further consideration,[218] though that was not a matter which fell within Angiolini's terms of reference.[219] In the context of these somewhat tantalising leaks, there have been several attempts to have Angiolini's report made public.

A full copy of Angiolini's report was first requested from the First and deputy First Ministers in November 2012, but the request was refused in April 2013 in reliance upon an exemption to the Freedom of Information Act 2000 providing that information held by a government department can be withheld if it relates to the formulation or development of a government policy.[220] The First and deputy

[215] Martin O'Brien, 'Keeping Faith in the Law: Martin O'Brien Meets Controversial Attorney General John Francis Larkin' (*The Irish Catholic*, 21 November 2013). Available at: www.irishcatholic.com/keeping-faith-in-the-law/.

[216] NIA (Official Report), 14 October 2013, vol 88, no 5, 25. Further information about the controversies referred to in this quotation is included in ch 7 at 216–217.

[217] 'Guardian of the Rule of Law: The Office of Attorney General for Northern Ireland' (n 206) 26. Also see: Attorney General for Northern Ireland, 'Tenth Annual Report – 2019/20' (n 207) paras 5 and 101–102.

[218] ibid para 45.

[219] As mentioned earlier, however, the Department of Justice consulted on this issue in 2012. See (n 113).

[220] Information Commissioner's Office, 'Freedom of Information Act 2000 Decision Notice FS50497952' (17 December 2013). The Office of the First Minister and deputy First Minister initially relied upon the Freedom of Information Act 2000, s 41(1), but withdrew its reliance upon that provision after an internal review of the decision and instead relied upon the exemption provided in s 35(1)(a).

First Ministers argued that Angiolini's report sought 'to inform the formulation of government policy and thinking around the role and post of Attorney General',[221] going on to say that the policy-making process was still 'in the early development stage' and that the information in question would 'form the basis of any future policy discussions concerning the role of the Attorney General'.[222] The individual who requested the report appealed to the Deputy Information Commissioner who, while holding that the information fell more squarely under 'development' of government policy rather than its 'formulation', was satisfied that the exemption was engaged and that it was in the public interest to maintain the exemption. In the course of his reasoning about the arguments in favour of disclosing the withheld information, the Commissioner noted that the First and deputy First Ministers had 'accepted that disclosure of the withheld information would provide greater transparency and accountability' which, it was said, had the potential to 'increase trust' in the office.[223] However the reasoning behind the Commissioner's final decision provided that, on balance, despite the existence of other information about the role of the Attorney General for Northern Ireland in the public domain and a series of controversies surrounding the office, it was considered fundamentally important for ministers to have a 'safe space' and an opportunity to consider all of their options 'without fear of premature disclosure'.[224] The Commissioner did find that the First and deputy First Ministers had failed to comply with the procedural requirements under section 17(1) of the 2000 Act and certain uncontentious extracts of Angiolini's report were released to the complainant in the course of proceedings.[225] However, these were largely hollow victories which did not reveal any of the substantive recommendations sought.

A further request for the disclosure of Angiolini's report was refused in August 2018 despite the passage of some time for the consideration of its findings.[226] The Executive Office (which is the new name for the Office of the First Minister and deputy First Minister)[227] acknowledged that Angiolini's report was completed some time ago and that there remains genuine interest in her conclusions, but maintained that these considerations were strongly outweighed by countervailing public interest factors which are recognised by the Freedom of Information Act 2000. In particular, it said that release of the report had 'the potential to prejudice the effective operation' of the Attorney General's office; that some information quoted in the report was protected by legal professional privilege and was provided to Angiolini on the understanding that it was not intended to be widely disclosed; and, most interestingly perhaps, that because the term of the Attorney General was due to expire in the near future there would be a need for decisions 'on the future,

[221] ibid para 14.
[222] ibid para 16.
[223] ibid para 19.
[224] ibid paras 26–27.
[225] ibid paras 35–37.
[226] Email to author from Richard Hill on behalf of the Executive Office (30 August 2018).
[227] Departments Act (Northern Ireland) 2016, s 1(1).

role and identity' of the office.[228] The urgency of this last consideration was emphasised with reference to the continued absence of Executive ministers in Northern Ireland at the time, which brings us neatly to the next sub-section of this chapter.

The Political Vacuum and its Consequences

The main institutions of devolved government in Northern Ireland stopped working at the beginning of 2017,[229] which resulted in a wide range of serious constitutional difficulties for the region that were not resolved until the institutions were restored in January 2020. Reflecting on the impact that this vacuum had on the work of the Attorney General for Northern Ireland at the start of August 2018, the office-holder at that time highlighted a number of operational consequences. Most obviously, he noted that 'the stream of work' involved in advising both Northern Ireland Ministers and the Executive Committee had naturally 'dried up' since the beginning of the impasse.[230] Despite the evaporation of this business area, which required considerable work on the part of the Attorney General between 2010 and 2017, the office-holder continued to exercise his other statutory and non-statutory functions in the light of the challenges to the constitutional framework for Northern Ireland at the time. Five brief examples may illustrate how the powers of the Attorney General continued and in some cases increased in importance during the absence of a working devolution settlement.

First, when Barra McGrory announced his intention to resign as DPP in May 2017 it fell to the Attorney General for Northern Ireland to seek applications for a successor to this constitutionally sensitive post in accordance with section 30(1)(a) of the Justice (Northern Ireland) Act 2002. In the exercise of his power of appointment under that provision, the Attorney General subsequently appointed Stephen Herron as the new DPP in January 2018.[231] Second, the Attorney General was required to consider whether to grant his authorisation of ex gratia payments at the request of certain charities in accordance with one of his various duties in that area of law.[232] The Attorney General in fact described the possibility of nobody

[228] After his initial appointment in May 2010, John Larkin was reappointed for a further term of two years in May 2014. In September 2015, the First and deputy First Ministers further extended his appointment until 23 May 2019. Subsequent to this statement on behalf of the Executive Office, in May 2019, the Secretary of State for Northern Ireland extended Larkin's tenure to 30 June 2020. He was then succeeded by Dame Brenda King, who first assumed the office in July 2020.

[229] For a synopsis of the reasons for the collapse, see: Dickson (n 30) 17–18. Also see: Jess Sargeant and Jill Rutter, 'Governing Without Ministers: Northern Ireland Since the Fall of the Power-Sharing Executive' (Institute for Government, 25 September 2019). Available at: www.instituteforgovernment.org.uk/publications/governing-without-ministers-northern-ireland. See further: Adam Evans, 'Northern Ireland, 2017–2020: An Experiment in Indirect Rule' [2021] *Public Law* 471.

[230] Constitutional Law Summer School 2018 (n 210).

[231] 'Appointment of the New Director of Public Prosecutions for Northern Ireland' (*Attorney General for Northern Ireland*, 2 January 2018). Available at: www.attorneygeneralni.gov.uk/news-centre/appointment-new-director-public-prosecutions-northern-ireland.

[232] Charities Act (Northern Ireland) 2008, s 47. There is scope for much more research on the broader role of the Attorney General for Northern Ireland in this area of law, especially given that tensions have arisen between the Attorney General and the Charity Commission for Northern Ireland on multiple

being in post to make decisions of this nature as a 'sobering thought', given their often sensitive nature.[233] Third, by running an 'It's Your Law' programme in relevant communities the Attorney General's office sought to address a perception of disconnection between the legal system and individuals affected by paramilitarism.[234] This scheme complemented a long-running effort on the part of the Attorney General to encourage engagement with the law among non-grammar school pupils by way of a 'Living Law' programme.[235]

Fourth, the Attorney General brought three new human rights documents into force in the exercise of his powers under section 8 of the Justice (Northern Ireland) Act 2004 during the political impasse.[236] This was possible because, as explained above, new guidance can come into effect if it has been published and laid before the Assembly subject to the negative resolution procedure before being commenced by order of the Attorney General.[237] The negative resolution procedure was still available during the political vacuum because the Northern Ireland Assembly had not been formally prorogued. This meant that although no MLAs had taken their seats since January 2017, draft statutory rules could still be laid before the empty chamber and then take effect when (inevitably) they were not resolved against. The constitutionality of this troubling practice was contemporaneously legitimised to some extent by the fact that the 'statutory period' during which the Assembly could annul secondary legislation made in this way was defined as either ten sitting days or 30 calendar days, whichever was the longest,[238] meaning that the three orders made by the Attorney General could be annulled by a future Assembly during the first ten sitting days of its return. Indeed, the Attorney General duly appeared before the Assembly's Committee for Justice to answer questions about these orders, among other things, shortly after the devolved institutions were restored in 2020.[239] To have used this law-making power in such constitutionally uncertain circumstances arguably warranted some criticism just the same.

Fifth and finally, the Attorney General's office faced a surge in work arising from devolution issues raised in the courts as a result of the political impasse. By far the most significant case of this nature was *Buick*, which essentially involved a challenge to the legality of decisions taken by civil servants in the absence of democratic oversight and without regard to certain procedures required by the

occasions. See, e.g., *Attorney General for Northern Ireland v Charity Commission for Northern Ireland* [2015] NICh 18.

[233] Constitutional Law Summer School 2018 (n 210).

[234] ibid.

[235] ibid.

[236] See the Attorney General's Human Rights Guidance (Domestic Abuse and Stalking) Order (Northern Ireland) 2018; the Attorney General's Human Rights Guidance (The Application of Section 5 of the Criminal Law Act (Northern Ireland) 1967 to Rape Victims and Those to Whom They Make Disclosures in Connection With a Claim for Social Security, Child Tax Credit or Anonymous Registration on the Electoral Roll) Order (Northern Ireland) 2018, and the Attorney General's Human Rights Guidance (The Use of the Irish Language) Order (Northern Ireland) 2019.

[237] Justice (Northern Ireland) Act 2004, s 8(3).

[238] Interpretation Act (Northern Ireland) 1954, s 41(2) (as amended).

[239] NIA (Official Report), 30 January 2020, Committee for Justice.

Northern Ireland Act 1998.[240] Although the Department for Infrastructure at the centre of the case announced that it did not intend to appeal a judgment handed down by the Court of Appeal in July 2018, and legislation has since been passed at Westminster which effectively annulled the effect of the *Buick* rulings,[241] inter alia, the Attorney General nonetheless made an independent decision to refer to the UK Supreme Court several questions arising from *Buick* about devolution issues.[242] His questions related mainly to a ruling of the Court of Appeal about the applicability of the Ministerial Code to civil servants, because he thought section 28A of the Northern Ireland Act 1998 had been wrongly interpreted.[243] The reference was intended to offer the UK Supreme Court 'the opportunity to give us authoritative guidance about the powers of departments to make important decisions' during the political stalemate,[244] but the court adjourned its proceedings arising from the reference because the issues had become moot and, as such, better 'determined against the backdrop of a clear factual matrix'.[245] In reaching this view, the Court also ruled that the Attorney General would be entitled to apply to intervene in relevant lower court proceedings which had been stayed pending the outcome of his reference, despite the fact that he had not been served with a formal devolution notice in those proceedings.[246]

The Appointment of Dame Brenda King

John Larkin QC served as the Attorney General for Northern Ireland for just over ten years.[247] While this lengthy tenure could be said to have operated as a

[240] *Re Buick's Application* [2018] NIQB 43; [2018] NICA 26. Also see: Conor McCormick, 'The Three Tiers of Executive Power in Northern Ireland' in Brice Dickson and Conor McCormick (eds), *The Judicial Mind: A Festschrift for Lord Kerr of Tonaghmore* (Hart Publishing 2021) 239–240; Gordon Anthony, 'The Quartet Plus Two: Judicial Review in Northern Ireland' in TT Arvind and others (eds), *Executive Decision-Making and the Courts* (Hart Publishing 2021) 277; Anurag Deb, 'The Legacy of Buick: Northern Ireland's Chaotic Constitutional Crucible' (2019) 23 *Edinburgh Law Review* 259; Dickson and McCormick (n 200) 1163–1164.

[241] Northern Ireland (Executive Formation and Exercise of Functions) Act 2018.

[242] The reference was purportedly made under the Northern Ireland Act 1998, Sch 10, para 34, but the UK Supreme Court itself raised preliminary questions over whether the matters referred by the Attorney were indeed valid devolution issues. See: *Reference by the Attorney General for Northern Ireland of Devolution Issues to the Supreme Court pursuant to Paragraph 34 of Schedule 10 to the Northern Ireland Act (No 2)* [2019] UKSC 1 at [9].

[243] ibid [4].

[244] Mark Devonport and Jayne McCormack, 'Arc21 Ruling: NI Attorney General Seeks Clarity Over Case' (*BBC News*, 10 August 2018). Available at: www.bbc.co.uk/news/uk-northern-ireland-45150319.

[245] *Reference by the Attorney General for Northern Ireland of Devolution Issues to the Supreme Court pursuant to Paragraph 34 of Schedule 10 to the Northern Ireland Act (No 2)* [2019] UKSC 1 at [28].

[246] ibid [29]–[30].

[247] As indicated at n 228 above, Larkin was first appointed by the First and deputy First Ministers in May 2010. He was reappointed for a further term of two years in May 2014. In September 2015, the First and deputy First Ministers further extended his appointment until 23 May 2019. In May 2019, the Secretary of State for Northern Ireland extended Larkin's tenure to 30 June 2020 under appointment powers conferred by the Northern Ireland (Executive Formation and Exercise of Functions) Act 2018, s 5, as amended by the Northern Ireland (Ministerial Appointment Functions) Regulations 2019.

source of continuity and stability during a period otherwise bedevilled by constitutional turmoil, it may also have made it difficult to disassociate the office of the Attorney General for Northern Ireland from Larkin's distinctive approach to the role. Larkin's tenure was considerably longer than any of his contemporaries in the UK law officer regime and overlapped with his appointment as a temporary (i.e., part-time, fee-paid) High Court judge.[248] The office of the Solicitor General for England and Wales, for instance, saw no fewer than seven different office-holders during Larkin's tenure. Against this backdrop, the appointment of Dame Brenda King as the second Attorney General for Northern Ireland appointed by the First and deputy First Ministers of Northern Ireland under section 22(2) of the Justice (Northern Ireland) Act 2002 was met with widespread interest.[249]

King's background is noticeably different from Larkin's, which was largely in private practice as a high-profile barrister, together with a brief stint in academia. King has spent most of her career as an in-house legal adviser to UK government departments (including the Northern Ireland Office) and as a leader of international standing within the Office of the Legislative Counsel at the Northern Ireland Assembly. Although King has been in office for over a year at the time of writing, it is difficult to discern any substantive changes that she may have introduced to the Attorney General's office because her first annual report has not yet been laid before the Assembly. Equally, King has kept a remarkably low public profile as compared to Larkin.[250] It is possible that King's background as a solicitor and a legislative draftsperson has resulted in a different set of priorities for her office, particularly in the context of Brexit and the COVID-19 pandemic. She may, for instance, have chosen to concentrate on the advisory work of her office and on the quality of legislation brought forward by the Northern Ireland Executive, rather than on opportunities to initiate and intervene in litigation. In any case, it is clear that, like her predecessor, King has faced context-specific challenges in connection with her duty to uphold the rule of law in Northern Ireland. Indeed, in the light of

[248] See: Alan Erwin, 'Attorney General John Larkin Appointed High Court Judge' (*Belfast Telegraph*, 31 January 2020). Available at: www.belfasttelegraph.co.uk/news/courts/attorney-general-john-larkin-appointed-temporary-high-court-judge-38913330.html. It should be noted that various members of the Northern Ireland Assembly, inter alios, raised concerns about the potential for actual and perceived conflicts of interests on account of this overlapping appointment. See, e.g., NIA (Official Report), 17 February 2020, Oral Answers to Questions by the Executive Office. Also see: NIA (Official Report), 30 January 2021, Committee for Justice.

[249] In July 2020, King was appointed for one year in the first instance, but with the option of an extension subject to the agreement of both parties. In July 2021, King's appointment was duly extended for a further year, such that her term of appointment was due to expire on 30 June 2022. However, just prior to the latest collapse of the devolved institutions, in February 2022, her term was extended by another three years such that it will now expire on 30 June 2025. See: 'Appointment of Attorney General' (*The Executive Office*, 3 February 2022). Available at: www.executiveoffice-ni.gov.uk/news/appointment-attorney-general.

[250] See ch 7 at 214 and 216–217.

an apparent decline in political respect for the rule of law and its requirements,[251] the role of the Attorney General for Northern Ireland remains both highly demanding and extremely important.

Conclusions

There are many features which genuinely distinguish the Advocate General for Northern Ireland and the Attorney General for Northern Ireland from other members of the UK law officer regime. The cognate nature of the former office and the statutory independence of the latter are perhaps the most striking of these distinguishing features, though they should not be permitted to cloud the fact that each office also carries out a notable bundle of functions that resemble those of their counterparts. This chapter has traced the historical development of both roles, albeit with much greater emphasis on the Attorney General's office, and fashioned a digestible outline of their constitutional functions today. As with the analyses provided in respect of the law officers for Scotland, England and Wales in earlier chapters, most of the controversies that have arisen in connection with each office and its functions have not yet been explored in any depth. Such matters form the focus of Chapter 7. However, it is probably apparent from some of the asides in this chapter that the office of the Attorney General for Northern Ireland has attracted a substantial level of controversy at times. It is unsurprising, therefore, that the unique features of that office have been reviewed at several points, though it is curious in this context that very little has occurred by way of substantive reform since its (re-)establishment in 2010. Indeed, neither the Department of Justice's consultation on the relationship between the Attorney General and the DPP[252] nor Dame Elish Angiolini's review of the Attorney General's relationship with the Northern Ireland Executive and its departments appear to have resulted in any meaningful constitutional change. Against this background, it is undoubtedly significant that a more comprehensive review into the operation of the office of the Attorney General for Northern Ireland was agreed upon and commissioned by the Northern Ireland Executive in the summer of 2021.[253] Nonetheless, it remains to be seen whether the recommendations of Sir John Gillen, who was engaged to carry out this exercise, will prove capable of reshaping the Attorney General's office in a way which enhances its constitutional legitimacy.

[251] For some worrying laments from the High Court bench, see: *McNern and Turley's Application* [2020] NIQB 57 (McAlinden J) and *Napier's Application* [2021] NIQB 86; [2021] NIQB 120 (Scoffield J). Also see *The Northern Ireland Human Rights Commission's Application* [2021] NIQB 91 at [104] (Colton J).

[252] Department of Justice (n 113).

[253] The First and deputy First Ministers' intention to establish this review was announced to the Northern Ireland Assembly in 2020: NIA (Official Report), 14 September 2020, Oral Answers to Questions by the Executive Office. In July 2021, the Executive Office revealed that ministers had agreed to the proposed review and invited Sir John Gillen to conduct it. See: 'Extension of Term of Appointment of Attorney General' (n 249).

7

Constitutional Controversy and Law Officer Legitimacy

Introduction

The arrangement of this book is premised on the view that normative evaluations of the UK law officer regime are likely to be weak and shallow unless they are informed by a detailed analysis of its constitutional circuitry. Thus, in the absence of any sufficiently holistic analyses in the existing literature, the four preceding chapters have attempted to assemble, disentangle and synthesise the historical and structural foundations of the UK law officer regime in its entirety. In addition, the potency of various differences within the constituent parts of the regime have been highlighted by way of a relatively unobtrusive comparative framework throughout. It may therefore be helpful at this juncture to review the way in which that framework – which was first explained in Chapter 1 and which draws on McHarg's idea of trivial, contextual, conservationist, symbolic and genuine differences[1] – has facilitated several useful insights about the UK law officer regime from a comparative point of view. Variations in respect of the procedural route by which legislative proposals are screened for the constitutionality of provisions with retrospective effect or early commencement, for instance, have been characterised as *trivial* differences. The role of the Lord Advocate in connection with the investigation of unexplained deaths in the absence of a coroners' system in Scotland has been noted, for example, as a *contextual* distinction. Statutory provisions protecting the 'retained functions' of the Lord Advocate have been explained, moreover, by reference to *conservationism* in respect of the historical role of that office in prosecutions and the investigation of deaths. As anticipated,[2] there have not been many instances of purely *symbolic* distinctions, though the absence of any royal involvement in the appointment process for the Attorney General for Northern Ireland may perhaps qualify. Numerous *genuine* distinctions between the constituent parts of the regime have been highlighted, however, such as the cognate nature of the office of the Advocate General for Northern Ireland in comparison to the standalone nature of the Advocate General for Scotland – despite the similarity of

[1] See ch 1 at 17–19.
[2] See ch 1 at 19.

their functional portfolios – and the strikingly different features of the law officer model that has developed in the form of the statutorily independent Attorney General for Northern Ireland.

This comparative exercise has clarified the richness and complexity of the UK law officer regime and exposed several loose conceptual threads to be picked up hereafter. Genealogically, it can be seen that the devolution reforms of 1998 unify the historical origins of the Counsel General for Wales, the Advocate General for Scotland, and the Advocate General for Northern Ireland to some extent, though the evolution of the Counsel General for Wales since that time has set its tale apart in particularly important ways. The Attorney General and Solicitor General for England and Wales, the Lord Advocate and the Solicitor General for Scotland, and the Attorney General for Northern Ireland, on the other hand, have individualistic ancestries which – despite evidence of some functional cross-pollination at various junctures (not least in 1998 and thereafter) – have produced a highly heterogeneous set of institutional histories. Analogically, the range of differences between these offices, which are visible both vertically and horizontally, may appear to overshadow their similarities. The comparative analysis would never come to an end, however, if it sought to rationalise all the similarities and differences it has revealed. It must therefore be enough, for now, to confirm that no more than an extremely ductile definition of what *constitutes* a law officer is maintainable in the UK. The absence of a ministerial advisory role on the part of the Attorney General for Northern Ireland between 2017 and 2020 supports this point in as much as the initial status of the Counsel General for Wales as a civil servant. Now, having established this abundantly clear appreciation for the constitutional diversity inherent in the UK law officer regime, it is time to return to the unifying constitutional values which appear to *legitimise* the variety of models encompassed by it.

A considerable proportion of social science scholarship 'converges on the idea that meaningful components of society – beliefs and values, practices and institutions, and associated individuals – do not have equal standing'.[3] Instead, it is thought that these phenomena are 'endowed with varying degrees of legitimacy on the basis of recognized levels of popular support, official validation, and cultural normativity'.[4] It is also commonly argued that vicissitudes in these variables can result in outbreaks of fundamental societal change, where the relevant variations are of a sufficient magnitude.[5] Clayman conceptualises this theoretical landscape by reference to three 'zones': a 'zone of consensus', a 'zone of legitimate controversy', and a 'zone of deviance'.[6] The first zone is host to topics which are essentially non-debateable because they are so broadly supported and culturally normative,

[3] Steven E Clayman, 'The Micropolitics of Legitimacy: Political Positioning and Journalistic Scrutiny at the Boundary of the Mainstream' (2017) 80 *Social Psychology Quarterly* 41, 42.

[4] ibid; David Beetham, *The Legitimation of Power* (Palgrave 1991) 12.

[5] Clayman (n 3) 43.

[6] ibid 42–43. See also: Daniel C Hallin, 'The Media, the War in Vietnam, and Political Support: A Critique of the Thesis of an Oppositional Media' 46 *The Journal of Politics* 2, 21.

whereas the third zone is home to social relations broadly regarded as 'marginal, nonnormative, or otherwise illegitimate'.[7] The middle zone, however, encompasses matters 'about which reasonable people may disagree and still remain within the societal mainstream'.[8] It is with reference to this middle zone that the term 'controversy' is used throughout this chapter. This is because indicators of fluctuating approval regarding the constitutional values of independence, accountability and trust that will be discussed hereafter (as a proxy for evaluating constitutional legitimacy in accordance with the methodology explained in Chapter 2 and further developed below) generally fall between the two poles of marginality and extremism envisaged by Clayman. Moreover, while many of the controversial incidents that follow share standard features that justify grouping them as controversies – such as longevity or widespread attention – they vary considerably in terms of the extent to which they register at the edges of the legitimate controversy zone and, therefore, the extent to which they border on consensus or deviance.

Each of the following sections in this chapter are concerned with analysing controversies, broadly construed in the foregoing sense, because they provide insightful settings for studying the 'institutional maintenance of legitimacy' in respect of the UK law officer regime.[9] This is largely because the phenomena that give rise to controversies can also be regarded as tests of legitimacy.[10] It will be recalled from Chapter 2 that the tests for legitimacy developed by Beetham and used for the purposes of this book consist of assessments about the legal validity of power, the justifiability of the rules governing power relationships by reference to the beliefs and values operating within a given regime, and evidence of consent as expressed through actions.[11] By virtue of the doctrinal legal study of powers and duties belonging to members of the UK law officer regime set out in Chapters 3 to 6, however, questions of legal validity do not feature prominently in the analyses that follow. As noted above, this chapter is primarily focused on charting episodes of legitimate controversy rather than searching for instances of illegality likely to be regarded as deviant. Nor does this chapter dwell on 'culturally specific' actions constituting expressions of consent,[12] which are easily evidenced in this constitutional context. The fact that individuals *elected* to an office within the UK law officer regime partake in well-established democratic procedures which condition their eligibility for appointment demonstrates enough evidence of popular consent to confer this element of legitimacy upon those office-holders. Where individuals are ministerially *appointed* to an office within the UK law officer regime by

[7] Clayman (n 3) 42–43.
[8] ibid.
[9] Gerardo Patriotta, Jean-Pascal Gond and Freiderike Schultz, 'Maintaining Legitimacy: Controversies, Orders of Worth, and Public Justifications' (2011) 48 *Journal of Management Studies* 1804, 1806.
[10] ibid.
[11] Beetham (n 4) 15–25. Also see ch 2 at 21–26.
[12] ibid 19.

ministers who are themselves elected, a lesser but nonetheless adequate measure of legitimacy is conferred upon those office-holders. In both these scenarios, the role of the Welsh and Scottish legislatures in appointment procedures for the Counsel General, the Lord Advocate and the Solicitor General for Scotland adds to this sense of legitimacy in a way that the legislatures in Westminster and Northern Ireland could easily replicate. The ceremonial role of the judiciary in respect of all appointments to the UK law officer regime also contributes to this effect.

Having thus addressed the aspects of legitimacy that involve assessments of legal validity and actions expressive of consent, the substantive sections of this chapter concentrate on evaluating the dominant justifications for powers exercised and duties carried out by members of the UK law officer regime. In keeping with Beetham's general conception of legitimacy, this analysis turns upon the beliefs and, most importantly for present purposes, the values that pertain within a given regime.[13] It should be remembered that the concepts of independence, accountability and trust emerged as dominant (though certainly not solitary) values 'immanent' in the materials consulted for the purposes of writing this book.[14] Consequently, the interpretive approach throughout has been to start with general understandings of those concepts before attempting to marry them with meanings that are specific to the UK law officer regime as manifested in relevant discourse. This represents the reflective ex post facto dimension of the theory, which is derived from Daly's values-based framework of analysis as set out in Chapter 1.[15] As such, the controversy discourse which follows has informed understandings of the constitutional values in as much as the constitutional values have informed understandings of the controversy discourse. The thematic method involved in this analysis is both deductive and inductive in this respect,[16] though the appearance of deductivism predominates because the themes that have been used to catalogue related patterns within the controversy discourse are based on the conceptual dimensions of each constitutional value set out in Chapter 2. Thematic analysis of this sort operates as a 'systematic and transparent' way of organising the high volume of literature about controversial episodes connected to the UK law officer regime and of grouping incidents with conceptual commonalities that have occurred in significantly different contexts.[17] The final section in this chapter

[13] ibid 17–18.

[14] Paul Daly, 'Administrative Law: Characteristics, Legitimacy, Unity' in Mark Elliott, Jason NE Varuhas and Shona Wilson Stark (eds), *The Unity of Public Law? Doctrinal, Theoretical and Comparative Perspectives* (Hart Publishing 2018) 108; Paul Daly, 'Administrative Law: A Values-Based Approach' in John Bell and others (eds), *Public Law Adjudication in Common Law Systems: Process and Substance* (Hart Publishing 2016) 25. Also see: Paul Daly, *Understanding Administrative Law in the Common Law World* (Oxford University Press 2021) ch 1.

[15] Daly, 'Administrative Law: Characteristics, Legitimacy, Unity' (n 14) 108; Daly, 'Administrative Law: A Values-Based Approach' (n 14) 25; Allan Beever and Charles Rickett, 'Interpretive Legal Theory and the Academic Lawyer' (2005) 68 *The Modern Law Review* 320, 324. Also see ch 1 at 15–16.

[16] On thematic analysis generally, see: Helene Joffe, 'Thematic Analysis' in David Harper and Andrew R Thompson (eds), *Qualitative Research Methods in Mental Health and Psychotherapy* (Wiley-Blackwell 2012) 210.

[17] ibid.

offers some conclusions about the relationship between the three values explored throughout.

Constitutional Controversy and the Value of Independence

In her 2016 monograph concentrating on Australian Solicitors-General, Appleby acknowledged and explored the continued relevance of Edwards' earlier observation that independence is a 'recurring theme' in law officer scholarship.[18] Having carefully considered some UK controversies which have arisen in connection with the independence of the Attorney General for England and Wales, Appleby's findings demonstrated the enduring importance of giving practical effect to the concept from an international perspective.[19] As mentioned in Chapter 1,[20] Appleby expressed disapproval toward the UK Government's response to reform proposals flowing from independence-related controversies which, in her view, exhibited a poor understanding of the 'non-political' law officer models adopted with some success in jurisdictions like Australia.[21] This book has revealed that Appleby's critical conclusions about the Attorney General for England and Wales could be similarly criticised, however, for the minimal extent to which they considered the 'non-political' law officer models which have been tried and tested to some extent in devolved regions of the UK. As highlighted in Chapters 4 to 6, the UK law officer regime has featured 'non-political' law officer models of various sorts in recent times. The civil service model initially adopted in respect of the Counsel General for Wales, Alex Salmond's decision as First Minister of Scotland to appoint an avowedly 'non-political' Lord Advocate in 2007, and the statutorily independent model still constitutive of the Attorney General for Northern Ireland all exemplify attempts to experiment with 'non-political' law officer models in the UK that are underpinned by heightened conceptions of independence. Just as the success of the Australian model is now open to some doubt based on subsequent controversies,[22] serious questions must be asked about the overall

[18] Gabrielle Appleby, *The Role of the Solicitor-General: Negotiating Law, Politics and the Public Interest* (Hart Publishing 2016) 254; John Ll J Edwards, *The Law Officers of the Crown: A Study of the Offices of Attorney-General and Solicitor-General of England with an Account of the Office of the Director of Public Prosecutions of England* (Sweet & Maxwell 1964) 11.

[19] Appleby, *The Role of the Solicitor-General* (n 18) ch 2; ch 7.

[20] See ch 1 at 13.

[21] ibid 47–48. Also see: Gabrielle Appleby, 'Reform of the Attorney General: Comparing Britain and Australia' [2016] *Public Law* 573.

[22] Henry Belot and Ashlynne McGhee, 'Solicitor-General Resigns Over "Broken" Relationship with Attorney-General George Brandis' (*ABC News*, 24 October 2016). Available at: www.abc.net.au/news/2016-10-24/justin-gleeson-resigns-as-solicitor-general/7960632; Gabrielle Appleby, 'Navigating a Complicated Relationship: The Role of the Solicitor-General' (2016) 29 *Law Society of NSW Journal* 70.

legitimacy of UK-based law officer models which have placed very strong, if not exclusive, weight on the constitutional value of independence. In the following sub-sections, this book examines several notable controversies that relate to the two main facets of Rubin's general theory of independence as set out in Chapter 2 above.[23] Outstanding questions about how to legitimately weigh this value alongside the constitutional values of accountability and trust will be revisited after those concepts have been considered on their own terms.

Inappropriate Interdependence

It should be recalled that Rubin prefers to theorise government by reference to an 'image of a network of interconnected institutions' over 'three-branch imagery' that is often used 'infelicitously' to represent the modern administrative state.[24] He persuasively contends that the latter imagery tends to inappropriately conflate the concept of independence with a distinctly judicial branch of government and that the former imagery sustains a more accurate model for 'understanding the internal structure and external connections of the institutions that constitute the bulk of the modern state'.[25] The basic argument made by Rubin here appears to be supported, in principle, by a number of jurists in the UK who emphasise that, contradictory though it may seem, the notion of *interdependence* is an integral aspect of *independence* in all but the most extreme conceptions of the latter. Thomas LCJ, for instance, has strongly endorsed the general idea of interdependence (though attached, perhaps confusingly, to some enduring three-branch imagery) given that it has been construed to embrace 'inter-institutional comity' and 'mutual respect' which, in his view, characterises the UK constitutional position well.[26] Similarly, a recent Solicitor General for England and Wales expressly indicated that while the offices of the Attorney General and Solicitor General for England and Wales may 'defy the US/Montesquieu vision' of a state with fully separated powers, he regarded that as a 'good thing' due to his own belief in 'a sense of greater comity'

[23] See ch 2 at 26–29.

[24] Edward L Rubin, 'Independence as a Governance Mechanism' in Stephen B Burbank and Barry Friedman (eds), *Judicial Independence at the Crossroads: An Interdisciplinary Approach* (Sage 2002) 57–63. Also see: Edward L Rubin, *Beyond Camelot: Rethinking Politics and Law for the Modern State* (Princeton University Press 2007) 65.

[25] ibid 61.

[26] Lord Thomas of Cwmgiedd, 'The Judiciary Within the State: The Relationship Between the Branches of the State' (A Speech by the Lord Chief Justice of England and Wales for the Michael Ryle Memorial Lecture, 15 June 2017), paras 15–19. Available at: www.judiciary.uk/wpcontent/uploads/2017/06/lcj-michael-ryle-memorial-lecture-20170616.pdf, citing Aileen Kavanagh, 'The Constitutional Separation of Powers' in David Dyzenhaus and Malcolm Thorburn (eds), *Philosophical Foundations of Constitutional Law* (Oxford University Press 2016). Also see: Lord Burnett, 'Becoming Stronger Together' (A Speech by the Lord Chief Justice of England and Wales to the Commonwealth Judges and Magistrates' Association, 10 September 2018), para 16. Available at: www.judiciary.uk/wp-content/uploads/2018/09/lcj-speech-brisbane-lecture-20180910.pdf.

across government and in the idea that 'familiarity breeds respect'.[27] In fact, the Solicitor General 'strongly' disagreed with strict adherents to the separation of powers doctrine because, based on his experience in office, he regarded the Attorney General and Solicitor General as 'very well placed to help maintain the necessary interrelationships between several arms of our unwritten constitution'.[28] With that said, this sub-section concerns several controversies about the UK law officer regime which appear to be correlated to under-appreciation of and misunderstanding about this significant facet to Rubin's general theory of independence. This is important because, as Elvin has said, it would be 'regrettable' if critics sought to unravel offices in the UK law officer regime based a misplaced 'vision of the separation of powers' that has 'never been a dominant feature' of UK constitutionalism.[29]

It has been noted at several points earlier in this book that the relationship between law officers and the Cabinet, i.e. the inner council of a particular government that is conventionally subject to collective responsibility, has been a source of considerable controversy over the years.[30] With respect to the Attorney General for England and Wales, in particular, it was noted in Chapter 1 that Edwards delineated several philosophical approaches to the proper role of a law officer by considering some of the historical evidence in this domain.[31] What is notable from Edwards' observations at this point, however, is the fact that both Silkin's 'doctrine of intimate but independent involvement' and Rawlinson's 'doctrine of independent aloofness' refer to independence in a manner which is premised on *some* continued relationship with the Cabinet.[32] In other words, both of the dominant philosophies identified by Edwards conceptualise the value of independence as containing a measure of interdependence in this respect. Even Shawcross' proposal to completely depoliticise the Attorney General for England and Wales by

[27] Robert Buckland, 'The Model of a Modern Solicitor General: Thoughts on the Constitution in the Time of Brexit' (A Speech by the Solicitor General for England and Wales to Politeia, 16 October 2017). Available at: www.politeia.co.uk/the-model-of-a-modern-solicitor-general-thoughts-on-the-constitution-in-the-time-of-brexit/.

[28] ibid.

[29] Rebecca Elvin, 'Who Should Decide Who Decides the Public Interest?' (*Judicial Power Project*, 15 February 2016). Available at: https://judicialpowerproject.org.uk/who-should-decide-who-decides-the-public-interest/. For a critic who argues in favour of reform on this basis, see: Alec Samuels, 'Abolish the Office of Attorney-General' [2014] *Public Law* 609.

[30] It should be noted that the same debate does not apply with equal force to the unique relationship between the Attorney General for Northern Ireland and the Northern Ireland Executive Committee because, unlike the position in other UK jurisdictions, collective responsibility does not form part of the constitutional package for Northern Ireland government established in 1998. Northern Ireland ministers are intended to have full executive authority in their respective areas of responsibility, subject to a broad Programme of Government agreed by the Committee and endorsed by the Assembly. See: *Re Buick's Application* [2018] NICA 26 at [22].

[31] See ch 1 at 10.

[32] Sam Silkin, 'The Functions and Position of the Attorney-General in the United Kingdom' (1978) 59 *The Parliamentarian* 149; Peter Rawlinson, 'A Vital Link in the Machinery of Justice' (1977) 74 *Guardian Gazette* 798.

advocating for the adoption of 'a non-elected, non-political, public servant model for the office',[33] which was rejected outright by Edwards for its failure to preserve sufficient parliamentary accountability, is premised on some continued relationship with the Cabinet in circumstances where the latter requires legal advice and so on.

The current position of the Attorney General for England and Wales which, as described at some length in Chapter 3,[34] is that of a government minister who *attends* Cabinet by invitation rather than as a *member* is, in this light, no more than a symbolic representation of independence. Arguments to the effect that this arrangement is practically useful because it prevents the Attorney General from being bound by collective responsibility in inappropriate circumstances are unpersuasive to the extent that they ignore the fact that such circumstances can be easily avoided by clear exceptions to the general rule. In Scotland, for example, it has been explained that there is a legislative provision which exempts the Lord Advocate from collective responsibility as a member of the Scottish Government in so far as the doctrine relates to his or her retained functions.[35] It is difficult to think of good reasons for believing that a similar proviso would not work effectively with respect to Cabinet membership. In truth, therefore, the distinction between 'Cabinet level status' and 'Cabinet membership' appears to have very few practical consequences, especially when it is borne in mind that the absence of a law officer from a Cabinet meeting in person carries 'no guarantee of insulation against the pressures inherent in their subsequent reading of the Cabinet minutes, in which the strength or urgency of the opinions expressed around the Cabinet table are permanently recorded'.[36] Indeed, any conception of independence with respect to the UK law officer regime which ignores the fundamentality of interdependence with the Cabinet, particularly with respect to the executive advisory functions of a law officer, is difficult to support. To the contrary, the Cabinet level status of a law officer has been referred to as an important source of their authority before other government units, such as the prosecuting authorities.[37] The fact that a law officer's decisions can often be presumed to have benefitted from the insights that come from access to ministerial discussions has thus been viewed as a strength rather than a weakness in those contexts.[38] These legitimising benefits complement the more commonly emphasised observation that by being 'present participants' in Cabinet, the law officers are better positioned to 'stand up for the rule of law' by telling their ministerial colleagues 'when there are things that, legally, they cannot do, or indeed must do'.[39] Nonetheless, a different conception of

[33] John Ll J Edwards, *The Attorney General, Politics and the Public Interest* (Sweet & Maxwell 1984) 65.

[34] See ch 3 at 46–48.

[35] Scotland Act 1998, s 52(5)(b).

[36] Edwards, *The Attorney General, Politics and the Public Interest* (n 33) 323.

[37] *The Government's Response to the Constitutional Affairs Select Committee Report on the Constitutional Role of the Attorney General* (Cm 7355, 2008) para 30.

[38] ibid passim.

[39] Buckland (n 27); Ben Yong, 'Risk Management: Government Lawyers and the Provision of Legal Advice within Whitehall' (The Constitution Society 2013) 60–61.

independence appears to have captured the public imagination in several episodes of recent controversy; one which characterises even the appearance of interdependence as inappropriate. Two examples can be provided to illustrate the point – one arising in respect of the Counsel General for Wales and one in respect of the Lord Advocate.

In January 2019, the newly appointed First Minister for Wales, Mark Drakeford, brought a motion before the Senedd seeking its approval in relation to his decision to recommend to the Queen that Jeremy Miles be (re-)appointed as the Counsel General for Wales.[40] Several Members of the Senedd refused to support the motion, however, because the Welsh Government and Miles himself had styled the appointment as 'Counsel General and Brexit Minister' on several digital platforms.[41] In light of the relevant provisions in the Government of Wales Act 2006 and its explanatory notes which constituted the Counsel General as a member of the Welsh Government with 'ministerial status', though not as a Welsh Minister per se,[42] the First Minister's critics regarded his implicit request for approval in respect of the title 'Counsel General and Brexit Minister' as 'highly irregular'.[43] The perceived irregularity of the request must have been regarded as implicit, it should be noted, because the actual motion laid before the Senedd proposed 'to appoint Jeremy Miles AM as Counsel General' only,[44] with no concurrent reference to the position of Brexit Minister as advertised by the Welsh Government and Miles himself online.

The First Minister's critics feared that the appointment they were being asked to approve might amount to a breach of section 49(9) of the Government of Wales Act 2006, which provides that a person holding office as a Welsh Minister under section 48, inter alia, 'may not be appointed as the Counsel General'. Interestingly, moreover, in his speech against the motion Rhun ap Iorwerth specifically complained that the Counsel General would not be able to 'operate truly independently of the Welsh Government, because he is listed by the Welsh Government … as one of their Ministers'.[45] The BBC also quoted ap Iorwerth as having posed the question, 'How can someone who's also a minister act independently of government?', drawing particular attention to the likelihood of the Counsel General having to advise himself on the complex legal issues arising from a Brexit portfolio.[46] In a similar vein, the political editor of BBC Wales, Felicity Evans, queried 'When is a minister not a minister?' before conjecturing, acerbically, 'When they're also Counsel General apparently'.[47] Concerns of this nature did not, however, persuade

[40] The Record of Proceedings, Plenary, 8 January 2019, para 339.
[41] The Record of Proceedings, Plenary, 8 January 2019, para 341–353.
[42] See ch 4 at 79.
[43] The Record of Proceedings, Plenary, 8 January 2019, para 344.
[44] The Record of Proceedings, Plenary, 8 January 2019, para 339.
[45] The Record of Proceedings, Plenary, 8 January 2019, para 348.
[46] 'Key Cabinet Appointment Is Legal, Says Mark Drakeford' (*BBC News Wales*, 8 January 2019). Available at: www.bbc.co.uk/news/uk-wales-politics-46801150.
[47] ibid.

a majority of the 51 members present to withdraw their support for the First Minister's motion, with the end result of the debate on it being 31 votes in favour, 6 against, and 14 abstentions.[48] This outcome followed several assurances made by the First Minister in response to his critics. Drakeford's reply to the allegation of illegality under the 2006 Act was that because Miles was not appointed Brexit Minister under the aegis of section 48, which would have entitled him to exercise statutory functions conferred upon the Welsh Ministers appointed by way of that provision, no inconsistency arose.[49] Miles' role as Brexit Minister had instead been specifically 'constructed' to ensure that statutory functions would not fall to him, with his responsibilities instead being:

> policy advice to the Welsh Government on Brexit strategy; representing the Welsh Government in negotiations; acting on behalf of the Welsh Government in discharging responsibilities arising from the inter-governmental agreement and other protocols; and co-ordinating activities.[50]

This controversial sequence of events, which came dangerously close to derailing the First Minister's chosen designate to the office of Counsel General, contains a number of telling assumptions about the concept of a minister in addition to subtle misunderstandings about the concept of independence (as theorised herein) which require careful evaluation in retrospect. On the question of legality, it is indeed constitutionally questionable whether the First Minister can create ministerial posts other than under the aegis of section 48 of the 2006 Act, given that the Act also contains a specific restriction on how many 'relevant Welsh Ministerial office[s]' may exist at any time prescribing that such offices (defined by reference to appointments made under section 48) cannot exceed 12 in number.[51] By 'constructing' the office of Brexit Minister in the way that he did, the First Minister may have avoided the limitation on 'relevant Welsh Ministerial office[s]' in the statute, but the constitutional validity of this arrangement is itself premised on the idea that ministerial offices can be created which are ineligible for the conferral of statutory functions by the legislature; which exist solely for the purpose of exercising non-statutory functions; and which have no specific basis in the 2006 Act. Whether this premise qualifies as something beyond 'highly irregular' is certainly open to some doubt, though it does seem that the First Minister's explanation has been accepted by the Welsh legislature given that there was no similar pushback when the current Counsel General, Mick Antoniw, was appointed 'Minister for the Constitution' concurrently with the office of Counsel General in May 2021.[52]

In any event, and leaving aside the lack of clarity in relation to these legitimate questions of legality, the most significant aspect of this debate for present

[48] The Record of Proceedings, Plenary, 8 January 2019, para 361.
[49] The Record of Proceedings, Plenary, 8 January 2019, para 354.
[50] The Record of Proceedings, Plenary, 8 January 2019, para 355.
[51] Government of Wales Act 2006, s 51.
[52] The Record of Proceedings, Plenary, 26 May 2021, paras 100–105.

purposes is the vividness with which it highlights the conceptual confusion about ministerialism that pervades the Government of Wales Act 2006 and, in particular, those parts of it which constituted the Counsel General. It has already been explained that, by giving the Counsel General 'ministerial status' within the Welsh Government but not according office holders the status of a Welsh Minister, the 2006 Act sought to enhance the perceived independence of the Welsh law officer. However, as this episode of controversy shows, that endeavour has resulted in a serious lack of conceptual transparency about the constitutional value of independence underpinning the office. The quotations of Rhun ap Iorwerth and Felicity Jones above clearly demonstrate how a largely symbolic endeavour to convey independence has created false public expectations about the level of interdependence necessary for the office of the Counsel General to function, which, to return to the general emphasis of this sub-section, is widely regarded as an important source of authority given that law officers very often 'stand at the point where the executive and the judicial, or at least the quasi-judicial, functions of [the UK] constitution intersect'.[53] The 'diverse and, some have suggested, paradoxical powers'[54] demanded by this position amid an especially varied web of government units do, of course, call for clear rules and principles about which signals may be sent or received between them. Before turning to address how this facet of Rubin's general conception of independence applies in the context of the UK law officer regime, however, a further example of constitutional controversy about the importance of interdependence as a component of independence is provided below to reinforce the credibility of the arguments set out in this sub-section thus far.

In the context of the newly established devolved settlement for Scotland, the Lord Advocate moved from being a full member of the Cabinet[55] to merely attending its meetings while 'not formally a member' under the first two Labour–Liberal Democrat administrations.[56] The former position was altered in due course partly because of critiques drawing attention to the perceived risk of unelected office-holders using the legitimacy they derived from being members of the Scottish Parliament 'to influence policy for which he [or she] ha[d] no mandate' through their membership of the Cabinet,[57] and partly because of arguments suggesting that Cabinet membership rendered quasi-judicial and prosecutorial decisions made by the Lord Advocate incompatible with Article 6 of the European Convention on Human Rights.[58] Even the latter position, involving regular attendance at Cabinet

[53] Nicholas Leyell, 'The Role of the Law Officers' (1988) 12 *Trent Law Journal* 1, 1.

[54] ibid.

[55] *Guide to Collective Decision Making* (Executive Secretariat, August 1999) para 4.2.

[56] *Guide to Collective Decision Making* (Scottish Executive, August 2003) para 4.2.

[57] Christine O'Neill, 'The Constitutional Position of the Lord Advocate' (*The Journal of the Law Society of Scotland*, 1 March 2000). Available at: www.journalonline.co.uk/Magazine/45-3/1000843.aspx; Noreen Burrows, *Devolution* (Sweet & Maxwell 2000) 155–156.

[58] Ian S Dickinson, 'The Lord Advocate, the Lord Chancellor and the ECHR' (2000) 5 *Scottish Parliament Law Review* 3. Arguments of this nature of course founded upon the 'independent and impartial tribunal' aspect of the requirements under Article 6 of the ECHR.

meetings while lacking formal membership, drew negative comment for the continued risk of unwarranted influence which some worried it might enable.[59] The Lord Advocate of the day did not share these concerns, however, reasoning that her attendance was necessary 'to ensure that the interests of [her] own department are taken into account in any discussions about for instance the resourcing or the structures of the Scottish Executive'.[60] In the Lord Advocate's absence, the responsibility for representing her department's needs would fall to a different Minister with their own competing priorities.[61] Indeed, in February 2007 the then Lord Advocate defended her relationship with the Cabinet by arguing, inter alia, that the independence of her office was *safeguarded* rather than *jeopardised* by same:

> The ability to address cabinet reinforces the strength of the office in fending off any potential for innocent, but inappropriate, incursions into my independent duties. The alternative would be to rely on some other Minister with a wider portfolio to do so. Just as the law and the need for legal advice permeates all of the activities of the Executive – the implications of enforcement of proposed policies will include repercussions for the prosecution – including costs and resources.
>
> Independence is not just about decision making in individual cases. It is about the resources and structures to make those decisions independently. A reliance or dependency on another Minister to bid for those resources may be construed as likely to diminish rather than enhance the independence of the office. Any changes in that arrangement would therefore need to ensure that these aspects are addressed.[62]

It was against this backdrop that in May 2007 the decision of the newly elected First Minister (Alex Salmond) to 'exclude' the Lord Advocate from Cabinet meetings was taken. It will be recalled from Chapter 5 that the then Lord Advocate, Elish Angiolini, was being retained in post despite a change in administrations.[63] Salmond explained the Cabinet-membership aspect of his decision to the Scottish Parliament in the following terms:

> [T]he involvement of the law officers in the political operations of Government is, in my view, unnecessary and inappropriate, so I have decided that the Lord Advocate will not be a member of the Cabinet and will not normally attend meetings. That will emphasise the apolitical and professional role that the Lord Advocate and I have agreed is appropriate in the provision of legal advice to Government.

[59] Frank Maguire, 'The Lord Advocate: A Suspicion of Bias Lingers' (*Scotsman*, 17 October 2006). Available at: www.scotsman.com/news/the-lord-advocate-a-suspicion-of-bias-lingers-1-721442; Lord McCluskey, 'Where now for the Lord Advocate?' (*Scotsman*, 10 October 2006). Available at: www.scotsman.com/news/where-now-for-the-lord-advocate-1-1143868.

[60] Peter Nicholson, 'Hearing and Answering' (*The Journal of the Law Society of Scotland*, 12 February 2007). Available at: www.journalonline.co.uk/Magazine/52-2/1003853.aspx.

[61] ibid.

[62] Elish Angiolini, 'The Lord Advocate in the 21st Century' (Speech by the Lord Advocate at the KPMG Annual Law Lecture, 28 February 2007).

[63] See ch 5 at 120.

> Naturally, if there is some particular matter relating to the prosecution function or some civil matter that should be discussed jointly by Cabinet, the Lord Advocate will attend. In addition, she has the right to address Cabinet, as she has the right to address this chamber. However, the separation from the political operation of Government will ensure that the law officers can focus on improving our prosecution service and providing the expert and impartial legal advice that Cabinet requires.[64]

The First Minister's decision naturally meant that the Lord Advocate was going to have to rely on another Minister to represent the interests of her department after all, and there was speculation on whether the Cabinet Secretary for Justice would have to be relied upon for that purpose.[65] This suggested a remarkable role reversal, given that prior to devolution the Lord Advocate had historically been the 'go to' conduit to the UK Cabinet for most Scottish matters. Salmond's new protocol was expressed as follows in the amended 'Guide to Collective Decision Making':

> The Lord Advocate is not a member of the Cabinet and does not normally attend meetings, although she receives all Cabinet papers. However, the Lord Advocate (or the Solicitor General as the Lord Advocate's deputy) retains the right to address Cabinet where he/she considers it appropriate to do so and will attend where the Cabinet is to discuss a matter relating to his/her retained functions or requires his/her advice on a particular issue.[66]

This move to 'depoliticise' the Scottish law officers did not, however, put the issue of Cabinet involvement to bed indefinitely. After two new individuals were installed as Lord Advocate (Frank Mulholland) and Solicitor General for Scotland (Lesley Thomson) to serve the second Scottish National Party administration which had been formed in 2011, the apparent regularity of their 'conspicuous presence' at Cabinet meetings caused some commentators to call the Government's reasoning for and commitment towards Cabinet exclusion into question.[67] Tickell, while highlighting the inconsistency seemingly apparent between the government's protocols and practices, situated the issue in a broader set of concerns about the proper constitutional status of the Lord Advocate and Solicitor General for Scotland. For Tickell, having Scottish law officers who are 'adherents to the political party of government' was not an inherently objectionable idea.[68] He pointed to

[64] SP (Official Report), 24 May 2007, col 105.

[65] 'Lord Advocate Post Excluded from Cabinet' (*The Journal of the Law Society of Scotland*, 23 May 2007). Available at: www.journalonline.co.uk/News/1004203.aspx#.WMVelY5BrEY.

[66] *Guide to Collective Decision Making* (Scottish Government, November 2008) para 4.2.

[67] Andrew Tickell, 'The Unpolitical: The SNP's Pied Lord Advocate' (*Lallands Peat Worrier*, 25 August 2012). Available at: http://lallandspeatworrier.blogspot.co.uk/2012/08/the-unpolitical-snps-pied-lord-advocate.html; Andrew Tickell, 'The Unpolitical Lord Advocate (Vol 2)' (*Lallands Peat Worrier*, 13 October 2013). Available at: http://lallandspeatworrier.blogspot.co.uk/2013/10/the-unpolitical-lord-advocate-vol-2.html.

[68] Andrew Tickell, 'The Unpolitical: The SNP's Pied Lord Advocate' (n 67). Tickell is not the only contemporary commentator on the Scottish situation to express preference for 'partisan legal advice'. See, e.g., Ian Smart, 'Pants on fire?' (*ianssmart*, 27 October 2012). Available at: http://ianssmart.blogspot.co.uk/2012/10/pants-on-fire.html.

the status of the Attorney General for England and Wales at UK Cabinet meetings who, as a Conservative Party MP, was able to offer legal advice to his colleagues 'as a practically-minded ally, conversant in the law, keen actively to identify alternative ways of realising the collective political goals of the party'.[69] Thus, the long-standing Westminster debate over whether the relationship between law officers and their executive clients ought to be one of 'intimate but independent involvement' or, rather, one of 'independent aloofness'[70] was revived by the Scottish National Party's attempt at depoliticisation in the devolved Scottish context.

It is plain to see that there was a familiar but important point of constitutional principle underlying this debate. By maintaining that the Lord Advocate and Solicitor General for Scotland have an 'apolitical status' which makes it inappropriate for them to attend Cabinet meetings,[71] the Scottish Government promoted a narrow understanding of the law officers' roles which is difficult to justify. In addition to their legal portfolio, the Lord Advocate and Solicitor General for Scotland continue to have ministerial powers and responsibilities. To suggest otherwise is misleading. Moreover, even if they are not members of the Cabinet, it should be remembered that the Lord Advocate and Solicitor General for Scotland are nonetheless, like the Counsel General for Wales, members of the Scottish Government ex officio. It was regarded as controversial, therefore, for the Scottish Government to have maintained its purported depoliticisation policy despite having 'found it necessary to reverse Salmond's commitment to the exclusion of Law Officers from his cabinet' approximately 50% of the time, according to figures published in October 2013.[72] This was viewed as controversial partly because, as Tickell put it:

> [A] gloss of independence makes the Lord Advocate and Solicitor General politically useful figures to embroil in political controversies. Their opponents and the media struggle to know how to treat them. Can you set them head-to-head against opposition MSPs who disagree with them? Should the interviewing tone be one of forensic critique and suspicion, as a politician would expect, or the more solicitous, less combative approach usually directed towards expert opinion?[73]

Reasons such as these illustrate the importance of bringing as much clarity as possible to bear upon the relations between law officers and other government units throughout the UK. Having highlighted the normativity of interdependence between law officers and other government units and the necessity of interdependence in order for office-holders to manifest the independence expected of them in

[69] Andrew Tickell, 'The Unpolitical: The SNP's Pied Lord Advocate' (n 67).

[70] Edwards, *The Attorney General, Politics and the Public Interest* (n 33) 67–79.

[71] Paul Hutcheon, 'Lord Advocate Role "Increasingly Political"' (*The Herald*, 13 October 2013). Available at: www.heraldscotland.com/news/13127048.Lord_Advocate_role__increasingly_political_/.

[72] Andrew Tickell, 'The Unpolitical Lord Advocate (Vol 2)' (n 67). Also see: Paul Hutcheon, 'SNP Government in Row Over Presence of Lord Advocate at Cabinet Meetings' (*The Herald*, 5 August 2018). Available at: www.heraldscotland.com/news/16399053.snp-government-in-row-over-presence-of-lord-advocate-at-cabinet-meetings/.

[73] Andrew Tickell, 'The Unpolitical: The SNP's Pied Lord Advocate' (n 67).

most cases, the next sub-section of this chapter turns to the significant question of how to regulate the extent of those relations.

Inappropriate Signals and Interferences

It should be recalled from Chapter 2 at this stage that the second important facet of Rubin's general theory of independence involves a taxonomy of 'signal' types that can be sent between different government units, in tandem with a second taxonomy of 'interference' types that can be drawn upon to achieve different forms and levels of independence between units.[74] It was explained that Rubin suggests a 'low level' of independence is achieved by prohibitive interferences which prevent performative signals only (like promises, requests and commands); a 'medium level' of independence is achieved by prohibitive interferences which prevent both performative signals and informative signals (which describe a state of affairs within a particular unit); and a 'high level' of independence is achieved by prohibitive interferences which prevent performative signals, informative signals and expressive signals (namely moral or political comments about the conduct of a particular unit).[75] Although Rubin does not say so expressly, it is presumed that these escalating levels of independence can also be achieved by different combinations of the three signal types involved (meaning that the prohibition of, say, performative signals and expressive signals would likewise achieve a medium level of independence). In addition to prohibitions, Rubin recognises that other forms of interference can be used in circumstances where the outright proscription of signals between units is undesirable, such as attenuation and expert filtering.[76] It is clear, however, that these methods are prone to implementation difficulties because it can be challenging for units to reach agreement on the norms or protocols required to make them sustainable.[77] In any event, Rubin admits that his 'network model of government' is inherently heuristic; it is not intended as a 'demonstrable truth' but as a more accurate model for facilitating analyses of governmental relations than those which are predicated on three-branch imagery.[78] Its real strength lies in the dissolution of terms like 'judicial independence' into their component parts, namely by replacing statements of status with descriptions of relationships.[79] In this light, it becomes clear that the constitution of a particular office or a particular function as one requiring 'independence' is an avoidably imprecise conceptual approach, because significantly greater clarity can be produced by prescribing the specific rules by which the necessary level of

[74] Rubin (n 24) 63–69; ch 2 at 27–29.
[75] ibid.
[76] Rubin (n 24) 66–67.
[77] ibid.
[78] ibid 68.
[79] ibid.

independence is to be accomplished.[80] Several episodes of controversy which have arisen in relation to the UK law officer regime by reason of insufficient conceptual clarity of this sort are thus the focus of this sub-section.

The first and perhaps most prominent set of controversies that are relevant to this point concern allegations of inappropriate influence by members of the UK Cabinet in circumstances where the Attorney General for England and Wales, like other members of the UK law officer regime in similar predicaments, has been expected to discharge his or her range of 'public interest functions'[81] with poorly defined forms and levels of independence. There is thus an overlap between the application of the first facet of Rubin's theory in this context, namely the importance of recognising some interdependence, and the second facet of his theory regarding the importance of specificity about legitimate signals and interferences.

The *Campbell* case is undoubtedly the most consequential controversy relating to perceptions of inappropriate influence by the UK Cabinet on prosecutorial decision-making by the Attorney General for England and Wales.[82] The relevant facts centred on an instruction by the Attorney General issued to the Director of Public Prosecutions in 1923, requiring that a prosecution be commenced against the acting editor of a communist publication, John Ross Campbell of the *Daily Worker*, for incitement to mutiny. Following representations made at a Cabinet meeting on 6 August 1924, however, the Attorney General made arrangements for the Campbell prosecution to be withdrawn. The Cabinet meeting itself had centred on the political impropriety of the prosecution given that it would draw attention to the causes of communism, contrary to the government's typical approach, together with questions that had been raised in Parliament about prosecuting Campbell, who, it turned out, was a decorated war amputee with various sympathisers on the opposition benches. The Cabinet had therefore added to its minutes an agreement made in the presence of the Attorney General that not only would the prosecution be dropped, but also that 'no public prosecution of a political character should be undertaken without the prior sanction of the Cabinet being obtained'.[83] When opposition MPs subsequently pressed the Prime Minister to clarify his role in the prosecution decision, out of concern for inappropriate political interference in the criminal process, he denied having been consulted on the institution or withdrawal of Campbell's prosecution and refused to refer the matter for investigation by a Select Committee. Consequent to this deceitful lack of transparency, the first Labour administration in UK history was defeated in a successful censure motion which forced its resignation. The succeeding Prime Minister subsequently

[80] ibid.

[81] See ch 3 at 62–71.

[82] Edwards, *The Law Officers of the Crown* (n 18) chs 10–11; Edwards, *The Attorney General, Politics and the Public Interest* (n 33) 310–318. The relevant facts described above are drawn from Edwards' detailed accounts.

[83] For a full excerpt of the minute, see: Edwards, *The Attorney General, Politics and the Public Interest* (n 33) 315.

gave directions that the offending minute be excised from the Cabinet's records on account of being 'unconstitutional, subversive of the administration of justice and derogatory to the office of Attorney General'.[84]

In order to fully appreciate the relevance of Rubin's theory of independence in this context, and before evaluating the *Campbell* case through that lens, two further points should be made. The first is that prior to the furore surrounding the *Campbell* case, many former Attorneys General and the governments to which they belonged had recognised the law officers' 'subservience to the views of other members of the executive in the institution of criminal proceedings against particular individuals'.[85] Speaking in 1896, for example, a former Lord Chancellor who had also served as Solicitor General for England and Wales, Lord Herschell, argued that 'the government cannot entirely detach itself' from the prosecutorial decision-making of a law officer and refuted any suggestion that a government could 'say that the whole matter is for the determination absolutely of the Attorney-General'.[86] This point serves to highlight that the strong presumptions about independence which arose in the *Campbell* case were driven in large part by their contemporary context, while also underscoring the historical inaccuracy of some normative claims on which those presumptions were based. The second point to note is that, subsequent to the *Campbell* case, the accepted relationship between the law officers and the Cabinet regarding public interest functions was eventually crystallised by Sir Hartley Shawcross qua the Attorney General for England and Wales into a doctrine that has been endorsed and legitimised by many office-holders and patrons since. Shawcross' statement, which was reproduced on pages 66–67 of this book, clarified the constitutional position by averring that while a law officer is perfectly entitled to consult his or her ministerial colleagues in order to inform the discharge of his or her prosecutorial functions, the assistance of those colleagues is confined to 'informing him [or her] of particular considerations which might affect his [or her] own decision'.[87] It 'does not consist, and must not consist', he said, in telling the law officer what his or her decision ought to be.[88]

With the benefit of this rounded view of the *Campbell* case, together with its historical prelude and aftermath, it is possible to draw upon Rubin's general theory of independence in order to discern with precision the source of controversy at the heart of the whole saga. Put simply, the illegitimacy of Cabinet influence in the *Campbell* case as compared with the legitimacy of Cabinet influence envisaged by the Shawcross statement can be reduced to a distinction between the types of signal interfered with by prohibitions in each paradigm. In the *Campbell* case, there is both little evidence of any prohibitive interferences between the relevant

[84] Edwards, *The Law Officers of the Crown* (n 18) 213.
[85] ibid 178.
[86] HL Deb 2 July 1896, vol 42, col 518.
[87] HC Deb 29 January 1951, vol 483, col 683.
[88] ibid.

government units (the Cabinet and the Attorney General) and clear evidence of a performative signal in the form of a command. The Cabinet minute, requiring its 'prior sanction' before the Attorney General would be permitted to make prosecutorial decisions in future cases with a political character, amounts to an obvious example of a performative signal. The case also displays evidence of informative and expressive signals, with the former being evident in the account provided by the Attorney General to the Cabinet at its meeting on 6 August 1924 and the latter being apparent in the Prime Minister's condemnatory remarks about the initial decision of the Attorney General to prosecute Campbell. With all three forms of signal being permitted to flow freely between the Cabinet and the Attorney General, a very low level of independence, if any, was generated between the relevant units. Once this state of affairs became public knowledge, opposition MPs and the broader public were capable of realising that their expectations of some independence had been frustrated. This much is unsurprising, in retrospect, given that the exceptionally subservient relationship that appears to have existed between the relevant units could scarcely have been described as one involving any form of independence recognised by Rubin.

The Shawcross statement, on the other hand, clearly delineated a specific type of interference that may legitimately condition the exchange of signals between relevant units while also spelling out the acceptability of other signal types. In particular, Shawcross indicated that performative signals were prohibited when he said that 'the responsibility for the eventual decision rests with the Attorney General, and he [or she] is not to be put, and is not put, under pressure by his colleagues in this matter'.[89] He did so while, at the same time, minimising any inappropriate expectations of 'high level' independence which might result in his ministerial responsibility for the director assuming a 'theoretical quality' of little practical significance.[90] This much was conveyed by his explanation that the Attorney General may 'consult with any of his colleagues in the Government' who, in turn, may inform the Attorney General 'of particular considerations which may affect his [or her] own decision'.[91] In this way, Shawcross made it clear that the receipt of informative and perhaps even expressive signals were a necessary part of the law officer's role in prosecutorial decision-making, without compromising the importance of preserving an important degree of independence by the prohibition of performative signals.

Despite the apparent perspicuity of Shawcross' 'classic pronouncement'[92] on the constitutional position between the Attorney General and the Cabinet in decisions pertaining to the public interest functions of the law officers, further

[89] ibid col 684.

[90] John Ll J Edwards, 'The Office of Attorney General – New Levels of Public Expectations and Accountability' in Philip C Stenning (ed), *Accountability for Criminal Justice: Selected Essays* (University of Toronto Press 1995) 310.

[91] HC Deb 29 January 1951, vol 483, col 683.

[92] Edwards, *The Attorney General, Politics and the Public Interest* (n 33) 318.

controversies about the legitimacy of the arrangement laid out in his statement have since occurred on several occasions. One particularly high-profile example must be explored at this juncture. It involved a further government unit in the form of the Serious Fraud Office and can thus be used to demonstrate the utility of Rubin's framework of analysis in scenarios involving more than two government units with a relationship to the Attorney General. It is also interesting and significant because it resulted in the creation of a further form of attenuating interference designed to avoid further controversies of a similar nature. The example in question relates to a series of events that were examined in the *Corner House* case which was considered in 2008 by the High Court and the Appellate Committee of the House of Lords; with the latter overturning the ruling of the former at first instance.[93]

The Director of the Serious Fraud Office, it should be recalled, discharges all his or her functions under the superintendence of the Attorney General for England and Wales by virtue of section 1(2) of the Criminal Justice Act 1987. One such function is the investigation of any suspected offence which appears on reasonable grounds to involve serious or complex fraud.[94] The courts in *Corner House* heard that, in the exercise of this statutory role, the Director had launched an investigation into allegations of corruption involving a company known as 'BAE' concerning, inter alia, 'a valuable arms contract between Her Majesty's Government and the Kingdom of Saudi Arabia for which BAE was the main contractor'.[95] In the course of this investigation, the Director faced resistance from BAE in response to requests for the disclosure of information which, BAE submitted, would adversely affect UK–Saudi relations and jeopardise the lucrative arms contract mentioned above. The director therefore contacted the Attorney General and together they put a 'Shawcross exercise' into motion, based on their view that it was 'appropriate to invite the views of other Government ministers, in order to acquaint themselves with all the relevant considerations, so as to enable them to assess whether it was contrary to the public interest for the investigation to proceed'.[96] Despite the generally off-putting responses to that exercise, including a letter from the Cabinet Secretary indicating that British security interests could be damaged if the investigation were to continue, the Director and the Attorney General decided that it was indeed in the public interest for the Serious Fraud Office investigation to proceed. However, just as the Serious Fraud Office was on the cusp of obtaining Swiss banking information to ascertain whether Saudi officials had been in receipt of certain payments, the Saudi authorities delivered an explicit threat to

[93] *R (Corner House Research & Ors) v Director of the Serious Fraud Office* [2008] EWHC 714 (Admin), [2008] UKHL 60, [2009] 1 AC 756. The relevant facts described above are drawn from a combination of these reports.

[94] Criminal Justice Act 1987, s 1(3).

[95] *R (Corner House Research & Ors) v Director of the Serious Fraud Office* [2008] UKHL 60, [2009] 1 AC 756 at [3].

[96] ibid at [6].

the UK Prime Minister's Chief of Staff. Those authorities specifically threatened to end negotiations in relation to the arms deal between Saudi Arabia and the UK, as well as Saudi cooperation in relation to both UK counter-terrorism measures and the pursuit of wider UK foreign policy objectives in the Middle East. The Prime Minister thereafter communicated to the Attorney General his 'judgment' that the risks posed by these representations were 'likely to have seriously negative consequences for the UK public interest in terms of both national security and our highest priority foreign policy objectives'.[97] In conveying these views to the Attorney General, the Prime Minister did, however, 'understand and respect the constitutional position' and the 'independent judgement' required of the Attorney General, emphasising that he simply believed it was his duty to share these perspectives with the law officer for consideration.[98] After the Director of the Serious Fraud Office had received similar warnings from the UK Ambassador to Saudi Arabia, who emphasised that the ongoing investigation posed a real threat to UK lives, both he and the Attorney General met to deliberate. The Attorney General expressed doubts about the sufficiency of evidence in the case rather than proposing to discontinue it on account of factors flowing from the threat by Saudi officials that had been conveyed by the Prime Minister and others. The Director decided to discontinue the investigation the following day, however, in light of the representations both he and the Attorney General had received, and it was that decision which the courts in *Corner House* had been invited to impugn.

Although the Director's decision was challenged on six grounds, only the sixth ground is directly relevant to the present analysis, which alleged that 'the Shawcross exercise was conducted improperly in that ministers expressed their opinions as to what the Director's decision should be'.[99] The High Court questioned the justiciability of this submission and decided that the case before it could be decided without resolving those doubts.[100] It did, however, make a number of telling obiter dicta about differing interpretations of the Shawcross exercise which had contributed so much to the controversy giving rise to the application. The government's interpretation was that, although 'ministers must not instruct the Attorney General to make a particular decision, and must not direct him what his decision ought to be', they are free to give 'their opinion as [to] where they think the public interest lies'.[101] Only performative signals were clearly prohibited, according to this interpretation. The wording of the sixth ground of review, however, involved an interpretation of independence on the part of the applicants which incorporated a prohibition on not only performative signals, but also

[97] *R (Corner House Research & Ors) v Director of the Serious Fraud Office* [2008] EWHC 714 (Admin) at [31].
[98] ibid.
[99] ibid [49].
[100] ibid [167].
[101] ibid [165].

certain expressive signals. As Moses LJ and Sullivan J put it, the applicants alleged that the Prime Minister had 'broke[n] the rules by forcefully expressing his opinion that the investigations should be halted'.[102] This carried a danger, in the court's view, of making it 'more difficult for the independent decision maker clearly to demonstrate that his decision was exercised independently and free from what Sir Hartley [Shawcross] describes as *pressure by his colleagues*'.[103] The court went so far as to suggest there would be 'some advantage in public clarification' about the ambiguity of the existing Shawcross statement.[104]

The House of Lords did not engage with the justiciability of the Shawcross exercise in any depth. Nor did it express any view on the most appropriate interpretation of the constitutional regulation provided therein. The Appellate Committee focused, instead, on a principle formulated by the High Court holding that 'submission to a threat is lawful only when it is demonstrated to a court that there is no alternative course open to the decision-maker',[105] which the committee rejected in the course of overturning the decision of the High Court at first instance and in ruling that the decision of the Director had, in fact, been lawful.[106] Importantly, however, controversy surrounding the decision of the Director to drop the Serious Fraud Office investigation of BAE was not assuaged by the House of Lords' confirmation of its legality. Together with several similar incidents involving allegations of inappropriate political pressure on the Attorney General and the prosecuting authorities under his or her superintendence, the BAE saga came to be characterised as having created 'perceptions of a lack of independence and of political bias' which risked eroding trust in the office of the Attorney General.[107] There was a stage at which legislative reform to the office of Attorney General appeared likely in response to these concerns,[108] but ultimately the Government abandoned those proposals in favour of non-legislative changes which, it had since been decided, were a more appropriate way of addressing the misplaced perceptions described above. In particular, the Lord Chancellor and Secretary of State for Justice of the time indicated that

> the Attorney has reached a new settlement with the Directors of Public Prosecutions, the Serious Fraud Office and Revenue and Customs Prosecutions to improve relationships, guarantee prosecutorial independence while ensuring an appropriate degree of accountability and to improve transparency about the relationship, as reflected in

[102] ibid [163].
[103] ibid [168]. Italics in original.
[104] ibid [166].
[105] ibid [99]; *R (Corner House Research & Ors) v Director of the Serious Fraud Office* [2008] UKHL 60, [2009] 1 AC 756 at [38].
[106] *R (Corner House Research & Ors) v Director of the Serious Fraud Office* [2008] UKHL 60, [2009] 1 AC 756 at [40]–[42].
[107] Constitutional Affairs Committee, *The Constitutional Role of the Attorney General* (HC 2006-07, 306) paras 43-46, 54; Select Committee on the Constitution, *Reform of the Office Attorney General* (HL 2007-08, 93) paras 15–16.
[108] Ministry of Justice, *Governance of Britain – Constitutional Renewal* (Cm 7342-I, 2008) paras 32–92.

> the new protocol setting out the respective responsibilities of the Attorney and the Directors.[109]

The extent to which the protocol in question clarified doubts about which signals, with respect to prosecutorial decisions, could legitimately flow between government ministers, the Attorney General, and the Director of the Serious Fraud Office, inter alios, remained questionable.[110] The following part of the protocol is especially noteworthy:

> In a few very exceptional cases the prosecutor, whether the Attorney General or the Directors, may conclude that it is appropriate to consult relevant Government Ministers as part of the decision making process. In such a case the Attorney General may seek Ministerial representations in a public interest consultation exercise …
>
> The purpose of the exercise is confined to identifying particular public interest considerations which are relevant to the prosecution decision of the Attorney General or the Director. The weight to be given to such representation is a matter for the Director or the Attorney General. Ministers are not able to dictate what the decision ought to be. The responsibility for the eventual decision rests with the Attorney General or with the Director, depending on the case …
>
> The Attorney General ensures that public interest consultation exercises are conducted with propriety, that Ministers who are consulted are informed that the decision is for the Director or the Attorney General alone; and that where such considerations are said to point away from prosecution, the Attorney General and the Director will probe rigorously the representations made where, and as far as, it appears to them appropriate to do so.[111]

It is clear from this excerpt that the protocol attempted to shift focus away from the types of signal that may be sent between the relevant government units toward the weight which a receiving unit is entitled to accord to those signals. This form of interference arguably amounts to what Rubin refers to as an 'attenuation' of informative and expressive signals, rather than a prohibition of the sort which has been established in respect of performative signals. While this approach avoids the recurring question about whether vigorously expressed ministerial signals that might be viewed as political pressurisation should be categorically prohibited, it demonstrates how attenuations can be used to enhance the level of independence enjoyed by receiving units. After ten years in operation, however, the attenuation achieved by this protocol was replaced in January 2019 with a new framework agreement between the law officers and the Director of the Serious Fraud Office.[112] A similar but separate agreement has been agreed between the law officers and the

[109] HC Deb 20 July 2009, col WS146.
[110] Attorney General's Office, *Protocol between the Attorney General and the Prosecuting Departments* (July 2009).
[111] ibid para 4(e).
[112] Attorney General's Office, *Framework Agreement between the Law Officers and the Director of the Serious Fraud Office* (21 January 2019); Justice Committee, *Oral Evidence by the Rt Hon Geoffrey Cox QC MP on the Work of the Attorney General* (HC 1887, 23 January 2019).

Director of the Crown Prosecution Service which supplants the 2009 protocol in a comparable manner.[113] The new framework agreements are a modified form of attenuation between the relevant units featuring a number of interesting changes. Some of these changes simply reflect the evolution of organisational relationships between the relevant units over the course of ten years and a need for modern governance arrangements to reflect those changes,[114] such as the establishment of a 'Ministerial Strategic Board' responsible for setting the strategic direction of an 'SFO Board'.[115] It is clear, however, that some changes were directly precipitated by high-profile controversy over disclosure failings on the part of prosecuting departments in the year prior to its publication (together with related questions about the extent to which the law officers were in a proper position to account for those failings).[116] The UK Government, for example, has stated that the new agreement is intended to achieve a 'strengthened' relationship of 'superintendence and sponsorship' between the law officers and prosecuting departments.[117] Although it has no statutory basis akin to superintendence, the latter reference to sponsorship is a particularly interesting descriptor of these relationships given that it suggests, among other things, a renewed emphasis on the need for the law officers to protect the independence of prosecuting departments by helping to ensure adequate government resourcing.[118] The statutory superintendence of the Attorney General for England and Wales over the Directors of the Serious Fraud Office and the Crown Prosecution Service is also broken down with interesting specificity in the new framework agreements. For present purposes it is especially interesting to note, for instance, that certain signals are expressly prohibited between the law officers and the Serious Fraud Office unless consultation is required by law (such as in cases requiring a law officer's consent to initiate a prosecution). In particular, the framework agreement adds clear and unambiguous language providing

[113] Attorney General's Office, *Framework Agreement between the Law Officers and the Director of Public Prosecutions* (18 December 2020). Moreover, for a recently agreed Protocol which emphasises the independence of the Crown Prosecution Service Inspectorate, see: Attorney General's Office, *Protocol between the Law Officers and Her Majesty's Chief Inspector of the Crown Prosecution Service* (29 January 2020).

[114] Letter from the Attorney General for England and Wales, Geoffrey Cox QC MP, to the Chair of House of Commons Justice Committee, Bob Neill MP (18 January 2019). Available at: www.parliament.uk/documents/commonscommittees/Justice/correspondence/2019-01-18-AG-Bob-Neill-MP.pdf.

[115] Attorney General's Office, *Framework Agreement between the Law Officers and the Director of the Serious Fraud Office* (21 January 2019) paras 21–25; Justice Committee, *Oral Evidence by the Rt Hon Geoffrey Cox QC MP on the Work of the Attorney General* (HC 1887, 23 January 2019).

[116] See, e.g., Justice Committee, *Disclosure of Evidence in Criminal Cases* (HC 2017–19, 859); Attorney General's Office, *Framework Agreement between the Law Officers and the Director of the Serious Fraud Office* (21 January 2019) para 63.

[117] Ministry of Justice, *Government Response to the Justice Select Committee's Eleventh Report of Session 2017–19: Disclosure of Evidence in Criminal Cases* (Cm 9744, 2018) para 15.

[118] The new framework agreement deals with practicalities involved in this financial accountability role at some length. See: Attorney General's Office, *Framework Agreement between the Law Officers and the Director of the Serious Fraud Office* (21 January 2019) paras 29–38.

that the law officers 'will never be consulted or otherwise engaged on any case' which either relates to a range of previously recognised reasons for not engaging in consultation, namely in cases relating to a Member of Parliament (including peers) or minister; to a political party or the conduct of elections, or which gives rise to any question of personal or professional conflict of interest.[119] The agreement also reiterates the regulation of appropriate signals that may flow between relevant government units in the 'few very exceptional cases' where a Shawcross exercise seeking ministerial representations on the public interest is deemed appropriate.[120]

The conceptual clarity that can be derived from analysing adjustments to a conception of independence using Rubin's theoretical framework is arguably exemplified by these observations. This sub-section could go on to apply Rubin's theory to a wide range of further examples involving controversies that have arisen from other law officers' functions, including episodes drawn from devolved contexts, but it does not do so because the central point about Rubin's utility has now been made and illustrated. To the extent that the framework leaves open questions about who should be held accountable for the final decisions taken by office-holders with differing levels of independence from various government units, a separate but related method of conceptual analysis is called for. The next section of this chapter turns to consider in more detail what that method might involve.

Constitutional Controversy and the Value of Accountability

There have been numerous occasions on which the constitutional value of accountability appears to have given rise to episodes of controversy about the UK law officer regime, in all its complexity, which have had an effect on the legitimacy of its members. The danger of over-generalisation in examining a selection of episodes from this wide range of controversies has been addressed, it is hoped, by deploying a relatively sophisticated conceptual framework for analysing the examples. To this end, Bovens' detailed definition of accountability has been drawn upon in preference to leaner definitions that, for instance, distinguish simply between 'sacrificial' and 'explanatory' forms of accountability. Bovens' definition bears repeating in full:

> [a]ccountability is a relationship between an actor and a forum, in which the actor has an obligation to explain and to justify his or her conduct, the forum can pose questions and pass judgement, and the actor may face consequences.[121]

[119] ibid para 64.
[120] ibid paras 53–55.
[121] Mark Bovens, 'Analysing and Assessing Accountability: A Conceptual Framework' (2007) 13 *European Law Journal* 447, 450. Emphasis removed.

As explained in Chapter 2,[122] the analytical capabilities provided by this definition are accentuated by Bovens' identification of four dimensions to it. These dimensions can be used to dissect any given social or institutional relation that fall within the definition. In the next sub-section hereafter, both the dimension relating to the importance of distinguishing between different *forums* and the dimension relating to the types of *conduct* that each forum takes account of are explored with due reference to the UK law officer regime. In the following sub-section, complications surrounding the identification of relevant *actors* that forums should hold to account in the context of a complex institutional structure like the UK law officer regime are considered. Those considerations are analysed alongside a brief review of several controversial episodes that appear to be premised on uncertainty surrounding the nature of *obligations* that pertain between actors and forums in the UK law officer regime. In addition to providing a framework for studying the 'mechanism' of accountability in this four-dimensional way, it should also be recalled at this point that Bovens acknowledges a role for the concept as a 'virtue' that can be used to assess excesses and deficits in the legitimacy of a given regime. Normative perspectives of this kind therefore feature throughout the remainder of this chapter, where appropriate, together with similar assessments flowing from other relevant standards for evaluating the legitimacy of the UK law officer regime (namely independence and trust).

Varied Forums with Varying Metrics

There are at least five types of forum that law officers in the UK confront in the course of exercising their functions – political, administrative, social, legal and professional – with each forum type generally restricting its attention to different kinds of conduct. Bovens has highlighted how these varied forms of accountability can come into conflict, where the 'problem of many eyes', as he puts it, results in confusion about what constitutes legitimate conduct.[123] In other words, because each forum type applies a different approval metric, controversies can occur, for example, where a law officer is blinkered towards satisfying one forum type and fails, as a result, to pay due attention to all the other forums which hold him or her to account in different ways. This makes it important for office-holders to assess the legitimacy of any actions they propose to take, to the largest extent possible, with reference to all forum types and each approval metric that they can be expected to apply. Moreover, there are some functional circumstances in which law officers themselves amount to forums of accountability for other actors. In these circumstances it becomes important for actors accounting to the law officers to realise that they constitute a special mixed sort of forum that can be expected to

[122] See ch 2 at 30–36.
[123] Bovens (n 121) 455.

apply a number of varying metrics, in order to maintain the legitimacy they enjoy by virtue of accountability to other forums.

There are a range of large government units, as Rubin would describe them, which might be loosely classified as political forums. Each of the legislatures in the UK are good examples, as are the Cabinets that have been formed in each jurisdiction (with the exception of Northern Ireland, where the Executive Committee is the nearest equivalent). Each of these units might be broken down into more specific sub-units for the purposes of establishing appropriate levels of independence, and indeed for the purpose of allocating responsibility to particular actors as discussed in the next sub-section, but generally speaking they can all be expected to apply political ideologies by way of an approval metric. The scope of conduct which different political forums may legitimately call upon a law officer to account for varies significantly, however, with a clear example of this being the ability of executive units to account for the quality of legal advice provided by law officers in a way which parliamentary units cannot.[124] Financial auditors are an important example of administrative forums, meanwhile, who must be borne in mind most particularly when law officers are exercising functions with significant budgetary implications.[125] Corporate governance principles like efficiency are the metric to be expected from this perspective, which are clearly evident in the framework documents which govern relationships between the law officers for England and Wales and the prosecuting departments they are responsible for sponsoring and superintending for example.[126]

Bovens acknowledges that social forums can be difficult to identify.[127] This is because, while there are plenty of public interest groups and charities that are affected by and comment on law officers' decisions in the UK, they often lack any direct ability to enforce consequences upon office-holders where the latter fail to provide adequate explanations of their conduct. It could be suggested, however, that the general public should be regarded as a forum in and of itself to the extent that law officers clearly feel obliged to account to the whole populace in some circumstances. The approval metric that should be borne in mind when thinking of this forum is fraught with ambiguity, however, which is perhaps why 'the public interest' has proved so troublesome a barometer of legitimacy.[128] Thus, while law officers have been known to proclaim that their overall concern is 'with

[124] Some recent controversies arising from the convention which prevents governmental legal advice provided by law officers from being disclosed to parliamentary units will be explored further below.

[125] On the provisions for managing and controlling the availability of central government funds, see: John McEldowney, 'Public Expenditure and the Control of Public Finance' in Jeffrey Jowell, Dawn Oliver and Colm O'Cinneide (eds), *The Changing Constitution* (8th edn, Oxford University Press 2015).

[126] Attorney General's Office, *Framework Agreement between the Law Officers and the Director of the Serious Fraud Office* (18 December 2020) paras 31–41; Attorney General's Office, *Framework Agreement between the Law Officers and the Director of Public Prosecutions* (21 January 2019) paras 29–38.

[127] Bovens (n 121) 457.

[128] Neil Walker, 'The Antinomies of the Law Officers' in Maurice Sunkin and Sebastian Payne (eds), *The Nature of the Crown: A Legal and Political Analysis* (Oxford University Press 1999) 150.

keeping the enforcement of the law in tune with current standards of public opinion' while not becoming 'subservient to it',[129] it is arguable that this variety of social forum is perhaps the least 'clearly demarcated, coherent and authoritative' one in existence.[130] To the extent that the Freedom of Information Act 2000 has added a degree of enforceability to the mechanism by making it possible for members of the public to demand information from or about most members of the UK law officer regime, moreover, the statutory limits on that right have plainly inhibited the power of the forum in practice. The contested saga involving an attempt to have a report prepared by Dame Elish Angiolini on the operation of the office of the Attorney General for Northern Ireland released at the request of individual members of the public is a clear case in point.[131]

Courts represent the most obvious legal forums that members of the UK law officer regime must account to, though of course they too can be expected to apply varying metrics based on their position in the judicial hierarchy and the effect of binding precedents from higher courts. Contextualised assessments of legality are the relevant metric here in any event, though the scope of law officer conduct which may be reviewed by a court of law has proved to be a particularly controversial topic over recent decades. For many years the position on this point was governed by judicial reasoning developed in a landmark challenge to the discretion of the Attorney General for England and Wales in deciding whether to grant his or her fiat to a relator action that arose in the case of *Gouriet*.[132] The dispute in question gave rise to a difference in opinion on the Court of Appeal between the views of Lord Denning sitting as Master of the Rolls and the opinions of both his fellow Lords Justices of Appeal. Lord Denning's view, put simply, was that it would be 'a direct challenge to the rule of law' for the Attorney General to prevent a citizen from enforcing rights of a public nature by refusing his consent to a relator action.[133] His Lordship hypothesised situations wherein an Attorney General '[c]onfronted with a powerful subject whom he feared to offend' might refuse his consent to a relator and thereby enable that subject 'to disregard the law with impunity'.[134] Circumstances such as these would, Lord Denning suggested, render it permissible for courts to indirectly override an Attorney's exercise of discretion. Sir Stephen Sedley has since suggested that the premise of Lord Denning's argument was 'not fanciful' given that it is to some extent reflected by the fact that 'courts have developed their own principles of standing' over the course of history instead of leaving it solely to members of the UK law officer regime to sieve out cases for substantive hearing according to their own conceptions of the public

[129] Sam Silkin, 'The Office of the Attorney General' (1976) 2 *Poly Law Review* 3, 6.
[130] Bovens (n 121) 457.
[131] See ch 6 at 162–164.
[132] *Gouriet v Union of Post Office Workers* [1977] QB 729 (CA); *Gouriet v Union of Post Office Workers* [1977] UKHL 5, [1978] AC 435.
[133] *Gouriet v Union of Post Office Workers* [1977] QB 729 (CA) 758.
[134] ibid 761.

interest.[135] Lawton LJ disagreed with Lord Denning, however, holding that 'the courts have no jurisdiction over the discretion of the Attorney-General as to when, and when not, he should seek to enforce the law having public consequences'.[136] Likewise, Ormrod LJ held that 'the Attorney-General's discretion is not subject to review by the court'.[137] Lord Denning's view was further castigated when on a further appeal to the Appellate Committee of the House of Lords a unanimous bench specifically and unequivocally rejected it. Lord Wilberforce emphasised that the courts were not 'fitted or equipped' to review the discretionary powers of Attorneys General when they involve assessments of what is in the public interest:

> The very fact that, as the present case very well shows, decisions are of the type to attract political criticism and controversy, shows that they are outside the range of discretionary problems which the courts can resolve. Judges are equipped to find legal rights and administer, on well-known principles, discretionary remedies. These matters are widely outside those areas.[138]

Viscount Dilhorne also felt compelled to address Lord Denning's remarks at some length because, speaking from experience as a former law officer, he considered it 'undesirable that any judicial observations suggesting that the exercise by the Attorney-General of [his or her] functions and duties is subject to control, supervision and review by the courts should be left unanswered'.[139] The suggestion that refusal to consent to a relator action might constitute a challenge to the rule of law was 'entirely misconceived' in his judgment.[140] Lords Diplock, Edmund-Davies and Fraser concurred with these rulings, with Lord Edmund-Davies even describing the discretion of the Attorney General for England and Wales as 'absolute and non-reviewable'.[141] In addition, Lord Fraser expressed his preference for the law officer being held to account by political forums in the following terms:

> If the Attorney-General were to commit a serious error of judgment by withholding consent to relator proceedings in a case where he ought to have given it, the remedy must in my opinion lie in the political field by enforcing his responsibility to Parliament and not in the legal field through the courts. That is appropriate because his error would not be an error of law but would be one of political judgment, using the expression of course not in a party sense but in the sense of weighing the relative importance of different aspects of the public interest.[142]

[135] Stephen Sedley, *Law and the Whirligig of Time* (Hart Publishing 2018) 110.
[136] *Gouriet v Union of Post Office Workers* [1977] QB 729 (CA) 768.
[137] ibid 772.
[138] *Gouriet v Union of Post Office Workers* [1977] UKHL 5, [1978] AC 435, 482. Inclinations toward judicial deference where public interest decisions are involved were likewise expressed in the *Corner House* case: *R (Corner House Research & Ors) v Director of the Serious Fraud Office* [2008] UKHL 60, [2009] 1 AC 756 at [31].
[139] ibid 488.
[140] ibid 495.
[141] ibid 512.
[142] ibid 524.

To the extent that this judicial reasoning would have once undermined the suggestion that courts should be regarded as legal forums which can hold members of the UK law officer regime to account for their decisions, three points must be emphasised by way of explanation. The first point is that, as a former Attorney General has put it, there is of course a degree of indirect accountability over advisory law officer functions through the courts because the 'legal advice of the law officers is often tested when the dispute in which the legal advice was relevant comes to be determined in court'.[143] Recently, for instance, when Suella Braverman qua the Attorney General for England and Wales made submissions to the Court of Appeal in connection with an unduly lenient sentencing referral, her argument was considered so ill-considered that the Court described it as both 'unusual', 'to say the least', and 'regrettable'.[144] As Rozenberg has observed, 'this is as scathing as it gets'.[145]

The second point is that senior judicial opinions appear to have evolved somewhat since *Gouriet*, though the precedent set by it has never been definitively overruled.[146] The decision that has come closest to doing so is *Mohit*, wherein Lord Bingham held that a statement from *Gouriet* on the non-reviewability of the prerogative power of the Attorney General for England and Wales to enter a nolle prosequi 'remains a binding statement of English law on cases covered by it'.[147] In addition to this finding, however, Lord Bingham implied that the ratio decidendi reached in *Gouriet* may need to be 'reviewed or modified' in light of the Appellate Committee's later ruling in *GCHQ*, which expanded the reach of judicial review to include prerogative decisions made by members of the executive.[148] Further still, Lord Bingham held that where a function of the Attorney General is based in statute – such as the requirement for his or her consent to commencement of certain prosecutions – there are no 'inherent constitutional objections to the jurisdiction of the courts being invoked'.[149] Indeed, the *Corner House* case discussed above

[143] Peter Goldsmith, 'Independence – Myth or Mystery?' (A Speech for the Annual Denning Lecture, 27 November 2007).

[144] *R v Long, Bowes and Cole* [2020] EWCA Crim 1729, [2021] 4 WLR 5 at [84]. Also see: Joshua Rozenberg, 'An Unusual Submission: Suella Braverman Fails to Persuade Judges that Three Killers Received Unduly Lenient Sentences' (*A Lawyer Writes*, 16 December 2020). Available at: https://rozenberg.substack.com/p/an-unusual-submission?r=8r17o&utm_campaign=post&utm_medium=web&utm_source=copy.

[145] ibid.

[146] For further commentary on these developments, see: Conor McCormick, 'Reviewing the Reviewability of the Attorney General for Northern Ireland' [2018] *Public Law* 22; Osita Mba, 'Judicial Review of the Prosecutorial Powers of the Attorney-General in England and Wales and Nigeria: An Imperative of the Rule of Law' (2010) 2 *Oxford University Comparative Law Forum*. Available at: https://ouclf.iuscomp.org/judicial-review-of-the-prosecutorial-powers-of-the-attorney-general-in-england-and-wales-and-nigeria-an-imperative-of-the-rule-of-law/#fn0sym; Edwards, 'New Levels of Public Expectations and Accountability' (n 90) 312–323; Barry Hough, 'Judicial Review Where the Attorney General Refuses to Act: Time for a Change' (1988) 8 *Legal Studies* 189, 193–200.

[147] *Mohit v Director of Public Prosecutions of Mauritius* [2006] UKPC 20, [2006] 1 WLR 3343, 3350.

[148] ibid, citing *Council of Civil Service Unions v Minister for the Civil Service* [1983] UKHL 6, [1985] AC 374.

[149] ibid.

involved the review of a decision by the Director of the Serious Fraud Office acting under the statutory superintendence of the Attorney General and is, therefore, a clear example of how *Mohit* has taken effect in practice.[150] It has been observed, moreover, that by ruling the Attorney General and the Director of the Serious Fraud Office had acted lawfully in circumstances of widespread controversy, judicial review operated as a timely source of legitimacy for the office-holders in *Corner House*.[151] No clear examples involving challenges to the exercise of prerogative powers by the Attorney General have yet reached the appellate courts, however, leaving some doubt about which of those functions are, in fact, judicially reviewable following *GCHQ*. Having critically reviewed the case law from a comparative perspective, Mba for one has concluded that the UK Supreme Court 'should subject the Attorney-General's prerogative prosecutorial powers to judicial review by expressly overruling the *Gouriet* line of cases whenever the opportunity presents itself'.[152]

The third point to note about *Gouriet* is that it deemed accountability by legal forums inappropriate in respect of the office of the Attorney General for England and Wales only. The case did not, as such, feature judicial reasoning about the particularities of the other law officer models in the UK that were highlighted throughout Chapters 3 to 6 of this book. The significance of this point was borne out in two recent applications for the judicial review of statutory inquest decisions taken by the Attorney General for Northern Ireland, wherein both Maguire J and Deeny J were invited to rule on the amenability of that office to review.[153] Neither judge felt it necessary to decide this jurisdictional question in order to resolve the cases before them, but the general tenor of their obiter remarks suggested a degree of acceptance that jurisdiction would in fact lie against certain decisions of the Attorney General for Northern Ireland. Maguire J, for example, said he was 'not persuaded that the AGNI when making a decision whether or not to order a fresh inquest … is immune from judicial review'.[154] It is arguably desirable that questions of amenability to judicial review about each member of the UK law officer regime should be considered from first principle in this manner, as and when relevant circumstances arise, on account of the considerably different levels of accountability that are applied to each office by other types of forum. It should be clear from Chapter 6, for instance, that political accountability over the office of the Attorney General for Northern Ireland is subject to a broad range of operational and statutory caveats at present which render the reasons expressed in *Gouriet* for immunising the Attorney General for England and Wales from judicial review less

[150] See the text at (n 93)–(n 120) above.
[151] Mba (n 146).
[152] ibid.
[153] *Re Johnstone's Application for Judicial Review* [2017] NIQB 33; *Re Johnstone's (Dorothy) Application for Leave* (HC, 17 June 2016); *Re Mulhern's (Francis) Application for Leave* [2016] NIQB 59. Also see *Re Dalton's (Rosaleen) and Johnstone's (Dorothy) Application* [2020] NICA 27.
[154] *Re Mulhern's (Francis) Application for Leave* [2016] NIQB 59 at [16].

applicable to the Northern Ireland Attorney.[155] Lord Fraser's preference for political accountability, for example, must be viewed with particular circumspection when considered alongside the limited availability of that forum type in connection with the modern office of the Attorney General for Northern Ireland.[156] This point also speaks to a more fundamental conceptual issue about overlaps in the scope of conduct which legal and political forums can legitimately oversee, in that each forum type appears to premise the limits on its on accountability role by reference to the operational functionality of other forums. As such, conceptual limits on the judicial role appear less convincing in the absence of a legislature; just as the absence of an adequate judicial system would presumably embolden legislative intervention in respect of orthodox judicial jurisdiction.

Moving on to professional forum types, the most relevant in the context of the UK law officer regime are the Inns of Court, the Bar Councils and the Law Societies in Northern Ireland and in England and Wales respectively, together with the Faculty of Advocates and Law Society in Scotland. Law officer literature features several references to the importance of professional legal ethics as a guiding influence on the exercise of their constitutional functions,[157] with the oversight of relevant professional bodies being a significant source of both reassurance and ammunition in times of controversy. Among the metrics that can be expected from this standpoint are duties of candour to the court and duties to decline instructions in areas of law outside the officer-holder's competence. With respect to the former, for example, Edwards has chronicled allegations of unprofessional conduct on the part of Sir John Hobson that were adjudicated upon by his fellow benchers of the Inner Temple while he occupied the office of the Attorney General for England and Wales:

> The original complaint arose out of the heated controversy engendered by the Government's refusal to grant political asylum to Chief Enaharo of Nigeria. The specific allegations directed against the attorney general were that, in the course of habeas corpus proceedings that preceded the deportation of Enaharo to stand trial for treason in Nigeria, Hobson had presented an affidavit sworn by the home secretary which he, the attorney general, knew to be inaccurate and misleading … Among the dispositions available to the Inner Temple benchers were a reprimand, suspension or disbarment. The attorney general was represented by counsel and gave evidence refuting the allegations made against him. At the conclusion of the hearing the assembled masters of the Inn of Court found that the charges were unfounded and that there were no grounds for criticizing the attorney general's conduct.[158]

[155] Also see: McCormick, 'Reviewing the Reviewability of the Attorney General for Northern Ireland' (n 146) 29–30.

[156] ibid.

[157] For an interesting analysis that challenges how standard theories of legal ethics apply to government lawyers, including law officers, see: Matthew Windsor, 'Government Legal Advisors through the Ethics Looking Glass' in David Feldman (ed), *Law in Politics, Politics in Law* (Hart Publishing 2015).

[158] Edwards, 'New Levels of Public Expectations and Accountability' (n 90) 299–300. See *R v Brixton Prison Governor, ex p Enaharo* [1963] 2 QB 455, [1963] 2 WLR 1260.

With respect to the latter metric involving a duty to refuse instructions beyond the competence or expertise expected by a practising lawyer with a particular specialism, a recent example is evidenced in commentary about whether Jeremy Wright qua the Attorney General for England and Wales held the requisite 'experience or, frankly, the legal fire-power' to resist a prominent legal challenge over the constitutional process for initiating Brexit given his background in criminal rather than constitutional law.[159] Scott noted the possibility of 'ignominous' professional accountability in this way:

> … if [Wright] were in fact to "lead" the Government's legal team (in the sense, as it is invariably understood in legal circles, to mean appearing as the leading Queen's Counsel in a case) it might even lay him open to the charge that he is in breach of rule C21.8 of the Barristers' Code of Conduct which provides that a barrister should not act in a case when he is: "… not competent to handle the particular matter or otherwise [does] not have enough experience to handle the matter." It would certainly be an ignominious experience were the Attorney-General, the Government's chief legal adviser and nominal head of the Bar of England and Wales, to be referred to his professional body for acting beyond his experience.[160]

Interestingly, Wright's own recognition of the fact that it would have been 'absolute folly'[161] for him to conduct this case in full has since been described in positive terms as something which enhanced his reputation as a law officer, in the sense that it demonstrated an honest appreciation of his professional limitations.[162] Conversely, Suella Braverman qua the Attorney General for England and Wales suffered serious reputational damage after deciding to appear personally in an unduly lenient sentencing hearing which an experienced criminal lawyer said she was 'not competent to conduct'.[163] Braverman was also reported to the Bar Standards Board (together with Michael Ellis qua the Solicitor General for England and Wales) by 'hundreds' of complainants in the context of an extremely serious controversy 'about whether the law officers were condoning breaches of international law',[164] which inflicted further damage on the law officers' professional

[159] *R (Miller) v Secretary of State for Exiting the European Union* [2017] UKSC 5, [2018] AC 61; Matthew Scott, 'In Its Battle for Brexit, the Government Is Bringing a Knife to the Legal Gunfight' *The Telegraph* (29 September 2016). Available at: www.telegraph.co.uk/news/2016/09/29/in-its-battle-for-brexit-the-government-is-bringing-a-knife-to-t/.

[160] ibid.

[161] 'Ministers Reflect: Jeremy Wright' (*Institute for Government*, 2020). Available at: www.institutefor-government.org.uk/ministers-reflect/person/jeremy-wright/.

[162] James Hand, 'The Attorney-General, Politics and Logistics – A Fork in the Road?' (2022) *Legal Studies*, forthcoming.

[163] The Secret Barrister (*Twitter*, 12 November 2020). Available at: https://twitter.com/BarristerSecret/status/1326849470676480000?s=20.

[164] Jemma Slingo, 'Reports Against Barristers Have Doubled, Says Regulator' (*The Law Society Gazette*, 1 June 2021). Available at: www.lawgazette.co.uk/news/reports-against-barristers-have-doubled-says-regulator-/5108674.article. Also see: Amanda Pinto, 'Chair of the Bar: The Law Officers Must Defend the Rule of Law, Even When it is Unpopular with the Government' (*The Bar Council*, 18 September 2020). Available at: www.barcouncil.org.uk/resource/

reputation for independence and trustworthiness. Indeed, one commentator said that Braverman and Ellis' failure to resign in this context meant that they had 'destroyed their legal reputations for the sake of their political careers'.[165] In another incident, albeit with reference to different provisions in the Code of Conduct, the reputation of Lord Keen qua the Advocate General for Scotland was negatively affected by a substantive decision of the Bar Standards Board which held that he had breached the Code by failing to abide strictly by the terms of his firearms licence.[166] However, Lord Keen's reputation was later replenished to some extent following his decision to resign when Braverman and Ellis did not.[167]

These examples make it quite clear that members of the UK law officer regime are not considered immune from the disciplinary processes of their professional bodies and must, as such, observe the same 'standards by which every lawyer is subject to the assessment of his peers'.[168] With that said, the reach of this immunity might be questioned from first principles by reference to the legal position in other common law jurisdictions. In Canada, for instance, while it is accepted that most provincial and territorial Attorneys General are subject to the disciplinary processes of their professional bodies, Flavelle Martin has observed that those office-holders are clearly immune from professional discipline in circumstances involving prosecutorial discretion, unless they have acted with bad faith; that they are probably immune from professional discipline in circumstances involving 'core' policy advice, unless they have acted in bad faith; and that they are absolutely immune from professional discipline with respect to anything said in the legislature to which they belong.[169]

chair-of-the-bar-the-law-officers-must-defend-the-rule-of-law-even-when-it-is-unpopular-with-the-government.html. For details on some other reputationally damaging incidents in connection with Braverman's particularly controversial tenure, see: Owen Bowcott, 'Attorney General Faces Calls to Resign After She Defends Dominic Cummings' (*The Guardian*, 25 May 2020). Available at: www.theguardian.com/politics/2020/may/25/attorney-general-faces-calls-to-resign-defends-dominic-cummings-suella-braverman; Joshua Rozenberg, 'Mixed Millers from the Attorney General: Moral: Know Your Cases Before Taking on Another QC' (*A Lawyer Writes*, 25 September 2020). Available at: https://rozenberg.substack.com/p/mixed-millers-from-the-attorney-general. On the other hand, for commentary which defends some of Braverman's conduct in office, see: Conor Casey and John Larkin, 'Crossing the Line? The Attorney General and the Law/Politics Divide' (*Policy Exchange*, 12 January 2022). Available at: www.policyexchange.org.uk/publication/crossing-the-line/; Richard Ekins, 'Braverman is Right to Seek Clarification from the Court of Appeal in the Colston Case' (*ConservativeHome*, 13 January 2022). Available at: www.conservativehome.com/thinktankcentral/2022/01/richard-ekins-braverman-is-right-to-seek-clarification-from-the-court-of-appeal-on-the-colston-case.html.

[165] David Allen Green, 'The Law Officers in the New Age of Politics' (*Prospect*, 18 September 2020). Available at: www.prospectmagazine.co.uk/politics/law-officers-suella-braverman-lord-keen-robert-buckland-brexit-internal-market-bill.

[166] Jemma Slingo, 'Lord Keen QC in Breach of Core Duty – But Cleared of Misconduct' (*The Law Society Gazette*, 29 October 2019). Available at: www.lawgazette.co.uk/news/lord-keen-qc-in-breach-of-core-duty-but-cleared-of-misconduct/5101978.article.

[167] Joshua Rozenberg, 'What Made Lord Keen Resign?' (*A Lawyer Writes*, 2 October 2020). Available at: https://rozenberg.substack.com/p/what-made-lord-keen-resign.

[168] Edwards, 'New Levels of Public Expectations and Accountability' (n 90) 300.

[169] Andrew Flavelle Martin, 'The Immunity of the Attorney General to Law Society Discipline' (2016) 94 *Canadian Bar Review* 413.

The exploration of forum types throughout this sub-section has highlighted that various lines of accountability which draw upon varying metrics for assessing the legitimacy of law officers' conduct tend to attract controversy where there is doubt over the scope of conduct which a given forum may enquire into or where there is ambiguity about the relevant approval metric in use. The most high-profile debate about scope is perhaps that in respect of the appropriate ambit of judicial review, while the public interest is perhaps the most contentious approval metric invoked. By using Bovens' definition of accountability to clarify this dimension of the constitutional value, however, it has been possible to avoid a further form of confusion which commonly besets discussions about the UK law officer regime; namely the tendency to characterise law officers' as being 'required to serve two masters, the government and the law'.[170] It is this tendency which goes to the heart of taxonomical classification problems encountered throughout Chapters 3 to 6, in that any attempt to frame a particular function with reference to a single forum or a single approval metric fails to account for the 'pervasiveness of wider considerations'.[171] It is thus suggested that characterisations of this nature invariably oversimplify the constitutional position, and should be eschewed wherever possible in favour of the more precise model of conceptualising this dimension of accountability made possible by Bovens' framework.

Ambiguous Procedures and Uncertain Obligations

The remaining dimensions to accountability identified by Bovens concern 'the problem of many hands' and the possibility of uncertainty as regards the strength of obligations applicable to particular relationships. With respect to the former, it should be remembered that Bovens identifies a number of strategies for coping with the complex ways in which actors may contribute to a particular government decision (namely unitary, individual, collective and personal accountability).[172] These strategies all aim to address the understanding that government decisions are normally implemented after having passed through many hands, and are premised on the idea that accountability is only effective where it provides for a clear method for singling out the most appropriate actor responsible for a final decision (taking into account any relevant chains of command and so forth).[173] With respect to the latter, it should be recalled that Bovens generalises the types of obligation that compel a particular actor to answer to a particular forum into three categories: mandatory obligations, voluntary obligations and intermediate obligations (which are conceptually related to notions of vertical, horizontal and

[170] Diana Woodhouse, 'The Attorney General' (1997) 50 *Parliamentary Affairs* 97, 97.
[171] Walker (n 128) 158.
[172] Bovens (n 121) 457–459.
[173] ibid.

diagonal accountability).[174] Bovens indicates that the type of obligation which pertains between an actor and a forum will depend to some extent on the relevant strategy that exists for coping with the problem of many hands. For instance, he suggests that the relationship between a minister and Parliament is emblematic of a hierarchical relationship giving rise to mandatory obligations which can be conveniently conceptualised as a vertical form of accountability. This can be contrasted, Bovens submits, with the horizontal accountability that arises between two bodies of equal standing (as, perhaps, in the case of two ministers) which is sustained by voluntary obligations operating mutually. The semblance between these two aspects of accountability underpins the decision to consider them together in this sub-section, the remainder of which is concerned with analysing controversial incidents connected to both aspects.

One brief example may be provided to illustrate some difficulties related to the problem of many hands within the UK law officer regime, namely the position of the Solicitor General for England and Wales and the Solicitor General for Scotland. While they are traditionally positioned at the apex of complex organisational structures for the provision of legal advice and identified as the ministers responsible for various subordinate units that deal with government functions well beyond advisory services, the status of these law officers as deputies technically means that those offices are ranked second from the top in the applicable hierarchies. The Solicitor General for England and Wales is below the Attorney General for England and Wales, while the Solicitor General for Scotland is below the Lord Advocate (though these distinctions are often either glossed over or ignored).[175] This ranking sits somewhat uneasily alongside the standalone formulation of the statutory powers for each office, however, with those pertaining to the Solicitor General for England and Wales, in particular, providing that the 'validity of anything done in relation to the Attorney General, or done by or in relation to the Solicitor General, is not affected by a vacancy in the office of Attorney General'.[176] The effect of this provision is that in the event of a vacancy in the office of Attorney General, the Solicitor General will be held accountable for decisions of the former regardless of whether the latter has actually been involved in taking those decisions. While the reverse applies at all other times, in that the Attorney General is conventionally expected to take primary responsibility for the exercise of powers carried out by the Solicitor General, this arrangement is sustained by the idea that both individuals work 'in the closest concert together' while in office.[177] Historically,

[174] ibid 460.

[175] For instance, when describing the position of the Attorney General and Solicitor General for England Wales above staff in the Government Legal Service, Archer states that 'at the apex of the pyramid are the two Law Officers': Peter Archer, *The Role of the Law Officers* (Fabian Society Research Series 339 1978) 3.

[176] Law Officers Act 1997, s 1(3).

[177] Hartley Shawcross, 'The Office of the Attorney General' (An Address at the Law Society's Hall, 18 February 1953) 17.

this has shielded the Solicitor General from 'dislike levelled principally against the [Attorney General]' for the exercise of their ostensibly shared functions.[178]

Whether this arrangement would survive certain types of controversy in modern times is open to question, however, as it must be doubted whether Parliament, for instance, would regard any Solicitor General in office following the departure of an outcast Attorney General as legitimately accountable for decisions taken by the latter while in office where it could be shown that the former played no influential part in taking those decisions. Whether the Attorney General for England and Wales or the Lord Advocate could evade accountability for decisions taken by a disgraced Solicitor General for England and Wales or Scotland, on the other hand, is open to less doubt on account of the hierarchical method for coping with the problem of many hands entrenched by statute and historical convention. With that said, if there were ever a severe breakdown in relations between the principal law officer and their deputy, it is easy to envisage calls to replace the present hierarchical accountability strategy with an individualistic one which would allow each office-holder to be 'judged on the basis of his [or her] actual contribution instead of on the basis of his [or her] formal position'.[179] Taken together, these observations about the status of the Solicitors General demonstrate how legitimate controversy may arise about the most appropriate strategy for coping with a need for accountability over the complex decision-making processes with which they are frequently involved.

In respect of controversies arising from the issue of uncertain obligations between actors and forums, two examples are illustrative. First, consider the position of unelected office-holders within the UK law officer regime past and present. The present status of the Attorney General for Northern Ireland as an unelected appointee, for instance, is the source of many difficulties in connection with delineating the appropriate extent to which office-holders should be permitted to participate in proceedings of the Northern Ireland Assembly.[180] In consequence, the ability of that particular forum to exercise accountability over the Northern Ireland Attorney has been significantly limited ever since the office was (re-) established in 2010.[181] Similarly weighty issues arose in relation to unelected individuals appointed to the office of the Lord Advocate on a number of occasions throughout the mid-twentieth century, due to a paucity of senior Scottish advocates among MPs loyal to the governing party.[182] Some of these appointments were made on an 'entirely non-political' basis; that is, by mutual agreement between Prime Minister and office-holder that the latter would discharge his (and it was always 'his') duties and enjoy the rights of office 'without participation in policy

[178] John Payne Collier, *Criticisms on the Bar* (Simpkin and Marshall 1819) 95–96.
[179] Bovens (n 121) 459.
[180] See ch 6.
[181] ibid.
[182] *The Laws of Scotland: Stair Memorial Encyclopaedia*, Constitutional Law Reissue, para 428; Ian S Dickinson, 'The Office of Lord Advocate' [1980] *Scots Law Times* (News) 69, 71.

and, of course, without a seat in the House [of Commons]'.[183] The nature of all such appointments meant that office-holders were sheltered from regular parliamentary accountability for the exercise of their functions notwithstanding their ability to influence some legislative business by roundabout means.[184] However, these arrangements proved difficult to maintain in some cases due to concerns that Parliament was being deprived of relevant expertise on Scots law. Dickinson notes, for example, that

> but for the need for Scottish legal expertise on the Government side in the House of Lords during the consideration by the House of the Scotland Bill, the Solicitor-General for Scotland … would probably have remained outside Westminster. In fact in 1976 to satisfy this need he was created a life peer.[185]

Controversies surrounding unelected office-holders within the UK law officer regime thus tend to revolve around a normative concern to minimise notions of democratic legitimacy that attach to office-holders who are closely associated with an elected legislature, together with related concerns about the possibility of office-holders using that platform in order to legitimise a continued role in government policy-making in the absence of a public mandate of their own.

By far the most intense form of controversy arising from uncertain obligations between members of the UK law officer regime and the variety of forums which hold them to account, however, concerns the convention of non-disclosure in respect of legal advice provided to government units of various sorts. The convention is traditionally understood to provide that 'neither the substance of any advice tendered by the law officers nor even the fact that they have given any advice may be disclosed outside government circles save in exceptional circumstances'.[186] One relatively minor issue to note here is the uncertain wording of the Welsh Ministerial Code over whether the consent of the Counsel General for Wales is enough to permit departure from the normal convention, or whether consent on the part of his or her 'government client' is also required (as is the convention elsewhere).[187] There is much greater doubt, however, over the 'exceptional circumstances' which may justify any such departure and, at a more fundamental level, who should be regarded as the law officer's client in such circumstances.[188]

[183] Letter from Lord Advocate Hugh Macmillan to Prime Minister Ramsay MacDonald, *The Times* (London, 9 February 1924), reproduced in James Casey, 'The First Labour Government and Office of Lord Advocate' (1975) 26 *Northern Ireland Legal Quarterly* 18.

[184] Lord Macmillan has candidly recounted his 'share in the promotion of' both the Conveyancing (Scotland) Act 1924 and the Church of Scotland (Property and Endowments) Act 1925, despite his being a non-political appointment to the office of Lord Advocate: Lord Macmillan, *A Man of Law's Tale* (Macmillan & Co 1952) 87–90.

[185] Dickinson (n 182) 70.

[186] Klearchos A Kyriakides, 'The Advisory Functions of the Attorney-General' (2003) 1 *Hertfordshire Law Journal* 73, 76.

[187] See ch 4 at 83–84.

[188] For an interesting Canadian perspective on the general dilemma of determining a lawyer's client in governmental contexts, see: Elizabeth Sanderson, *Government Lawyering: Duties and Ethical Challenges of Government Lawyers* (LexisNexis 2018).

While the Attorney General for England and Wales, for instance, is regarded as being primarily 'accountable to the Prime Minister for the quality and correctness of the advice he [or she] gives to the government', it has been argued that the 'accountability for that advice would seem to pass to Parliament' where government ministers justify their actions on the basis of legal advice they have received from the law officer.[189]

Although there are now quite a number of occasions on which the 'gist' of law officers' legal advice has been disclosed to satisfy calls for greater accountability,[190] there appear to be just three episodes in recent history which resulted in disclosure of the full legal advice provided by the Attorney General or Solicitor General for England and Wales.[191] These episodes emanated from exceptional circumstances surrounding the Westland Affair,[192] the Iraq war,[193] and Brexit.[194] In addition to such full public disclosures, there have been a further two occasions in recent history where the actual advice provided by a law officer has been disclosed outside government circles by virtue of its relevance to certain judicial proceedings (namely in respect of the *Factortame* litigation and the Scott Inquiry).[195] There was no evidence of similar disclosures made in respect of government legal advice provided by law officers at the devolved level until that record was disrupted recently by publication of the Lord Advocate's advice to the Scottish Government in respect of harassment allegations against the former First Minister of Scotland, Alex Salmond.[196]

[189] Woodhouse (n 170) 104.

[190] HL Deb 12 January 2004, col WA64.

[191] For a discussion of older incidents, see: Edwards, *The Law Officers of the Crown* (n 18) 256–261.

[192] *Review of Intelligence on Weapons of Mass Destruction* (14 July 2004, HC 898) para 373. The disclosure of advice provided to Michael Heseltine by the Solicitor General for England and Wales on this occasion was carried out by way of a leak. See: Pat Srickland, *Law Officers' Advice* (HC Library Standard Note SNHA/2942, 2004) 5–6.

[193] Yong (n 39) ch 6.

[194] Department for Exiting the European Union, *Publication of the Attorney General's Legal Advice to Cabinet on the Withdrawal Agreement and the Protocol on Ireland/Northern Ireland* (5 December 2018). Available at: www.gov.uk/government/publications/exiting-the-eu-publication-of-legal-advice.

[195] *Review of Intelligence on Weapons of Mass Destruction* (14 July 2004, HC 898) para 373; HL Deb 12 January 2004, col WA64.

[196] See 'Legal advice related to the Parliamentary Inquiry into the Scottish Government's Handling of Harassment Complaints (SGHHC)' (*Scottish Government*, 2 March 2021). Available at: www.gov.scot/publications/legal-advice-related-to-the-parliamentary-inquiry-into-the-scottish-governments-handling-of-harassment-complaints-sghhc/. Note, moreover, that legal advice by the Attorney General for Northern Ireland was recently leaked to a local journalist: Sam McBride, 'DUP-Civil Service Showdown Could Be Days Away, and the Implications are Vast' (*Belfast Telegraph*, 29 January 2022). Available at: www.belfasttelegraph.co.uk/opinion/columnists/Sam-mcbride/dup-civil-service-showdown-could-be-days-away-and-the-implications-are-vast-41290094.html. For earlier attempts to have the advice of law officers at the devolved level disclosed, see, e.g., *Department of Health, Social Services and Public Safety v Information Commissioner, McDermott and the Attorney General for Northern Ireland* (EA/2013/0081, 13 November 2013). In this case, the First-Tier Tribunal overturned a decision by the Information Commissioner in favour of a gay rights activist who had requested the disclosure of legal advice provided by the Attorney General for Northern Ireland to the above-named department. The advice related to a lifetime ban on blood donations by men who have sex with men in Northern Ireland, which had been challenged in separate judicial review proceedings (see *Re JR65's Application* [2016] NICA 20). The Counsel General for Wales also provided a written submission to the

Underpinning all these controversial episodes lie complex issues about the nature of any obligations owed between law officers and their varied accountability forums. The recurring tendency to judge circumstances involving requests for disclosure beyond government on a case-by-case basis, however, leaves this aspect of the law officers' accountability obligations to forums outside government subject to much uncertainty. It is difficult to find any official support for the late Lord Bingham's extra-curial suggestion, for example, that with respect to a law officer's opinion on the lawfulness of war 'it is not unrealistic … to regard the public, those who are to fight and perhaps die, rather than the government, as the client'.[197] Likewise, Appleby's laudable attempt to define 'at least two circumstances' where there is a strong case for the disclosure of government legal advice to Parliament (namely where Parliament is considering Bills of 'uncertain constitutional validity' and where it is exercising its 'constitutional function of holding the government to account') runs in tension with the continuation of an official narrative which favours a very strong presumption of confidentiality.[198] For instance, commenting on his recent decision to disclose legal advice provided to Cabinet in respect of the EU Withdrawal Agreement, following a finding of contempt by Parliament, Sir Geoffrey Cox qua Attorney General for England and Wales stated:

> The release of this advice does not set a precedent for any future release of Law Officers' advice. It remains a fundamental Constitutional Convention that neither the fact, nor the content, of Law Officers' advice is disclosed outside Government without the Law Officers' consent. That Convention provides the fullest guarantee that the business of Governments is conducted at all times in the light of thorough and candid legal advice, which may also enter into matters of acute sensitivity to the public interest … The constitutional tensions created between the expression of the will of the House of Commons by these means on the one hand, and the public interest in the Law Officers' Convention on the other, are not themselves conducive to the proper conduct of public affairs. It is necessary that the public has confidence in the ability of Government and Parliament to work together at a time of national decision-making of the most profound significance. The standing of the House of Commons is also of prime importance. For these reasons, having tested the will of the House twice, the Government will respect

Tribunal, in support of the argument against disclosure that was successfully advanced on behalf of the Attorney General for Northern Ireland. Note, too, that in a recent decision of the Court of Session the Outer House ruled that the Lord Advocate (and Advocate Deputes acting in his or her name) is entitled to rely on legal advice privilege in respect of any advice he or she receives from officials in the Crown Office and Procurator Fiscal Service: *Whitehouse & Anr v HM Advocate* [2019] CSOH 38, 2019 SLT 573.

[197] Lord Bingham, 'The Rule of Law' (2007) 66 *Cambridge Law Journal* 67, 83.

[198] Gabrielle Appleby, 'Releasing Government's Advice Would Help Parliament Better Scrutinise Laws' (*The Conversation*, 16 December 2015). Available at: http://theconversation.com/releasing-governments-advice-would-help-parliament-better-scrutinise-laws-50593. Also see David Kenny and Conor Casey, 'A One Person Supreme Court? The Attorney General, Constitutional Advice to Government, and the Case for Transparency' (2019) 42 *Dublin University Law Journal* 89; Conor Casey, 'The Law Officers: The Relationship Between Executive Lawyers and Executive Power in Ireland and the United Kingdom' in Oran Doyle, Aileen McHarg and Jo Murkens (eds), *The Brexit Challenge for Ireland and the UK* (Cambridge University Press 2021).

> its decision and, in these exceptional circumstances and to resolve for the present those constitutional tensions, it has decided, with my consent, to publish this advice.[199]

Thus, it remains 'impossible to be dogmatic and to assert either the principle of absolute confidentiality or, on the other hand, a rule requiring the government to reveal in full or in part the contents of the opinions' it is given by members of the UK law officer regime.[200] Rather, it is submitted that the nature of these obligations, in common with all the dimensions of accountability considered in this sub-section, are best mediated by a value-based evaluation of the independence and trust called for by a particular set of circumstances. Before reaching a fuller discussion of this trifocal model of legitimacy, however, a little more must be said about the value of trust and its constitutional relationship with the UK law officer regime in times of controversy.

Constitutional Controversy and the Value of Trust

The last two sections of this chapter have connected specific conceptual frameworks for analysing independence and accountability to controversy discourses that illustrate various dimensions of those frameworks by either explicitly referencing relevant conceptual terms and ideas or by implicitly drawing upon those ideas. While the same approach can and will be adopted in outlining the relationship between trust and the controversial phenomena analysed in this section, that analysis should be prefaced by a more general point concerning the underestimation of trust in each of the controversy episodes considered throughout this chapter so far. It is arguably by reason of this underestimation, among other things, that there are fewer explicit references to trust in the controversy discourse. This, in turn, is why the analysis in this section relies more heavily on implicit connections between aspects of the controversy discourse and the elements of trust outlined in chapter two.[201] A comparatively limited number of explicit references to the value of trust comes as no surprise, of course, given that an under-appreciation of its relevance as a missing link between the values of independence and accountability is a central tenet of this book.

With that said, explicit references to the concept of trust are certainly not confined to the margins of relevant discourses. For instance, the 2007 government

[199] HC Deb 5 December 2018, col WS1142. For a critical perspective on this particular controversy, see: Rupert Bowers and Margherita Cornaglia, 'Advice from the Attorney General Does Not Attract Privilege' (*The Law Society Gazette*, 7 December 2018). Available at: www.lawgazette.co.uk/commentary-and-opinion/advice-from-the-attorney-general-does-not-attract-privilege/5068625.article. For further details, see: Conor McCormick and Graeme Cowie, *The Law Officers: A Constitutional and Functional Overview* (House of Commons Library, Research Briefing, 28 May 2020), 53–55. Available at: https://commonslibrary.parliament.uk/research-briefings/cbp-8919/.

[200] Edwards, *The Law Officers of the Crown* (n 18) 259–260.

[201] See ch 2 at 36–41.

consultation paper canvassing a number of possible reforms to the office of the Attorney General for England and Wales in response to a recent catalogue of controversies (including the BAE saga discussed above) was conducted in order to demonstrate overtly that the government was 'fully committed to enhancing public confidence and *trust* in the office of Attorney General'.[202] Indeed, it stated that all of the options outlined in the consultation paper were 'directed to that end'.[203] Moreover, in a 2017 speech about his office the former Lord Advocate James Wolffe said that 'in reflecting on the constitutional trust bestowed on the office of Lord Advocate' he thought it proper to 'say something about independence and accountability'.[204] Wolffe elaborated by explaining that promoting the integrity and independence of prosecutorial decision-making was a 'significant aspect of the Lord Advocate's constitutional trust', while also insisting that 'the principle of independence is not inconsistent with appropriate mechanisms of accountability' (which he illustrated by reference to some mechanisms for judicial and public scrutiny alongside parliamentary oversight).[205] Wolffe made it clear that he also regards statutory duties attached to the office of the Lord Advocate, together with responsibilities flowing from a general responsibility to uphold the rule of law (including a duty to ensure that the government acts lawfully at all times), as expressions of the constitutional trust placed in and expected of his office.[206] In addition, the speeches made by quite a number of Attorneys and Solicitors General over the years contain references to trust as an important legitimising factor in respect of debates about the unique combination of functions vested in their offices and, in particular, by way of a justification for maintaining a close relationship with their ministerial colleagues. Speaking as the Solicitor General for England and Wales in 2010, for instance, Sir Edward Garnier said that:

> the current arrangement, as awkward as it may look on paper, like so many eccentricities in our constitution, works because it puts at the heart of Government an independent lawyer who is *trusted* by those he advises and because he is one of them.[207]

Likewise, speaking as the Attorney General for England and Wales in 1978, Sir Sam Silkin referred to the importance of acquiring trust, together with the relevance of accountability to its acquisition, in the following terms:

> every decision which I make, every letter which I sign or which is signed on my behalf, every statement which is published by my office is made or signed or published in the

[202] *Governance of Britain: A Consultation on the Role of the Attorney General* (Cm 7192, 2007) 2. Emphasis added.

[203] ibid.

[204] James Wolffe, 'A Constitutional Trust' (A Speech by the Lord Advocate for the James Wood Lecture 2017 at Glasgow University, 15 November 2017).

[205] ibid.

[206] ibid.

[207] Edward Garnier, 'The Law Officers and Legislative Procedure' (A Speech by the Solicitor General to the Constitutional and Administrative Law Bar Association, 17 July 2010). Available at: www.gov.uk/government/speeches/speech-to-the-constitutional-and-administrative-law-bar-association. For a reiteration of this statement by another Solicitor General, see: Oliver Heald, 'The Role of the Law

> knowledge that a time may come when I shall be questioned on it and criticised for it and required to answer for it in Parliament. *That knowledge is a powerful influence – not to court popularity, but to try to acquire*, however difficult it may be, *trust* and a reputation for integrity, courage and sound judgement.[208]

Silkin, of course, was no stranger to controversy. Indeed, on a later occasion he remarked:

> I am a very introverted person and when I accepted the appointment [of Attorney General for England and Wales] it did not for one moment occur to me that before long the media would be referring to me frequently as the controversial Attorney-General. Since then I have discovered that all Attorneys-General are controversial, although some disguise it more successfully than others. It is a necessarily controversial post.[209]

While Silkin's first statement clearly demonstrates an appreciation for the significance of trust, his second suggests a contestable understanding of how to achieve it. This book posits that to avoid controversy, and thereby sustain legitimacy, members of the UK law officer regime generally do not and normatively should not concern themselves with efforts to 'disguise' the balancing of conflicting principles that arise from their unique constitutional position. Rather, it suggests that office-holders should assess the legitimacy of their conduct with reference to the sociological understandings of trust outlined in Chapter 2 of this book (in just the same way that assessments of legitimacy should be performed with reference to the conceptual understandings of independence and accountability as illustrated earlier in this chapter). It should be recalled from Chapter 2 at this point that trust is a term that relates to various appurtenant concepts, the most notable being reliance, risk and expectation. Moreover, the preferred conception adopted for the purposes of this book accepts that to achieve an 'optimal' form of trust it is necessary to combine 'cognitive' and 'affective' approaches to it (namely approaches which recognise a place for rational-choice motivations to trust alongside innate moral inclinations to trust). Finally, the 'trust test' proposed by Seldon as a practical method of measuring whether certain actions add or subtract from trust is a particularly significant aspect of earlier explanations for present purposes. It should be remembered that the trust test proposed by Seldon consists of a qualitative judgement informed by reference to two interacting continuums: an individualist–collectivist continuum and an ideology–regulation continuum.[210]

Officers' (A Speech by the Solicitor General to Kent Law School, 18 October 2012). Available at: www.gov.uk/government/speeches/the-role-of-the-law-officers accessed 21 April 2018. Emphasis added.

[208] Sam Silkin, 'The George Bean Memorial Lecture' (A Speech by the Attorney General in Manchester, 29 October 1978). Emphasis added.

[209] Sam Silkin, 'Magistrates Address' (A Speech by the Attorney General to Somerset & South Avon Magistrates, 23 February 1979).

[210] Anthony Seldon, *Trust: How We Lost It and How to Get It Back* (Biteback 2009) 26–29.

Figure 7.1 Intersecting Trust Continuums

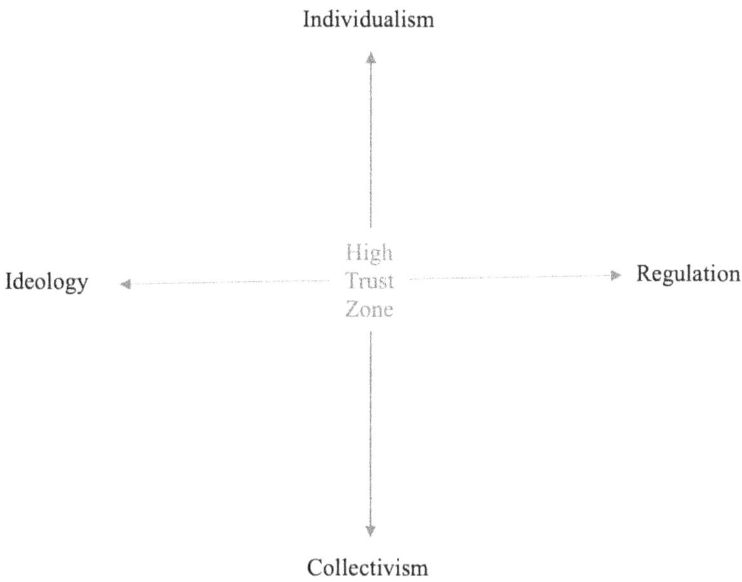

These ideas will be considered and developed further in the following two sub-sections, with reference to common sources of controversy that might be mapped onto the relevant continuums to achieve a higher level of trust in the appropriate office-holders and, by proxy, to attach a stronger degree of legitimacy to their offices. The intersecting relationship between both continuums, which is illustrated in the diagram above, should be borne in mind throughout these investigations. Placing both continuums together to form a cross usefully highlights the middle ground between all four conceptual poles, a middle ground which Seldon terms the 'high trust' zone.[211] His theory of trust, and the trust test arising from it, rests on two related premises: first, that where individuals and organisations operate in this high trust zone 'there will be a natural tendency for the actions to help build trust' and, second, that if individuals and organisations operate at the outer margins 'there will be a tendency to spread mistrust'.[212]

Inappropriate Individualism or Collectivism

Seldon thinks that trust 'requires a balance of individual and collective needs' for the following reasons:

> If an individual action is too individualistic and rides over others, then it will be a selfish and untrusting act. If the collective impulse is too strong, then individuality will

[211] ibid 28.
[212] ibid.

> be swamped … if the government is too collectivist, it stifles individual and corporate enterprise.[213]

Crude though this explanation might seem, Seldon's reasons are clearly informed by his distinguished background in political history and philosophy.[214] As such, it may be assumed that Seldon's model of trust has been influenced by the mature body of scholarship concerning individualism and collectivism that has exercised philosophers from those disciplines for many years,[215] though he does not expressly acknowledge the full range of ideas underpinning his attempt to delineate an accessible and practical account of trust. All the same, a highly apposite notion derived from scholarship of this nature is the concept of proportionality. That concept has particular relevance to the constitutional value of trust as it relates to the UK law officer regime because it has been shaped by both political theory and legal theory. In particular, the concept has been adopted and developed by the UK judiciary in recent times for the purpose of substantively reviewing justiciable public decisions in some contexts. This, in turn, has had a notable effect on the way in which administrative government units assess the constitutional legitimacy of their conduct.[216] Though the legal reasoning required in performing proportionality assessments is formulated differently according to context, the leading common law formulation involves establishing (a) whether the objective of a government measure is sufficiently important to justify the limitation of a right; (b) whether that measure is rationally connected to the objective; (c) whether a less intrusive measure could have been used; and (d) whether 'having regard to these matters and to the severity of the consequences, a fair balance has been struck between the rights of the individual and the interests of the community'.[217] Multi-limbed formulations of this sort have given rise to some debate over whether each and every stage of the test used where human rights are engaged is suitable in other contexts[218] but, for present purposes, only two further points need be made about the relevance of proportionality to the conception of trust at hand.

First, the majority of remaining arguments against the use of proportionality as a conceptual yardstick for evaluating the legitimacy of government decision making are premised on constitutional concerns about the appropriate reach of

[213] ibid 26.

[214] See, e.g., Dennis Kavanagh and Anthony Seldon, *The Powers Behind the Prime Minister: The Hidden Influence of Number Ten* (HarperCollins 1999); Brian Brivati, Julia Buxton and Anthony Seldon, *The Contemporary History Handbook* (Manchester University Press 1996); David Marquand and Anthony Seldon, *The Ideas That Shaped Post-War Britain* (Fontana Press 1996).

[215] Notable examples include: Dycus F Miller and Jeffrey Paul, *The Communitarian Challenge to Liberalism* (Cambridge University Press 1996); John O'Neill (ed), *Modes of Individualism and Collectivism* (Gregg Revivals 1993); John Kingdom, *No Such Thing as Society? Individualism and Community* (Open University Press 1992); Shlomo Avineri and Avner de-Shalit (eds), *Communitarianism and Individualism* (Oxford University Press 1992).

[216] See, e.g., Government Legal Department, *The Judge Over Your Shoulder – A Guide to Good Decision-Making* (18 July 2016) 40–42.

[217] *Bank Mellat v Her Majesty's Treasury (No 2)* [2013] UKSC 39, [2014] AC 700 at [20].

[218] See: Hanna Wilberg and Mark Elliott (eds), *The Scope and Intensity of Substantive Review: Traversing Taggart's Rainbow* (Hart Publishing 2017).

judicial review and the purported risk that it poses to matters such as administrative effectiveness.[219] These arguments are not applicable in the present context because the argument here is that a proportionality assessment, if carried out by members of the UK law officer regime *themselves*, is likely to maintain the legitimacy of their offices by sustaining trust in their approach to the unique mixture of constitutional responsibilities called for by those offices. As such, leaving whether it is normatively desirable for a court to conduct its own review of initial proportionality assessments aside, this book contends that members of the UK law officer regime should normalise proportionality assessments of their own conduct in any event given that the judiciary is not the only accountability forum relevant to the maintenance of their legitimacy. Proportionate actions, at the centre of the relevant political philosophies encapsulated by Seldon's individualist–collectivist continuum, are less likely to attract significant controversy from the wide spectrum of political representatives in the UK than actions which operate at the margins of individualism or collectivism.

The second point is that, regardless of how many limbs to the proportionality test are preferred by a particular office-holder or accountability forum, such evaluations are inherently heuristic in any event. That is to say, breaking the reasoning underpinning a particular decision down into some number of distinct elements can simply help 'make value judgments more explicit'.[220] There being no exact science for quantifying such matters, as with trust and legitimacy generally, the overriding suggestion made by this book is that a balancing exercise of some kind should be performed by members of the UK law officer regime deciding how to discharge their functions ab initio in order to avoid damaging trust and thereby embroiling their offices in avoidable controversy. Indeed, the heuristic nature of this exercise should be strongly emphasised given that a strict understanding of the dichotomy could be challenged by reference to the complementary relationship between individualism and collectivism in some contexts. Harris and others note, for example, how the original purpose of the European Convention on Human Rights 'was not primarily to offer a remedy for particular *individuals* who had suffered violations of the Convention but to provide a *collective*, inter-state guarantee that would benefit individuals generally'.[221]

It would seem that a sure way of failing to strike a fair balance between individualism and collectivism is to mismanage the proper role of consultation in official decision-making. Failure to consult all relevant parties may create an impression that the decision-maker has adopted a blinkered, individualistic view of how to discharge their function, for instance, while if they consult too widely the views of the collective may drown out or overpower the voice of individuals

[219] ibid.
[220] *Bank Mellat v Her Majesty's Treasury (No 2)* [2013] UKSC 39, [2014] AC 700 at [74].
[221] DJ Harris and others, *Harris, O'Boyle & Warbrick: Law of the European Convention on Human Rights* (4th edn, Oxford University Press 2018) 39. Emphasis added.

who will be directly affected by their decision. Whereas there are some functions belonging to members of the UK law officer regime which explicitly require consultation with others by virtue of statute and thereby obviate this danger (the Attorney General for Northern Ireland, for instance, may only appoint someone as the Director of Public Prosecutions after consulting the Advocate General for Northern Ireland[222]), the matter is unregulated in respect of most functions. As a result, several controversies have arisen from consultations which appear to strike an unfair balance between individualism and collectivism in this context. In 2013, for example, the Attorney General for Northern Ireland made public statements to the effect that 'there should be no further police investigations, inquests or inquiries into any relevant killings that took place before the signing of the Good Friday Agreement in 1998'.[223] Media coverage from the time suggests that these remarks damaged trust in the Attorney on the part of various forums by virtue of, inter alia, the office-holder's failure to 'consult the Stormont Executive about his proposals before making them public'[224] and 'without any apparent engagement with those most affected'[225] notwithstanding the fact that they were made as a contribution to public debate rather than as an official policy announcement.

Instead of traversing further historical episodes to demonstrate this particular point, it is submitted more broadly that all decisions described as having been taken 'in the public interest' or 'to uphold the rule of law' should be reconceptualised to highlight the trust-sustaining role of proportionality in the relevant reasoning processes. This would arguably go some way toward remedying the skewed emphasis on collectivism suggested by law officer functions that have been conceptualised solely with reference to the public interest (such as fiat decisions as regards relator actions). This could reduce the likelihood of controversy raised by reliance on such a vague but ostensibly collectivist construct given that, as Walker puts it, 'within our pluralist political culture, the content of the public interest or even the means by which it might be ascertained are often deeply contested'.[226] Likewise, those law officer roles typically associated with the rule of law and human rights (such as pre-legislative scrutiny opinions) could benefit from being determined with greater emphasis on the role of proportionality, in order to avoid any perception that individualism is unduly privileged over collectivism by virtue of how those functions have been labelled. Taking these observations into account, references to members of the UK law officer regime as 'guardians of the public interest' and 'guardians of the rule of law' might seem ill-judged. If the dominant

[222] Justice (Northern Ireland) Act 2002, s 43(1).

[223] Vincent Kearney, 'NI Attorney General John Larkin Calls for End to Troubles Prosecutions' (*BBC News NI*, 20 November 2013). Available at: www.bbc.co.uk/news/uk-northern-ireland-24999051.

[224] ibid.

[225] 'NIHRC Responds to Attorney General's Comments on Dealing with the Past' (*Northern Ireland Human Rights Commission*, 20 November 2013). Available at: www.nihrc.org/news/detail/nihrc-responds-to-attorney-generals-comments-on-dealing-with-the-past.

[226] Walker (n 128) 150.

purpose of those labels is to help law officers maintain the trust of all the government units and accountability forums which contribute to the maintenance of their legitimacy, perhaps 'guardians of the public interest *and* the rule of law' or 'guardians of proportionate government' would be more fitting.

Inappropriate Ideology or Regulation

The second continuum forming part of Seldon's trust test calls for a balance between ideology and regulation. Seldon justifies this prescription as follows:

> Ideologies can … be damaging of trust in society if, like Marxism or extreme environmentalism, they place the achievement of their ends above human needs … At the other end of the scale, one can place the modern drive for scientific managerialism in the form of regimentation and accountability. Too much of it belittles values, marginalises ethics and chokes trust.

While members of the UK law officer regime should be wary of adhering too doggedly to any single ideology, bearing in mind the range of approval metrics that will be applied by their varied accountability forums, this aspect of Seldon's trust test is perhaps best considered and remembered with reference to the other two constitutional values which mainly contribute to the legitimacy of their offices – namely independence and accountability. The argument here is certainly not that those values qualify as political ideologies in the Marxist sense, for instance, of ideas that work to conceal the contradictions of a capitalist society.[227] Rather, it is that they are, as Bell understood them, an action-orientated system of beliefs that motivate people to do certain things or to refrain from doing certain things.[228] Like Heywood, this book does not regard ideologies as 'good nor bad, true nor false, open nor closed, liberating nor oppressive – they can be all of these things'.[229] Understood in this way, the term ideology is not just appropriate for describing major political belief systems like liberalism, conservatism, socialism and fascism – or indeed major legal theories like positivism, realism and natural law. It also captures 'thought-practices' of different shapes and sizes that are performed by the actors who regularly participate in a particular system.[230] Members of the UK law officer regime who perform their roles strictly in accordance with the tenets of any action-orientated belief system thus lay themselves open to a charge of ideological extremism in this sense. In line with Seldon's model of trust, a key part of evaluating the conduct of law officers for inappropriate adherence to a particular ideology is the assessment of its dominance over competing action-orientated

[227] Andrew Heywood, *Political Ideologies* (5th edn, Palgrave Macmillan 2012) 6–8.
[228] Daniel Bell, *The End of Ideology: On the Exhaustion of Political Ideas in the 1950s* (5th edn, Harvard University Press 2000).
[229] Heywood (n 227) 10.
[230] Michael Freeden, 'Ideology and Political Theory' (2006) 11 *Journal of Political Ideologies* 3, 19.

belief systems. In other words, it is implicit in Seldon's account of trust that only hegemonic ideological behaviour is likely to court controversy, reduce trust and damage the overall legitimacy of offices like those that constitute the UK law officer regime (that is, behaviour which elevates one ideology above all others regardless of societal disagreement as to the merits of those beliefs).

The most obvious illustration of ideological extremism within the UK law officer regime is in relation to excessive interpretations of independence that appear to have motivated the controversial actions of various law officers over the years, but especially office-holders who have been appointed on a 'non-political' basis. Many of these controversies were examined in the subsection on independence above, but from the present vantage point the damage that can be caused by inappropriate understandings of independence is made even clearer. For instance, consider how the statutory requirement providing that functions of the modern-day Attorney General for Northern Ireland 'shall be exercised by him [or her] independently of any other person' has provided the basis for adherence to a controversially conceptualised understanding of independence which has resulted in significant challenges to the legitimacy of the office.[231] Three incidents driven by this ideology may help to illustrate the issue. One incident prompted the UK Government to distance itself 'from an attempt by Northern Ireland's Attorney General to intervene in an adoption case involving two Austrian lesbians'.[232] The Attorney General had intervened in a case at the European Court of Human Rights to argue that 'regions like Austria and Northern Ireland should be allowed to opt out of same sex adoption law', but the Foreign and Commonwealth Office subsequently informed the Strasbourg court that the Attorney General's intervention did 'not represent the views of the UK Government', nor 'the position throughout the United Kingdom'.[233] The second incident involved an attempt by the Attorney General to prosecute Peter Hain for publishing remarks describing Girvan J (as he had been) as not only 'high-handed and idiosyncratic' but 'off his rocker'.[234] Although the Attorney General withdrew this charge after Hain agreed to write an addendum, Pannick notes that the proceedings 'attracted very considerable criticism' on account of the Attorney General's contestable assumption that Girvan LJ (as he later became) should be shielded from public criticism of this nature to protect the independence of the judiciary.[235] This excessive conception

[231] Justice (Northern Ireland) Act 2002, s 22(5).

[232] Liam Clarke, 'Government Distances Itself from Attorney General John Larkin over Austrian Lesbian Case' (*Belfast Telegraph*, 25 October 2012). Available at: www.belfasttelegraph.co.uk/news/northern-ireland/government-distances-itself-from-attorney-general-john-larkin-over-austrian-lesbian-case-28877682.html.

[233] ibid.

[234] David Pannick, '"We Do Not Fear Criticism, Nor Do We Resent It": Abolition of the Offence of Scandalising the Judiciary' [2014] *Public Law* 5, 8.

[235] ibid. Also see: Pete Baker, 'NI Attorney General: "Citizens Are Entitled to Have Confidence in the Administration of Justice"' (*Slugger O'Toole*, 25 April 2012). Available at: https://sluggerotoole.com/2012/04/25/ni-attorney-general-citizens-are-entitled-to-have-confidence-in-the-administration-of-justice.

of independence was considered so flawed that the UK Parliament was persuaded to abolish 'scandalising the judiciary' as a common law criminal offence in the aftermath of the controversy.[236] The relevant offence was likewise abolished in Northern Ireland.[237] The third incident arose from circumstances whereby the Attorney General had offered to act as 'counsel and questioner' on behalf of the Justice Committee at the Northern Ireland Assembly in relation to a proposed investigation concerning the opening of an abortion clinic in Belfast.[238] The advice of the Assembly's own lawyers on whether to accede to the offer of the Attorney General was leaked. It cautioned, inter alia, that 'for the Attorney to act as counsel and questioner amounts to participation in Assembly proceedings, and is therefore currently not permitted by the [Justice (Northern Ireland) Act 2002]'.[239] This incident is a particularly clear illustration of how a decision taken on the basis of a particular ideology can undermine legitimising regulation, contrary to the need for a balance between ideology and regulation in order to maintain trust. The controversial nature of the incident was further compounded by reference to a radio interview in which John Larkin had 'compared abortion to shooting a newborn baby' prior to assuming the office of the Attorney General for Northern Ireland, which naturally raised questions 'about how much personal baggage he [brought] to his consideration of the issue'.[240]

Seldon's enjoinder as regards the ability of over-regulation to do violence to trust is also applicable to the UK law officer regime more generally. Although various controversies arising from imprecise conceptions of accountability were studied at length earlier in this chapter, some of those concerns appear more pronounced than others when viewed through a trust lens. In particular, the present context enables appropriate emphasis to be placed on the danger of excessive accountability arrangements which have the effect of stifling other important values like independence and trust. As O'Neill memorably put it: just as 'plants don't flourish when we pull them up too often to check how their roots are growing', neither are officials likely to flourish if we constantly 'uproot' them to 'demonstrate that everything is transparent and trustworthy'.[241] Quite to the contrary, O'Neill cogently argues that while the 'pursuit of ever more perfect accountability provides citizens … with more information, more comparisons [and] more complaints systems' it also 'builds a culture of suspicion, low morale, and may ultimately

[236] Crime and Courts Act 2013, s 33.

[237] Criminal Justice Act (Northern Ireland) 2013, s 12.

[238] Liam Clarke, 'Revealed: Advice Given to MLAs on Attorney General's Abortion Row Intervention' (*Belfast Telegraph*, 17 November 2012).

[239] ibid.

[240] Mark Devenport, 'Attorney General John Larkin Hits Headlines for Wrong Reasons' (*BBC News NI*, 24 October 2012). Available at: www.bbc.co.uk/news/uk-northern-ireland-20054111. Also see: Marie-Louise Connolly, 'Doctor Quits Over NI Attorney General's Abortion Interventions' (*BBC News NI*, 14 September 2016). Available at: www.bbc.co.uk/news/uk-northern-ireland-37353825.

[241] Onora O'Neill, *A Question of Trust* (Cambridge University Press 2002) 19.

lead to professional cynicism' and public mistrust.[242] Concern to avoid excessive regulation is evident in some literature, for instance, which resists proposals to establish a dedicated parliamentary select committee to scrutinise prosecutorial decisions taken by the Attorney General and Solicitor General for England and Wales. Thomas, for example, places particular weight on the fact that additional accountability of this sort would divert the already limited resources available to those law officers away from their substantive responsibilities.[243] A similar reticence towards excessive regulation is borne out by deliberations of the Northern Ireland Assembly concerning the appropriate extent of parliamentary accountability over some of the functions of the Attorney General for Northern Ireland. It may be recalled from Chapter 6,[244] in particular, that the Committee of Procedures decided not to recommend any amendments to the Standing Orders of the Assembly in relation to some of the Attorney's functions out of recognition towards several risks posed by over-formalisation.[245]

Conclusions

This chapter has revealed that a majority of the discourse about controversies which have arisen in respect of law officers has generally centred on accusations that either a particular office or a particular function has been situated at the wrong point on a conceptual continuum between independence and accountability, or, more commonly, because at least one of those values has been poorly conceptualised in the first instance. Importantly, however, it has also suggested that a bifocal view of independence and accountability alone is a conceptually incomplete framework for understanding the legitimacy of law officers and that it is therefore incapable of adequately explaining the causes of constitutional controversies that afflict the regime. The incompleteness of this bifocal model of evaluation has arguably resulted from a failure to take proper cognisance of trust as another important value underpinning the constitutional legitimacy of the UK law officer regime.

[242] ibid 57.

[243] Rosamund M Thomas, 'The Attorney-General for England and Wales, and Northern Ireland: His Role in Civil and Criminal Proceedings' (1991) 57 *International Review of Administrative Sciences* 209, 219–220; Rosamund M Thomas, *Espionage and Secrecy: The Official Secrets Acts 1911–1989 of the United Kingdom* (Routledge 1991) 114. Cf Klearchos A Kyriakides, 'The Law Officers of the Crown and the Rule of Law in the United Kingdom' in Gabrielle Appleby, Patrick Keyzer and John M Williams (eds), *Public Sentinels: A Comparative Study of Australian Solicitors-General* (Routledge 2014) 201–202.

[244] See ch 6 at 145.

[245] Committee on Procedures, *Inquiry into the extent to which Standing Orders should permit the Attorney General for Northern Ireland to participate in proceedings of the Assembly: Part 1 – Impartiality of the Office of AGNI, Registration of Interests and Participation of the AGNI in Assembly Proceedings in respect of areas other than Statutory Rules* (NIA 232/11-16, 24 February 2015) paras 64–90.

From this vantage point, another interesting observation emerges from the findings of this chapter, namely that the level of trust placed in a particular law officer by constitutional actors with more discrete and readily identifiable sources of legitimacy appears to determine their ideal position on a continuum of independence and accountability. This idea – that investigating indicators of trust enjoyed by law officers can be used to discern whether their powers have been vested in a way which reflects optimal measures of independence and accountability – further engenders a second argument about the synergistic relationship between these three core values. It is submitted that the values are much more mutually inclusive than a bifocal view of them might otherwise suggest. It seems, as such, that the level of independence which a law officer displays also regulates their position on a continuum of trust and accountability and, correspondingly, that a law officer's accountability appears to govern their position on a trust–independence continuum. It is proposed, therefore, that this synergistic relationship of legitimising constitutional values is better captured by a conceptual model of evaluating the law officers which is trifocal rather than bifocal. In the course of offering some concluding remarks on the overall findings of this book, the following chapter will attempt to draw these shared meanings closer together by way of a structured theoretical model for thinking about the constitutional legitimacy of law officers in the UK – a model which is both prescriptive and evaluative to the extent that it is suggested as a tool for guiding the conduct of law officers, and as a mechanism for benchmarking criticism.

8

Conclusions

Introduction

The main aim of this book was to present the most persuasive conceptual basis for analysing the constitutional legitimacy of law officers in the UK. Armed with the foregoing findings, the most plausible framework of analysis may now be stated as follows. The UK law officer regime comprises a diverse range of offices responsible for a diverse range of functions. In the performance of any given function, it is clear that the legitimacy of a law officer cannot be evaluated by referring to the *interests* of a particular client that may or may not be advanced by their conduct. There is simply too much conceptual confusion about who a law officer's client is in such diverse functional contexts to make this a viable conceptual basis for analysing the legitimacy of their conduct in all circumstances. Instead, it is submitted that the constitutional legitimacy of law officers in the UK is best analysed with reference to three *values*, namely: independence, accountability and trust.

For such a framework to be effective, however, it is necessary to adopt clear conceptual understandings for each value in order to avoid controversies borne from misunderstanding. A clear conception of independence will take into account the importance of interdependence and contain lucid rules as regards the kinds of signal that can be sent to and from the law officers.[1] A clear conception of accountability will acknowledge both the range of forums that UK law officers account to and the varying approval metrics employed by each type of forum.[2] A clear conception of accountability will also incorporate strategies for dealing with decisions made by multiple officials and distinguish between different forms of obligation that may pertain between the law officers and their accountability forums.[3] Finally, a clear conception of trust will recognise the significance of balancing individual and collective interests while also specifying the importance of resisting extreme incarnations of ideology or regulation.[4]

[1] See ch 7 at 173–192.
[2] See ch 7 at 192–208.
[3] ibid.
[4] See ch 7 at 208–218.

A Trifocal and Relativistic Model of Legitimising Values

Having set out the main conclusions resulting from this book in summary terms – namely that the most persuasive basis for analysing the constitutional legitimacy of law officers in the UK is with reference to clearly defined understandings of independence, accountability and trust – it must now be emphasised that the relationship between these values should not be regarded as linear nor fixed, for they appear to be trifocal and relativistic. In other words, this book does not only argue that trust is a useful concept for understanding how the weighting of independence and accountability factors in the exercise of a given function can contribute to the maintenance of institutional legitimacy. It also argues that the concept of independence is an equally important part of understanding how the weighting of accountability and trust considerations may have stabilising or destabilising effects on the constitutional legitimacy of UK law officers. Similarly, it argues that the concept of accountability is a helpful part of any analysis on how positive or negative constitutional effects are achieved by the practical manifestations of independence and trust.

Bearing this trifocal model of conceptual relations in mind, which is illustrated in the diagram below, the necessarily relativistic nature of each concept becomes obvious: they each fall to be weighted differently according to context, with concomitant adjustments to the weighting of their legitimising counterparts. This point should provide pause for thought for anyone tempted to describe the constitutional legitimacy lost and won by members of the UK law officer regime as the result of an even 'balancing' of the three values central to that legitimacy. It would be futile, no doubt, to suggest a procrustean formula for their weighting in all circumstances. In some contexts, for example, a particularly strong demand for accountability might justify incursions upon the normal requirements of trust and independence. It is arguable that this occurred, for instance, when the Attorney General for England and Wales decided to disclose to Parliament the legal advice he had provided to the UK Cabinet in relation to the EU Withdrawal Agreement, even though doing so was obviously in tension with his assessment as to the requirements of independence and trust in those circumstances. In other contexts, however, a particularly heavy emphasis on the concept of independence may inflict damage on the legitimacy of a law officer because of the way in which accountability and trust requirements are relegated by doing so. The way in which the office of the Attorney General for Northern Ireland has been framed and practiced is arguably an example of this nature.

The final conceptual point to reflect on at this stage is with respect to the necessarily polydimensional nature of the trifocal model proposed. That is to say, inherent in the conceptions of each value outlined hitherto is the idea that law officers do not derive their legitimacy from one source and should not therefore be evaluated from just one perspective. This is most evident in the dimension of accountability that relates to the problem of many eyes, but it is also evident in the need for clearly defined relations with the numerous government units mandated by a clear concept of independence. One of the drawbacks borne from building an original conceptual model based on a range of antecedent scholarship from different disciplines, however, is a certain level of divergence with respect to the terminology used by various theorists when referring to much the same thing. As such, when analysing the constitutional legitimacy of law officers in the UK, it is recommended that reference should be made to their 'patrons' (rather than, say, their accountability forums or the government units with which they interact).

Figure 8.1 A Trifocal and Relativistic Model of Legitimising Values

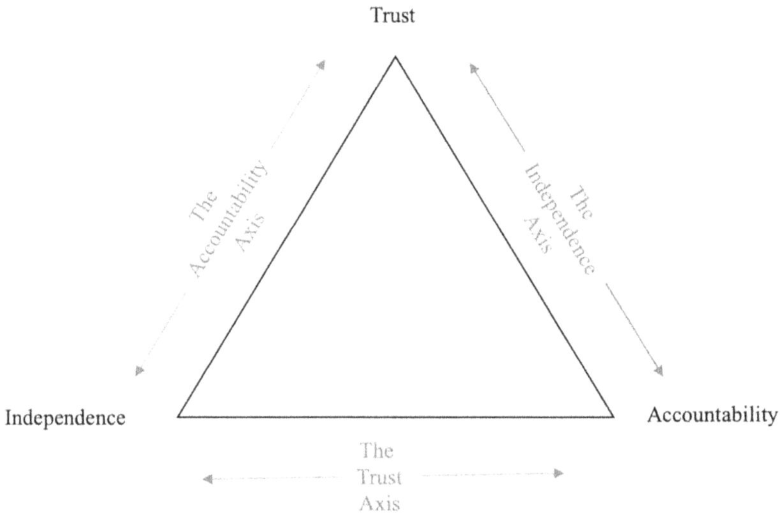

It is the unique web of relationships between law officers and patrons identified throughout this book that calls for polydimensional conceptions of trust, accountability and independence. This is a constitutionally pluralist view, consonant with the scholarship of thinkers like Bottoms and Tankebe,[5] given that it does not interpret the notion of legitimacy as a derivative of some absolute form of institutional sovereignty. It instead interprets legitimacy as something attained only through a contestable consensus among relevant patrons. Envisioning the trifocal model of legitimising values as polydimensional is a necessary outworking of this view in order to account for the different constitutional priorities each legitimising patron (like each of the central and devolved executives, legislatures and courts, for example) may bring to bear when assessing the legitimacy of a law officer's conduct. This,

[5] See ch 1 at 16. Also see Paul Daly, *Understanding Administrative Law in the Common Law World* (Oxford University Press 2021) ch 1.

in turn, may mean that the relevant axes of trust, accountability and independence that characterise the trifocal model proposed may be constituted in different measures according to whichever perspective is employed. Put simply, each legitimising value must be satisfied from the perspective of all relevant patrons, which is likely to operate as a buffer between potentially conflicting interests while providing principled justifications for difficult decisions. Although it might be argued that this model cages the discretion of law officers in something akin to a governmental-politico-legal neutral zone, this book views that as an inevitable consequence of their sources of legitimacy. Determining the constitutional limits that can be gleaned from this heuristic model might not be easy or ideal, but it is the most persuasive conceptual basis for analysing the legitimacy of UK law officers.

Conclusions

This book has argued that the constitutional legitimacy of law officers in the UK is best analysed with reference to a trifocal and relativistic model of legitimising values, and that those values should be anchored in clear conceptual definitions if they are to survive controversy. The parameters of the research leading to these findings were initially canvassed in Chapter 1, which also clarified some terminological issues before reviewing the most significant scholarly literature that has critiqued the law officer regime to date. Chapter 2 then examined several foundational understandings in connection with the concepts of constitutional legitimacy, independence, accountability and trust. As part of the introductory groundwork in these opening chapters, it was explained that the research which underpins this book was largely based on a values-based framework of analysis first developed by Daly for the purpose of studying the legitimacy of judicial review. It was then explained that Daly's values-based framework of analysis – featuring historical, descriptive, interpretive, prescriptive and evaluative dimensions – would be supplemented by a comparative dimension in accordance with the specific objectives of this UK-wide study.

Consistent with those plans, Chapters 3 to 6 delivered an extensive analysis of the UK law officer regime consisting of predominantly historical, descriptive and comparative dimensions. As a result of those endeavours, these chapters contain a constitutionally holistic and balanced account of the UK law officer regime which highlights in detail, for the first time, the magnitude of the constitutional differences that pertain between the law officer models operating in this jurisdiction. The interpretive, evaluative and prescriptive dimensions to the book executed primarily over the course of Chapter 7 could not have been carried out without the new understandings made possible by those preceding analyses. In sum, therefore, this book offers two new contributions to the literature in this area of research, namely a holistic account of how the UK law officer regime has evolved into the form that it takes today, and a trifocal and relativistic model of legitimising values for conceptually analysing the constitutional legitimacy of that regime.

Due to practical limitations, however, there remain a number of avenues for further study in what has proved to be a very fertile field of research. Foremost among these is the theoretical character of the arguments developed herein, though those arguments are based, of course, on a rigorous analysis of the publicly accessible resources available. It is hoped that the conceptual foundations provided by these necessarily falsifiable arguments will usefully inform any empirical research that might be conducted in order to build a more sociologically based account of the offices to which they relate. Any studies of this kind could, for example, test the analytical premises and conclusions borne from this book through formal interviews with members of the UK law officer regime, past and present, or by way of surveys issued to their patrons. Indeed, studies of this nature are to be strongly encouraged now that an in-depth understanding of how the UK law officer regime has evolved into the form that it takes today is available alongside a theoretical basis for conceptually analysing the legitimacy of the regime. Illuminated by these new insights, it is sincerely hoped that greater scholarly attention will gravitate towards this important set of domestic institutions and their unique place in the UK constitution.

BIBLIOGRAPHY

Ad-hoc Committee, *Second Report on the Justice (Northern Ireland) Bill and the Criminal Justice Review – Implementation Plan* (January 2002).

Adler, M, 'Understanding and Analysing Administrative Justice' in Michael Adler (ed), *Administrative Justice in Context* (Hart Publishing 2010).

Angiolini, E, 'Legislation, Litigation and Prosecution: The Role of a Scottish Law Officer' (2003) *Juridical Review* 219.

Angiolini, E, 'The Lord Advocate in the 21st Century' (Speech by the Lord Advocate at the KPMG Annual Law Lecture, 28 February 2007).

Angiolini, E, 'Role still independent' (*Scotsman*, 1 August 2007). Available at: www.scotsman.com/news/role-still-independent-1-911529.

Angiolini, E, 'A Speech by the Lord Advocate to the Law Society of Scotland Annual Conference' (8 May 2009).

Angiolini, E, 'Review of the Attorney General's Relationship with the Executive and Departments (Extracts from the Introduction and Background Sections of the Report)' (31 October 2012).

Anthony, G, 'The Devolution of Policing and Criminal Justice' (2011) 17 *European Public Law* 197.

Anthony, G, 'The St Andrews Agreement and the Northern Ireland Assembly' (2008) 14 *European Public Law* 151.

Anthony, G, *Judicial Review in Northern Ireland* (2nd edn, Hart Publishing 2014).

Anthony, G, 'The Quartet Plus Two: Judicial Review in Northern Ireland' in TT Arvind and others (eds), *Executive Decision-Making and the Courts* (Hart Publishing 2021).

Antoniw, M, 'Written Statement: Legal Challenge to the UK Internal Market Act 2020 – Update' (*Welsh Government*, 29 June 20201). Available at: https://gov.wales/written-statement-legal-challenge-uk-internal-market-act-2020-update.

Antoniw, M, 'A National Civic Conversation About Our Constitutional Future' (A Speech by the Counsel General to the Wales Governance Centre at Cardiff University, 5 July 2021). Available at: www.cardiff.ac.uk/__data/assets/pdf_file/0003/2532405/Counsel-General-Speech.pdf.

Appleby, G, 'Releasing Government's Advice Would Help Parliament Better Scrutinise Laws' (*The Conversation*, 16 December 2015). Available at: http://theconversation.com/releasing-governments-advice-would-help-parliament-better-scrutinise-laws-50593.

Appleby, G, 'Navigating a Complicated Relationship: The Role of the Solicitor-General' (2016) 29 *Law Society of NSW Journal* 70.

Appleby, G, 'Reform of the Attorney General: Comparing Britain and Australia' [2016] *Public Law* 573.

Appleby, G, *The Role of the Solicitor-General: Negotiating Law, Politics and the Public Interest* (Hart Publishing 2016).

Appleby, G, Keyzer, P and Williams, JM, (eds), *Public Sentinels: A Comparative Study of Australian Solicitors-General* (Routledge 2014).

Archer, P, *The Role of the Law Officers* (Fabian Society Research Series 339 1978).

Assembly and Executive Review Committee, *First Report on the Arrangements for the Devolution of Policing and Justice Matters Together with the Minutes of Proceedings of the Committee Relating to the Report, the Minutes of Evidence and Other Relevant Documents* (NIA 22/08/09R, 6 January 2009).

Assembly and Executive Review Committee, *First Report on the Inquiry into the Devolution of Policing and Justice Matters: Volume 1 – Minutes of Proceedings Relating to the Report, Minutes of Evidence, Papers from the NIO* (NIA 22/07/08R, 26 February 2008).

Assembly and Executive Review Committee, *Second Report on the Arrangements for the Devolution of Policing and Justice Matters: Volume 2 – Together with the Minutes of Proceedings of the Committee Relating to the Report, the Minutes of Evidence and Other Relevant Documents* (NIA 42/09/10R, 25 February 2010).

Attorney General's Human Rights Guidance No 1, 'Human Rights Standards Relevant to the Right to Life' (*Office of the Attorney General for Northern Ireland*, 22 March 2013). Available at: www.attorneygeneralni.gov.uk/sites/ag/files/guidance-on-human-rights-protection-of-the-right-to-life.pdf.

Attorney General's Human Rights Guidance No 2, 'Human Rights Guidance for Forensic Science Northern Ireland' (*Office of the Attorney General for Northern Ireland*, 8 May 2013). Available at: www.attorneygeneralni.gov.uk/sites/ag/files/human-rights-guidance-for-fsni.pdf.

Attorney General for Northern Ireland, 'Sixth Annual Report – 2015/16'. Available at: www.attorneygeneralni.gov.uk/sites/ag/files/media-files/AGNI%20Annual%20Report%202015-16_0.pdf.

Attorney General for Northern Ireland, 'Solicitor Trainee Scheme' (6 June 2018). Available at: www.attorneygeneralni.gov.uk/sites/ag/files/AGNI18042%202018%20Trainee%20Solicitor%20Terms%20%26%20Conditions%20%28Revised%29.pdf.

Attorney General for Northern Ireland, 'Tenth Annual Report – 2019/20'. Available at: www.attorneygeneralni.gov.uk/sites/ag/files/media-files/Attorney%20General%20for%20Northern%20Ireland%20Annual%20Report%20201920_0.pdf.

Attorney General's Office, *Protocol between the Attorney General and the Prosecuting Departments* (July 2009).

Attorney General's Office, *Use of the Common Law Offence of Conspiracy to Defraud* (November 2012). Available at: www.gov.uk/guidance/use-of-the-common-law-offence-of-conspiracy-to-defraud--6.

Attorney General's Office, *Framework Agreement between the Law Officers and the Director of the Serious Fraud Office* (21 January 2019).

Attorney General's Office, *Framework Agreement between the Law Officers and the Director of Public Prosecutions* (18 December 2020).

Attorney General's Office, *Protocol between the Law Officers and Her Majesty's Chief Inspector of the Crown Prosecution Service* (29 January 2020).

Attorney General's Office, *The Law Officers' Approach to Contempt of Court Referrals* (15 September 2021). Available at: www.gov.uk/guidance/the-law-officers-approach-to-contempt-of-court-referrals.

Austin, JL, *How to do Things with Words* (2nd edn, Harvard University Press 1962).

Avineri, S and de-Shalit, A (eds), *Communitarianism and Individualism* (Oxford University Press 1992).

Baker, P, 'NI Attorney General: "Citizens Are Entitled to Have Confidence in the Administration of Justice"' (*Slugger O'Toole*, 25 April 2012). Available at: https://sluggerotoole.com/2012/04/25/ni-attorney-general-citizens-are-entitled-to-have-confidence-in-the-administration-of-justice.

Bamforth, N, 'Ultra Vires and Institutional Interdependence' in Christopher Forsyth (ed), *Judicial Review and the Constitution* (Hart Publishing 2000).

Barber, NW, *The United Kingdom Constitution: An Introduction* (Oxford University Press 2021).

Barradas de Freitas, R and Lo Iacono, Sergio (eds), *Trust Matters: Cross-Disciplinary Essays* (Hart Publishing 2021).

Bartole, S, 'Internal Ordering in the Unitary State' in Michel Rosenfeld and András Sajó (eds), *The Oxford Handbook of Comparative Constitutional Law* (Oxford University Press 2012).

Beetham, D, *The Legitimation of Power* (Palgrave 1991).

Beever, A, and Rickett, C, 'Interpretive Legal Theory and the Academic Lawyer' (2005) 68 *Modern Law Review* 320.

Bell, D, *The End of Ideology: On the Exhaustion of Political Ideas in the 1950s* (5th edn, Harvard University Press 2000).

Bell, RE, 'The Office of Director of Public Prosecutions for Northern Ireland' (PhD thesis, Queen's University Belfast 1988).

Belot, H and McGhee, A, 'Solicitor-General Resigns Over "Broken" Relationship with Attorney-General George Brandis' (*ABC News*, 24 October 2016). Available at: www.abc.net.au/news/2016-10-24/justin-gleeson-resigns-as-solicitor-general/7960632.

Bingham, Lord, 'The Rule of Law' (2007) 66 *Cambridge Law Journal* 67.

Birrell, D, *Comparing Devolved Governance* (Palgrave Macmillan 2012).

Blackburne, E, *Life of the Right Hon Francis Blackburne* (Macmillan and Co 1874).

Blick, A, *The Codes of the Constitution* (Hart Publishing 2016).

Bogdanor, V, *Devolution in the United Kingdom* (Oxford University Press 1999).

Bogdanor, V, 'Parliament and the Judiciary: The Problem of Accountability' (*UK Public Administration Consortium*, 9 February 2006). Available at: https://ukpac.wordpress.com/bogdanor-speech/.

Bottoms, A, and Tankebe, J, 'Beyond Procedural Justice: A Dialogic Approach to Legitimacy in Criminal Justice' (2012) 102 *Journal of Criminal Law and Criminology* 119.

Bovens, M, 'Analysing and Assessing Accountability: A Conceptual Framework' (2007) 13 *European Law Journal* 447.

Bovens, M, 'Two Concepts of Accountability: Accountability as a Virtue and as a Mechanism' (2010) 33 *West European Politics* 946.

Bovens, M, Goodin RE and Schillemans, T, 'Public Accountability' in Mark Bovens, Robert E Goodin and Thomas Schillemans (eds), *The Oxford Handbook of Public Accountability* (Oxford University Press 2014).

Bovens, M, Schillemans, T and Hart, P, 'Does Public Accountability Work? An Assessment Tool' (2008) 86 *Public Administration* 225.

Bowcott, O, 'Attorney General Faces Calls to Resign After She Defends Dominic Cummings' (*The Guardian*, 25 May 2020). Available at: www.theguardian.com/politics/2020/may/25/attorney-general-faces-calls-to-resign-defends-dominic-cummings-suella-braverman.

Bowers, R and Cornaglia, M, 'Advice from the Attorney General Does Not Attract Privilege' (*The Law Society Gazette*, 7 December 2018). Available at: www.lawgazette.co.uk/commentary-and-opinion/advice-from-the-attorney-general-does-not-attract-privilege/5068625.article.

Boyd, C, 'Ministers and the Law' (2006) *Juridical Review* 179.

Boyle, K, Hadden, T and Hillyard, P, *Law and State: The Case of Northern Ireland* (Martin Robertson 1975).

Brazier, R, *Ministers of the Crown* (Oxford University Press 1997).

Bregman, R, *Humankind: A Hopeful History* (Bloomsbury 2020).

Brivati, B, Buxton, J and Seldon, A, *The Contemporary History Handbook* (Manchester University Press 1996)

Bryett, K and Osborne, P, *Criminal Prosecutions Procedure and Practice: International Perspectives* (TSO 2000).

Buckland, R, 'Role of Law Officers on Devolution and Bills' (A Speech by the Solicitor General to Public Law Wales, 20 December 2016). Available at: www.gov.uk/government/speeches/role-of-law-officers-on-devolution-and-bills.

Buckland, R, 'The Model of a Modern Solicitor General: Thoughts on the Constitution in the Time of Brexit' (A Speech by the Solicitor General for England and Wales to Politeia, 16 October 2017). Available at: www.politeia.co.uk/the-model-of-a-modern-solicitor-general-thoughts-on-the-constitution-in-the-time-of-brexit/.

Buckland, R, 'The History and Role of the Law Officers' (*Inner Temple Lecture*, 18 February 2019). Available at: www.robertbuckland.co.uk/news/history-and-role-law-officers.

Burbank, SB, 'The Architecture of Judicial Independence' (1999) 72 *Southern California Law Review* 315.

Burbank, SB, and Friedman, B, 'Reconsidering Judicial Independence' in Stephen B Burbank and Barry Friedman (eds), *Judicial Independence at the Crossroads: An Interdisciplinary Approach: An Interdisciplinary Approach* (Sage 2002).

Burnett, Lord, 'Becoming Stronger Together' (A Speech by the Lord Chief Justice of England and Wales to the Commonwealth Judges and Magistrates' Association, 10 September 2018). Available at: www.judiciary.uk/wp-content/uploads/2018/09/lcj-speech-brisbane-lecture-20180910.pdf.

Burrows, N, *Devolution* (Sweet & Maxwell 2000).

Burrows, N and Greaves, R, *The Advocate General and EC Law* (Oxford University Press 2007).

Cabinet Office, *Ministerial Code* (August 2019). Available at: www.gov.uk/government/publications/ministerial-code.

Cabinet Office, *List of Ministerial Responsibilities Including Executive Agencies and Non-Ministerial Departments* (March 2021). Available at: https://assets.publishing.service.gov.uk/government/uploads/system/uploads/attachment_data/file/968352/List-of-Ministerial-Responsibilities.pdf.

Cabinet Office, *List of Cabinet Committees* (21 October 2021). Available at: www.gov.uk/government/publications/the-cabinet-committees-system-and-list-of-cabinet-committees.

Calvert, H, *Constitutional Law in Northern Ireland: A Study in Regional Government* (Stevens & Sons 1968).

Canivet, G, Andenas, M and Fairgrieve, D (eds), *Independence, Accountability and the Judiciary* (British Institute of International and Comparative Law 2006).

Carrubba, CJ, 'A Model of the Endogenous Development of Judicial Institutions in Federal and International Systems' (2009) 71 The *Journal of Politics* 55.

Carswell, Lord, 'Founding a Legal System: The Early Judiciary of Northern Ireland' in Felix M Larkin and Norma M Dawson (eds), *Lawyers, the Law and History* (Four Courts Press 2013).

Carter, H, 'Local Government and Administration in Wales 1536–1939' in JA Andrews (ed), *Welsh Studies in Public Law* (University of Wales Press 1970).

Casey, C, 'The Law Officers: The Relationship Between Executive Lawyers and Executive Power in Ireland and the United Kingdom' in Oran Doyle, Aileen McHarg and Jo Murkens (eds), *The Brexit Challenge for Ireland and the UK* (Cambridge University Press 2021).

Casey, C and Kenny, D, 'The Gatekeepers: Executive Lawyers and the Executive Power in Comparative Constitutional Law' (2022) *International Journal of Constitutional Law*, forthcoming.

Casey, J, 'The First Labour Government and Office of Lord Advocate' (1975) 26 *Northern Ireland Legal Quarterly* 18.

Casey, J, *The Irish Law Officers: Roles and Responsibilities of the Attorney General and Director of Public Prosecutions* (Sweet & Maxwell 1996).

Clark, L, 'The Role of the Advocate General for Scotland in the New Constitutional Settlement' in Alan Boyle and others (eds), *Human Rights and Scots Law* (Hart Publishing 2002).

Clarke, L, 'Government Distances Itself from Attorney General John Larkin over Austrian Lesbian Case' (*Belfast Telegraph*, 25 October 2012). Available at: www.belfasttelegraph.co.uk/news/northern-ireland/government-distances-itself-from-attorney-general-john-larkin-over-austrian-lesbian-case-28877682.html.

Clarke, L, 'Revealed: Advice Given to MLAs on Attorney General's Abortion Row Intervention' (*Belfast Telegraph*, 17 November 2012).

Clayman, SE, 'The Micropolitics of Legitimacy: Political Positioning and Journalistic Scrutiny at the Boundary of the Mainstream' (2017) 80 *Social Psychology Quarterly* 41.

Clyde, Lord, 'Memorandum on the Law Officers of Scotland' *The Times* (London, 7 February 1924).

Collier, JP, *Criticisms on the Bar* (Simpkin and Marshall 1819).

Committee on Procedures, *Standing Orders in Respect of the Attorney General for Northern Ireland* (28 September 2010). Available at: http://archive.niassembly.gov.uk/record/committees2010/Procedures/100928_StandingOrdersinRespectofAttorneyGeneral.htm.

Committee on Procedures, *Inquiry into the extent to which Standing Orders should permit the Attorney General for Northern Ireland to participate in proceedings of the Assembly: Part 1 – Impartiality of the Office of AGNI, Registration of Interests and Participation of the AGNI in Assembly Proceedings in respect of areas other than Statutory Rules* (NIA 232/11-16, 24 February 2015).

Committee on the Administration of Justice, *Commentary on the 'Inquiry into how the Attorney General for Northern Ireland will Participate in Proceedings of the Northern Ireland Assembly* (CAJ Submission No 268, October 2010). Available at: www.caj.org.uk/files/2010/11/01/s._268_Inq_into_how_Attorney_General_NI_will_participate_NIA,_Oct_2010_.pdf.

Connolly, M-L, 'Doctor Quits Over NI Attorney General's Abortion Interventions' (*BBC News NI*, 14 September 2016). Available at: www.bbc.co.uk/news/uk-northern-ireland-37353825.

Conor, C and Larkin, J, 'Crossing the Line? The Attorney General and the Law/Politics Divide' (*Policy Exchange*, 12 January 2022). Available at: www.policyexchange.org.uk/publication/crossing-the-line/.

Constitutional Affairs Committee, *The Constitutional Role of the Attorney General* (HC 2006-07, 306).

Cook, KS, Hardin, R and Levi, M, *Cooperation Without Trust?* (Russell Sage Foundation 2005).

Cotterrell, R, 'Trusting in Law: Legal and Moral Concepts of Trust' (1993) 46 *Current Legal Problems* 75.

Cotterrell, R, 'Is It So Bad to Be Different? Comparative Law and the Appreciation of Diversity' in Esin Orucu and David Nelken (eds), *Comparative Law: A Handbook* (Hart Publishing 2007).

Craig, P and de Búrca, G, *EU Law: Text, Cases and Materials (UK Version)* (7th edn, Oxford University Press 2020).

Crawford, J, *Brownlie's Principles of Public International Law* (9th edn, Oxford University Press 2019).

Criminal Justice Review, *Report of the Criminal Justice Review in Northern Ireland* (TSO 2000).

Cross, FB, 'Law and Trust' (2004) 93 *Georgetown Law Journal* 1457.

Daintith, T and Page, A, *The Executive in the Constitution: Structure, Autonomy, and Internal Control* (Oxford University Press 1999).

Daly, P, *Understanding Administrative Law in the Common Law World* (Oxford University Press 2021).

Daly, P, 'Administrative Law: A Values-Based Approach' in John Bell and others (eds), *Public Law Adjudication in Common Law Systems: Process and Substance* (Hart Publishing 2016).

Daly, P, 'Administrative Law: Characteristics, Legitimacy, Unity' in Mark Elliott, Jason NE Varuhas and Shona Wilson Stark (eds), *The Unity of Public Law? Doctrinal, Theoretical and Comparative Perspectives* (Hart Publishing 2018).

Daniell, ER, *A Treatise on the Practice of the High Court of Chancery with Some Practical Observations on the Pleadings in That Court: Volume 1* (J & WT Clarke 1837).

de Londras, F, and Dzehtsiarou, K, *Great Debates on the European Convention on Human Rights* (Palgrave 2018).

de Montesquieu, B, *The Spirit of Laws* (Thomas Nugent tr, Batoche Books 2001).

Deacon, R, *Devolution in the United Kingdom* (2nd edn, Edinburgh University Press 2012).

Deacon, R, Denton, A and Southall, R, *The Government and Politics of Wales* (Edinburgh University Press 2018).

Deb, A, 'The Legacy of Buick: Northern Ireland's Chaotic Constitutional Crucible' (2019) 23 *Edinburgh Law Review* 259.

Department for Exiting the European Union, *Publication of the Attorney General's Legal Advice to Cabinet on the Withdrawal Agreement and the Protocol on Ireland/Northern Ireland* (5 December 2018). Available at: www.gov.uk/government/publications/exiting-the-eu-publication-of-legal-advice.

Department of Justice, *Governance and Accountability of the Public Prosecution Service* (8 February 2012).

Devonport, M, 'Attorney General John Larkin Hits Headlines for Wrong Reasons' (*BBC News NI*, 24 October 2012). Available at: www.bbc.co.uk/news/uk-northern-ireland-20054111.

Devonport, M and McCormack, J, 'Arc21 Ruling: NI Attorney General Seeks Clarity Over Case' (*BBC News*, 10 August 2018). Available at: www.bbc.co.uk/news/uk-northern-ireland-45150319.

Dickinson, IS, 'The Office of Lord Advocate' (1980) *Scots Law Times* (News) 69.

Dickinson, IS, 'The Lord Advocate, the Lord Chancellor and the ECHR' (2000) 5 *Scottish Parliament Law Review* 3.

Dickson, B, *Law in Northern Ireland* (3rd edn, Hart Publishing 2018).

Dickson, B, 'Devolution in Northern Ireland' in Jeffrey Jowell and Colm O'Cinneide (eds), *The Changing Constitution* (9th edn, Oxford University Press 2019).

Dickson, B and McCormick, C, 'Northern Ireland Dimensions to the First Decade of the United Kingdom Supreme Court' (2020) 83 *Modern Law Review* 1133.

Duhs, E and Rao, I, *Retained EU Law: A Practical Guide* (The Law Society 2021).

Dyzenhaus, D, 'The Legitimacy of the Rule of Law' in David Dyzenhaus, Murray Hunt and Grant Huscroft (eds), *A Simple Common Lawyer: Essays in Honour of Michael Taggart* (Bloomsbury Publishing 2009).

Edwards, J Ll J, *The Law Officers of the Crown: A Study of the Offices of Attorney-General and Solicitor-General of England with an Account of the Office of the Director of Public Prosecutions of England* (Sweet & Maxwell 1964).

Edwards, J Ll J, *Ministerial Responsibility for National Security as it relates to the Offices of Prime Minister, Attorney General and Solicitor General of Canada* (A Study Prepared for the Commission of Inquiry Concerning Certain Activities of the Royal Canadian Mounted Police 1980).

Edwards, J Ll J, *The Attorney General, Politics and the Public Interest* (Sweet & Maxwell 1984).

Edwards, J Ll J, 'The Attorney General and the Charter of Rights' in Robert J Sharpe (ed), *Charter Litigation* (Butterworths 1986).

Edwards, J Ll J, 'The Office of Attorney General – New Levels of Public Expectations and Accountability' in Philip C Stenning (ed), *Accountability for Criminal Justice: Selected Essays* (University of Toronto Press 1995).

Elliott, M, *The Constitutional Foundations of Judicial Review* (Hart Publishing 2001).

Elvin, R, 'Who Should Decide Who Decides the Public Interest?' (*Judicial Power Project*, 15 February 2016). Available at: https://judicialpowerproject.org.uk/who-should-decide-who-decides-the-public-interest/.

Endicott, T, *Administrative Law* (5th edn, Oxford University Press 2021).

Erwin, A, 'Attorney General John Larkin Appointed High Court Judge' (*Belfast Telegraph*, 31 January 2020). Available at: www.belfasttelegraph.co.uk/news/courts/attorney-general-john-larkin-appointed-temporary-high-court-judge-38913330.html.

Ekins, R, 'Braverman is Right to Seek Clarification from the Court of Appeal in the Colston Case' (*ConservativeHome*, 13 January 2022). Available at: www.conservativehome.com/thinktankcentral/2022/01/richard-ekins-braverman-is-right-to-seek-clarification-from-the-court-of-appeal-on-the-colston-case.html.

Evans, A, 'Northern Ireland, 2017–2020: An Experiment in Indirect Rule' [2021] *Public Law* 471.

Fard, HD and Rostamy, AAA, 'Promoting Public Trust in Public Organizations: Explaining the Role of Public Accountability' (2007) 7 *Public Organization Review* 331.

Feldman, D, 'Constitutionalism, Deliberative Democracy, and Human Rights' in John Morison, Kieran McEvoy and Gordon Anthony (eds), *Judges, Transition, and Human Rights* (Oxford University Press 2007).

Ferguson, PR and McDiarmid, C, *Scots Criminal Law: A Critical Analysis* (2nd edn, Edinburgh University Press 2014).

Finlay, J, 'James Henryson and the Origins of the Office of King's Advocate in Scotland' (2000) 79 *The Scottish Historical Review* 17.

Fordham, M, 'The Counsel General for Wales' Intervention in the Prorogation Case' in Daniel Clarry (ed), *The UK Supreme Court Yearbook, Volume 10: 2018–2019* (Appellate Press 2021).

Fox, C, 'New Hope for the Criminal Justice Review? A Commentary on the Implementation Process' (2003) 54 *Northern Ireland Legal Quarterly* 437.

Fraser, J, 'Section 8 "Human Rights" Guidance and its Relevance to Practitioners' (2014) 222 *The Writ – The Journal of the Law Society of Northern Ireland* 10.

Freeden, M, 'Ideology and Political Theory' (2006) 11 *Journal of Political Ideologies* 3.

Gardner, D, *Administrative Law and the Administrative Court in Wales* (University of Wales Press 2016).

Garnier, E, 'The Law Officers and Legislative Procedure' (A Speech by the Solicitor General to the Constitutional and Administrative Law Bar Association, 17 July 2010). Available at: www.gov.uk/government/speeches/speech-to-the-constitutional-and-administrative-law-bar-association.
Gee, G and others, *The Politics of Judicial Independence in the UK's Changing Constitution* (Cambridge University Press 2015).
Genki Kimura, 'Towards Persuasive Accountability: Accountability in the Post-Truth Era' (Questions of Accountability Conference, Online, November 2021).
Goldsmith, P, 'Government and the Rule of Law in the Modern Age' (A Speech by the Attorney General for the LSE Law Department and Clifford Chance, 22 February 2006). Available at: www.lse.ac.uk/website-archive/publicEvents/pdf/20060222-Goldsmith.pdf.
Goldsmith, P, 'The Role of the Attorney General in Changed Constitutional Circumstances' (A Lecture at Birmingham College of Law, 2006).
Goldsmith, P, 'Independence – Myth or Mystery?' (A Speech for the Annual Denning Lecture, 27 November 2007).
Gordon, LI, 'Lord Advocate and the Crown Office' in MR McLarty and G Campbell H Paton (eds), *A Source Book and History of Administrative Law in Scotland* (William Hodge and Company 1956).
Gordon, R, '*Miller* and Devolution: How Wales Approached the Issues' in Daniel Clarry (ed), *The UK Supreme Court Yearbook, Volume 8: 2016–2017* (Appellate Press 2018).
Government Legal Department, *The Judge Over Your Shoulder – A Guide to Good Decision-Making* (18 July 2016).
Gow, N, 'Judicial Tenure and the Advocate General' [1998] SLT 87.
Gowan, I, 'Government in Wales in the Twentieth Century' in JA Andrews (ed), *Welsh Studies in Public Law* (University of Wales Press 1970).
Green, DA, 'The Law Officers in the New Age of Politics' (*Prospect*, 18 September 2020). Available at: www.prospectmagazine.co.uk/politics/law-officers-suella-braverman-lord-keen-robert-buckland-brexit-internal-market-bill.
Grieve, D, 'Contempt of Court: Why It Still Matters' (A Lecture by the Attorney General in Honour of Michael Kalisher, 12 October 2010).
Grieve, D, 'Parliament and the Judiciary' (A Speech by the Attorney General to BPP Law School, 25 October 2012). Available at: www.gov.uk/government/speeches/parliament-and-the-judiciary.
Grieve, D, 'The Role of Human Rights in a Law Officer's Work: Challenges Facing the HRA and the ECHR' [2012] *Judicial Review* 101.
Habermas, J, *The Theory of Communicative Action* (Thomas McCarthy tr, Beacon Press 1984).
Hadfield, B, *The Constitution of Northern Ireland* (SLS Legal Publications (NI) 1989).
Hall, MA, 'The Importance of Trust for Ethics, Law, and Public Policy' (2005) 14 *Cambridge Quarterly of Healthcare Ethics* 156.
Hallin, D, 'The Media, the War in Vietnam, and Political Support: A Critique of the Thesis of an Oppositional Media' 46 *The Journal of Politics* 2.
Hand, J, 'Ministerial Maternity Leave' (*UK Constitutional Law Association Blog*, 1 March 2021). Available at: https://ukconstitutionallaw.org/2021/03/01/james-hand-ministerial-maternity-leave/.
Hand, J, 'The Attorney-General, Politics and Logistics – A Fork in the Road?' (2022) *Legal Studies*, forthcoming.
Hanham, HJ, 'The Creation of the Scottish Office 1881–1887' (1965) *Juridical Review* 205.
Hanlon, F, 'An Analysis of the Office of Attorney General in Australia and Directions for the Future' (PhD thesis, University of Melbourne 2007).
Hardin, R, *Trust and Trustworthiness* (Russell Sage Foundation 2004).
Hardin, R, *Trust* (Polity Press 2006).
Harlow, C, 'Accountability as a Value in Global Governance and for Global Administrative Law' in Gordon Anthony and others (eds), *Values in Global Administrative Law* (Hart Publishing 2011).
Harlow, C, 'The Human Rights Act and "Coordinate Construction": Towards a "Parliament Square" Axis for Human Rights?' in NW Barber, Richard Ekins and Paul Yowell (eds), *Lord Sumption and the Limits of Law* (Hart Publishing 2016).

Harlow, C and Rawlings, R, 'Promoting Accountability in Multilevel Governance: A Network Approach' (2007) 13 *European Law Journal* 542.
Harris, DJ and others, *Harris, O'Boyle & Warbrick: Law of the European Convention on Human Rights* (4th edn, Oxford University Press 2018).
Hart, AR, *A History of the Bar and Inn of Court of Northern Ireland* (The General Council of the Bar of Northern Ireland 2013).
Hart, HLA, *The Concept of Law* (3rd edn, Oxford University Press 2012).
Harvey, C, 'Bringing Humanity Home: A Transformational Human Rights Culture for Northern Ireland?' in Anne-Marie McAlinden and Clare Dwyer (eds), *Criminal Justice in Transition: The Northern Ireland Context* (Hart Publishing 2015).
Hazell, R, 'Out of Court: Why Have the Courts Played No Role in Resolving Devolution Disputes in the United Kingdom?' (2007) 37 *Publius: The Journal of Federalism* 578.
Heald, O, 'The Role of the Law Officers' (A Speech by the Solicitor General to Kent Law School, 18 October 2012). Available at: www.gov.uk/government/speeches/the-role-of-the-law-officers.
Heywood, A, *Political Ideologies* (5th edn, Palgrave Macmillan 2012).
Himsworth, CMG and Munro, CR, *The Scotland Act 1998* (2nd edn, Sweet & Maxwell 2000).
Hollis, M, *Trust Within Reason* (Cambridge University Press 1998).
Hope, Lord, *Lord Hope's Diaries: UK Supreme Court … and Afterwards (2009–2015)* (Avizandum Publishing Ltd 2019).
Horne, A, *The Law Officers* (HC Library Standard Note SN/PC/04485, 2014).
Hosking, G, *Trust: A History* (Oxford University Press 2014).
Hough, B, 'Judicial Review Where the Attorney General Refuses to Act: Time for a Change' (1988) 8 *Legal Studies* 189.
Humphreys, R, *Beyond the Border: The Good Friday Agreement and Irish Unity After Brexit* (Merrion Press 2018).
Hutcheon, P, 'Lord Advocate Role "Increasingly Political"' (*The Herald*, 13 October 2013). Available at: www.heraldscotland.com/news/13127048.Lord_Advocate_role__increasingly_political_/.
Hutcheon, P, 'SNP Government in Row Over Presence of Lord Advocate at Cabinet Meetings' (*The Herald*, 5 August 2018). Available at: www.heraldscotland.com/news/16399053.snp-government-in-row-over-presence-of-lord-advocate-at-cabinet-meetings/.
Hyde, J, 'Ex-Attorney General Cox Earning £468,000 a Year as Law Firm Consultant' (*The Law Society Gazette*, 30 August 2021). Available at: www.lawgazette.co.uk/news/ex-attorney-general-cox-earning-468000-a-year-as-law-firm-consultant/5109621.article.
Jackson, J, *Special Advocates in the Adversarial System* (Routledge 2021).
Jenkins, D, 'Law and Government in Wales Before the Act of Union' in JA Andrews (ed), *Welsh Studies in Public Law* (University of Wales Press 1970).
Jennings, I, *The Law and the Constitution* (University of London Press 1959).
Joffe, H, 'Thematic Analysis' in David Harper and Andrew R Thompson (eds), *Qualitative Research Methods in Mental Health and Psychotherapy* (Wiley-Blackwell 2012).
Justice Committee, *Oral Evidence by the Rt Hon Jeremy Wright QC MP on the Work of the Attorney General* (HC 409, 15 September 2015).
Justice Committee, *Oral Evidence by the Rt Hon Geoffrey Cox QC MP on the Work of the Attorney General* (HC 1887, 23 January 2019).
Justice Committee, *Oral Evidence by Robert Buckland QC MP on the Work of the Solicitor General* (HC 1837, 4 April 2019).
Justice Committee, *Disclosure of Evidence in Criminal Cases* (HC 2017–19, 859).
Justice Committee, *Oral Evidence by the Rt Hon Suella Braverman QC MP on the Work of the Attorney General* (HC 462, 21 July 2020).
Justice Committee, *Role and Purpose of the Crown and Procurator Fiscal Service* (25 April 2017, SP Paper 123.1).
Kavanagh, A, 'The Constitutional Separation of Powers' in David Dyzenhaus and Malcolm Thorburn (eds), *Philosophical Foundations of Constitutional Law* (Oxford University Press 2016).

Kavanagh, D and Seldon, A, *The Powers Behind the Prime Minister: The Hidden Influence of Number Ten* (HarperCollins 1999).

Kearney, V, 'NI Attorney General John Larkin Calls for End to Troubles Prosecutions' (*BBC News NI*, 20 November 2013). Available at: www.bbc.co.uk/news/uk-northern-ireland-24999051.

Keen, Lord, 'The Rule of Law and the Role of the Law Officers' (Speech by the Advocate General for Scotland to the SPLG Conference, 11 June 2018). Available at: www.gov.uk/government/news/the-rule-of-law-and-the-role-of-the-law-officers.

Keeton, GW, *A Liberal Attorney-General: Being the Life of Lord Robson of Jesmond (1852–1918) with an Account of the Office of Attorney-General* (James Nisbet & Co 1949).

Kennon, A, 'Legal Advice to Parliament' in Alexander Horne, Gavin Drewry and Dawn Oliver (eds), *Parliament and the Law* (Bloomsbury Publishing 2013).

Kenny, D and Casey, C, 'A One Person Supreme Court? The Attorney General, Constitutional Advice to Government, and the Case for Transparency' (2019) 42 *Dublin University Law Journal* 89.

Kingdom, J, *No Such Thing as Society? Individualism and Community* (Open University Press 1992).

Komorowski, J, 'The Accountability Deficit: Control of the Lord Advocate in Light of the McKie Case' (2007) *Juridical Review* 73.

Kyriakides, KA, 'The Advisory Functions of the Attorney-General' (2003) 1 *Hertfordshire Law Journal* 73.

Kyriakides, KA, 'The Law Officers of the Crown and the Rule of Law in the United Kingdom' in Gabrielle Appleby, Patrick Keyzer and John M Williams (eds), *Public Sentinels: A Comparative Study of Australian Solicitors-General* (Routledge 2014).

Lamb, RD, *Rethinking Legitimacy and Illegitimacy: A New Approach to Assessing Support and Opposition Across Disciplines* (Rowman & Littlefield 2014).

Larkin, J, 'Establishing the Office of the Attorney General for Northern Ireland' (August 2009).

Le Sueur, A, 'Developing Mechanisms for Judicial Accountability in the UK' (2004) 24 *Legal Studies* 73.

Leyell, N, 'The Role of the Law Officers' (1988) 12 *Trent Law Journal* 1.

Liebling, A, 'A "Liberal Regime Within a Secure Perimeter"?: Dispersal Prisons and Penal Practice in the Late Twentieth Century' in Anthony Bottoms and Michael Tonry (eds) *Ideology, Crime and Criminal Justice* (Routledge 2002).

Lines, K, *18 Months of Covid-19 Legislation in England: A Rule of Law Analysis* (Bingham Centre for the Rule of Law, 16 October 2021). Available at: https://binghamcentre.biicl.org/publications/18-months-of-covid-19-legislation-in-england-a-rule-of-law-analysis.

Lipset, SM, 'Some Social Requisites of Democracy: Economic Development and Political Legitimacy' (1959) 53 *The American Political Science Review* 69.

Lipset, SM, 'Social Conflict, Legitimacy, and Democracy' in William Connolly (ed), *Legitimacy and the State* (Basil Blackwell 1984).

Loughlin, M, 'The State, the Crown and the Law' in Maurice Sunkin and Sebastian Payne (eds), *The Nature of the Crown: A Legal and Political Analysis* (Oxford University Press 1999).

Luhmann, N, *Trust and Power* (Wiley & Sons 1979).

Mackintosh, JP, *The British Cabinet* (Stevens 1962).

Macmillan, Lord, *A Man of Law's Tale* (Macmillan & Co 1952).

MacRae, R, 'The Attorney General's Role in Relation to Charities' [2018] *The Jersey & Guernsey Law Review* 34.

Magrath, P, 'Why Can't We Read Prince Philip's Will?' (*Transparency Project*, 26 September 2021). Available at: www.transparencyproject.org.uk/why-cant-we-read-prince-philips-will/.

Maguire, F, 'The Lord Advocate: A Suspicion of Bias Lingers' (*Scotsman*, 17 October 2006). Available at: www.scotsman.com/news/the-lord-advocate-a-suspicion-of-bias-lingers-1-721442.

Malcolm, CA, 'The Solicitor General for Scotland (Part I)' (1942) *Juridical Review* 67.

Malcolm, CA, 'The Solicitor General for Scotland (Part II)' (1942) *Juridical Review* 125.

Mansergh, N, *The Government of Northern Ireland: A Study in Devolution* (George Allen & Unwin Ltd 1936).

Marshall, G, *Constitutional Conventions: The Rules and Forms of Political Accountability* (Oxford University Press 1987).

Marston, G, 'Armed Intervention in the 1956 Suez Canal Crisis: The Legal Advice Tendered to the British Government' (1988) 37 *International and Comparative Law Quarterly* 773.

Martin, AF, 'The Immunity of the Attorney General to Law Society Discipline' (2016) 94 *Canadian Bar Review* 413.

Marquand, D and Seldon, A, *The Ideas That Shaped Post-War Britain* (Fontana Press 1996).

Mashaw, JL, *Bureaucratic Justice: Managing Social Security Disability Claims* (Yale University Press 1983).

Mawdsley, G, 'The Historical Purpose and Role of Fatal Accident Inquiries' [2021] SLT 157.

Mayhew, P, 'The Role of the Law Officers in England and Wales' (1992) 1 *Inter Alia* 18.

Mba, O, 'Judicial Review of the Prosecutorial Powers of the Attorney-General in England and Wales and Nigeria: An Imperative of the Rule of Law' (2010) 2 *Oxford University Comparative Law Forum*. Available at: https://ouclf.iuscomp.org/judicial-review-of-the-prosecutorial-powers-of-the-attorney-general-in-england-and-wales-and-nigeria-an-imperative-of-the-rule-of-law/#fn0sym.

McBride, PG, 'Law Officers are Impartial' (*Scotsman*, 2 August 2007). Available at: www.scotsman.com/news/law-officers-are-impartial-1-911758.

McBride, S, 'DUP–Civil Service Showdown Could Be Days Away, and the Implications are Vast' (*Belfast Telegraph*, 29 January 2022). Available at: www.belfasttelegraph.co.uk/opinion/columnists/Sam-mcbride/dup-civil-service-showdown-could-be-days-away-and-the-implications-are-vast-41290094.html.

McCaffrey, B, 'Declassified Documents Reveal Army Lobbied Attorney General Not to Prosecute Soldiers' (*thedetail*, 15 April 2013). Available at: www.thedetail.tv/articles/declassified-documents-reveal-army-lobbied-attorney-general-not-to-prosecute-soldiers.

McCaffrey, R, 'Speaking Rights of Attorneys General/Law Officers in Legislatures' (NIAR Briefing Paper 154-13, 19 February 2013).

McCluskey, Lord, 'Where now for the Lord Advocate?' (*Scotsman*, 10 October 2006). Available at: www.scotsman.com/news/where-now-for-the-lord-advocate-1-1143868.

McCorkindale, C, 'Devolution in Scotland and the Supreme Court: A Question of Interpretation?' (2020) 1 *Materiali Per Una Storia Della Cultura Giuridica* 67.

McCorkindale, C, 'The UNCRC and European Charter of Self-Government Bill References: Once (and Twice) More unto the Breach?' (*Centre on Constitutional Change*, 26 April 2021). Available at: www.centreonconstitutionalchange.ac.uk/news-and-opinion/uncrc-and-european-charter-local-self-government-bill-references-once-and-twice.

McCorkindale, C and Hiebert, JL, 'Vetting Bills in the Scottish Parliament for Legislative Competence' (2017) 21 *Edinburgh Law Review* 319.

McCorkindale, C and McHarg, A, 'Litigating Brexit' in Oran Doyle, Aileen McHarg and Jo Eric Khushal Murkens (eds), *The Brexit Challenge for Ireland and the United Kingdom* (Cambridge University Press 2021).

McCorkindale, C, McHarg, A and Scott, PF, 'The Courts, Devolution, and Constitutional Review' (2017) 36 *University of Queensland Law Journal* 289.

McCormick, C, 'Expanding the Portfolio of the Counsel General to the National Assembly for Wales' (*UK Constitutional Law Association Blog*, 28 July 2016). Available at: https://ukconstitutionallaw.org/2016/07/28/conor-mccormick-expanding-the-portfolio-of-the-counsel-general-to-the-national-assembly-for-wales/.

McCormick, C, 'Book Review: Public Sentinels: A Comparative Study of Australian Solicitors-General' (2017) 10 *Irish Yearbook of International Law* 315.

McCormick, C, 'Judicial Review of Administrative Action in the United Kingdom: The Status of Standards Between 1890 and 1910' (2018) 10 *Italian Journal of Public Law* 49.

McCormick, C, 'Reviewing the Reviewability of the Attorney General for Northern Ireland' [2018] *Public Law* 22.

McCormick, C, 'The Three Tiers of Executive Power in Northern Ireland' in Brice Dickson and Conor McCormick (eds), *The Judicial Mind: A Festschrift for Lord Kerr of Tonaghmore* (Hart Publishing 2021).
McCormick, C and Cowie, G, *The Law Officers: A Constitutional and Functional Overview* (House of Commons Library, Research Briefing, 28 May 2020). Available at: https://commonslibrary.parliament.uk/research-briefings/cbp-8919/.
McCrudden, C, 'Northern Ireland and the British Constitution' in Jeffrey Jowell and Dawn Oliver (eds), *The Changing Constitution* (3rd edn, Oxford University Press 1994).
McEldowney, J, 'Public Expenditure and the Control of Public Finance' in Jeffrey Jowell, Dawn Oliver and Colm O'Cinneide (eds), *The Changing Constitution* (8th edn, Oxford University Press 2015).
McEvoy, K, Mallinder L and Bryson, A, *Lawyers in Conflict and Transition* (Cambridge University Press 2022).
McHarg, A, 'Public Law in Scotland: Difference and Distinction' in Aileen McHarg and Tom Mullen (eds), *Public Law in Scotland* (Avizandum 2006).
McHarg, A, 'Unity and Diversity in the United Kingdom's Territorial Constitution' in Mark Elliott, Jason NE Varuhas and Shona Wilson Stark (eds), *The Unity of Public Law? Doctrinal, Theoretical and Comparative Perspectives* (Hart Publishing 2018).
McHarg, A, 'Devolution in Scotland' in Jeffrey Jowell and Colm O'Cinneide (eds), *The Changing Constitution* (9th edn, Oxford University Press 2019).
McHarg, A and McCorkindale, C, 'The Supreme Court and Devolution: The Scottish Continuity Bill Reference' (2019) 2 *Juridical Review* 190.
McKenzie, R, 'Interview: Elish Angiolini' (*The Journal of the Law Society of Scotland*, 1 January 2002). Available at: www.journalonline.co.uk/Magazine/47-1/1000046.aspx.
McKerrell, N, 'The Lord Advocate: A Need for Reform or Reflection?' (*The Constitution Society*, 1 April 2021). Available at: https://consoc.org.uk/the-lord-advocate-a-need-for-reform-or-reflection/.
Miles, J, 'Discrimination and Public Law: Promoting Equalities for a Fairer and More Equal Wales' (A Speech by the Counsel General to the Public Law Wales Conference, 26 March 2018). Available at: https://publiclawproject.org.uk/content/uploads/2018/05/Public-Law-Wales-Project-final-speech-for-publication.pdf.
Miles, J, 'Written Statement: Legal Challenge to the UK Internal Market Act 2020' (*Welsh Government*, 19 January 2021. Available at: https://gov.wales/written-statement-legal-challenge-uk-internal-market-act-2020.
Miller, DF and Paul, J, *The Communitarian Challenge to Liberalism* (Cambridge University Press 1996).
Milne, D, *The Scottish Office and Other Scottish Government Departments* (George Allen & Unwin 1957).
Ministry of Justice, *Governance of Britain – Constitutional Renewal* (Cm 7342-I, 2008).
Ministry of Justice, *Government Response to the Justice Select Committee's Eleventh Report of Session 2017-19: Disclosure of Evidence in Criminal Cases* (Cm 9744, 2018).
Misztal, B, *Trust in Modern Societies: The Search for the Bases of Social Order* (Polity Press 1996).
Mitchell, J, *Governing Scotland: The Invention of Administrative Devolution* (Palgrave Macmillan 2003).
Mitchell, J, *Devolution in the UK* (Manchester University Press 2009).
Mitchell, JDB, 'The Merits of Disharmony' [1956] *Public Law* 6.
Monateri, PG, 'Methods in Comparative Law: An Intellectual Overview' in Pier Giuseppe Monateri (ed), *Methods of Comparative Law* (Edward Elgar 2012).
Morison, J and Livingstone, S, *Reshaping Public Power: Northern Ireland and the British Constitutional Crisis* (Sweet & Maxwell 1995).
Mulholland, S, 'An Interview with the Attorney General for Northern Ireland' [2010] *The Verdict* 5.
Munby, J, 'The Role of the Attorney General in Appointing Advocates to the Court or Special Advocates in Family Cases' (Guidance from the President of the Family Division, 26 March 2015).
Munro, CR, *Studies In Constitutional Law* (2nd edn, Oxford University Press 1999).
Munro, J, *Public Law* (2nd edn, W Green & Son 2007).

Ng, Y-F, 'Book Review: The Role of the Solicitor General' (2017) 26 *Social & Legal Studies* 658.

Nicholson, P, 'Hearing and Answering' (*The Journal of the Law Society of Scotland*, 12 February 2007). Available at: www.journalonline.co.uk/Magazine/52-2/1003853.aspx.

Normand, WG, 'The Public Prosecutor in Scotland' (1938) 54 *Law Quarterly Review* 345.

Northern Ireland Office, *The Belfast Agreement* (10 April 1998).

Northern Ireland Office, *Criminal Justice Review Implementation Plan* (2 November 2001).

Norton-Kyshe, JW, *The Law and Privileges Relating to the Attorney-General and Solicitor-General of England* (Stevens and Haynes 1897).

Norton, E, 'Applications to the Attorney-General and s 13 of the Coroners Act 1988' (*Liberty*, 6 October 2016). Available at: www.publiclawproject.org.uk/data/resources/249/PLP-paper-Emma-Norton.pdf.

O'Brien, M, 'Keeping Faith in the Law: Martin O'Brien Meets Controversial Attorney General John Francis Larkin' (*The Irish Catholic*, 21 November 2013). Available at: www.irishcatholic.com/keeping-faith-in-the-law/.

O'Connell, R and others, *Applying an International Human Rights Framework to State Budget Allocations: Rights and Resources* (Routledge 2014).

O'Neill, A, 'Human Rights and People and Society' in Elaine E Sutherland and others (eds), *Law Making and the Scottish Parliament: The Early Years* (Edinburgh University Press 2011).

O'Neill, C, 'The Constitutional Position of the Lord Advocate' (*The Journal of the Law Society of Scotland*, 1 March 2000). Available at: www.journalonline.co.uk/Magazine/45-3/1000843.aspx

O'Neill, J (ed), *Modes of Individualism and Collectivism* (Gregg Revivals 1993).

O'Neill, O, *A Question of Trust* (Cambridge University Press 2002).

O'Neill, O, 'Trust, Trustworthiness, and Accountability' in Nicholas Morris and David Vines (eds), *Capital Failure: Rebuilding Trust in Financial Services* (Oxford University Press 2014).

Office of the Advocate General for Scotland, 'Involvement in Cases' (19 August 2021). Available at: www.gov.uk/government/publications/involvement-in-cases.

Office of the First Minister and deputy First Minister, 'Response to the Recommendations on the Report by John Larkin QC on Establishing the Office of the Attorney General for Northern Ireland' (23 March 2010).

Office of the Secretary of State for Wales, *Better Governance for Wales* (Cm 6582, 15 June 2005).

Oliver, D, *Government in the United Kingdom: The Search for Accountability, Effectiveness and Citizenship* (Open University Press 1991).

Oliver, D, *Common Values and the Public-Private Divide* (Butterworths 1999).

Oliver, D, *Constitutional Reform in the United Kingdom* (Oxford University Press 2006).

Oliver, D, 'Accountability and the Foundations of British Democracy – the Public Interest and Public Service Principles' in Nicholas Bamforth and Peter Leyland (eds), *Accountability in the Contemporary Constitution* (Oxford University Press 2013).

Omond, GWT, 'The Lord Advocates of Scotland: Second Series: 1834–1880' (Andrew Melrose 1914).

Owen, G, 'Constitutional Quick Guides – Research Briefing' (*Welsh Parliament/Senedd Research*, 27–29 November 2021). Available at: https://research.senedd.wales/media/qssa4cmf/21-19.pdf.

Page, A, 'A Parliament that is Different? The Law-Making Process in the Scottish Parliament' in Elaine E Sutherland and others (eds), *Law Making and the Scottish Parliament: The Early Years* (Edinburgh University Press 2011).

Page, A, *Constitutional Law of Scotland* (Scottish Universities Law Institute Ltd 2015).

Palley, C, 'The Evolution, Disintegration and Possible Reconstruction of the Northern Ireland Constitution' (1972) 1 *Anglo-American Law Review* 368.

Pannick, D, '"We Do Not Fear Criticism, Nor Do We Resent It": Abolition of the Offence of Scandalising the Judiciary' [2014] *Public Law* 5.

Parrillo, NR (ed), *Administrative Law from the Inside Out: Essays on Themes in the Work of Jerry L. Mashaw* (Cambridge University Press 2018).

Patriotta, G, Gond, J-P and Schultz, F, 'Maintaining Legitimacy: Controversies, Orders of Worth, and Public Justifications' (2011) 48 *Journal of Management Studies* 1804.

Picarda, H, *The Law and Practice Relating to Charities* (4th edn, Bloomsbury Professional 2010).

Picarda, H, *The Law and Practice Relating to Charities – Supplement to the Fourth Edition* (Bloomsbury Professional 2014).
Pinker, S, *Words and Rules: The Ingredients of Language* (Basic Books 1999).
Pinto, A, 'Chair of the Bar: The Law Officers Must Defend the Rule of Law, Even When it is Unpopular with the Government' (*The Bar Council*, 18 September 2020). Available at: www.barcouncil.org.uk/resource/chair-of-the-bar-the-law-officers-must-defend-the-rule-of-law-even-when-it-is-unpopular-with-the-government.html.
Pritchard, H, 'Revisiting Legal Wales' (2019) 23 *Edinburgh Law Review* 123.
Quekett, AS, *The Constitution of Northern Ireland: Part I – The Origin and Development of the Constitution* (HM Stationery Office 1928).
Quekett, AS, *The Constitution of Northern Ireland: Part II – The Government of Ireland Act 1920 and Subsequent Enactments* (HM Stationery Office 1933).
Rawlings, R, 'Law Making in a Virtual Parliament: The Welsh Experience' in Robert Hazell and Richard Rawlings (eds), *Devolution, Law Making and the Constitution* (Imprint Academic 2005).
Rawlings, R, *Delineating Wales: Constitutional, Legal and Administrative Aspects of National Devolution* (University of Wales Press 2003).
Rawlings, R, 'The Strange Reconstitution of Wales' [2018] *Public Law* 62.
Rawlings, R, 'The Welsh Way / Y Ffordd Gymreig' in Jeffrey Jowell and Colm O'Cinneide (eds), *The Changing Constitution* (9th edn, Oxford University Press 2019).
Rawlinson, P, 'A Vital Link in the Machinery of Justice' (1977) 74 *Guardian Gazette* 798.
Reynolds, P, 'Legitimate Expectation and the Protection of Trust in Public Officials' [2011] *Public Law* 330.
Rich, B, 'Small Change: Charity and the National Debt' (2018) 24 *Trusts & Trustees* 741.
Richards, Z, *Responsive Legality: The New Administrative Justice* (Routledge 2018).
Roughan, N, 'The Legitimacy of Whom?' in Wojciech Sadurski, Michael Sevel and Kevin Walton (eds), *Legitimacy: The State and Beyond* (Oxford University Press 2019).
Rozenberg, J, 'Mixed Millers from the Attorney General: Moral: Know Your Cases Before Taking on Another QC' (*A Lawyer Writes*, 25 September 2020). Available at: https://rozenberg.substack.com/p/mixed-millers-from-the-attorney-general.
Rozenberg, J, 'What Made Lord Keen Resign?' (*A Lawyer Writes*, 2 October 2020). Available at: https://rozenberg.substack.com/p/what-made-lord-keen-resign.
Rozenberg, J, 'An Unusual Submission: Suella Braverman Fails to Persuade Judges that Three Killers Received Unduly Lenient Sentences' (*A Lawyer Writes*, 16 December 2020). Available at: https://rozenberg.substack.com/p/an-unusual-submission?r=8r17o&utm_campaign=post&utm_medium=web&utm_source=copy.
Rozenberg, J, 'New Figures Suggest Better Sentencing: Steady Decline in Proportion of Unduly Lenient Sentences Increased on Appeal' (*A Lawyer Writes*, 26 August 2021). Available at: https://rozenberg.substack.com/p/new-figures-show-better-sentencing?r=8r17o&utm_campaign=post&utm_medium=web&utm_source=.
Rubin, EL, 'Independence as a Governance Mechanism' in Stephen B Burbank and Barry Friedman (eds), *Judicial Independence at the Crossroads: An Interdisciplinary Approach* (Sage 2002).
Rubin, EL, *Beyond Camelot: Rethinking Politics and Law for the Modern State* (Princeton University Press 2007).
Sadurski, W, Sevel, M and Walton, K, (eds), *Legitimacy: The State and Beyond* (Oxford University Press 2019).
Samuels, A, 'Abolish the Office of Attorney-General' [2014] *Public Law* 609.
Sanderson, E, *Government Lawyering: Duties and Ethical Challenges of Government Lawyers* (LexisNexis 2018).
Sargeant, J and Rutter, J, 'Governing Without Ministers: Northern Ireland Since the Fall of the Power-Sharing Executive' (*Institute for Government*, 25 September 2019). Available at: www.instituteforgovernment.org.uk/publications/governing-without-ministers-northern-ireland.
Schaar, JH, *Legitimacy in the Modern State* (Transaction 1981).

Scott, M, 'In Its Battle for Brexit, the Government Is Bringing a Knife to the Legal Gunfight' *The Telegraph* (29 September 2016). Available at: www.telegraph.co.uk/news/2016/09/29/in-its-battle-for-brexit-the-government-is-bringing-a-knife-to-t/.

Scottish Government, 'A Fairer, Greener Scotland: Programme for Government 2021-2022' (September 2021). Available at: www.gov.scot/publications/fairer-greener-scotland-programme-government-2021-22/documents/.

Searle, JR, *Speech Acts: An Essay in the Philosophy of Language* (Cambridge University Press 1969).

Seaton, R, 'A Monster of the Constitution: Scotland's Lord Advocate' (2001) 1 *Common Law Review* 40.

Sedley, S, *Law and the Whirligig of Time* (Hart Publishing 2018).

Seldon, A, *Trust: How We Lost It and How to Get It Back* (Biteback 2009).

Select Committee on the Constitution, *Reform of the Office Attorney General* (HL 2007-08, 93).

Seymour-Ure, C, 'The Disintegration of the Cabinet and the Neglected Question of Cabinet Reform' (1971) 24 *Parliamentary Affairs* 196.

Shawcross, H, 'The Office of the Attorney General' (An Address at the Law Society's Hall, 18 February 1953).

Shawcross, H, 'The Office of the Attorney-General' (1953) 7 *Parliamentary Affairs* 380.

Shute, S, 'Prosecution Appeals Against Sentence: The First Five Years' (1994) 57 *Modern Law Review* 745.

Silkin, S, 'The Office of the Attorney General' (1976) 2 *Poly Law Review* 3.

Silkin, S, 'The Functions and Position of the Attorney-General in the United Kingdom' (1978) 59 *The Parliamentarian* 149.

Silkin, S, 'The George Bean Memorial Lecture' (A Speech by the Attorney General in Manchester, 29 October 1978).

Silkin, S, 'Magistrates Address' (A Speech by the Attorney General to Somerset & South Avon Magistrates, 23 February 1979).

Slingo, J, 'Lord Keen QC in Breach of Core Duty – But Cleared of Misconduct' (*The Law Society Gazette*, 29 October 2019). Available at: www.lawgazette.co.uk/news/lord-keen-qc-in-breach-of-core-duty-but-cleared-of-misconduct/5101978.article.

Slingo, J, 'Reports Against Barristers Have Doubled, Says Regulator' (*The Law Society Gazette*, 1 June 2021). Available at: www.lawgazette.co.uk/news/reports-against-barristers-have-doubled-says-regulator-/5108674.article.

Smart, I, 'Pants on fire?' (*ianssmart*, 27 October 2012). Available at: http://ianssmart.blogspot.co.uk/2012/10/pants-on-fire.html.

Smith, BC, *Judges and Democratization: Judicial Independence in New Democracies* (Routledge 2017).

Smith, BT, 'Scottish Public Prosecution, Policy and Practice: Issues of Independence and Accountability' (1999) *Juridical Review* 141.

Smith, SA, *Contract Theory* (Oxford University Press 2004).

Sofronoff, W, 'Book Review: The Role of the Solicitor General' (2017) 91 *Adelaide Law Journal* 683.

Spigelman, J, 'The Integrity Branch of Government' (2004) 78 *Australian Law Journal* 724.

Srickland, P, *Law Officers' Advice* (HC Library Standard Note SNHA/2942, 2004).

Stott, G, *Lord Advocate's Diary 1961–1966* (Aberdeen University Press 1991).

Styles, SC, 'How the Roles of Lord Advocate Could Be Split and Why It Could Help Pursuit of Indy' (*The National*, 14 June 2021). Available at: www.thenational.scot/news/19369788.roles-lord-advocate-split-help-pursuit-indy/.

The Secret Barrister (*Twitter*, 12 November 2020). Available at: https://twitter.com/BarristerSecret/status/1326849470676480000?s=20.

Thomas, A, 'The Counsel General – A Quick Constitution Guide' (*National Assembly for Wales Research Service*, March 2018). Available at: https://senedd.wales/media/0bdjk3cj/18-019-web-english.pdf.

Thomas, A, 'Why did the Counsel General intervene in the Supreme Court?' (*In Brief*, 3 August 2018). Available at: https://seneddresearch.blog/2018/08/03/why-did-the-counsel-general-intervene-in-the-supreme-court/.

Thomas, Lord, 'The Judiciary Within the State: The Relationship Between the Branches of the State' (A Speech by the Lord Chief Justice of England and Wales for the Michael Ryle Memorial Lecture, 15 June 2017). Available at: www.judiciary.uk/wpcontent/uploads/2017/06/lcj-michael-ryle-memorial-lecture-20170616.pdf.

Thomas, RM, 'The Attorney-General for England and Wales, and Northern Ireland: His Role in Civil and Criminal Proceedings' (1991) 57 *International Review of Administrative Sciences* 209.

Thomas, RM, *Espionage and Secrecy: The Official Secrets Acts 1911–1989 of the United Kingdom* (Routledge 1991).

Tickell, A, 'The Unpolitical: The SNP's Pied Lord Advocate' (*Lallands Peat Worrier*, 25 August 2012). Available at: http://lallandspeatworrier.blogspot.co.uk/2012/08/the-unpolitical-snps-pied-lord-advocate.html.

Tickell, A, 'The Unpolitical Lord Advocate (Vol. 2)' (*Lallands Peat Worrier*, 13 October 2013). Available at: http://lallandspeatworrier.blogspot.co.uk/2013/10/the-unpolitical-lord-advocate-vol-2.html.

Trench, A, 'Washing Dirty Linen in Private: The Processes of Intergovernmental Relations and the Resolution of Disputes' in Alan Trench (ed), *Devolution and Power in the United Kingdom* (Manchester University Press 2007).

Turner, R, 'Cornish Fisherman Ordered to Pay £50,000 for Taking Scallops from Welsh Waters' (*Wales Online*, 3 April 2014). Available at: www.walesonline.co.uk/news/wales-news/cornish-fisherman-ordered-pay-50000-6915013.

Tushnet, M, *The New Fourth Branch: Institutions for Protecting Constitutional Democracy* (Cambridge University Press 2021).

Twomey, A, 'Book Review: The Role of the Solicitor General' (2016) 39 *UNSW Law Journal* 1466.

Vitale, D, 'A Trust Network Model for Social Rights Fulfilment' (2018) 38 *Oxford Journal of Legal Studies* 706.

Vitale, D, 'Leaving the EU: A Matter of "Trust"?' (*UK Constitutional Law Association Blog*, 9 April 2019). Available at: https://ukconstitutionallaw.org/2019/04/09/david-vitale-leaving-the-eu-a-matter-of-trust/.

Wade, HWR and Forsyth, CF, *Administrative Law* (10th edn, Oxford University Press 2009).

Walker, DM, *The Scottish Legal System: An Introduction to the Study of Scots Law* (7th edn, Sweet & Maxwell 1997).

Walker, N, 'The Antinomies of the Law Officers' in Maurice Sunkin and Sebastian Payne (eds), *The Nature of the Crown: A Legal and Political Analysis* (Oxford University Press 1999).

Wallace of Tankerness, Lord, 'The Role of the Advocate General and its Constitutional Context' (A Speech by the Advocate General for Scotland to a 1st Year Public Law Class at Edinburgh University, 10 June 2013). Available at: www.gov.uk/government/speeches/the-role-of-the-advocate-general-and-its-constitutional-context.

Watkin, TG, *The Legal History of Wales* (2nd edn, University of Wales Press 2012).

Weeks, G, *Soft Law and Public Authorities: Remedies and Reform* (Hart Publishing 2016).

Welsh Government, 'Cabinet, Cabinet Secretaries and Ministers' (3 November 2017).

Welsh Government, 'Ministerial Code' (August 2021). Available at: https://gov.wales/cabinet-members-and-ministers.

Welsh Government, 'Cabinet Members and Ministers' (1 November 2021). Available at: https://gov.wales/cabinet-members-and-ministers.

White, RM, 'The Career Path of Recent Scottish Law Officers Revisited: Lord Advocate Becomes Solicitor, Solicitor Becomes Lord Advocate, and Other Surprises' (2007) 29 *Scots Law Times* 223.

Wilberg, H and Elliott, M (eds), *The Scope and Intensity of Substantive Review: Traversing Taggart's Rainbow* (Hart Publishing 2017).

Willock, ID, 'Some Lessons of Khaliq' (1984) *Scottish Legal Action Group* 124.

Windsor, M, 'Government Legal Advisors through the Ethics Looking Glass' in David Feldman (ed), *Law in Politics, Politics in Law* (Hart Publishing 2015).

Wolffe, J, 'A Constitutional Trust' (A Speech by the Lord Advocate for the James Wood Lecture 2017 at Glasgow University, 15 November 2017).

Wolffe, J, 'The Renton Lecture 2020: Devolution and the Statute Book' (2021) 42 *Statute Law Review* 121.
Woodhouse, D, 'The Attorney General' (1997) 50 *Parliamentary Affairs* 97.
Wright, J, 'The Attorney General on Who Should Decide What the Public Interest Is' (A Speech at University College London's Law Faculty, 9 February 2016). Available at: www.gov.uk/government/speeches/the-attorney-general-on-who-should-decide-what-the-public-interest-is.
Yong, B, 'Risk Management: Government Lawyers and the Provision of Legal Advice within Whitehall' (The Constitution Society 2013).
Yong, B, Davies, G and Leston-Bandeira, C, 'Tacticians, Stewards, and Professionals: The Politics of Publishing Select Committee Legal Advice' (2019) 46 *Journal of Law and Society* 367.
'Appointment of the New Director of Public Prosecutions for Northern Ireland' (*Attorney General for Northern Ireland*, 2 January 2018). Available at: www.attorneygeneralni.gov.uk/news-centre/appointment-new-director-public-prosecutions-northern-ireland.
'Counsel General Calls for Distinct Welsh Legal System' (*Welsh Government*, 7 October 2016). Available at: https://gov.wales/newsroom/improvingpublicservices/2016/58652062/?lang=en.
'Counsel General for Wales' (*Law Wales*, 15 May 2018).
'Extension of Term of Appointment of Attorney General' (*The Executive Office*, 1 July 2021). Available at: www.executiveoffice-ni.gov.uk/news/extension-term-appointment-attorney-general.
'Follow-Up Review of Fatal Accident Inquiries' (*Scottish Government*, August 2019). Available at: www.gov.scot/publications/follow-up-review-fatal-accident-inquiries/.
'Guardian of the Rule of Law: The Office of Attorney General for Northern Ireland' (2013) 87 *Frontline* 8.
'Judges' verdict on Lord Advocate' (*The Scotsman*, 8 November 2008). Available at: www.scotsman.com/news/judges-verdict-on-lord-advocate-1-1301097.
'Key Cabinet Appointment Is Legal, Says Mark Drakeford' (*BBC News Wales*, 8 January 2019). Available at: www.bbc.co.uk/news/uk-wales-politics-46801150.
'Law Officers sworn in' (*Attorney General's Office*, 23 September 2021). Available at: www.gov.uk/government/news/law-officers-sworn-in.
'Legal advice related to the Parliamentary Inquiry into the Scottish Government's Handling of Harassment Complaints (SGHHC)' (*Scottish Government*, 2 March 2021). Available at: www.gov.scot/publications/legal-advice-related-to-the-parliamentary-inquiry-into-the-scottish-governments-handling-of-harassment-complaints-sghhc/.
'Lord Advocate Post Excluded From Cabinet' (*The Journal of the Law Society of Scotland*, 23 May 2007). Available at: www.journalonline.co.uk/News/1004203.aspx#.WMVelY5BrEY.
'Lord Advocate Vows to Act Independently as She is Sworn In' (*Crown Office and Procurator Fiscal Service*, 22 June 2021). Available at: www.copfs.gov.uk/media-site-news-from-copfs/1961-lord-advocate-vows-to-act-independently-as-she-is-sworn-in.
'Lord Keen of Elie QC Appointed as Lords Spokesperson' (*Office of the Advocate General for Scotland*, 19 July 2016). Available at: www.gov.uk/government/news/lord-keen-of-elie-qc-appointed-as-lords-spokesperson.
'Lord Stewart of Dirleton QC Sworn in as Advocate General for Scotland (*Office of the Advocate General for Scotland*, 8 December 2020). Available at: www.gov.uk/government/news/lord-stewart-of-dirleton-qc-sworn-in-as-advocate-general-for-scotland.
'Mick Antoniw MS: Counsel General and Minister for the Constitution' (*Welsh Government*). Available at: https://gov.wales/mick-antoniw-ms.
'Ministers Reflect: Dominic Grieve' (*Institute for Government*, 2015). Available at: www.instituteforgovernment.org.uk/ministers-reflect/person/dominic-grieve/.
'Ministers Reflect: Jeremy Wright' (*Institute for Government*, 2020). Available at: www.instituteforgovernment.org.uk/ministers-reflect/person/jeremy-wright/.
'NIHRC Responds to Attorney General's Comments on Dealing with the Past' (*Northern Ireland Human Rights Commission*, 20 November 2013). Available at: www.nihrc.org/news/detail/nihrc-responds-to-attorney-generals-comments-on-dealing-with-the-past.

'Northern Ireland's New Attorney General Brenda King Sworn In at Belfast's Royal Courts of Justice' (*Belfast Telegraph*, 18 August 2020). Available at: www.belfasttelegraph.co.uk/news/courts/northern-irelands-new-attorney-general-brenda-king-sworn-in-at-belfasts-royal-courts-of-justice-39459371.html.

'Opposition Parties Consider Vote of No-Confidence in Lord Advocate' (*Scottish Legal News*, 16 November 2020). Available at: www.scottishlegal.com/article/opposition-parties-consider-vote-of-no-confidence-in-lord-advocate.

'Scots Lawyers Call for Role of Lord Advocate to be Split' (*Scottish Legal News*, 5 March 2021). Available at: www.scottishlegal.com/article/scots-lawyers-call-for-role-of-lord-advocate-to-be-split.

'The Future of Welsh Law: A Programme for 2021 to 2026' (*Welsh Government*, 21 September 2021). Available at: https://gov.wales/the-future-of-welsh-law-accessibility-programme-2021-to-2026-html.

'The Role and Functions of the Lord Advocate' (*Scottish Government*, 16 August 2021). Available at: www.gov.scot/publications/lord-advocate-role-and-functions/.

'The Role of the Lord Advocate: Time for Radical Change or Cautious Reform?' (*Scottish Legal News*, 4 March 2021). Available at: www.scottishlegal.com/article/the-role-of-the-lord-advocate-time-for-radical-change-or-cautious-reform.

'"Well-qualified" Attorney General is Sworn In' (*Belfast News Letter*, 9 June 2010). Available at: www.newsletter.co.uk/news/well-qualified-attorney-general-is-sworn-in-1-1848319

Annual Report for the Scotland Office and the Office of the Advocate General (2011–2012) (HC 70, 16 July 2012).

Annual Report for the Scotland Office and the Office of the Advocate General (2020–2021) (HC 423, 13 July 2021).

Consents to Prosecute (Crown Prosecution Service). Available at: www.cps.gov.uk/legal-guidance/consents-prosecute.

Consents to Prosecution (Law Com No 255, 1998).

Constitutional Affairs Committee, *The Constitutional Role of the Attorney General* (HC 2006-07, 306).

Form and Accessibility of the Law Applicable in Wales (Law Com No 366, 2016).

Form and Accessibility of the Law Applicable in Wales: A Consultation Paper (Law Com CP No 223, 2015).

Governance of Britain: A Consultation on the Role of the Attorney General (Cm 7192, 2007).

Guide to Collective Decision Making (Scottish Government, November 2008).

Halsbury's Laws of England (2014) vol 20, Constitutional and Administrative Law.

Halsbury's Laws of England (2014) vol 29, Crown and Crown Proceedings.

Home Office Memorandum to the Departmental Committee on Section 2 of the Official Secrets Act 1911 (Cmnd 5104, 1972).

Justice in Wales for the People of Wales (The Commission on Justice in Wales Report, October 2019). Available at: https://gov.wales/commission-justice-wales-report.

Review of Intelligence on Weapons of Mass Destruction (14 July 2004, HC 898).

Scottish Ministerial Code 2018 Edition (Scottish Government, 8 February 2018).

Select Committee on the Constitution, *Reform of the Office Attorney General* (HL 2007-08, 93).

The Government's Response to the Constitutional Affairs Select Committee Report on the Constitutional Role of the Attorney General (Cm 7355, 2008).

The Laws of Scotland: Stair Memorial Encyclopaedia, Constitutional Law Reissue.

The Laws of Scotland: Stair Memorial Encyclopaedia, Criminal Procedure 2nd Reissue.

INDEX

www.ingramcontent.com/pod-product-compliance
Ingram Content Group UK Ltd.
Pitfield, Milton Keynes, MK11 3LW, UK
UKHW020220041026
15470UKWH00012B/864